America's Longest War
The United States and Vietnam, 1950–1975

America's Longest War

The United States and Vietnam, 1950–1975

FOURTH EDITION

George C. Herring
University of Kentucky

Boston   Burr Ridge, IL   Dubuque, IA   Madison, WI   New York
San Francisco   St. Louis   Bangkok   Bogotá   Caracas   Kuala Lumpur
Lisbon   London   Madrid   Mexico City   Milan   Montreal   New Delhi
Santiago   Seoul   Singapore   Sydney   Taipei   Toronto

McGraw-Hill Higher Education

A Division of The McGraw-Hill Companies

AMERICA'S LONGEST WAR: THE UNITED STATES AND VIETNAM 1950–1975
Published by McGraw-Hill, an imprint of The McGraw-Hill Companies, Inc.
1221 Avenue of the Americas, New York, NY, 10020. Copyright © 2002, 1996,
1986, 1979 by The McGraw-Hill Companies, Inc. All rights reserved. No part of this
publication may be reproduced or distributed in any form or by any means, or
stored in a database or retrieval system, without the prior written consent of The
McGraw-Hill Companies, Inc., including, but not limited to, in any network or other
electronic storage or transmission, or broadcast for distance learning.
Some ancillaries, including electronic and print components, may not be available to
customers outside the United States.

This book is printed on acid-free paper.

5 6 7 8 9 0 DOC/DOC 0 9 8 7 6

ISBN-13:   978-0-07-241755-5
ISBN-10:   0-07-241755-2

Publisher: *Lyn Uhl*
Developmental editor: *Kristen Mellitt*
Marketing manager: *Janise Fry*
Project manager: *Jean R. Starr*
Production supervisor: *Debra R. Sylvester*
Senior designer: *Jenny El-Shamy*
Senior media producer: *Sean Crowley*
Associate supplement producer: *Vicki Laird*
Photo research coordinator: *Jeremy Cheshareck*
Photo researcher: *PoYee Oster*
Cover design: *Jenny El-Shamy*
Cover photograph: *"Night Patrol" by Larry Powell*
Typeface: *10/12 Palatino*
Compositor: *Shepherd Incorporated*
Printer: *R. R. Donnelley & Sons Company*

Library of Congress-in-Publication Data

Herring, George C., 1936–
    America's longest war : the United States and Vietnam, 1950-1975 / George C.
Herring.—4th ed.
        p. cm.
    Includes bibliographical references and index.
    ISBN 0-07-241755-2 (alk. paper)
      1.Vietnamese Conflict, 1961-1975—United States. 2. Vietnam—History—
1945-1975. 3. United States—History—1945- 4. United States—Foreign relations—
Vietnam. 5. Vietnam—Foreign relations—United States.

DS558.H45 2002
959.704'3373—dc21   2001052123

www.mhhe.com

For
Christy, John, Andrew, and Madeline
and
Lisa, Peter, and Caili

Contents

Maps

Foreword

"The United States always wins the war and loses the peace," runs a persistent popular complaint. Neither part of the statement is accurate. The United States barely escaped the War of 1812 with its territory intact. In Korea in the 1950s, the nation was forced to settle for a stalemate. A decade later in Vietnam, the United States clearly lost the war. At Paris in 1783, and again in 1898, American negotiators drove hard bargains to win notable diplomatic victories. Yet the myth persists, along with the equally erroneous American belief, that we are a peaceful people. Our history, in fact, is studded with conflict and violence. From the Revolution to the Cold War, Americans have been willing to fight for their interests, their beliefs, and their ambitions. The United States has gone to war for many objectives—for independence in 1775, for honor and trade in 1812, for territory in 1846, for the Union in 1861, for humanity and empire in 1898, for neutral rights in 1917, and for national security in 1941. Since 1945, the nation has been engaged in two limited wars in Asia with disappointing outcomes, a successful air war in the Balkans, and a brief conflict in the Middle East that ended in a decisive victory.

This volume on the Vietnam War is part of a series of books designed to examine in detail critical periods relating to American involvement in foreign wars. George Herring originally wrote it in the late 1970s, at a time when most Americans preferred to forget the recent fiasco. Drawing on the Pentagon Papers, newly opened documents in the presidential libraries, and contemporary articles, books, and memoirs, he was able to offer a comprehensive and balanced account of the American role from 1950 to 1975. In subsequent editions, Herring drew on the expanding literature on the Vietnam War, weaving the new scholarly findings into his account of the conflict. In the fourth edition, he continues that process, incorporating the latest insights on Ho Chi Minh's leadership, on the Tet offensive, and on the impact of the peace movement at home. He pays special attention to new sources dealing with decision making in Hanoi, the international context of the war, and the personal responsibility of two key American leaders, presidents Lyndon Johnson and Richard Nixon, for escalating and extending the conflict.

While acknowledging the errors made by Johnson and Nixon, Herring views American participation in the Vietnam War as the logical culmination of the containment policy that began under Harry Truman in the late 1940s. Successive administrations never questioned the assumption that the national interest required the denial of South Vietnam to communism. The result was a gradual, yet inescapable, intervention in a local civil conflict. The United States sought at first to uphold French control, then to build and maintain South Vietnamese independence, and finally to deny victory to North Vietnam. Five presidents struggled with the dilemma of Vietnam; none was successful. Throughout, as Herring makes clear, no one in Washington examined the basic premises—the importance of South Vietnam to America's position in the world and the viability of South Vietnam as a political entity. The ultimate failure in Vietnam, Herring concludes, revealed the flaws in a policy of global containment. Yet he understands that the Vietnam story was not a simple case of diplomatic failure; the strength of his account lies in his portrayal of the complex challenge that Vietnam posed for the United States and varied responses it evoked from the American people.

Robert A. Divine

Preface

"Vietnam, Vietnam. . . . There are no sure answers." So wrote the veteran Southeast Asian correspondent Robert Shaplen in the midst of a long and perplexing war that would inflict enormous suffering and tragedy on the people of the United States and especially of Vietnam.*

More than three decades have passed since Shaplen penned these words. During that time, millions of pages of documents have been declassified and thousands of books and articles have been written. We now know a great deal more about the Vietnam War, but answers to many of the basic questions remain murky and contested. Why did the United States make such a vast commitment in an area of so little apparent importance? What did it attempt to do during the quarter century of its involvement there? Why, despite the expenditure of more than $150 billion, the loss of more than 58,000 lives, the application of its vast technological apparatus, and the employment of a huge military arsenal, did the world's most powerful nation fail to achieve its objectives and suffer its first defeat in war, a humiliating and deeply frustrating experience for a people accustomed to success? What have been the consequences for Americans, Vietnamese, and others of the nation's longest and most divisive war?

---

*Robert Shaplen, *The Road from War: Vietnam, 1965–1970* (New York, 1970), p. 283.

This book seeks to provide some answers to these still contro-versial questions and to place America's involvement in Vietnam in historical perspective. I have given the most detailed treatment to the years 1963–1973, the decade of heaviest U.S. involvement. But I have also devoted considerable attention to the period 1950–1963. The assumptions that led to the crucial commitments took form during these years. In addition, as CIA operative Edward Lansdale, himself a key player in these events, once observed, without an un-derstanding of this formative period, "one is like a spectator arriv-ing in the middle of a complex drama, without true knowledge of the plot or of the identity and motivation of those in the drama."**

This is not primarily a military history. Rather, in keeping with the purpose of the "America in Crisis" series, it seeks to integrate military, diplomatic, and political factors in such a way as to explain America's involvement and ultimate failure in Vietnam. My focus is on the United States, but I have sought to provide sufficient analysis of the Vietnamese side to make these events comprehensible. I have attempted to show the important role played by other nations such as the Soviet Union and China in the origins and outcome of the war.

The first three editions of this book, although relying on the al-ready sizable secondary literature on the war, also used recently declassified documents as they became available. It was especially exciting in the first edition, while trying to make a recent, still quite traumatic event part of history, to unearth new discoveries, chal-lenge old conventional wisdoms, and contribute to the growth of Vietnam scholarship as well as synthesize it.

This scholarship has literally exploded in volume over the past ten years, providing new information, new insights, and new chal-lenges for those of us who seek to interpret the war. It has also been exciting to witness this phenomenon and especially to observe the emergence of a new Vietnam scholarship by a new generation of scholars, some of them conversant in the Vietnamese language and well versed in Vietnamese history and culture. All of us who study the subject are grateful for the splendid recent work that has been done. I would like to think as a "pioneer" in the field that I have in some small way helped this process along. I know the new scholar-

**Quoted in W. Scott Thompson and Donaldson D. Frizzell, *The Lessons of Vietnam* (New York, 1977), p. 43.

ship has broadened my understanding of the war, and I hope that understanding is reflected in these pages.

I have attempted to explain American decision making on Vietnam in the broader context of the nation's domestic politics and especially of its global outlook and foreign policies for the quarter century between 1950 and 1975. Fear of the domestic political consequences of "losing" Vietnam haunted American policymakers from Harry Truman to Richard Nixon. More important, I think, U.S. involvement in Vietnam was a logical, if not inevitable, outgrowth of a world view and a policy—the policy of containment—that Americans in and out of government accepted without serious question for more than two decades. The commitment in Vietnam expanded as the containment policy itself grew. In time, it outlived the conditions that had given rise to that policy. America's failure in Vietnam called into question some of the basic premises of that policy and provoked a searching reappraisal of American attitudes toward the world and their place in it.

It is too easy, however, simply to conclude that Americans responded like automatons to the dictates of ideology, and recent scholarship reaffirms the importance of personality in the decision-making process. A strange sequence of events conspired to place Lyndon Baines Johnson and Richard Milhous Nixon in office at crucial points in the history of U.S. involvement in Vietnam. I hope these pages will show the ways in which the personalities and leadership styles of these powerful but deeply insecure individuals exerted crucial influence on the decisions to go to war, the manner in which the war was fought and ended, and especially the ways in which dissent at home was handled.

Much has changed since the first edition of this book appeared in 1979. The Cold War has ended. The United States enjoys a position of economic and military primacy quite unprecedented in world history; its ideology appears triumphant. The nation that defeated it in 1975, by contrast, languishes in poverty, desperately clinging to the ideology that sparked its revolution and drove it to victory in the face of a major new assault from the forces of globalization and Americanization.

These stunning changes have not altered my basic interpretations of the war. I believe now, as I did then, that U.S. intervention in Vietnam was misguided. It can be argued that the containment policy worked in Europe, contributing significantly, perhaps even decisively, to the outcome of the Cold War. This said, I still believe that containment was misapplied in Vietnam. Obsessed with their determination to stop the advance of communism, abysmally ignorant of the Vietnamese people and their history, Americans profoundly misread the nature of the struggle in Vietnam, its significance for their national interests, and its susceptibility to their power.

Defeat came hard, and it has been fashionable for many Americans to argue in its aftermath that victory could have been attained if the war had been fought differently. Such views are perhaps comforting for a people spoiled by success, and they accord with what the English scholar, D. W. Brogan, once called "the illusion of American omnipotence," the belief, almost an article of faith among Americans, that the difficult we do tomorrow, the impossible may take awhile. But the enduring lesson of the Vietnam War is that power, no matter how great, has its limits. American power was constrained in Vietnam by the Cold War, in whose name, ironically, the Vietnam War was fought. It was limited by the weakness of America's client, South Vietnam, and by the determination and willingness to pay any price of its foes, the North Vietnamese and the National Liberation Front of South Vietnam. Given these circumstances, I do not believe that the war could have been won in any meaningful sense or at a moral or material price Americans would—or should—have been willing to pay.

The costs of these mistakes—crimes some would say—still stagger the imagination: 58,000 Americans dead, a deep wound to the American psyche, deepseated and still lingering domestic divisions. For the Vietnamese the cost was much, much higher: millions dead, as many as 300,000 North Vietnamese and NLF still missing in action, and the devastation of a beautiful country. These costs, many of which are still being paid on both sides, make it urgent even today that Americans understand one of the most traumatic events in their history and come to terms with what it can tell them about themselves and the way they deal with other peoples.

NEW LEARNING TOOLS

A pronunciation guide, prepared by Tri C. Tran of the Department of East Asian Languages and Literatures at the University of

California–Irvine, has been added to this edition to assist students with proper pronunciation of Vietnamese names and places. Also new to this edition is a supporting website (www.mhhe.com/herring), where students will find quizzes, web-based research exercises, and links to sites relevant to the Vietnam War, and instructors will find a gallery of maps to use in presentations.

ACKNOWLEDGMENTS

Numerous people and institutions have assisted in the preparation of this edition, and I can acknowledge only a few here. From the time I first proposed this book in the summer of 1975, Professor Robert A. Divine has been the most helpful and supportive of editors. Lyn Uhl of McGraw-Hill encouraged this revision. Her colleague, Kristen Mellitt, has kept me busier than I would have liked this summer trying to meet a deadline that seemed to slip further and further into the past, but she has been an excellent editor and I have greatly enjoyed working with her. Many colleagues and students have taken the time to point out things that should be revised. Stephanie May of the University of Kentucky and Travis Hardy of the University of Richmond provided indispensable research assistance.

I am grateful to reviewers of the third edition, who offered helpful suggestions for revision:

J. Garry Clifford, University of Connecticut
Robert C. Cottrell, California State University, Chico
Leonard Gambrell, University of Wisconsin, Eau Claire
Gerald Herman, Northeastern University
David Hunt, University of Massachusetts, Boston
Adrian R. Lewis, University of North Texas
Jeffery C. Livingston, California State University, Chico
Kyle Longley, Arizona State University
John Ohl, Mesa Community College
John M. Simpson, Pierce College
Melvin Small, Wayne State University
Peter Trubowitz, University of Texas at Austin
Kenneth Winkle, University of Nebraska

I began the revisions for this edition during my semester as Douglas Southall Freeman Professor at the University of Richmond, and I am grateful to Professor Hugh West and his colleagues in the UR history department for providing me a most congenial environment in which to work. Debbie Govoruhk and Mary Ann Wilbourne provided indispensable technical assistance, Debbie especially in my continuing education in the, to me, still quite mysterious realm of computers. I immensely enjoyed and profited from daily conversations with my colleague and friend Ernie Bolt, many of them related to our mutual interest in the Vietnam War. Bob Kenzer lured me away for regular walks around the beautiful Richmond campus, a source both of relaxation and intellectual stimulation. The "red meat group," which met regularly for ribs, brisket, and other such culinary delights, provided special enjoyment during my months in Richmond.

Dottie Leathers typed the manuscript for the first edition of this book. The wonders of word-processing have spared her repeat performances on subsequent editions, but, as my wife of the last six years, she has been a source of constant encouragement and support. I am daily grateful for her love and companionship.

My students at the University of Otago in New Zealand, the U.S. Military Academy, West Point, the University of Richmond, and especially at the University of Kentucky, my academic home now for more than thirty years, have contributed far more to my work on the Vietnam War than they can ever realize or I can properly acknowledge. The research they have done has added immeasurably to my knowledge of the war. The stimulation they have provided has helped sustain my interest in the subject for more than a quarter century. Their curiosity has compelled me to keep learning; their questions have prevented me from becoming complacent with my answers. It has been a joy to learn with and from them. Their influence is present in these pages far more than the footnotes and bibliography will indicate.

I have dedicated this book, with all my love, to my children John and Lisa; to their spouses, Christy and Peter; and to my very special grandchildren, Andrew, Madeline, and Caili.

George C. Herring

About the Author

GEORGE C. HERRING is Alumni Professor of History at the University of Kentucky. He is a graduate of Roanoke College, Salem, Virginia. After service in the U.S. Navy, he earned the Ph.D. degree from the University of Virginia. He has taught at Ohio University as well as the University of Kentucky, where he has been a member of the faculty since 1969.

Dr. Herring served as editor of the scholarly journal *Diplomatic History* from 1982 to 1986 and was President of the Society for Historians of American Foreign Relations in 1990. He has been a Visiting Fulbright Scholar at the University of Otago, Dunedin, New Zealand. In 1993–94, he was a visiting professor at the U.S. Military Academy, West Point and in 2001, he was Douglas Southall Freeman Professor of History at the University of Richmond. He has been awarded fellowships from the National Endowment for the Humanities and the Guggenheim Foundation.

Dr. Herring has been teaching about and researching the Vietnam War for more than twenty-five years and has lectured on the subject throughout the United States and abroad. He is the author of numerous books, articles, and essays on the war, including most importantly, *The Secret Diplomacy of the Vietnam War: The Negotiating Volumes of the Pentagon Papers* (1983) and *LBJ and Vietnam: A Different Kind of War* (1994).

America's Longest War
The United States and Vietnam, 1950–1975

Ho Chi Minh, March 1946
The charismatic and indefatigable Ho Chi Minh
(the name means "he who enlightens") led the
Vietnamese revolution from its inception until
his death in 1969, and his organizational genius
and indomitable will were instrumental to
Vietnamese victories over France and the
United States.
Photographic collection of Wayne DeWitt Larabee

CHAPTER 1

A Dead-End Alley

The United States, France, and the First Indochina War, 1950–1954

When Ho Chi Minh proclaimed the independence of Vietnam from French rule on September 2, 1945, he borrowed liberally from Thomas Jefferson, opening with the words "We hold these truths to be self-evident. That all men are created equal." During independence celebrations in Hanoi later in the day, American warplanes flew over the city, U.S. Army officers stood near the reviewing stand, and a Vietnamese band played the "Star-Spangled Banner." Toward the end of the festivities, Vo Nguyen Giap spoke warmly of Vietnam's "particularly intimate relations" with the United States—something, he noted, "which it is a pleasant duty to dwell upon."[1] The prominent role played by Americans at the birth of modern Vietnam appears in retrospect one of history's most bitter ironies. Despite the glowing professions of friendship on September 2, the United States in 1945 acquiesced in the return of France to Vietnam and from 1950 to 1954 actively supported French efforts to suppress Ho's revolution, the first phase of a quarter-century American struggle to control the destiny of Vietnam.

HO CHI MINH AND THE VIETMINH REVOLUTION

The August revolution of 1945—the most celebrated event in modern Vietnamese history—marked yet another milestone in Vietnam's centuries-old struggle against foreign domination. For roughly one thousand years, the land of Nam Viet had been the

---

[1]Quoted in R. Harris Smith, *OSS: The Secret History of America's First Central Intelligence Agency* (Delta ed.; New York, 1973), p. 354.

southern-most province of China, and while absorbing Chinese culture and institutions, the Vietnamese during much of this millennium fiercely resisted the rule of their larger northern neighbor. Perhaps the most famous of Vietnamese heroes, the Trung sisters, mounted elephants in the first century A.D. to lead the first major rebellion against a much superior Chinese force, and when defeated drowned themselves in a lake in Hanoi. Another woman, Trieu Au, led yet another unsuccessful revolt in 248 A.D. In the tenth century the Vietnamese won their independence by luring an attacking Chinese fleet into a river bed in which iron-tipped spikes had been planted. Three times in the thirteenth century, the Vietnamese repulsed the legendary Mongol warrior Kublai Khan, their leader Tran Hung Dao pioneering methods of guerrilla warfare later used against the French and Americans. Another legendary figure, Le Loi, defeated the Chinese in 1426 and secured independence for Vietnam.

Expansion to the south forms as important a part of the Vietnamese heritage as resistance to northern invaders. Following their defeat of the Mongols, they moved southward against the kingdom of Champa, and after nearly two centuries of fighting destroyed the capital of Indrapura. National unity was always a fragile matter, however, and civil war continued until the late nineteenth century, when the French imposed a form of order through colonization.

The Vietnamese resisted French imperialism as persistently as Chinese. A scholars movement sought unsuccessfully to remove the French and restore the old imperial order. Emulating Japanese and Chinese models, early-twentieth-century nationalists like Phan Boi Chau attempted to mold traditional opposition to outside domination into modern, pro-Western republicanism. In the meantime, French colonial policies had transformed the Vietnamese economic and social systems, giving rise to an urban middle class and proletariat, and exploitation of the country and its people stimulated more radical revolutionary activity. In 1930, a Nationalist party headed by urban intellectuals launched the abortive Yen Bay revolt in northern Vietnam, while peasant and worker rebellions, backed by the Communists, erupted throughout the central part of the country. The French brutally suppressed the latter, jailing as many as 10,000 dissidents and even using aircraft to drop bombs on demonstrators.

The revolution of 1945 was in many ways the personal creation of the charismatic patriot and revolutionary agitator Ho Chi Minh, called by his biographer "one of the most influential figures of the twentieth century." Born in the province of Nghe An, the cradle of Vietnamese revolutionaries, Ho inherited from his mandarin father a sturdy patriotism and an adventurous spirit. Departing Vietnam in 1911 as a cook aboard a French merchant steamer, Ho eventually settled in France with a colony of Vietnamese nationalists. When the Paris Peace Conference ending World War I rejected his petition for democratic reforms for Vietnam, he became a founding member of the French Communist Party. Then known as Nguyen Ai Quoc (Nguyen the Patriot), he worked for more than two decades as a party functionary and revolutionary organizer in the Soviet Union, China, Thailand, and Vietnam, hiding behind aliases, eluding French, Chinese, and British police, spending time in prison, and on one occasion being reported dead. In 1930, he organized the Indochinese Communist Party. A frail and gentle man who radiated warmth and serenity, he was also a tireless worker, a master organizer, and a determined revolutionary—a "fiery stallion" in the words of an associate. His dark, piercing eyes revealed the intensity of his commitment to the cause to which he devoted his life, and he was willing to sanction the most cold-blooded methods to achieve his aims.

When Hitler conquered France in 1940 and Japan began to establish control over Vietnam, Ho returned to his homeland. Establishing headquarters in caves near the Chinese border, by a mountain he named Karl Marx and a river he called Lenin, Ho founded the Vietminh political organization and conceived the strategy that would eventually drive the French from Vietnam. He and the other Communists who constituted the Vietminh leadership skillfully tapped the deep reservoir of Vietnamese nationalism, muting their commitment to social revolution and adopting a broad platform stressing independence and "democratic" reforms. Displaying an organization and discipline far superior to competing nationalist groups, many of which spent as much time fighting each other as the French, the Vietminh established itself as the voice of Vietnamese nationalism.[2]

---

[2]See especially William J. Duiker, *Ho Chi Minh: A Life* (New York, 2000), pp. 1–306.

The Vietminh capitalized on the uniquely favorable circumstances of World War II to launch its revolution. The Japanese had permitted the French colonial authorities to retain nominal power throughout most of the war, but the ease with which Japan had established its position discredited the French in the eyes of the Vietnamese. The hardships imposed by the Japanese and their French puppets, along with a devastating famine, fanned popular discontent. By the spring of 1945, Ho had mobilized a base of mass support in northern Vietnam and, with the assistance of Giap, a former professor of history, he had raised an army of 5,000 soldiers. After the Japanese deposed the French puppet government in March 1945, the Vietminh, with limited assistance from a U.S. Office of Strategic Services (OSS) intelligence unit (hence the American presence on September 2), began the systematic harassment of their new colonial masters. When Japan surrendered in August 1945, the Vietminh opportunistically filled the vacuum, occupying government headquarters in Hanoi. Wearing the faded khaki suit and rubber sandals that would become his trademark, Ho Chi Minh stood before cheering throngs on September 2 and proclaimed the independence of his country.[3]

Independence would not come without a struggle, however, for the French were determined to regain the empire they had ruled for more than half a century. Conscious of their nation's declining position in world affairs, many French politicians felt that France could "only be a great power so long as our flag continues to fly in all the overseas territory."[4] French Indochina, comprising Cambodia, Laos, and the three Vietnamese colonies of Annam, Tonkin, and Cochin China, was among the richest and most prestigious of France's colonial possessions. The Vietminh had been unable to establish a firm power base in southern Vietnam, and with the assistance of British occupation forces, which had been given responsibility for accepting the Japanese surrender south of the sixteenth parallel, the French expelled the Vietminh from Saigon and reestablished control over the southern part of the country.

For more than a year, France and the Vietminh attempted to negotiate an agreement, but their goals were irreconcilable. French

---

[3]Ellen Hammer, *The Struggle for Indochina* (Stanford, Calif., 1966), pp. 11–53, 94–105; and John T. McAlister, Jr., *Vietnam: The Origins of Revolution* (Anchor ed.; New York, 1971), passim.

[4]Jean-Jacques Juglas quoted in Ronald E. Irving, *The First Indochina War: French and American Policy, 1945–1954* (London, 1975), p. 144.

FRENCH INDOCHINA

colonial policy had always stressed assimilation, full French citizen-
ship, rather than independence or dominion status, and France
hedged on the Vietminh's demand for immediate self-government
and eventual independence. For the Vietminh, unification of their
country represented not only fulfillment of the centuries-old dream
of Vietnamese nationalists but also an economic necessity, since the
south produced the food surplus necessary to sustain the overpop-
ulated, industrial north. The French were determined to keep
Cochin China separate from Annam and Tonkin and to maintain
absolute control in the southern colony, where their economic interests were greatest. Negotiations dragged on inconclusively, mutual
suspicions increased, and violence proliferated. After fighting
broke out in Haiphong in November 1946, a French warship
shelled the city, killing 6,000 civilians and setting off a war that in
its various phases would last nearly thirty years.[5]

The French went to war in 1946 confident of victory, but Ho
predicted the nature and outcome of the conflict more accurately.
"If ever the tiger [Vietminh] pauses," he said, "the elephant
[France] will impale him on his mighty tusks. But the tiger will not
pause, and the elephant will die of exhaustion and loss of blood."[6]
The Vietminh retreated into the countryside, evading major engagements, mobilizing popular support, and harassing French outposts. France held the major towns and cities, but a series of unsuccessful and costly offensives and relentless hit-and-run raids by
Vietminh guerrillas placed a growing strain on French personnel
and resources and in time produced war-weariness at home.

THE UNITED STATES AND
THE FIRST INDOCHINA WAR

Before 1940, Vietnam had been of little concern to the United States,
but by the outbreak of World War II American strategists had come
to view it as important to the nation's global interests. A relative
newcomer to the region, America established itself as a Pacific power
in 1898 with the acquisition of Hawaii and the Philippines. Eager for

[5]Hammer, *Struggle for Indochina*, pp. 148–202.
[6]Quoted in Jean Lacouture, *Ho Chi Minh: A Political Biography* (New York, 1968),
p. 171.

new markets and investments in East Asia, America had also promoted an "open-door policy" in China while working within the
prevailing imperial system. French monopolies sharply limited trade
and contact with Indochina, and a single consul attended to American interests in all of Vietnam. In the interwar years, the United
States established increasingly important economic interests in the
resource-rich Dutch and British East Indies. Southeast Asia provided
about 90 percent of America's crude rubber and 75 percent of its tin,
and U.S. oil companies produced about 27 percent of the sizable out-
put of the East Indies. Support for China, concern for the Philippines,
and a considerable stake in Southeast Asian raw materials put the
United States on a collision course with Japan in the 1930s, and
Americans grew increasingly alarmed by Japanese designs for a
Greater East Asia Co-Prosperity Sphere. Tokyo's move into Indochina in 1940 first impressed on U.S. officials the strategic importance of the French colonies as a gateway to China, the Philippines,
and Southeast Asia, leading to the imposition of sanctions on Japan
and eventually to the Japanese attack on Pearl Harbor.

For a time during World War II, the United States actively opposed the return of Indochina to France. Some U.S. officials perceived the growth of nationalism in Vietnam and feared that a
French attempt to regain control of its colony might provoke a long
and bloody war, bringing instability to an area of economic and
strategic significance. Even if France should succeed, they reasoned, it would restore monopolistic controls that would deny the
United States access to raw materials and naval facilities. President
Franklin D. Roosevelt seems instinctively to have recognized that
colonialism was doomed and that the United States should identify
with the forces of nationalism in Asia. Roosevelt profoundly dis-
liked France and its leader, Charles de Gaulle, moreover, and he regarded the French as "poor colonizers" who had "badly misman-
aged" Indochina and exploited its people. At the same time, like
most Americans, he viewed the "Annamites" as an inferior race,
backward, politically immature, and unready to govern themselves
without extended tutelage from an advanced western nation. He
therefore advocated placing Indochina under international trusteeship in preparation for independence.[7]

[7]Mark Philip Bradley, *Imagining Vietnam and America: The Making of Postcolonial Vietnam, 1919–1950* (Chapel Hill, N.C. 2000), pp. 76–80.

The United States also contributed at least indirectly to the success of the August Revolution. The OSS group that parachuted into Ho's remote base furnished small arms and other vital supplies and provided rudimentary military training in return for assistance in locating American fliers shot down in the region. Recognizing the potential importance of the United States to his success, Ho carefully cultivated his guests. The American presence at the independence day ceremonies gave the Vietminh legitimacy with other Vietnamese and at least the appearance of international support. General Philip Gallagher, sent to Vietnam in August 1945 as an adviser to the Chinese occupation forces, helped prevent conflict between the Chinese and French, giving Ho precious breathing space to coopt or eliminate his Vietnamese rivals and to prepare for serious negotiations with the French.[8]

Increasingly, however, the United States shifted toward support of France. In early 1945, Roosevelt retreated sharply from his seemingly forthright stand. Fearing for their own colonies, the British had strenuously opposed his trusteeship scheme, and many of Roosevelt's top advisers urged him not to antagonize an important ally by forcing the issue.[9] At Yalta in February 1945, the President endorsed a proposal under which colonies would be placed in trusteeship only with the approval of the mother country. In view of France's announced intention to return to its former colony, this plan implicitly precluded a trusteeship for Indochina.

After Roosevelt's death in April 1945, the United States adopted a policy even more favorable to France. Harry S. Truman did not share his predecessor's personal interest in Indochina or his concern about colonialism. American thinking about the postwar world also underwent a major reorientation in the spring of 1945. Military and civilian strategists perceived that the war had left the Soviet Union the most powerful nation in Europe and Asia, and the

[8]David Marr, *Vietnam 1945: The Quest for Power* (Berkeley, Calif., 1995), pp. 287–289; Peter M. Worthing, "Strangers in Hanoi: Chinese, Americans, and the Vietnamese August Revolution of 1945," *The Journal of American–East Asian Relations* 6 (Summer–Fall 1997):141–142.

[9]Significantly, some Vietminh officials were also wary of Roosevelt's trusteeship scheme, considering it only one step removed from colonialism. See Robert K. Brigham, "Cautious Allies: The Vietminh and the O.S.S., 1945" (paper delivered at the annual meeting of the Society for Historians of American Foreign Relations, June 1991).

subjugation of Eastern Europe raised growing fears that Joseph Stalin had broader, perhaps global, designs. Assigning top priority to the promotion of stable, friendly governments in Western Europe that could stand as bulwarks against Russian expansion, the Truman administration concluded that the United States "had no interest" in "championing schemes of international trusteeship" that would weaken and alienate the "European states whose help we need to balance Soviet power in Europe."[10] France assumed special importance in the new scheme of things, and the State Department insisted that the United States must repair the rift that had opened under Roosevelt by cooperating "wholeheartedly" with France and allaying "her apprehensions that we are going to propose that territory be taken away from her."[11] The Truman administration quickly scrapped what remained of Roosevelt's trusteeship plan and in the summer of 1945 assured de Gaulle that it would not stand in the way of restoration of French sovereignty in Indochina.

The United States viewed the outbreak of war in Indochina with concern. Along with revolutions in Burma, Malaya, and Indonesia, the Indochinese war underscored the explosiveness of nationalism in Southeast Asia. France's stubborn pursuit of outmoded colonial goals seemed to preclude anything except a military solution, but the State Department's Far Eastern Office doubted France's capacity to subdue the revolution and feared that a French defeat would eliminate Western influence from an area of economic and strategic importance. The State Department's Asian experts warned of the dangers of identifying with French colonialism and pressed the administration to force France to come to terms with Vietnamese nationalism.

American skepticism about French policy in Asia continued to be outweighed by European concerns. In the Spring of 1947, through the Truman Doctrine, the United States formally committed

---

[10]Office of Strategic Services, "Problems and Objectives of United States Policy," April 2, 1945, Harry S. Truman Papers, Harry S. Truman Library, Independence, Mo., Rose Conway File, Box 15.
[11]James Dunn memorandum, April 23, 1945, 851G.00/4-2345, Department of State Records, National Archives, Washington, D.C. See also George C. Herring, "The Truman Administration and the Restoration of French Sovereignty in Indochina," *Diplomatic History* 1 (Spring 1977): 97–117.

itself to contain a perceived Soviet threat to Greece and Turkey. The following year, the Marshall Plan committed massive funds for the reconstruction of Western Europe to further this policy of containment. During this time, attention was riveted on France, where economic stagnation and political instability aroused grave fears of a Communist takeover. Warned by moderate French politicians that outside interference in colonial matters would play into the hands of the French Communist Party, the United States left France to handle Indochina in its own way. An "immediate and vital interest" in retaining a "friendly government to assist in the furtherance of our aims in Europe," the State Department concluded, must "take precedence over active steps looking toward the realization of our objectives in Indochina."[12]

By early 1947, moreover, the Truman administration had drawn conclusions about Ho's revolution that would determine U.S. policy in Vietnam for the next two decades. From the outset, the Vietminh and United States viewed each other through badly distorted lenses. Isolated in the northern mountains of Vietnam and cut off from the outside world, Vietminh leaders clung to hopes that the friendly demeanor of the OSS representatives might reflect official American views toward their revolution. On numerous occasions, therefore, Ho appealed for U.S. support, even suggesting that Vietnam would be a "fertile field for American capital and enterprise" and raising the possibility of a naval base at Cam Ranh Bay. Ho emphatically denied that he was a "Moscow puppet," noting that he had received more support from the United States than from the Soviet Union. "You Americans ought to remember," he told those who questioned the Vietminh's capacity to win, "that a ragged band of barefoot farmers defeated the pride of Europe's best armed professionals."[13] In April 1947, the Vietminh dispatched an emissary to Bangkok to convince the United States of its moderation and to seek political and economic support. In meetings with lower-level Americans, the emissary stressed that his people sought primarily independence from France. Speaking language he

---

[12]Department of State, "Policy Statement on Indochina," September 27, 1948, in Department of State, *Foreign Relations of the United States, 1948* (Washington, D.C., 1974), 6:48. Hereafter cited as *FR* with date and volume number.

[13]Duiker, *Ho Chi Minh,* pp. 342–343, 379.

thought would appeal to capitalists, he offered tax-free monopolies for U.S. imports and for the rice export trade.

Such inducements had no impact in Washington. American political reporting about Vietnam was devoid of expertise and based on racial prejudices and stereotypes that reflected deep-seated convictions about the superiority of Western culture. In U.S. eyes, the Vietnamese were a passive and uninformed people, totally unready for self-government. The "Annamites" were not "particularly industrious," said one diplomat, nor were they noted for "honesty, loyalty, or veracity."[14] U.S. officials thus concluded that even if the Vietnamese were to obtain independence from France, they would be susceptible to the establishment of a Communist police state and vulnerable to external control.

Ho's long-standing ties with Moscow reinforced such fears. U.S. diplomats in Vietnam could find no evidence of direct Soviet contact with the Vietminh and stressed that regardless of ideology, Ho had established himself as the "symbol of nationalism and the struggle for freedom to the overwhelming majority of the population."[15] Also, Stalin was preoccupied with Europe at this time, and ideological conflicts with Ho dating to the 1920s influenced his aloofness toward the Vietminh revolution. Such subtleties were lost on Americans increasingly obsessed with the Communist menace in Europe. Intelligence reports stressed that Ho had remained loyal to Moscow throughout his career. The lack of close ties with the Soviet Union simply meant that he was trusted to carry out Stalin's plans without supervision. In the absence of irrefutable evidence to the contrary, the State Department concluded, the United States could not "afford to assume that Ho is anything but Moscow-directed." Unwilling, as Secretary of State George C. Marshall put it, to see "colonial empires and administrations supplanted by philosophies and political organizations emanating from the Kremlin," the administration refused to do anything to facilitate a "Communist" triumph in Indochina.[16]

---

[14]Quoted in Mark Bradley, "An Improbable Opportunity: America and the Democratic Republic of Vietnam's 1947 Initiative," in Jayne S. Werner and Luu Doan Huynh (eds.), *The Vietnam War: Vietnamese and American Perspectives* (New York, 1993), pp. 13–14.

[15]"Policy and Information Statement on Indochina," July 1947, Philippine and Southeast Asia Branch File, Department of State Records, Box 10.

[16]George C. Marshall to U.S. Embassy Paris, February 3, 1947, *FR, 1947*, 6: 67–68.

Thus, during the first three years of the Indochina war, the United States maintained a distinctly pro-French "neutrality." Fearful of antagonizing its European ally and of assisting the Vietminh even indirectly, the United States refused to acknowledge Ho's appeals for support and to use its leverage to end the fighting. After several unproductive meetings, the contact in Thailand was quietly terminated. Unwilling to support colonialism openly, the Truman administration provided "indirect" financial and military aid. Ships turned over to France under the wartime lend-lease program transported French troops to Vietnam, and the United States extended credits for the purchase of additional transports. Washington provided weapons for use in Europe that were, in fact, employed in Vietnam, and Marshall Plan funds enabled France to divert its own resources to the war in Indochina.

Some contemporaries and later historians have argued that the United States missed a splendid opportunity to do the right thing—and avert a looming disaster—by reaching an accommodation with the Vietminh in 1945 and preventing France from returning to Indochina. In the aftermath of the long and bloody wars in Vietnam, such a course had obvious appeal, and Ho Chi Minh's apparent flexibility made it seem entirely feasible. It is always easier to find such opportunities in retrospect than at the time, of course. After World War II, Vietnam was a very small blip on a very large American radar screen; France was far more important. In any event, as historian Mark Bradley has demonstrated, the cultural and ideological differences between the United States and the Vietminh were sufficiently large, the misperception and mutual misunderstanding so great, that likelihood of a fruitful relationship was at best "improbable." It is a sad fact of history that people often cannot see at the time the necessity of steps that later seem altogether obvious.[17]

INTERNATIONALIZATION OF THE WAR

Chinese Communist assistance to the Vietminh and U.S. aid for France transformed by 1950 a localized anticolonial struggle into a major and increasingly dangerous theater in the emerging Cold

---

[17]Bradley, *Imagining Vietnam and America*, pp. 146–176.

War. Isolated diplomatically and desperately in need of external assistance, the Vietminh finally turned to Mao Zedong's Chinese Communists for help. Recently triumphant in their own civil war, the Chinese proudly viewed their revolution as a model for other nations in the region, and they were encouraged by Stalin to take the lead in Asia. China thus leaned toward the Vietminh out of its "glorious internationalist duty." The Chinese also viewed with growing alarm the threat posed by the United States, and they saw support for the Vietminh as a means of securing their southern border. In early 1950, Mao created a Chinese Military Advisory Group and sent some of his best officers to help organize and train the Vietminh armies and plan strategy. He committed increasing volumes of military and nonmilitary equipment, provided sanctuaries for training troops, and took a keen personal interest in the planning and execution of Vietminh military operations. Not surprisingly, the two ancient and often hostile neighbors eyed each other suspiciously, and relations between them were frequently tense. But aid from China was vital to the survival of the Vietminh at this crucial point in the war and to its military success thereafter.[18]

In 1949 and 1950, the United States shifted from neutrality to open and soon massive support for the French. This dramatic and hugely significant policy change resulted from the intensification of the Cold War in Europe, its extension to Asia, and the establishment of direct links between the Vietminh and the Soviet Union and Communist China. These momentous events in turn generated domestic political pressures and a major reassessment of Cold War policies that produced not only a decision to support the French in Indochina but also a set of beliefs that would shape U.S. policies in Vietnam for the next twenty years and would lead to full-scale involvement.

Between 1947 and 1950, the Cold War in Europe escalated to dangerous proportions. The United States solidified its position in Western Europe with the North Atlantic Treaty Organization of 1949, the first "entangling alliance" to which it had been a party since 1801. The Soviet Union overthrew a neutralist government in Czechoslovakia, installed Stalinist regimes throughout Eastern Europe, and

[18]Qiang Zhai, "Transplanting the Chinese Model: Chinese Military Advisers and the First Vietnam War, 1950–1954," *Journal of Military History* 57 (October 1993): 689–715; Jian Chen, "China and the First Indochina War, 1950–1954," *China Quarterly* (March 1993): 85–110.

bound the region tightly to itself through economic agreements and a military alliance. The Berlin Blockade of 1948 brought the two nations perilously close to hot war. By 1950, negotiations had all but ceased, massive rearmament had begun on both sides, and two hostile power blocs ominously confronted each other along a line in Central Europe.

A series of stunning events in 1949 further heightened tensions, sending shock waves throughout the United States and arousing grave concerns for the nation's security. The Soviet Union's explosion of an atomic bomb in the summer came much sooner than most Americans had expected. It eliminated the U.S. nuclear monopoly and raised fears that an already aggressive Stalin might take greater risks.

The Communist triumph in China also had a profound effect in the United States. For years, many Americans had nourished the beliefs that China was their special protégé and that, with their guidance, it would be a close friend and reliable ally. The "loss" of China to communism at a pivotal moment in the early Cold War thus had especially unsettling consequences. It extended to East Asia a conflict that had been confined largely to Europe. In one stroke, it appeared to shift the global balance of power against the United States, and it created the notion that communism was on the move and the West increasingly on the defensive. It left frustrated and fearful Americans asking the portentuous—and pretentious—question: who lost China?

Revelations of Soviet espionage in the United States seemed, to some nervous Americans, to provide answers to otherwise unanswerable questions. Soviet spies had speeded Stalin's nuclear timetable by stealing U.S. secrets, it was alleged. Communist sympathizers within the U.S. government, in the words of a young California politician named Richard M. Nixon, had ensured, in the case of China, that the "deck was stacked on the communist side of the table."

Stunned from their complacency, a people who through much of their history had enjoyed relatively free security reacted with near panic. They took unprecedented steps to shore up their defenses against a sinister and ominous threat. They sought political retribution against those deemed responsible. They identified scapegoats for their newfound predicament. A Cold War culture of near hysterical fear, paranoiac suspiciousness, and stifling conformity began to take shape, and militant anticommunism came to dominate foreign and domestic policies. In February 1950, a heretofore obscure Wisconsin senator by the name of Joseph R. McCarthy, in a major speech in Wheeling, West Virginia, claimed to have the names of more than 200 communists working in the State Department, initiating the witch-hunt that would bear his name.[19]

The decision to aid France in Vietnam came out of this frantic milieu. The fall of China set loose powerful domestic political pressures to prevent the loss of additional Asian real estate to communism. Already under fire from Republicans and some Democrats for "losing" China, the Truman administration felt compelled to hold the line somewhere, and it attempted to divert attention from China and demonstrate its resolve by focusing on Southeast Asia. Significantly, the first aid extended to the French for Vietnam came from a fund originally appropriated for Nationalist China. The Truman administration thus took this first fateful step in Indochina without a Congressional debate and without justifying what it was doing.[20]

The crisis of 1949 also produced a sweeping reassessment of U.S. national security policy that assigned major significance to previously peripheral areas. This universalist worldview was best expressed in National Security Council (NSC) document 68, one of the key statements of U.S. Cold War policies. Drafted in early 1950, NSC 68 set as its fundamental premise that the USSR, "animated by a new fanatical faith," was seeking to "impose its absolute authority on the rest of the world." In this emotionally supercharged atmosphere, U.S. policymakers also concluded that Soviet expansion had reached a point beyond which it must not be permitted to go. "Any substantial further extension of the area under the control of the Kremlin," NSC 68 warned, "would raise the possibility that no coalition adequate to confront the Kremlin with greater strength could be assembled." In this context, then, of a world divided into two hostile power blocs, a fragile balance of power, a zero-sum game in which any gain for communism was automatically a loss for the United States, and the possibility if not likelihood of global war, the Truman administration initiated plans to increase American military capabilities, shore up the defense of Western Europe, and extend the containment policy to East Asia.[21]

[19]See especially Stephen J. Whitfield, *The Culture of the Cold War* (Baltimore, Md., 1991).
[20]Robert M. Blum, *Drawing the Line: The Origin of the American Containment Policy in East Asia* (New York, 1982).
[21]NSC 68, April 14, 1950, printed in *Naval War College Review* (May–June 1975): 51–108.

In the dramatically altered strategic context of 1950, support for France in Vietnam came to be considered essential for the security of Western Europe. Massive expenditures for the war in Indochina had retarded France's economic recovery and political stabilization. Preliminary proposals for the defense of Western Europe required France to raise sizable numbers of troops and provided for West German rearmament, measures the French would likely resist. The administration thus feared that if it did not meet its ally's appeals for aid in Indochina, France might reject its strategic design for Western Europe.

The strategic reassessment of 1950 also assigned high priority to previously marginal areas, and Southeast Asia was a region of particular concern. The raging conflict in Indochina and insurgencies in Burma, Malaya, and Indonesia all sprang from indigenous roots, but in a seemingly polarized world their mere existence and their leftist orientation persuaded anxious Americans that Southeast Asia was the "target of a coordinated offensive directed by the Kremlin." Should the region be swept by communism, the NSC warned, "we shall have suffered a major political rout the consequences of which will be felt throughout the world." The loss of an area so large and populous would tip the balance of power against the United States and might tempt the Europeans to reach an accommodation with the Soviet Union. The United States and its allies would be denied access to major markets. America's European allies desperately needed dollars to rebuild their devastated economies. To secure these dollars, the United States had to be able to purchase raw materials from former colonial areas in Southeast Asia, who then bought finished products from Western Europe, thus making up the "dollar gap" and permitting them to buy U.S. goods. Southeast Asia was the world's largest producer of natural rubber and a vital source of oil, tin, tungsten, and other strategic commodities. Its loss would threaten control of air and sea routes between Australia and the Middle East, thus imperiling nations such as Japan, India, and Australia in which the West retained predominant influence.

The impact on Japan, America's most important East Asian ally and the richest economic prize in the area, was viewed as potentially disastrous. Even before the fall of China, the United States was pushing for the reintegration of Japan with Southeast Asia, a region that had served as its rice bowl and breadbasket and an es-

CHINA

Red River

Quemoy
Island

Hong Kong

TAIWAN

BURMA

NORTH
VIETNAM

Hanoi

Haiphong

LAOS

Gulf of
Tonkin

HAINAN
ISLAND

Rangoon

Mekong River

Hue

Da Nang

Paracel Islands

LUZON

THAILAND

Bangkok

SOUTH
VIETNAM

Manila

PHILIPPINES

Andaman
Sea

CAMBODIA

Phnom
Penh

Saigon

South China Sea

Dangerous
Ground

Sulu Sea

Gulf of
Siam

Spratly Islands

NORTH BORNEO
BRUNEI

MALAYA

SARAWAK

Singapore

SUMATRA

INDONESIA

BORNEO

CELEBES

Java Sea

Djakarta

Indian Ocean

JAVA

SOUTHEAST ASIA, 1954

From By Sea, Air and Land: An Illustrated History of the U.S. Navy and
the War in Southeast Asia *by Edward J. Marolda, 1994, p. 2. Naval
Historical Center.*

sential source of its raw materials and markets. With China already lost to communism, U.S. officials feared that the loss of Southeast Asia would compel Japan to come to terms with the enemy. The United States thus set out to defend a "vital segment" of the "great crescent" of containment extending from Japan to India.[22]

By 1950, moreover, Americans viewed Vietnam as the key to keeping Southeast Asia out of communist hands, an importance it would retain for nearly a quarter century. Soviet and Chinese recognition of the Vietminh in January confirmed long-standing beliefs about Ho's allegiance, revealing him, in Secretary of State Dean Acheson's words, in his "true colors as the mortal enemy of native independence in Indochina."[23] It was also misinterpreted as a "significant and ominous" sign of Stalin's intention to "accelerate the revolutionary process" in Southeast Asia. Ho's increasingly well-organized and equipped guerrillas had already scored major gains against France and with increased Soviet and Chinese aid might force a French withdrawal, removing the last bulwark between China and Southeast Asia. Indochina was in the "most immediate danger," the State Department concluded, and was therefore "the most strategically important area of Southeast Asia."[24]

Indochina was considered intrinsically important for its raw materials, rice, and naval bases, but it was deemed far more significant for the presumed effect its loss would have on other areas. By early 1950, U.S. policy makers had firmly embraced what would become known as the domino theory, the belief that the fall of Indochina would cause in rapid succession the collapse of the rest of Southeast Asia. Acceptance of this concept reflected the perceived fragility of the region in 1950 as well as the experience of World War II, when Hitler had overrun Western Europe in three months and the Japanese had seized most of Southeast Asia in even less

[22]Michael Schaller, "Securing the Great Crescent: Occupied Japan and the Origins of Containment in Southeast Asia," *Journal of American History* 69 (September 1982): 392–413; Ronald McGlothen, *Controlling the Waves: Dean Acheson and U.S. Foreign Policy in Asia* (New York, 1993), pp. 191–201.

[23]*Department of State Bulletin* (February 13, 1950): 244; Charles Yost memorandum, January 31, 1950, *FR, 1950,* 6: 710–711.

[24]Dean Rusk to James H. Burns, March 7, 1950, U.S. Congress, Senate Subcommittee on Public Buildings and Grounds, *The Pentagon Papers (The Senator Gravel Edition)* (4 vols.; Boston, 1971), 1:363. Hereafter cited as *Pentagon Papers (Gravel).*

time. First employed to justify aid to Greece in 1947, the idea, once applied to Southeast Asia, became an article of faith.[25]

The strategic reassessment of 1950 thus ended American "neutrality" and produced in early March a commitment to furnish France military and economic assistance for the war against the Vietminh. It established principles that would form the basis for U.S. policy in Vietnam for years to come and would lead to large-scale U.S. military involvement.

THE BAO DAI SOLUTION

The creation of nominally independent governments in Indochina made it easier for the United States to rationalize support of France. Unable to defeat the Vietminh militarily, the French had attempted to undercut it politically by forming "free states" within the French Union in Laos, Cambodia, and Vietnam, the latter headed by the former Emperor of Annam, Bao Dai. Many U.S. officials were rightly skeptical of the so-called Bao Dai solution, warning that it was only a smoke screen for continued French domination and could not succeed. The State Department acknowledged the strength of these arguments, but Bao Dai seemed the only alternative to "Commie domination of Indochina," as Acheson put it, and while American support did not guarantee his success, the lack of it would ensure his failure.[26] By backing Bao Dai, moreover, the United States would at least avoid the appearance of being an accomplice of French imperialism. In February 1950, the Truman administration formally recognized the Bao Dai government and the free states of Laos and Cambodia and initiated plans to support them with economic and technical assistance.

The assumptions on which American policy makers acted in 1950 were misguided. The Southeast Asian revolutions were not inspired by Moscow, and although the Soviet Union and China at times sought to direct and control them, their capacity to do so was limited by their lack of military and especially naval power and by

[25]For a cultural explanation that traces the metaphor back to Woodrow Wilson, see Frank Ninkovich, *Modernity and Power: A History of the Domino Theory in the Twentieth Century* (Chicago, 1994).
[26]Dean Acheson to U.S. Embassy Manila, January 7, 1950, *FR, 1950*, 6: 692; Gary R. Hess, "The First American Commitment in Indochina: The Acceptance of the Bao Dai Solution," *Diplomatic History* 2 (Fall 1978): 331–350.

the strength of local nationalism. American assessment of the situation in Vietnam was off the mark. Because of old disputes, Stalin did not trust Ho Chi Minh, and the Soviet Union provided the Vietminh virtually no assistance until 1949. Although a dedicated Communist, Ho was no tool of Moscow, and while he was willing to accept help from the major Communist powers—indeed, he had no choice but to do so—he was not prepared to subordinate Vietnamese independence to them. Vietnam's historic fears of its larger northern neighbor made submission to China especially unlikely. "It is better to sniff French shit for a while than eat China's all our life," Ho once said, graphically expressing a traditional principle of Vietnamese foreign policy.[27] Perhaps most important, regardless of his ideology, Ho by 1950 had captured the standard of Vietnamese nationalism, and by supporting France, even under the guise of the Bao Dai solution, the United States attached itself to a losing cause.

U.S. policy makers were not unaware of the pitfalls. Should the United States commit itself to Bao Dai and he turn out to be a French puppet, a State Department Asian specialist warned, "we must then follow blindly down a dead-end alley, expending our limited resources . . . in a fight that would be hopeless."[28] Some officials even dimly perceived that the United States might get sucked into direct involvement in Vietnam. But the initial commitment seemed limited and the risks smaller than those of inaction. Caught up in a global struggle reminiscent of World War II, with Russia taking Germany's place in Europe and China Japan's place in Asia, U.S. officials were certain that if they did not back France and Bao Dai, Southeast Asia might be lost, leaving the more awesome choice of a "staggering investment" to recover the losses or a "much contracted" line of defense in the western Pacific.[29]

By the time the United States committed itself to assist France, the Vietminh had gained the military initiative in Indochina. Ho Chi Minh controlled an estimated two-thirds of the countryside, and Vietminh regulars and guerrillas numbered in the hundreds of thousands. The Chinese provided sanctuaries and large stocks of weapons. With Chinese encouragement, Giap, by early 1950, felt

[27]Quoted in Lacouture, *Ho Chi Minh*, p. 119.
[28]Charles Reed to C. Walton Butterworth, April 14, 1949, 851G.00/4–1449, Department of State Records.
[29]Acheson to Truman, May 14, 1950, Truman Papers, Confidential File. For an excellent discussion of the initial commitment in Indochina, see Blum, *Drawing the Line*. pp. 198–213.

sufficiently confident to take the offensive. The French maintained tenuous control in the cities and the major production centers, but at a very high cost, suffering 1,000 casualties per month and in 1949 alone spending 167 million francs on the war. Even in the areas under nominal French control, the Vietminh spread terror after dark, sabotaging power plants and factories, tossing grenades into cafes and theaters, and brutally assassinating French officials. "Anyone with white skin caught outside protected areas after dark is courting horrible death," an American correspondent reported.[30]

The Bao Dai solution, Bao Dai himself ruefully conceded, was "just a French solution."[31] The much-maligned "playboy Emperor" was in fact a tragic figure. An intelligent man, genuinely concerned about the future of his nation, he had spent most of his life as a puppet of France and then Japan, whiling away the years by indulging an apparently insatiable taste for sports cars, women, and gambling. The agreement of February 1950 gave him little to work with. Under this impossibly complex document of 258 pages, the French retained control of Vietnam's treasury, commerce, and foreign and military policies. They refused even to turn over Saigon's Norodom Palace as the seat of the new government. The government itself was composed largely of wealthy southern landowners, many of them more European than Vietnamese and in no sense representative of the people. Nationalists of stature refused to support Bao Dai, and the masses either backed the resistance or remained aloof. The emperor may have wished to become a leader, but he lacked the temperament to do so. Introverted and given to moods of depression and indolence, he lived in isolation in one of his palaces or aboard his 600-ton air-conditioned yacht or escaped to the French Riviera, all the while salting away large sums of money in Swiss bank accounts. Not "the stuff of which Churchills are made," U.S. Ambassador Donald Heath lamented with marvelous understatement.[32]

The onset of the Korean War in the summer of 1950 added new dangers. North Korea's invasion of South Korea confirmed U.S. suspicions that the Soviet Union sought to conquer all of Asia, even at the risk of war, and the defense of Indochina assumed even

---

[30]Tilman Durdin, "War 'Not for Land but for People,' " *New York Times Magazine,* May 28, 1950, 48.

[31]Robert Shaplen, *The Lost Revolution: The U.S. in Vietnam, 1946–1966* (New York, 1966), p. 64.

[32]Heath to John Foster Dulles, April 28, 1953, *FR, 1952–1954,* 13: 523; Ellen Hammer, "The Bao Dai Experiment," *Pacific Affairs* 23 (March 1950): 58.

greater importance. The United States responded in June 1950 by extending the containment policy already applied in Europe to East Asia, sending its own military forces to help defend South Korea, placing the Seventh Fleet between Taiwan and the Chinese mainland to protect Chiang Kai-shek's exile government, and stepping up aid to the French in Indochina. These crucial decisions would shape U.S. policies in Asia for many years to come.

By the end of the year, however, the United States and France had suffered major reversals. Chinese intervention in Korea forced General Douglas MacArthur into headlong retreat from the Yalu River. In the meantime, Giap had inflicted upon France its "greatest colonial defeat since Montcalm had died at Quebec," trapping an entire army at Cao Bang in northeastern Vietnam and costing the French more than 6,000 troops and enough equipment to stock an entire Vietminh division.[33] Chinese intervention in Korea raised fears of a similar plunge into Vietnam, and American policy makers were increasingly concerned that growing defeatism and war-weariness in France would raise demands for withdrawal from Indochina.

THE FRANCO-AMERICAN
PARTNERSHIP IN VIETNAM

Against this background of stunning defeat, the Truman administration struggled to devise a workable policy for Indochina. With large numbers of U.S. troops committed to Korea and with Europe seemingly vulnerable to a possible Soviet invasion, the Joint Chiefs of Staff (JCS) agreed that even should the Chinese invade Indochina, the United States could not commit military forces to its defense. France must bear primary responsibility for that war. More certain than ever that Indochina was essential to American security, the administration had to rely on military assistance to bolster French defenses. In late 1950, the United States committed more than $133 million for aid to Indochina and ordered immediate delivery of large quantities of arms and ammunition, naval vessels, aircraft, and military vehicles.

Most Americans agreed, however, that military equipment would not be enough. As early as May, Acheson complained that

---

[33]Bernard Fall, *Street without Joy* (New York, 1972), p. 33.

the French seemed "paralyzed, in a state of moving neither forward or backward."[34] A fact-finding mission dispatched to Indochina before the Cao Bang disaster reported that the French state of mind was "fatuous, even dangerous," and warned that unless France prosecuted the war with greater determination, used native personnel more effectively, and moved boldly and generously to win over the Vietnamese, the United States and its ally might be "moving into a debacle which neither of us can afford."[35] The JCS proposed that the United States condition its military aid on French pledges to take drastic measures, including the promise of eventual independence.

The administration approached this question with great caution. Acheson conceded that if the United States supported France's "old-fashioned colonial attitudes," it might "lose out." But the French presence was essential to defend Indochina against communism, he quickly added, and the United States could not press France to the point where it would say, "All right, take over the damned country. We don't want it." Admitting the inconsistency of American policy, he saw no choice but to encourage the French to remain until the crisis had eased but at the same time persuade them to "play with the nationalist movement and give Bao Dai a chance really to get the nationalists on his side."[36] The administration would go no further than gently urge France to make symbolic concessions and build a Vietnamese army, in the meantime holding Bao Dai's "feet to the fire" to get him to assert effective leadership under French tutelage.[37]

To strengthen the governments of Indochina and increase their popular appeal, the United States between 1950 and 1952 spent more than $50 million for economic and technical assistance. American experts provided fertilizer and seeds to increase agricultural production, constructed dispensaries, developed malaria control programs, and distributed food and clothing to refugees. To ensure

[34]Minutes of meeting, National Security Council, May 4, 1950, Truman Papers, President's Secretary's File.
[35]Melby Mission Report, August 6, 1950, *FR, 1950*, 6: 843–844; Policy Planning Staff Memorandum, August 16, 1950, ibid., 857–858.
[36]U.S. Congress, Senate, *Reviews of the World Situation: 1949–1950 Hearings Held in Executive Session before the Committee on Foreign Relations* (Washington, D.C., 1974), pp. 266–268, 292–293.
[37]Livingston Merchant to Dean Rusk, October 19, 1950, *FR, 1950*, 6: 901–902.

achievement of its objectives, the United States insisted that the aid go directly to the native governments. To secure maximum propaganda advantage, zealous U.S. aid officials tacked posters on pagoda walls and air-dropped pamphlets into villages indicating that the programs were gifts of the United States and contrasting the "real gains" with "Communism's empty promises." The U.S. Information Service even prepared a Vietnamese-language edition of the *Outline History of the United States* with an introduction by President Truman expressing hope that an "account of the progress of the American people toward a just and happy society can be an inspiration to those Vietnamese who today know something of the same difficulties as they build a new nation."[38]

The Truman policy brought limited results. Their hopes of victory revived by the prospect of large-scale American assistance, the French in late 1950 appointed the flamboyant General Jean de Lattre de Tassigny to command the armed forces in Indochina and instructed him to prosecute the war vigorously. A born crusader and practitioner of what he called *dynamisme,* de Lattre announced upon arriving in Vietnam that he would win the war within fifteen months, and under his inspired leadership French forces repulsed a major Vietminh offensive in the Red River Delta in early 1951. But when de Lattre followed up his success by attacking Vietminh strongholds just south of Hanoi, France suffered its worst defeat of the war. De Lattre himself would die of cancer in early 1952, and the French military position was more precarious than when he had come to Vietnam.

In other areas as well there was little progress. Desperately short of personnel, the French finally put aside their reluctance to arm the Vietnamese, and de Lattre made determined efforts to create a Vietnamese National Army (VNA), a process the French called *jaunissement* or yellowing. The Vietnamese were understandably reluctant to fight for a French cause, however, and by the end of 1951 the VNA numbered only 38,000 soldiers, far short of its projected strength of 115,000. Responding to American en-

---

[38]Mutual Security Agency, *Dateline Saigon: Our Quiet War in Indochina* (Washington, D.C., 1952). Roger Tubby to Joseph Short, March 8, 1951, Truman Papers, Official File 203-F. The French dismissed as the "height of national egotism" the fact that this first book translated by Americans into Vietnamese was a history of the United States. Heath to Secretary of State, June 14, 1951, *FR, 1951,* 6:425–427.

treaties, the French vaguely promised to "perfect" the independence of the Associated States, but the massive infusion of American supplies and de Lattre's early victories seemed to eliminate any need for real concessions. The French were unwilling to fight for Vietnamese independence and never seriously considered the only sort of concession that would have satisfied the aspirations of Vietnamese nationalism. France transferred to the "free states" some additional responsibilities, but they remained shadow governments lacking authority and popular support.

By 1952, the United States was bearing roughly one-third of the cost of the war, but it was dissatisfied with the results and with its inability to influence French military policy. A small Military Assistance and Advisory Group (MAAG) had been sent to Vietnam in 1950 to screen French requests for aid, assist in training Vietnamese soldiers, and advise on strategy. By going directly to Washington to get what he wanted, however, de Lattre reduced the MAAG to virtual impotence. Proud, sensitive, and highly nationalistic, he ignored the American "advisers" in formulating strategy, denied them any role in training the Vietnamese, and refused even to inform them of what he was doing.[39]

Deeply suspicious of American intrusion into their domain, the French expressed open resentment against the aid program and placed numerous obstacles in its way. De Lattre bitterly complained that there were too many Americans in Vietnam spending too much money, that U.S. aid was making France "look like a poor cousin in Vietnamese eyes," and that Americans were "fanning the flames of extreme nationalism." At a dinner for the U.S. consul in Hanoi in the spring of 1951, he launched into an anti-American tirade that lasted until 1:00 A.M., raving like a "madman," according to a British diplomat, and accusing the United States of trying to replace France in Vietnam. French officials attempted to block projects that did not contribute directly to the war and encouraged Vietnamese suspicions by warning that American aid contained "hidden traps" to subvert their "independence." Largely as a result of French obstructionism, the aid program touched only a small number of people. American officials conceded that its "beneficial

---

[39]Ronald H. Spector, *Advice and Support: The Early Years, 1941–1960* (Washington, D.C., 1983), pp. 115–121.

psychological results were largely negated because the United States at the same time was pursuing a program of [military] support to the French." America was looked upon "more as a supporter of colonialism than as a friend of the new nation."[40]

While firmly resisting U.S. influence, France demanded additional military assistance, and the United States could do little but comply. By early 1952, the domino theory was firmly rooted as a principle of U.S. foreign policy. Policy makers agreed that Southeast Asia must not be permitted to "fall into the hands of the Communists like a ripe plum" and that a continued French presence in Indochina was essential to that end.[41] Aware that the threat to Indochina had increased since 1950 and fearful that the French might pull out if their requests were not met, the administration in June 1952 approved $150 million in military assistance. Although thoroughly dissatisfied with France's performance in the war and deeply annoyed by its secretiveness and obstructionism, Truman and Acheson rejected Defense Department proposals to use the leverage afforded by aid to force France to adopt a "dynamic program" to "produce positive improvement in the military and political situation." The State Department feared that if it "pressed the French too hard they would withdraw and leave us holding the baby."[42]

America's Indochina policy continued to be a hostage to its policy in Europe. Since 1951, the United States had pushed for allied approval of the European Defense Community, a plan to integrate French and German forces into a multinational army originally put forward by France to delay German rearmament. The French repeatedly warned that they could not furnish troops for European defense without generous American support in Indochina, a ploy Acheson accurately described as "blackmail." The European Defense Community had also become a volatile political issue in France, where there was strong resistance to surrendering the iden-

---

[40]Shaplen, *Lost Revolution,* pp. 86–89; Embassy Saigon to Secretary of State, May 15, 1951, *FR, 1951,* 6: 419; Frank Gibbs to R. H. Scott, April 28, 1951, FO 371/92420, Foreign Office Records, Public Record Office, London.

[41]NSC 124/2, June 24, 1952, *Pentagon Papers (Gravel),* 1:385–386; "Pacific Security Pact," January 2, 1952, Truman Papers, President's Secretary's File, Churchill-Truman Meetings, Box 116.

[42]Quoted in John M. Allison, *Ambassador from the Prairie, or Allison Wonderland* (New York, 1976), pp. 191, 194.

tity of the French army and collaborating with a recent, and still despised, enemy. With the question awaiting ratification by the French parliament, Acheson later recalled, no one "seriously advised" that it would be "wise to end, or threaten to end, aid to Indochina unless an American plan of military and political reform was carried out."[43]

Despite a considerable investment in Indochina, Truman and Acheson left to their successors a problem infinitely more complex and dangerous than the one they had taken on in 1950. What had begun as a localized rebellion against French colonialism had expanded into an international conflict of major proportions. The United States was now bearing more than 40 percent of the cost of the war and had established a stake in its outcome. Chinese aid to the Vietminh had increased from 400 tons of military equipment and supplies per month to more than 3,000, and Chinese advisers trained the Vietminh army and helped plan its major campaigns. The war had spilled over into neighboring Laos and Thailand, where China and the Vietminh backed insurgencies against governments supported by the United States and France. In Vietnam itself, French control had been reduced to enclaves around Hanoi, Haiphong, and Saigon, and a narrow strip along the Cambodian border, and France faced a new and much more ominous military threat. "The enemy, once painted as a bomb-throwing terrorist or hill sniper lurking in night ambush," American journalist Theodore White observed, "has become a modern army, increasingly skillful, armed with artillery, organized into divisional groups.[44]

French military operations had settled into a frustrating and debilitating pattern. The Vietminh were deeply entrenched in the Red River Delta, using the rugged terrain and exceptional skills as camouflage to conceal themselves. In late 1952, the French high command launched Operation Lorraine, its largest operation of the war, mobilizing nearly 30,000 troops plus tanks and artillery to attack the Vietminh's delta strongholds. Hoping to draw the enemy into a set-piece battle where superior firepower could chew them up, French forces plunged deep into Vietminh territory without

[43]Dean G. Acheson, *Present at the Creation* (New York, 1969), p. 676.
[44]Theodore H. White, "France Holds On to the Indo-China Tiger," *New York Times Magazine,* June 8, 1952, 9.

meeting significant resistance. When the roadbound French con-
voys sought to withdraw, however, they were caught in a series of
deadly ambushes and chopped to pieces. Not for the last time, the
French would not get their set-piece battle. Operation Lorraine cost
nearly a battalion in casualties and tied up large-scale forces desperately needed elsewhere.[45]

The French had naively hoped that American aid might be a
substitute for increased sacrifice on their own part, but they had
come to realize that it only required more of them. Fearful of their
nation's growing dependence on the United States and aware that
victory would require an all-out effort, in late 1952 some French political leaders outside the Communist party began for the first time
to recommend withdrawal from Indochina. The "real" problem,
Acheson warned the incoming administration, was the "French will
to carry on the . . . war."[46]

EISENHOWER, DULLES, AND VIETNAM

The Republican administration of Dwight D. Eisenhower accepted
without modification the principles of Indochina policy bequeathed
by the Democrats. Eisenhower and his secretary of state, John Foster Dulles, agreed that Ho Chi Minh was an instrument of international communism and that the fall of Indochina would cause the
loss of all Southeast Asia with disastrous political, economic, and
strategic consequences for the United States. In the campaign of
1952, the Republicans had attacked the Democrats for failing to halt
the advance of communism, and they were even more determined
than their predecessors to prevent the fall of Indochina. While vow-
ing to wage the Cold War vigorously, Eisenhower and Dulles had
also promised cuts in defense spending, and their "New Look" defense policy called for sharp reductions in American ground forces.
They were even more reluctant than Truman and Acheson to commit American combat troops to Southeast Asia and agreed that
France must continue to bear the burden.

The changes introduced by the Republicans were changes of
mood and tactics rather than substance. As would happen so often

---

[45]Fall, *Street without Joy*, pp. 61–106.
[46]Henry Cabot Lodge, Jr., *As It Was* (New York, 1976), p. 36.

during the long history of American involvement in Vietnam, a new administration came into office confident that new methods or the more persistent application of old ones could reverse a deteriorating situation. The Republicans quickly concluded that the United States and France had made critical errors. Eisenhower insisted that the French generals in Indochina were a "poor lot" and that new leadership was needed. The U.S. military deplored France's cautious, defensive strategy and its reluctance to use Vietnamese troops, and diplomat Rob McClintock insisted that the United States should refuse to pay the bill unless the French stopped "sitting in their Beau Geste forts on champagne cases." The United States Army had achieved success in Korea by training South Korean troops and employing aggressive, offensive tactics. The JCS therefore concluded that France could win the war within a year if it made greater use of Vietnamese forces and adopted an aggressive strategy to destroy the enemy's regular units. Most U.S. officials also agreed that France had not done enough to win nationalist support by making timely and substantive political concessions. Eisenhower and Dulles felt that the Truman administration had carelessly squandered the leverage available to it, and they concurred with General J. Lawton Collins that it was time to "put the squeeze on the French to get them off their fannies."[47]

The new administration set out zealously to correct the mistakes of its predecessor. Alarmed by growing signs of war-weariness in France, Eisenhower and Dulles gave firm assurances of continued assistance and promised that French "tiredness" would "evaporate in the face of a positive and constructive program."[48] The administration also made clear, however, that continued aid would depend on detailed and specific information about French plans and military operations and on firm pledges to expand the VNA and develop an aggressive strategy with an explicit timetable for victory. Eisenhower himself impressed on the French the importance of appointing a "forceful and inspirational leader, empowered with the

[47]British Embassy, Saigon, to Foreign Office, April 24, 1953, PREM 11/645, Public Record Office; JCS meeting, April 24, 1953, FR, 1952–1954, 13:500.
[48]Dulles to American Embassy Paris, March 27, 1953, U.S. Congress, House Committee on Armed Services, United States–Vietnam Relations, 1945–1967: A Study Prepared by the Department of Defense (Washington, D.C., 1971), Book 9, 20. Hereafter cited as USVN with book number.

means and authority to win victory," and of making "clear and un-equivocal public announcements, repeated as often as may be desir-able," that complete independence would be granted when the war was won.[49]

Under mounting pressure to do something or withdraw from Indochina, the French government responded quickly. In early May 1953, it appointed General Henri Navarre to command its forces in Indochina. Two months later, a new cabinet, headed by Joseph Laniel, promised to "perfect" the independence of the Associated States by giving them additional responsibilities. Shortly after, the French presented for American approval a new strategic concept, the so-called Navarre Plan. Tailored to specifications set forth by the American JCS, the plan proposed a vast augmentation of the VNA along with the commitment to Indochina of an additional nine bat-talions of French regulars. Navarre proposed to withdraw his scat-tered forces from their isolated garrisons, combine them with the new forces available to him, and initiate a major offensive in the Red River Delta. In a secret report to Paris, he warned that the war could not be won in a strictly military sense and that the best that could be hoped for was a draw. The Laniel government apparently adopted the plan as a last-ditch measure to salvage some return on a huge in-vestment and to ensure continued American support. It also at-tached a high price tag, advising Washington that without an addi-tional $400 million in aid, it could not implement the plan and would have to consider withdrawal from Indochina.

Although dubious of French intentions and capabilities, Wash-ington felt compelled to go along. Eisenhower privately com-plained that Laniel's promise of independence had been made "in an obscure and roundabout fashion—instead of boldly, forthrightly and repeatedly."[50] The JCS doubted France's willingness and abil-ity to pursue the Navarre Plan vigorously. By this time, however, the two nations were caught in a tangle of mutual dependence and spiraling commitments. The JCS concluded that the Navarre Plan at least offered a chance of success. The State Department warned that Laniel's fall would bring in a government committed to a negoti-

---

[49]Eisenhower to C. Douglas Dillon, May 6, 1953, Dwight D. Eisenhower Papers, Dwight D. Eisenhower Library, Abilene, Kans., International File: France, 1953(3), Box 10.
[50]Eisenhower to Ralph Flanders, July 7, 1953, Eisenhower Papers, Diary Series, Box 2.

ated settlement resulting in "the eventual loss to Communism not only of Indochina but of the whole of Southeast Asia."[51] After extracting a formal French promise to pursue the plan with determination, the administration in September 1953 agreed to provide an additional $385 million in military assistance. With characteristic bravado, Dulles proclaimed that the new French strategy would "break the organized body of Communist aggression by the end of the 1955 fighting season."[52]

THE DIEN BIEN PHU CRISIS

Within six months, the military and political situation in Indochina drastically deteriorated. Navarre was forced to scrap his ill-fated plan in its initial stages. In the fall of 1953, he began mobilizing forces for the anticipated offensive in the delta. Giap, recognizing that he must strike a decisive blow before the impact of expanded American aid could be felt, invaded central and southern Laos, intensified guerrilla activity in the delta, and prepared for a major strike into northern Laos. The only response Navarre could devise was to scatter the forces he had just combined to counter the new Vietminh thrusts.

By early 1954, both sides had committed major forces to the remote village of Dien Bien Phu in the northwest corner of Vietnam. Navarre established a position at the intersection of several major roads near the Laotian border to cut off the anticipated invasion and lure Vietminh units into open battle. He hastily dispatched twelve battalions of regulars supported by aircraft and heavy artillery. His commander, the flamboyant aristocrat, Colonel Christian Marie Ferdinand de la Croix de Castries, constructed a garrison ringed with barbed wire and bunkers and protected by a series of artillery bases in the outlying hills, each, according to legend, named for one of the colonel's mistresses. Giap took the "bait." After a quick strike into Laos, he retraced his steps and encircled the French garrison. Navarre now found 12,000 of his elite forces isolated in a far corner

[51]State Department report to National Security Council, August 5, 1953, *USVN*, Book 9, 128.
[52]Quoted in Bernard Fall, *The Two Vietnams: A Political and Military Analysis* (New York, 1967), p. 122.

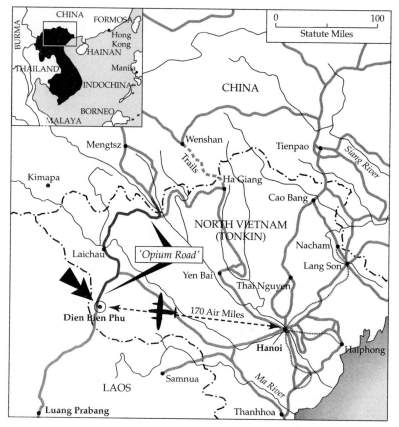

The Battle of Dien Bien Phu
©*AP Wide World Photos. Reprinted with permission.*

of Vietnam. Although increasingly uncertain they could hold out against superior Vietminh numbers, he decided to stay.

In the meantime, an outburst of Vietnamese nationalism further undercut France's already tenuous political position. When the French opened negotiations to "perfect" Vietnamese independence, non-Communist nationalists, including some of Bao Dai's associates, demanded not only complete independence but also severance of all ties with France. The United States found itself in a predicament. Although it had taken a forthright stand in favor of eventual independence, it feared that the Vietnamese demands would provoke a French withdrawal, and it was certain that the

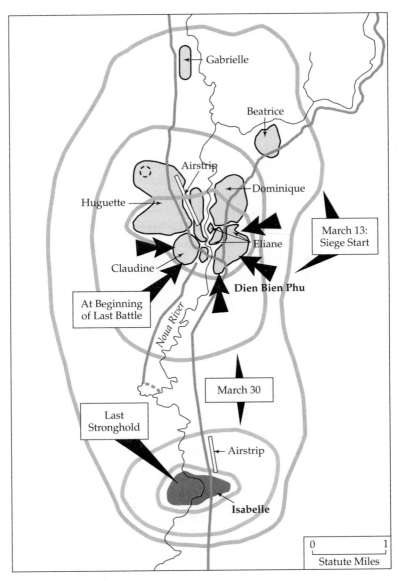

Progress of the Battle

Bao Dai government could not survive by itself. Ambassador Heath charged the Vietnamese with "childlike" and "irresponsible" behavior. Dulles angrily denounced the "ill-considered" actions of the nationalists and dangled before them promises of large-scale aid if they behaved.[53] The U.S. embassy in Saigon pressed the Vietnamese to tone down their demands—"We are the last French colonialists in Indochina," an American diplomat remarked with wry humor.[54] Despite United States attempts to mediate, the French and Vietnamese could not agree on the status of an independent Vietnam.

The political crisis of late 1953, along with a major shift in Soviet and Chinese foreign policies, heightened French tendencies toward a negotiated settlement. Many French politicians concluded that Vietnamese association with the French Union, if only symbolic, was all that could be salvaged and that without this there was no reason to prolong the agony. The leaders who had assumed power in the Kremlin after Stalin's death in February had taken a conciliatory line on a number of major Cold War issues, Indochina included, and the French government hoped that Soviet influence would make possible a favorable settlement. Over Dulles's vigorous opposition, France in early 1954 agreed to place Indochina on the agenda of an East-West conference scheduled to meet in Geneva to consider Asian problems.

Eisenhower and Dulles could only acquiesce. Distrustful of the Soviet overtures and skeptical of French wisdom, they could not openly oppose peaceful settlement of a major international crisis. Moreover, despite Dulles's threats of an "agonizing reappraisal" of U.S. commitments, the French still refused to ratify the European Defense Community, and the new Soviet line complicated the prospect by easing European fears of Russia. Like Acheson before him, Dulles hesitated to press France too hard on Indochina lest it reject the European Defense Community altogether, splitting the Western alliance and playing into the hands of the Russians.

In January 1954, the United States for the first time faced the prospect of direct military intervention in Indochina. Speaking with "great force," Eisenhower expressed to the NSC firm opposition to

[53]Heath to State Department, October 18, 1953, *FR, 1952–1954*, 13:836; Dulles to American Embassy Saigon, October 21, 1953, *USVN*, Book 9, 169–170.
[54]Quoted in Hammer, *Struggle for Indochina*, p. 319.

putting American troops into the jungles of Indochina. He went on to insist, however, that the United States could not forget its vital interests there. Comparing the region to a "leaky dike," he warned that it was "sometimes better to put a finger in than to let the whole structure wash away."[55] American officials especially feared that French war-weariness would result in a surrender at Geneva. A special committee reviewing Indochina policy recommended in mid-March that the United States should discourage defeatist tendencies in France and use its influence at Geneva to ensure that no agreements were reached. If, despite its efforts, the French accepted an unsatisfactory settlement, the United States might have to arrange with the Associated States and other interested nations to continue the war without France.[56]

While Eisenhower and his advisers pondered U.S. intervention, Giap tightened the noose around Dien Bien Phu. In one of the most spectacular logistical feats in the history of warfare, the Vietminh moved an army of 50,000 into the hills around the French fortress. Thousands of porters including a "long-haired army" of women moved tons of equipment and supplies over the hundred miles of rugged trails from staging areas near the Chinese border to Dien Bien Phu. On March 13, the Vietminh launched the first all-out attack and within twenty-four hours seized outposts Gabrielle and Beatrice. American and French experts had predicted that it would be impossible to get artillery up to the high ground surrounding the garrison. But the Vietminh formed "human anthills," carrying disassembled weapons up piece by piece, then reassembling them and camouflaging them so effectively that they were impervious to artillery and strafing. The heavy Vietminh guns quickly knocked out the airfield, making resupply impossible except by parachute drop and leaving the garrison of 12,000 soldiers isolated and vulnerable.

The spectacular Vietminh success at Dien Bien Phu raised the prospect of immediate U.S. intervention. During a visit to Washington in late March, French chief of staff General Paul Ely still estimated a "50-50 chance of success" and merely requested the transfer of additional American aircraft to be used by France for attacks on Vietminh lines around the fortress. Ely was deeply concerned about

---

[55]Record of NSC meeting, January 8, 1954, *FR, 1952–1954*, 13: 949, 952.
[56]*Pentagon Papers (Gravel)*, 1: 90–92.

the possibility of Chinese intervention, however, openly inquiring how the United States would respond in such a contingency.[57] Much less optimistic, the JCS chairman, Admiral Arthur Radford, seized upon a scheme originally devised by French and American officers in Saigon. Code-named VULTURE, the plan in its various manifestations called for the bombing of Vietminh supply lines and entrenchments around Dien Bien Phu by U.S. B-29s, possibly unmarked or camouflaged with French markings and flown by either French crews, American military pilots, or U.S. military pilots temporarily assigned to the French Foreign Legion. Some discussion was given to the use of tactical nuclear weapons. Radford's enthusiasm for the plan led Ely to believe that U.S. approval would be forthcoming should the French formally request it.[58]

In fact, VULTURE won little support in Washington. Eisenhower briefly toyed with the idea of a "single strike [flown by U.S. pilots in unmarked planes], if it were almost certain this would produce decisive results." "Of course . . . we'd have to deny it forever," he quickly added.[59] Dulles was prepared to consider air and naval operations in Indochina, but only as a last resort. Less worried about the immediate threat to Dien Bien Phu than about the long-range threat to Southeast Asia, the secretary preferred what he called "United Action," the formation of a coalition composed of the United States, Great Britain, France, Australia, New Zealand, the Philippines, Thailand, and the Associated States, to guarantee the security of Southeast Asia. Such a coalition, by its very existence, might deter Chinese intervention in the Indochina War and Chinese aggression elsewhere in Asia, and United Action, as some scholars have suggested, may have been primarily a bluff. Or, if

[57]Memorandum of conversation, Ely and Dulles, March 23, 1954, 751G.00/32354, Department of State Records. For a more detailed discussion of these events, see George C. Herring and Richard H. Immerman, "Eisenhower, Dulles, and Dien Bien Phu: 'The Day We Didn't Go to War' Revisited," *Journal of American History* 71 (September 1984): 343–363.

[58]Laurent Cesari and Jacques de Folin, "Military Necessity, Political Impossibility: The French Viewpoint on Operation *Vautour*," in Lawrence S. Kaplan, Denise Artaud, and Mark R. Rubin (eds.), *Dien Bien Phu and the Crisis of Franco-American Relations, 1954–1955* (Wilmington, 1990), pp. 105–120.

[59]Memorandum of conversation, Eisenhower and Dulles, March 24, 1954, Lot 64D199, Box 222, Department of State Records; James Hagerty Diary, April 1, 1954, James Hagerty Papers, Dwight D. Eisenhower Library, Abilene, Kans.

military intervention became necessary, it would remove the stigma of a war for French colonialism and ensure that the entire burden did not fall upon the United States. In keeping with the New Look defense policy, local and regional forces could bear the brunt of the ground fighting while the United States provided air and naval support, furnished money and supplies, and trained indigenous troops.

Dulles and Eisenhower were also unwilling to intervene unless they could extract concessions from the French. Dulles warned that if the United States intervened, its prestige would be "engaged to a point where we would want to have a success. We could not afford a defeat that would have world-wide repercussions."[60] The administration attributed France's failure to its mishandling of the Vietnamese and its refusal to wage the war aggressively. Persistent efforts to change French attitudes had failed. Indeed, Ely had only recently rebuffed a proposal to expand the role of the American military advisory group, bitterly complaining about the "invading nature" of the Americans and their "determination to control and operate everything of importance."[61] Dulles and Eisenhower agreed that the United States must not risk its prestige in Indochina until France agreed to keep its troops there, accelerate the move toward independence, and permit the United States a larger role in training indigenous forces and formulating strategy.

Most of Eisenhower's top military advisers raised serious objections to air intervention at Dien Bien Phu. Some questioned whether an air strike could relieve the siege without destroying the fortress itself; others wondered whether intervention could be kept limited—"One cannot go over Niagara Falls in a barrel only slightly," a Defense Department analyst warned.[62] Among the JCS, only Air Force General Nathan F. Twining approved the proposal, and he insisted on attaching conditions that the French were unlikely to accept. The other chiefs warned that air intervention posed major risks and would not decisively affect the outcome of the war. Army Chief of Staff Matthew Ridgway was particularly outspoken, responding to Radford's query about the proposed air strike with an "emphatic and immediate 'No.' " Alarmed by "the old delusive

[60]Dwight D. Eisenhower, *Mandate for Change, 1953–1956* (New York, 1963), p. 345.
[61]Radford to Eisenhower, March 29, 1954, *USVN*, Book 9, 283–284.
[62]*Pentagon Papers (Gravel)*, 1: 89.

idea . . . that we could do things the cheap and easy way," Ridgway warned Eisenhower that air power alone could not ensure victory and that ground forces would have to fight under the most difficult logistic circumstances and in a uniquely inhospitable terrain.[63]

Although profoundly skeptical about the proposed air strike, the administration was sufficiently alarmed by the emerging crisis in Indochina to seek congressional support for possible military intervention. The fall of Dien Bien Phu seemed certain by early April. Eisenhower and Dulles preferred to act in concert with other nations, but they feared that a defeat might produce a French collapse before plans for United Action could be put into effect, leaving American naval and air power the only means to save Indochina. Sensitive to Truman's fate in Korea, they were unwilling to act without backing from Congress, and Eisenhower instructed Dulles to explore with congressional leaders the conditions under which the use of American military power might be approved. The purpose of the dramatic meeting at the State Department on April 3 was not to secure approval for an immediate air attack but to gain discretionary authority to employ American naval and air forces—with allies if possible, without them if necessary—should the fall of Dien Bien Phu threaten the loss of Indochina.

The administration encountered stubborn resistance. Dulles and Radford grimly warned that failure to act might cost the United States Southeast Asia and advised that the president should have the power to use naval and air forces "if he felt it necessary in the interest of national security." No one questioned their assessment of the gravity of the situation, but the congressmen insisted that there must be "no more Koreas, with the United States furnishing 90% of the manpower," and made clear they would approve nothing until the administration had obtained firm commitments from other nations. Dulles persisted, assuring the legislators that the administration had no intention of sending ground troops to Indochina and indicating that he could more easily gain commitments from allies if he could specify what the United States would

[63]Ridgway memorandum for the Joint Chiefs, April 2, 1954, Matthew B. Ridgway Papers, U.S. Army Military History Institute, Carlisle Barracks, Pa.; Matthew B. Ridgway, *Soldier* (New York, 1956), pp. 276–277.

do. The congressmen were not swayed. "Once the flag is committed," they warned, "the use of land forces would surely follow." Sharing the administration's distrust of France, they also insisted that the United States must not go to war in support of colonialism. They would only agree that if "satisfactory commitments" could be secured from Great Britain and other allies to support military intervention and from France to "internationalize" the war and speed the move toward independence, they would support a resolution authorizing the president to commit U.S. forces. Congressional insistence on prior allied commitments, particularly from Great Britain, eliminated the option of unilateral American intervention and placed major obstacles in the way of United Action.[64]

The April 3 session doomed an air strike at Dien Bien Phu. Although unenthusiastic about the prospect of American intervention in any form, the French government eventually concluded that an air strike offered the only hope of saving the beleaguered fortress and on April 5 requested implementation of the plan. Eisenhower promptly rejected the French request as "politically impossible."[65] At a meeting on April 6, the NSC agreed that planning and mobilization for possible later intervention should "promptly be initiated," while the administration attempted to meet the essential preconditions for United Action.[66]

With the fate of Dien Bien Phu hanging in the balance, the United States frantically promoted United Action. Dulles immediately departed for London and Paris to consult with British and French leaders. Eisenhower penned a long personal letter to Prime Minister Winston Churchill urging British support for a coalition that would be "willing to fight" to check Communist expansion in Southeast Asia. At a much publicized news conference on April 7, the president laid the foundation for possible U.S. intervention. Outlining in simple language principles that had formed the basis for American policy for four years, he emphasized that Indochina was an important source of tin, tungsten, and

[64]Dulles memorandum, April 5, 1954, "Conference with Congressional Leaders, April 3, 1954," John Foster Dulles Papers, Dwight D. Eisenhower Library, Abilene, Kans.
[65]Record of telephone conversation, Eisenhower and Dulles, April 5, 1954, Eisenhower Papers, Diary Series, Box 3.
[66]Record of NSC meeting, April 6, 1954, *FR, 1952–1954*, 13: 1253.

rubber and that having lost China to "Communist dictatorship," the United States "simply can't afford greater losses." More important, he warned, should Indochina fall, the rest of Southeast Asia would "go over very quickly," like a "row of dominoes" when the first one is knocked down, causing much greater losses of raw materials and people, jeopardizing America's strategic position in the Far East, and driving Japan into the communist camp. "So the possible consequences of the loss," he concluded, "are just incalculable to the free world."[67]

The flurry of American diplomatic activity in April 1954 exposed fundamental cleavages between the United States and its allies. The Churchill government was prepared to join a collective security arrangement after Geneva, but it adamantly opposed immediate intervention in Indochina. Churchill and his foreign secretary, Anthony Eden, did not share the American fear that the loss of all or part of Indochina would bring the fall of Southeast Asia. They were convinced that France retained sufficient influence to salvage a reasonable settlement at Geneva, and they feared that outside military intervention would destroy any hope of a negotiated settlement and perhaps even provoke a war with China. Most important, they had no desire to entangle Britain in a war they were certain could not be won.

Dulles's discussions with France made clear the hugely divergent approaches of the two nations toward the war and the Geneva negotiations. The United States was willing to intervene in Indochina, but only on condition that France resist a negotiated settlement at Geneva, agree to remain in Indochina and fight indefinitely, concede to its ally a greater role in planning strategy and training indigenous forces, and accept Vietnamese demands for complete independence. The French insisted that Vietnam must retain ties with the French Union. They wanted nothing more than an air strike to relieve the siege of Dien Bien Phu. They opposed internationalization of the war, which would undermine their prestige in Indochina and remove control from their hands. Dulles may have hoped that by offering to help France he could yet save the European Defense Community, but the French government made

---

[67]Eisenhower, *Mandate for Change*, pp. 346–347; *Dwight D. Eisenhower, Public Papers, 1954* (Washington D.C., 1955), pp. 382–384.

clear that the EDC could not be approved if France obligated itself to keep troops in Indochina indefinitely.

The administration was deeply annoyed by the response of its allies. U.S. officials complained that the British were "weak-kneed," and Eisenhower privately lamented that Churchill and Eden showed a "woeful unawareness" of the risks of inaction in Southeast Asia.[68] Dulles misinterpreted Eden's willingness to discuss long-range security arrangements as a tentative commitment to United Action, and when informed of the actual British position, he was incensed. The White House and State Department were outraged by French intransigence. Eisenhower blamed the French for their present plight: they had used "weasel words in promising independence," he wrote a friend, "and through this reason as much as anything else have suffered reverses that have been inexcusable." He refused to consider intervention on France's terms. The French "want us to come in as junior partners and provide materials, etc., while they themselves retain authority in that region," and he would "not go along with them on any such notion."[69]

Congressional opposition reinforced the administration's determination to avoid unilateral intervention. In a speech that won praise from both sides of the aisle, Senator John F. Kennedy, a Democrat from Massachusetts, warned that no amount of military aid could conquer "an enemy of the people which has the support and covert appeal of the people." Victory could not be attained in Indochina as long as France remained. When a "high administration source," subsequently identified as Vice President Richard M. Nixon, remarked "off the record" that if United Action failed, the United States might have to act alone, the reaction was immediate and strong.[70]

Thus, even when France relented a bit, continued British opposition settled the fate of United Action. In late April, Foreign Minister

[68]Hagerty Diary, April 25, 1954, Hagerty Papers; Eisenhower Diary, April 27, 1954, Eisenhower Papers, Diary Series, Box 3.

[69]Eisenhower to E. E. Hazlett, April 27, 1954, Eisenhower Papers, Diary Series, Box 4; record of telephone conversation, Eisenhower and Walter Bedell Smith, April 24, 1954, ibid., Box 3.

[70]The Nixon statement has sometimes been regarded as a trial balloon, but it was unauthorized and did not reflect the administration's thinking at this time. See Hagerty Diary, April 17, 1954, Hagerty Papers; and Richard M. Nixon, RN: The Memoirs of Richard Nixon (New York, 1978), pp. 152–153.

Georges Bidault, whom Dulles described as "close to the breaking point," made a last desperate appeal for American support, warning that only a "massive" air attack would save Dien Bien Phu and hinting that France was prepared to internationalize the war. His hopes of implementing United Action suddenly revived, Dulles informed Bidault that if the British could be persuaded to go along, the administration would seek a congressional resolution authorizing intervention. Over the next three days, the secretary frantically attempted to convert Eden, urgently warning that without support from its allies, France might give up the fight. The British would have none of it, however, and the administration was forced to back off. Eisenhower informed congressional leaders on April 26 that it would be a "tragic error to go in alone as a partner of France" and made clear that the United States would intervene only as part of a "grouping of interested nations." Three days later, the NSC formally decided to "hold up for the time any military action in Indo China until we see how Geneva is coming along."[71]

It remains difficult to evaluate Eisenhower's handling of the Dien Bien Phu crisis. Whether he wanted to intervene militarily and was blocked by Congress and the allies or whether United Action was a clever bluff designed to shift blame for nonintervention elsewhere cannot be determined with certainty. If they had made up their minds what to do, Eisenhower and Dulles covered their tracks so skillfully that they confounded contemporaries and baffled future scholars. Thus, as Leslie Gelb and Richard Betts have concluded, they can be charged with "egregious bumbling saved only by the unwillingness of allies to participate and the restraint of enemies," or they can be praised for a "dazzling display of neutralizing potential domestic opposition and of deterring hostile states bent on total victory."[72]

Whatever the case, the decision sealed Dien Bien Phu's doom. Without U.S. airpower, France had no means to save the fortress. After pounding it mercilessly with artillery and mounting a series of costly human-wave attacks, the Vietminh closed in through an

[71]Dulles to State Department, April 22, 23, 1954, Eisenhower Papers, Ann Whitman File; summary of meeting, April 26, 1954, Eisenhower Papers, "Cleanup" File, Box 16; Hagerty Diary, April 29, 1954, Hagerty Papers.
[72]Leslie Gelb with Richard Betts, *The Irony of Vietnam: The System Worked* (Washington, 1978), p. 56.

elaborate system of networks and tunnels. The isolated and hope-lessly outnumbered French forces finally surrendered on May 7 after fifty-five days of stubborn but futile resistance.

Dien Bien Phu remains one of the most important battles of the twentieth century. It was enormously costly for both sides, the French losing 1,500 killed, 4,000 wounded, and as many as 10,000 missing or captured, the Vietminh 25,000 wounded and 10,000 killed. It brought an end to the First Indochina War and marked the first time in the postwar era that anticolonial forces had defeated a western power on its own terms. For much of the nine-week siege, the attention of the world was riveted on that beleaguered outpost in that remote part of the globe. The battle left a deep mark on those involved. The French felt betrayed by a United States that had pushed them to fight and then left them to die. Americans attributed the debacle to the French army's incompetence, especially its "bunker psychosis," ignoring what the battle could teach them about Vietminh tactics and reinforc-ing their confidence in their own aggressive way of war. For the Viet-minh, Dien Bien Phu vindicated "peoples' war" and became a cele-brated part of their larger historical legend of exploiting human resources to expel powerful outside invaders. They would seek a sim-ilar battle with similar results to defeat the United States in the war that would soon follow.[73]

THE GENEVA CONFERENCE

With the fall of Dien Bien Phu, the attention of belligerents and inter-ested outside parties immediately shifted to Geneva, where the fol-lowing day consideration of Indochina was to begin. Buoyed by its victory, the Vietminh savored the prize for which it had been fight-ing for more than seven years. Its influence in northern Vietnam re-duced to a small pocket around Hanoi, France began preparations to abandon the north and salvage as much as possible below the six-teenth parallel. The French delegation came to Geneva, Bidault lamented, holding a "two of clubs and a three of diamonds."[74]

[73]Dennis Showalter, "Dien Bien Phu in Three Cultures," *War and Society* 16 (October 1998): 93–108.
[74]Quoted in Chester Cooper, *The Lost Crusade: America in Vietnam* (New York, 1970), p. 79.

The United States was a reluctant participant at Geneva. Negotiation with any Communist nation was anathema in those years, but the presence of Communist China made the conference especially unpalatable. Dulles remained in Geneva only briefly and, in the words of a biographer, conducted himself with the "pinched distaste of a puritan in a house of ill repute."[75] He once remarked that the only way he and Chinese delegate Zhou EnLai would meet was if their cars collided; when they actually met face-to-face and Zhou extended his hand, the secretary reportedly turned his back. The administration had long feared that the conference would provide a fig leaf of respectability for a French surrender, and the fall of Dien Bien Phu increased its concern. After departing Geneva, Dulles instructed his delegation to participate in the conference only as an "interested nation," not as a "belligerent or a principal in the negotiations," and not to endorse an agreement that in any way impaired the territorial integrity of the Associated States.[76] Given the military position of the Vietminh when the conference opened, he was saying that the United States would approve no settlement at all.

Indeed, the administration probably hoped there would be no agreement, and during the first five weeks of the conference it kept alive the prospect of military intervention. When Laniel requested American military support should the Chinese stall the talks while the Vietminh pressed on for military victory, Dulles and Eisenhower seriously considered a new plan for intervention. The JCS drew up detailed contingency plans for deploying U.S. forces, agreeing that nuclear weapons would be used if it were militarily advantageous. Administration officials drafted a congressional resolution authorizing the president to employ military forces in Indochina.

As before, the United States and France could not agree on the terms. This time, the administration did not make intervention conditional on British backing, but it stiffened the concessions demanded of France, insisting on an unequivocal advance commitment to internationalize the war and a guarantee that the Associated States could withdraw from the French Union at any time. The French indicated a willingness only to discuss the American conditions and

[75]Townsend Hoopes, *The Devil and John Foster Dulles* (Boston, 1973), p. 222.
[76]Dulles to Smith, May 12, 1954, *USVN*, Book 9, 457–459.

added unacceptable demands of their own, including at least a token commitment of American ground forces and a prior commitment to employ airpower should the Chinese intervene. As the discussions dragged on inconclusively, each side grew wary. The French government eventually concluded that it must exhaust every possibility of a negotiated settlement before prolonging the war. Eisenhower and Dulles surmised that France was keeping alive the possibility of U.S. intervention primarily "as a card to play at Geneva," and they were unwilling to grant an "indefinite option on us." The talks all but ended by mid-June.[77]

In the meantime, the conferees at Geneva struggled toward an agreement. Under pressure from the Chinese and Russians, the Vietminh reluctantly accepted a temporary partition of Vietnam to permit regrouping of military forces following a cease-fire. Laniel had made firm commitments to Bao Dai not to accept partition, but his cabinet fell on June 12 and was replaced by a government headed by Pierre Mendès-France. The new prime minister was flexible on the issue of partition and upon taking power also promised to resign if a settlement were not reached by July 21. Although many details remained to be worked out, the outlines of a political agreement had begun to take form when the heads of delegations agreed to a short recess on June 19.

At this point, the Eisenhower administration adopted a change of policy with momentous long-range implications. Recognizing that the war could not be prolonged without unacceptable risks and that part of Vietnam would probably be lost at Geneva, the administration began to plan for the defense of the rest of Indochina and Southeast Asia. Dulles informed congressional leaders on June 24 that any agreement that emerged from Geneva would be "something we would have to gag about," but he expressed optimism that the United States might still be able to "salvage something" in Southeast Asia "free of the taint of French colonialism." The United States would have to take over responsibility for defending Laos, Cambodia, and that part of Vietnam beneath the sixteenth parallel. The first step was to draw a line that the Communists would not cross and then "hold this area and fight subversion within it with all the strength we have" by providing economic assistance and building a

---

[77]Dulles to American Consulate Geneva, June 8, 1954, ibid., 541.

strong military force. The United States would also have to take the lead in forming a regional defense grouping "to keep alive freedom" in Southeast Asia.[78]

Over the next few weeks, Dulles worked relentlessly to get an agreement that would enable the United States to follow this plan. He secured British concurrence to a set of principles that would constitute an "acceptable" settlement, including the freedom of Laos, Cambodia, and southern Vietnam to maintain "stable, noncommunist regimes" and to accept foreign arms and advisers. He applied extreme pressure, even threatening to disassociate the United States entirely from Geneva, until Mendès-France accepted the so-called seven points as the basis for the French bargaining position. Although armed with firm British and French promises, Dulles still approached the last stages of the conference cautiously and was determined to retain complete freedom of action. The United States should play no more than a passive role in the negotiations, he instructed the head of the American delegation, Walter Bedell Smith. If the agreement lived up to its standards, the administration would issue a unilateral statement of endorsement. Otherwise, it would reserve the freedom to "publicly disassociate itself." Under no circumstances would it be a "cosignatory with the Communists," and it would not guarantee the results.[79]

When the conference reconvened, pressures for a settlement had increased significantly. The July 21 deadline was rapidly approaching for Mendès-France, and Anglo-American support strengthened his bargaining position. Perhaps more important, although the Vietminh's military position gave it a strong claim to influence throughout Vietnam, both the Russians and Chinese exerted heavy pressure for a compromise peace. The Soviet Union had only limited interests in Southeast Asia and appears to have pursued a conciliatory line toward France to encourage rejection of the EDC. Bloodied from the war in Korea and eager to concentrate on pressing domestic issues, the Chinese sought mainly to prevent the Indochina war from expanding. They seem to have taken seriously Dulles's bluster and feared that a breakdown of negotiations might bring U.S. intervention. They persuaded a reluctant Vietminh to remove its forces from

[78]Hagerty Diary, June 23, 24, 28, 1954, Hagerty Papers.
[79]Pentagon Papers (Gravel), 1:152.

and accept neutrality for Laos and Cambodia and to agree to a temporary partition of Vietnam. "After French withdrawal, the whole of Vietnam will be yours," China's chief negotiator, Zhou EnLai, assured nervous Vietminh leaders.[80] For reasons of their own, the Chinese and Soviets moderated Vietminh demands and played a crucial role in arranging a settlement.

The Geneva Accords of 1954 reflected these influences. Vietnam was to be partitioned along the sixteenth parallel to permit the regrouping of military forces from both sides. The division was to be only temporary and was not to be "interpreted as constituting a political or territorial boundary." The country was to be reunified by elections scheduled for the summer of 1956 and supervised by an international commission composed of Canada, Poland, and India. To insulate Vietnam against a renewal of conflict during the transitional period, troops were to be withdrawn from the partition zones within 300 days, and the introduction of new forces and equipment and the establishment of foreign military bases were prohibited. Neither portion of Vietnam was to join a military alliance. Cease-fire arrangements for Laos and Cambodia explicitly recognized the two nations' right to self-defense, but to ease Chinese fears of American intervention, they were not to enter military alliances or permit foreign bases on their soil except in cases where their security was clearly threatened.

In the words of Canadian diplomat John Holmes, the Geneva agreements constituted a "nasty bargain accepted by all parties as the only way to avoid a dangerous confrontation."[81] The major issues over which the war was fought were not settled. The terms were vague in crucial places, and different people viewed their meaning quite differently. The manner in which the accords were handled was unusual if not unique and reflected the tenuous nature of the understandings themselves. The United States and South Vietnam refused to associate themselves with the formal agreements. Other nations signed only the cease-fire agreement, merely listing their names on the political "instruments."

---

[80]Quoted in Qiang Zhai, *China and the Vietnam Wars, 1950–1975* (Chapel Hill, N.C., 2000), p. 58.
[81]Quoted in James Eayrs, *In Defence of Canada: Indochina and ·Roots of Complicity* (Toronto, 1983), p. 225.

For many Vietminh, Geneva represented at best a bittersweet victory. They found partition difficult to accept, even temporarily, and they had hoped that the line would be drawn further south and the elections held sooner. The leadership seems to have recognized, however, that they could not get better terms. They had committed huge resources to Dien Bien Phu, suffered enormous losses, and were in no position to follow up with major campaigns elsewhere. Without support from the Soviet Union and China they could do nothing more, and prolonging the war risked U.S. intervention. Ever the pragmatist, Ho Chi Minh cautioned those "intoxicated with victories" that the "struggle for peace is a hard and complex one" and that they must work within the framework of the Geneva Accords to attain the goals of independence and national unity.[82]

The Eisenhower administration also took a mixed view toward Geneva. The settlement produced some domestic political backlash; California Republican senator William Knowland called it "the greatest victory the communists have won in twenty years." The administration itself viewed with concern the loss of northern Vietnam—"the keystone to the arch of Southeast Asia"—but Eisenhower and Dulles realized, as Smith put it, that "diplomacy has rarely been able to gain at the conference table what cannot be held on the battlefield." The administration protected itself against domestic criticism and retained its freedom of action by refusing to associate itself directly with the agreements. In a unilateral statement, Smith simply "took note" of the Geneva Accords and said that the United States would not "disturb them" by the "threat or the use of force."[83]

The administration was not altogether displeased, however. The agreements were better than had been anticipated when the conference opened, and they allowed sufficient latitude to proceed along the lines Dulles had outlined. Partition was unpalatable, but it gave the United States the opportunity to build up non-Communist forces in southern Vietnam, a challenge Eisenhower and Dulles took up eagerly. The accords placed some limits on outside intervention, to be sure, but the administration did not view them as prohibitive. And some of the terms seemed advantageous. Eisenhower and Dulles agreed, for example, that if elections were held immediately,

---

[82]Quoted in Duiker, *Ho Chi Minh,* pp. 460–461.
[83]*Pentagon Papers (Gravel),* 1:571–572.

Ho Chi Minh would be an easy victor. But the two-year delay gave the United States "fairly good time" to get ready, and Canada's presence on the commission would enable it to "block things."[84]

Eisenhower and Dulles viewed the apparent demise of French colonialism in Southeast Asia with equanimity, if not outright enthusiasm. From the start, the Franco-American partnership in Indochina had been marked by profound mutual suspicion and deep-seated tensions. From 1950 to 1954, the United States had provided France more than $2.6 billion in military aid, but its efforts to influence French policies by friendly persuasion and by attaching strings had failed, and the commitment to France had indeed turned out to be a "dead-end alley." The Americans attributed France's failure primarily to its misguided attempts to perpetuate colonialism in Indochina, and they were confident that without the problems posed by France, the United States could find a viable non-Communist alternative to the Vietminh. "We must work with these people, and then they themselves will soon find out that we are their friends and that they can't live without us," Eisenhower observed.[85] Conceding that the Geneva Accords included "many features he did not like," Dulles still insisted that they contained many "good aspects," most important, the "truly independent status" of Laos, Cambodia, and southern Vietnam. The "important thing," he concluded, was "not to mourn the past but to seize the future opportunity to prevent the loss in Northern Vietnam from leading to the extension of communism throughout Southeast Asia and the Southwest Pacific."[86]

[84]Record of telephone conversation, Eisenhower and Dulles, July 20, 1954, Eisenhower Papers, Diary Series, Box 4.
[85]Hagerty Diary, July 23, 1954, Hagerty Papers.
[86]Dulles news conference, July 23, 1954, John Foster Dulles Papers, Seely G. Mudd Manuscript Library, Princeton, N.J.

The Ngo Family
With American assistance, Ngo Dinh Diem played a major role in the
founding of South Vietnam, but his increasing isolation and reliance on his
family ultimately contributed to his undoing.
AP/Wide World Photos

CHAPTER 2

Our Offspring

Nation Building in South Vietnam, 1954–1961

"The fundamental tenets of this nation's foreign policy . . . depend in considerable measure upon a strong and free Vietnamese nation," Senator John F. Kennedy proclaimed in 1956. "Vietnam represents the cornerstone of the Free World in Southeast Asia, the keystone in the arch, the finger in the dike." Should the "red tide of Communism" pour into it, Kennedy warned, much of Asia would be threatened. Vietnam's economy was essential to the economy of Southeast Asia, the senator went on to say, its "political liberty" an "inspiration to those seeking to obtain or maintain their liberty in all parts of Asia—and indeed of the world." The United States had special obligations to Vietnam that extended beyond mere considerations of the national interest, Kennedy stressed in conclusion: "It is our offspring, we cannot abandon it, we cannot ignore its needs."[1]

Kennedy was addressing the American Friends of Vietnam, and he may have been indulging in after-dinner hyperbole, but his speech summed up the rationale of American policy in South Vietnam in the 1950s, touched on the pivotal role played by the United States at its birth, and highlighted the importance it came to assume. Certain that its fall to communism would lead to the loss of all Southeast Asia, the Eisenhower administration after Geneva set out to create in the southern part of the country a nation that would stand as a bulwark against Communist expansion and serve as a proving ground for democracy in Asia. Originating from the exigencies of the Cold War, the experiment in nation

[1] John F. Kennedy, "America's Stake in Vietnam," *Vital Speeches* 22 (August 1, 1956): 617–619.

building tapped the wellsprings of American idealism and took on many of the trappings of a crusade. Begun as a high-risk gamble, it appeared for a time one of the great success stories of postwar U.S. foreign policy. Only at the end of the decade, when South Vietnam was swept by revolution, did Americans begin to perceive the magnitude and complexity of the problem they had taken on.

A GOOD STOUT EFFORT

Warning that Geneva had been a "disaster" that had made possible a "major forward stride of Communism," the National Security Council (NSC) in the summer of 1954 called for a "new initiative" to shore up the U.S. position in Southeast Asia. The NSC recommended, among other actions, the use of "all available means" to undermine the infant Vietminh regime in northern Vietnam.[2] Throughout the rest of the year, a CIA team stationed in Saigon and headed by Colonel Edward Lansdale devised numerous clandestine methods to harass the Hanoi government. Paramilitary groups infiltrated across the demilitarized zone on sabotage missions, attempting to destroy the government's printing presses and pouring contaminants into the engines of buses to demobilize the transportation system. The teams also carried out "psywar" operations to embarrass the Vietminh regime and encourage emigration to the south. They distributed fake leaflets announcing the harsh methods the government was prepared to take and even hired astrologers to predict hard times in the north and good times in the south.[3]

In the meantime, Dulles hastened off to Manila and negotiated the Southeast Asian security pact he had promoted so vigorously during the Dien Bien Phu crisis. The Southeast Asian Treaty Organization (SEATO) had obvious weaknesses. The major neutralist

---

[2]NSC, "Review of U.S. Policy in the Far East," August 1954, U.S. Congress, House Committee on Armed Services, *United States–Vietnam Relations, 1945–1967: A Study Prepared by the Department of Defense* (Washington, D.C., 1971), Book 10, 731–741. Hereafter cited as *USVN* with book number.

[3]Neil Sheehan et al., *The Pentagon Papers as Published by the New York Times* (New York, 1971), pp. 16–18. Hereafter cited as *Pentagon Papers (NYT)*.

nations of the region—Burma, India, and Indonesia—declined to join, and because of restrictions imposed by the Geneva Accords, Laos, Cambodia, and southern Vietnam could not formally participate. Eisenhower and Dulles admitted that the "western colorization" of the alliance was "unfortunate," but they conceded that it was necessary because of the weakness of the nations in the area. The member nations bound themselves only to "meet common danger" in accordance with their own "constitutional processes" and to "consult" with each other.

From Dulles's standpoint, however, SEATO was more than satisfactory. Eager to minimize expenses and risks from the alliance, he successfully avoided NATO-like commitments and made clear that the United States would not underwrite a Marshall Plan for the area. The mere existence of the alliance, in Dulles's eyes, might deter Communist aggression in the region. More important, a separate protocol specifically designated Laos, Cambodia, and southern Vietnam as areas that, if threatened, would "endanger" the "peace and security" of the signatories. During the Dien Bien Phu crisis, Dulles had felt hampered by the lack of a legal basis for intervention in Indochina. The SEATO protocol not only remedied this defect but also established the foundation, should United Action become necessary in the future, and gave South Vietnam a semblance of international status as a "free" nation.[4]

The key to the new American "initiative" was South Vietnam. The NSC recommended that the United States "make every possible effort, not openly inconsistent with the U.S. position as to the armistice agreements . . . to maintain a friendly non-Communist South Vietnam and to prevent a Communist victory through all-Vietnam elections."[5] Violating the spirit and sometimes the letter of the Geneva Accords, the Eisenhower administration in 1954 and after firmly committed itself to the fragile government of Ngo Dinh Diem, eased the French out of Vietnam, and used its resources unsparingly to construct in southern

[4]The members of SEATO were the United States, the United Kingdom, France, Australia, New Zealand, Thailand, the Philippines, and Pakistan. For an insightful view of Dulles's attitudes toward the alliance, see Richard Bissell oral history interview, Dulles Papers, Princeton, N.J.
[5]NSC, "Review of U.S. Policy in the Far East," August 1954, *USVN*, Book 10, 731–741.

Vietnam a viable, non-Communist nation that would stand as the "cornerstone of the Free World in Southeast Asia."

Had it looked all over the world, the United States could not have chosen a less promising place for an experiment in nation building. The partition settlement left an estimated 14 of 25 million Vietnamese above the seventeenth parallel. The North Vietnamese regime was not without internal opposition, and it faced an enormous challenge of postwar reconstruction. At the same time, it had a large, reasonably well-equipped army and a tightly organized government. Ho Chi Minh was the best-known nationalist leader in all of Vietnam, and the Vietminh had won broad popular respect for leading the struggle against France. Ho and his cohorts remained deeply committed to unification, and they left between 10,000 and 15,000 operatives in the south to promote that goal by legal and extralegal means.

In southern Vietnam, chaos reigned. The colonial economy depended entirely on exports of rice and rubber to finance essential imports. It had been devastated by nearly fourteen years of war and was held together by enormous French military expenditures that would soon cease. The French had finally granted unqualified independence to the State of Vietnam in June 1954, but the government, still nominally presided over by Bao Dai, was a fiction. Assuming the premiership in the summer of 1954, the staunchly anti-French Ngo Dinh Diem inherited antiquated institutions patterned on French practices and ill-suited to the needs of an independent nation—an "oriental despotism with a French accent," one American scornfully labeled it. Diem's government lacked experienced civil servants. Tainted by its long association with France, it had no base of support in the countryside or among the non-Communist nationalists in Saigon. Its army had been created by the French out of desperation in the last stages of the war and was accurately dismissed by General Navarre as a "rabble."[6]

The French had employed the classical imperialist device of divide and conquer to rule their Indochinese colonies, and political

[6]Robert McClintock to State Department, May 20, 1953, and May 8, 1954, in Department of State, *Foreign Relations of the United States, 1952–1954* (Washington, D.C., 1981), 13: 575, 1519. Hereafter cited as *FR* with date and volume number.

fragmentation was the fundamental fact of life in post-Geneva South Vietnam. The French army remained, and the French government stubbornly persisted in trying to exert influence in its former colony. The Vietminh retained pockets of control, even on the doorstep of Saigon. The so-called sects, politico-religious organizations with their own governments and armies, ruled the Mekong Delta and the suburbs of Saigon as their private fiefdoms. Viewing a mass emigration from North Vietnam as a possible means of tipping the political balance toward the south and perhaps even winning the 1956 elections, the French and Americans actively encouraged northerners to cross the seventeenth parallel. Within weeks after Geneva, northern Catholics began pouring into predominantly Buddhist South Vietnam at the rate of 7,000 a day, adding new religious and ethnic tensions to an already volatile mix.

Some U.S. officials issued stern warnings about the pitfalls of nation building in South Vietnam. A National Intelligence Estimate of August 1954 admonished that even with solid support from the United States, the chances of establishing a strong, stable government were "poor."[7] When asked to formulate a program for training a South Vietnamese army, the Joint Chiefs of Staff (JCS) demurred, advising that it would be "hopeless" to build an army without a "reasonably strong, stable civil government in control."[8] Agreeing that the situation in South Vietnam was "utterly hopeless," Secretary of Defense Charles E. Wilson urged the United States to get out as "completely and as soon as possible." In words that would take on the ring of prophecy, he warned that he could "see nothing but grief in store for us if we remained in that area."[9]

Eisenhower and Dulles were not deterred by these gloomy forecasts. Dulles admitted that the chances of success might not exceed 1 in 10. On the other hand, he and the president agreed that to do nothing risked the probable loss to communism of a vital area. The administration could not afford to act only when success was assured, Dulles explained to the Senate Foreign Relations Committee,

[7]National Intelligence Estimate 63-5-54, "Post-Geneva Outlook in Indochina," August 3, 1954, *USVN*, Book 10, 692.
[8]Joint Chiefs of Staff to Secretary of Defense, August 4, 12, 1954, ibid., 701–702, 759–760.
[9]Record of National Security Council meeting, October 26, 1954, *FR, 1952–1954*, 13:2184–2186.

and Vietnam was one of those places where it was necessary to "put up a good stout effort even though it is by no means certain that we will succeed." They seem also to have felt that because of the purity of its motives and the superiority of its methods, the United States might succeed where the French had failed in creating a strong South Vietnamese army and a viable government. In its first two years in office, moreover, the administration with limited effort had toppled unfriendly governments in Iran and Guatemala, and Eisen hower and Dulles may have concluded that they could beat the odds in Vietnam as well. Admitting that he was indulging in the "familiar hen-and-egg argument as to which comes first," Dulles flatly informed the JCS that a strong army would do more than any-thing else to stabilize the government of South Vietnam.[10]

His arguments eventually prevailed with the president. At an NSC meeting on October 22, 1954, Eisenhower affirmed with "great conviction" that "in the lands of the blind, one-eyed men are kings," by which he presumably meant that despite the obstacles the United States had the resources and ingenuity to succeed.[11] Shortly after, the administration committed itself to a major aid program for South Vietnam. The commitment was carefully limited and conditioned on Diem's instituting major reforms, but its signifi-cance was unmistakable: the experiment in nation building was under way.

NGO DINH DIEM

The man to whom Eisenhower made the fateful commitment had impeccable credentials as a nationalist and, from the American standpoint, more important, as an anti-Communist. One of nine children of Ngo Dinh Kha, an official at the imperial court of Hue, Ngo Dinh Diem attended French Catholic schools in Hue and the school of public administration in Hanoi, where, after finishing at the top of his class, he was given an appointment in the bureaucracy of the protectorate of Annam. A devout Catholic, he became a

---

[10]Dulles to Charles E. Wilson, August 18, 1954, *USVN*, Book 10, 728–729.
[11]Record of National Security Council meeting, October 22, 1954, *FR, 1952–1954*, 13: 2157.

staunch opponent of communism before he became a nationalist. As a village supervisor in central Vietnam, he unearthed a Communist-inspired uprising in 1929 and severely punished its leaders. The French rewarded him with an appointment as minister of the interior, the highest position in the government, but when they refused to enact the reforms he had proposed, he resigned and would not return to his post even when threatened with deportation. For most of the next two decades, Diem was a virtual exile in his own land, living as a scholar-recluse and refusing offers from the Japanese, the Vietminh, and Bao Dai to participate in the various governments formed after World War II. He eventually traveled to Rome and then settled at a Maryknoll seminary in Lakewood, New Jersey. While in the United States he lectured widely, and his fervent appeals for an independent, non-Communist Vietnam attracted him to such luminaries as Francis Cardinal Spellman and Democratic Senators John F. Kennedy and Mike Mansfield.[12]

Diem's nationalism and administrative experience made him a logical choice for the premiership of an independent Vietnam, but he lacked many of the qualities required for the imposing challenges he faced. His most noteworthy characteristics seem to have been a stubborn determination to persist in the face of great danger and a remarkable penchant for survival. A man of principle, he inclined toward an all-or-nothing integrity that deprived him of the flexibility necessary to deal with the intractable problems and deep-seated conflicts he confronted. His love for his country in the abstract was profound, but he was an elitist who had little sensitivity to the needs and problems of the Vietnamese people. Not perceiving the extent to which the French and Vietminh had destroyed traditional political processes and values, he looked backward to an imperial Vietnam that no longer existed. He had no blueprint for building a modern nation or mobilizing his people. Introverted and self-absorbed, he lacked the charisma of Ho Chi Minh. "He was a short, broadly built man with a round face and a shock of black hair, who walked and moved jerkily, as if on strings," Robert Shaplen has recalled. "He always dressed in white and looked as if he were made out of ivory." A compulsive

---

[12]Frances FitzGerald, *Fire in the Lake: The Vietnamese and the Americans in Vietnam* (Boston, 1972), pp. 80–84, 98–99.

talker—"a single question was likely to provoke a dissertation for an hour or more"—he was a poor listener who seemed almost indifferent to the reaction he evoked in others.[13]

Diem's route to the premiership of South Vietnam remains obscure. He approached the U.S. government as early as 1951, attacking Bao Dai's leadership and expressing "somewhat wistfully" his hope that American troops might be used in Vietnam. Diem's virulent Francophobia seems to have been too much for Dean Acheson's State Department, and American diplomats regarded the self-exiled nationalist as too rigid, too Catholic, and too "monkish" to be an effective leader. Diem also came to the attention of General William Donovan, chief of U.S. intelligence in World War II, who at this time was orchestrating from his Wall Street office a global network of anti-Communist operations. Donovan and prominent Catholic-Americans such as Spellman and Mansfield, with or without the support of the CIA, may have forced Diem on a reluctant Bao Dai. More likely, the emperor turned to Diem as a means of getting the American support he needed to break free from French dominance.[14]

Although the United States may have influenced the appointment, many top U.S. officials found little encouragement in Diem's assumption of power. Indeed, what is striking in retrospect is the extent to which early on-the-scene estimates of the prime minister's leadership potential anticipated the problems that would develop later. From Geneva, Walter Bedell Smith did express hope that Diem might be a "modern political Joan of Arc" who could "rally the country behind him." In Paris, however, Ambassador Douglas Dillon was reassured by the emergence of this "Yogi-like mystic" only because the standard set by his predecessors had been so low. Within weeks after Diem took office, Chargé Robert McClintock in Saigon characterized him as a "messiah without a message," com-

[13]Robert Shaplen, *The Lost Revolution: The U.S. in Vietnam, 1946–1966* (New York, 1966), p. 104.

[14]Acheson to Legation Saigon, January 16, 1951, document #3051, William J. Donovan Papers, U.S. Army Military History Institute, Carlisle Barracks, Pa. Donovan's anti-Communist activities are discussed in Anthony Cave Brown, *The Last Hero: Wild Bill Donovan* (New York, 1984), pp. 820–822, 828. For possible Catholic lobby and CIA involvement in Diem's rise to power, see Congressional Research Service, *The U.S. Government and the Vietnam War*, Part I (Washington, D.C., 1983), pp. 261–262.

plained of his "narrowness of view," and commented scornfully that his only "formulated policy is to ask immediate American assistance in every form."[15]

Throughout the fall and winter of 1954–1955, Diem was the focal point of a bitter and protracted conflict between the United States and France. Controversy was probably inevitable given the accumulated tensions of four years of uneasy partnership, and it was sharpened by profound mutual suspicions that extended from top policy levels in Paris and Washington down to the operational level in Saigon. The French doubted Diem's capacity to lead, viewed him as a threat to implementation of the Geneva Accords, and actively sought to get rid of him. The Americans feared, probably without justification, that Paris was playing a double game, seeking to maintain its position in the south while attempting to build bridges to Hanoi. U.S. officials also feared that the French inclination to let the best man win the upcoming election would bring about a Ho Chi Minh victory. The French had always resented American intrusion in Vietnam, and they suspected that the United States was using Diem to supplant them. Diem has that "one rare quality, so precious in Asia," a French journalist snarled, "he is proAmerican."[16] Differences over Vietnam were exacerbated by French rejection of the European Defense Community, which strained Franco-American relations to the breaking point and, at least momentarily, left the Western alliance in disarray.

In Vietnam, the United States now held most of the cards, and it eventually imposed its will on a recalcitrant France. The French still depended on American aid to support their army in Vietnam, and Washington used this leverage in the fall of 1954 to extract a commitment to support Diem. The Eisenhower administration also insisted on giving its economic and military aid directly to the Diem government rather than funneling it through the French mission in Saigon, as Paris had proposed. Throughout the winter of 1954–1955, French officials insisted that Diem was incapable of running the government and proposed that he be replaced by Bao Dai or some other reputable nationalist figure. But Dulles would have

---

[15]T. B. Miller (ed.), *Australian Foreign Minister: The Diaries of R. G. Casey, 1951–1960* (London, 1972), p. 159; Dillon to State Department, May 24, 1954, *FR, 1952–1954,* 13:1608–1609; McClintock to State Department, July 4, 1954, ibid., 1783–1784.
[16]Quoted in *FR, 1952–1954,* 13: 2333.

none of it. If Bao Dai was the only person who could save Vietnam, the Secretary concluded, "then indeed we must be desperate." He conceded Diem's shortcomings but accepted Ambassador Donald Heath's argument "that there is no one to take his place who would serve US interests better."[17] More than any other single factor, the unstinting support provided by Dulles and the United States enabled Diem to remain in power against strong French opposition.

Timely American support also enabled Diem to thwart a series of military plots against his government. The U.S. embassy foiled a coup attempt in the fall of 1954 by making known that a change of government would result in termination of American aid. Lansdale singlehandedly stopped another coup in November. A former advertising executive, he had served in the Office of Strategic Services during World War II and afterward had assisted Philippine President Ramon Magsaysay in suppressing the Huk rebellion. A flamboyant and imaginative operator whose schemes ranged from the macabre to the bizarre, he had quickly ingratiated himself with Diem and became one of the prime minister's most trusted advisers and vocal supporters. Learning that a group of army officers was plotting to overthrow the government, Lansdale lured several of the ringleaders out of the country with an expense-paid trip to Manila, and the scheme quickly collapsed.[18]

The United States also enabled Diem to cope with some of the enormous problems he confronted in his first year. Responding to the fervent appeals of the northern Catholic hierarchy that "Christ has gone to the south" and to warnings that their lives would be in danger if they remained under communism, an estimated 900,000 refugees, most of them Catholics, fled the north after Geneva. The United States organized a task force of some fifty ships in what was dubbed "Passage to Freedom" and, along with private charities, established reception centers offering emergency food, clothing, and medical care to the newcomers. Himself a northerner and Catholic, Diem was sympathetic to the refugees, and his government gave them funds to build new dwellings and purchase clothing and food. Foreign Operations Administrator Harold Stassen called Pas-

[17]Embassy Paris to State Department, December 19, 1954, *USVN*, Book 10, 826–834; Heath to Walter Robertson, December 17, 1954, ibid., 824–825.
[18]Sheehan et al., *Pentagon Papers (NYT)*, p. 20.

sage to Freedom "one of the epochs" of modern history, and Diem's effective handling of the short-term problems created by the refugees was cited as early evidence of his ability to govern South Vietnam under American tutelage. The long-range problem of re-settlement and integration proved much more difficult, however, and Diem's favoritism for the northerners was one of the major arti-cles in the later indictment against him.[19]

THE SECTS CRISIS

Even with American help, Diem barely survived the sects crisis of 1955. The Cao Dai and Hoa Hao represented the most potent politi-cal forces in the fragmented society of post-Geneva Vietnam. Orga-nized along the lines of the Catholic Church with a pope as head, the Cao Dai claimed two million adherents, maintained an army of 20,000, and exercised political control over much of the Mekong Delta. Also centered in the delta, the Hoa Hao had as many as one million followers and an army of 15,000. The Binh Xuyen, a mafia-like organization headed by a colorful brigand named Bay Vien, had an army of 25,000 men, earned huge revenues from gambling and prostitution in Saigon, and actually ran the city's police force. Unable to subdue the sects while fighting the Vietminh, the French had given them virtual autonomy. Accustomed to running their own affairs, they refused to surrender their power or fortunes to the new national government.[20]

Diem's divide-and-conquer tactics at first united the sects against him. To win their support, he offered the Cao Dai and Hoa Hao cabinet posts, and Lansdale journeyed deep into the jungles near the Cambodian border and bribed the most important Cao Dai leaders to work with the government. The U.S. embassy backed Diem by warning that if the sects overthrew the president, Ameri-can aid would be withdrawn, leaving South Vietnam at the mercy of the Vietminh. Diem stubbornly refused to negotiate with the

[19]Stassen to Eisenhower, June 7, 1955, Dwight D. Eisenhower Papers, Dwight D. Eisenhower Library, Abilene, Kans., Office File 181-B, Box 862; Gertrude Samuels, "Passage to Freedom," *National Geographic* 107 (June 1955): 858–874.
[20]FitzGerald, *Fire in the Lake*, pp. 56–57.

Binh Xuyen, however, and his rapprochement with the Cao Dai and Hoa Hao broke down when he refused their demands for autonomy within their own territories. In the spring of 1955, the sects joined the Binh Xuyen in an all-out assault against the government. By March, government forces and sect armies waged open warfare in the streets of Saigon.

Diem's mishandling of the sects persuaded top French and American officials in Saigon that he must be removed. General Paul Ely, the French high commissioner for Vietnam, advised the U.S. Embassy that Diem verged on megalomania, that he probably could not be saved, and that if he were, "we shall have spared for Vietnam the worst Prime Minister it ever had." General J. Lawton Collins, whom Eisenhower had appointed ambassador to Vietnam in December, concurred. Collins had expressed misgivings about Diem from the time he arrived, and the sects crisis convinced him that he had been correct.

In late April, Collins returned to Washington to plead for Diem's removal. Dulles stood his ground, arguing that Diem's problems were caused by French intrigue and Vietnamese "warlords" and that if the French viewpoint won out, "we will be paying the bill and the French calling the tune."[21] Collins was able to persuade the president, however, and Dulles and the State Department could do nothing more than arrange a face-saving compromise by which Diem would be retained as president, a largely titular position, while the actual power was given to someone else.

While Collins was en route to Vietnam to implement the change, a sudden turn of events gave Diem's American backers another chance. When the Binh Xuyen launched a mortar attack against the presidential palace, Diem ordered his army into battle, and to the surprise of everyone, it quickly drove the opposition back into Cholon, the Chinese district of Saigon. Although instructed to remain neutral, many Americans openly sided with Diem. General John W. O'Daniel, the chief of the U.S. military mission, "rode past the Vietnamese troops in his sedan, flying the American flag . . . and gave them the thumbs-up sign, shouting 'Give 'em hell, boys.' "[22] Lansdale convinced a skeptical embassy

---

[21]Hagerty Diary, March 30, April 12, 20, 1955, James Hagerty Papers, Dwight D. Eisenhower Library, Abilene, Kans.; *USVN*, Book 10, 909.
[22]Edward G. Lansdale, *In the Midst of Wars* (New York, 1972), p. 288.

that the successful counterattack demonstrated the loyalty of the army and Diem's strength as a leader. At a critical moment in the struggle, moreover, the ubiquitous CIA agent persuaded Diem to ignore a cable from Bao Dai demanding his resignation.

Diem's success against the Binh Xuyen produced an American policy reversal of momentous significance. Senate leaders, including Mansfield and California Republican William Knowland, lobbied furiously for Diem's retention. Having lost the first round to Collins, Dulles, with the support of his brother, CIA director Allen Dulles, ably exploited the developments in Saigon. Arguing that Diem was the only means to "save South Vietnam and counteract revolution" and that he must be supported "wholeheartedly," the secretary persuaded the president to stick by a man whose political career had appeared doomed just days before.[23]

The American commitment to Diem provoked a final—and, from the American standpoint, not unwelcome—crisis with France. In a dramatic confrontation in Paris in mid-May, Prime Minister Edgar Faure argued heatedly that Diem was "not only incapable but mad" and that France could "no longer take risks with him": if the United States persisted in its support, France would have to withdraw from Vietnam.[24] Dulles perceived that the French presence had permitted the United States to avoid major commitments in the region and to blame failures on its ally. He also recognized, as the Joint Chiefs warned, that a French withdrawal, although desirable from a long-term standpoint, would leave the new nation highly vulnerable for the short term.

By the spring of 1955, however, Dulles concluded that the French had outlived their usefulness in the region, and resolution of the German problem permitted the United States for the first time to deal with Indochina issues on their own merits. Dulles thus persuaded the French to remain and support Diem until the Vietnamese could settle the future of their country through elections. He also let it be known that the United States would frame its policies independently and would not feel bound to consult France before acting. In all, it was a bravura performance. This "gentleman's agreement" ensured French support for the short run but separated

---

[23]Dulles to State Department, May 8, 1955, *USVN*, Book 10, 962–963.
[24]Ibid.

the United States from France and opened the way for bilateral relations with South Vietnam. Frustrated by Dulles and Diem and faced with rebellion in their North African colonies, the French abandoned what remained of their dreams of influence and began a phased withdrawal from what had been the most glittering jewel in the French Union. The United States in the meantime had already begun to replace France by assuming primary responsibility for the survival of the Saigon regime.[25]

Buoyed by his successes and by assurances of American support, Diem quickly consolidated his power. His army drove the Binh Xuyen deep into the swamps east of Saigon, where it eventually surrendered, and routed Hoa Hao forces in the Mekong Delta. Now isolated, the Cao Dai saw no choice but to come over to Diem's side. With American assistance, a "national" referendum was hastily arranged between Diem and Bao Dai. U.S. advisers informed the prime minister that 60 percent would be a more than adequate majority, but Diem and his brother Ngo Dinh Nhu left nothing to chance, securing 98.2 percent of the vote and winning more than 605,000 votes from the 405,000 registered voters in Saigon. Facing near certain downfall in May 1955, Diem, largely as a result of American support, had established uncontested control over South Vietnam by the end of the year.

With firm American backing, Diem also blocked the elections called for by the Geneva Accords. Such a position was awkward for the United States, given its traditional advocacy of free elections and its current policies in Germany and Korea. Even Diem's most uncritical supporters realized, however, that Ho Chi Minh's reputation as a nationalist leader made elections risky and that, in any event, the more populous north—operating under iron Communist discipline—was "mathematically certain" of winning.

Washington and Saigon used various devices to get around the Geneva provisions for elections. They cited North Vietnamese truce violations to justify their own noncompliance. They resorted to legalism, insisting that the Geneva articles calling for elections had no "juridical value" but merely expressed a "pious wish" that commit-

---

[25]Kathryn Statler, "The Diem Experiment: Franco-American Conflict Over South Vietnam, July 1954–May 1955," *The Journal of American-East Asian Relations* 6 (Summer–Fall 1997): 168–173.

ted no one. For the sake of appearances, the United States urged South Vietnam to state publicly that it would participate in genuinely free elections. Such a position was "unassailable in intent," Dulles argued, and held out little danger, since Communist nations never permitted a free and open political process.[26] When Diem refused even to do this, the United States artfully shifted its ground to self-determination, publicly stating that the matter should be left to the Vietnamese, privately assuring Diem that it would not force him into consultations. Under U.S. pressure, Diem finally issued a statement supporting the principle of free elections but making clear he would not be bound by the Geneva Accords and would not participate in consultations with North Vietnam. The consultations did not take place, and the elections called for by Geneva were not held.[27]

Absorbed in other matters, the major powers acquiesced. Soviet leader Nikita Khrushchev was unwilling to permit a dispute over elections in Vietnam to interfere with his newly proclaimed policy of "peaceful coexistence" with capitalist nations. The Soviet Union in 1957 even backed the admission of both Vietnams to the United Nations. Preoccupied with domestic problems and not inclined at this point to challenge Moscow, China would do no more than issue perfunctory protests. As cosponsors of the Geneva Conference, the British at first were more intent on implementing the accords than on containing communism. They shared France's low estimate of Diem and feared that with U.S. backing he might destroy the precarious peace in Vietnam. Privately, they scoffed at U.S. willingness to support free elections only when they seemed likely to produce "the desired result." At the same time, they conceded their inability to influence their more powerful ally. "We are treated like Australia," Prime Minister Anthony Eden moaned in April 1955. Unwilling to jeopardize their "special relationship"

[26]Dulles to State Department, May 8, 1955, *USVN*, Book 10, 962–963.

[27]Tran Van Chuong, "Comment on the Viet Minh's Request for General Elections in Viet Nam," document #4051, Donovan Papers; American Friends of Vietnam, "The Election Issue," n.d., copy in Hans Morgenthau Papers, Library of Congress, Washington, D.C.; Dulles news conference, August 30, 1955, Dulles Papers, Princeton, N.J., Box 95; Herbert Hoover, Jr., to Embassy Saigon, June 23, 1955, in Department of State, *Foreign Relations of the United States* (Washington, D.C., 1985), 1: 465–466; David Anderson, *Trapped by Success: The Eisenhower Administration and Vietnam, 1953–1961* (New York, 1991), pp. 122–127.

with America for no more than marginal interests in Vietnam, the British abdicated. "If the U.S. take the responsibility," Eden affirmed, "they will have to shoulder it before the world."[28]

Diem's refusal to participate in the elections ended, at least temporarily, any chance for the reunification of Vietnam, and the division of the country increasingly took on permanent form. Diem refused to permit any traffic with the north, including even a postal arrangement, and the seventeenth parallel became one of the most restricted boundaries in the world. The breakdown of the Geneva Accords all but assured at some future point the resumption of war in Vietnam.

NATION BUILDING IN SOUTH VIETNAM

Having ensured the survival of the Diem regime through its tumultuous first years, the United States supported it lavishly for the rest of the decade. The preservation of an independent South Vietnam as a bulwark against further Communist penetration of Southeast Asia remained the fundamental goal of U.S. policy. During the mid-1950s, the major battleground of the Cold War shifted from Europe to the newly emerging nations of Asia and Africa, where the United States and the Soviet Union vied for influence and sought to demonstrate the superiority of their respective systems. In this context, South Vietnam assumed even greater importance as a testing ground for the viability of American ideology and institutions in underdeveloped nations.

The experiment in nation building launched on a crash basis quickly assumed the form of a crusade. Private charitable agencies distributed food, soap, toothbrushes, and emergency medical supplies and worked zealously to improve amenities in refugee camps. Nongovernmental organizations such as CARE and Catholic Relief Services (CRS) set out to teach villagers modern methods of farming, fishing, and forestry, created health and sanitation programs to curb disease, and initiated self-help projects to promote economic development, in the process seeking to educate the South Viet-

---

[28]Quoted in Arthur Combs, "The Path Not Taken: The British Alternative to U.S. Policy in Vietnam, 1954–1956," *Diplomatic History* 19 (Winter 1995): 51.

namese in the values of democratic capitalism. The International Rescue Committee (IRC) went further. Originally established to assist refugees from Nazi Germany, the IRC had since shifted its efforts to the Cold War. In Vietnam, it professed to stand as a "lighthouse of inspiration" for those eager to preserve and broaden "concepts of democratic culture." It staged anti-Communist plays in the villages, and in the cities sponsored recitals and art exhibitions built around democratic themes. It also established Freedom Centers in Saigon, Hue, and Dalat to win over disaffected Vietnamese intellectuals and students through such diverse and apparently contradictory efforts as research into "pure Vietnamese culture" and English language courses.[29]

Meanwhile, in the United States, liberals and conservatives joined hands to form the American Friends of Vietnam (AFV), a group headed by Donovan and created to enlighten Americans about the "realities" in Vietnam and lobby the U.S. government to support Diem. "A free Vietnam means a greater guarantee of freedom in the world," the AFV affirmed in its statement of purpose. "There is a little bit of all of us in that faraway country," General O'Daniel, a charter member, would write in 1960.[30]

Already deeply committed to South Vietnam, the Eisenhower administration needed no urging from private lobby groups. From 1955 to 1961, the United States poured more than $1 billion in economic and military assistance into South Vietnam, and by 1961, Diem's government ranked fifth among all recipients of American foreign aid. By the late 1950s, there were more than 1,500 Americans in South Vietnam, assisting the government in various ways, and the U.S. mission in Saigon was the largest in the world.

The American aid program accorded top priority to building a South Vietnamese army. Dulles had insisted from the outset that the development of a strong, modern army was an essential first step in promoting a stable government. The withdrawal of the French Expeditionary Force; the presence of large, experienced armies in the

---

[29]Robert McAlister reports to IRC, May–October 1955, document #4084, Donovan Papers. For CARE and CRS, see Delia Pergande, "Private Voluntary Aid in Vietnam: The Humanitarian Politics of Catholic Relief Services and CARE, 1954–1965" (Ph.D. diss., University of Kentucky, 1999), especially pp. 43–157.

[30]American Friends of Vietnam, "Statement of Purpose," n.d., copy in Morgenthau Papers; John W. O'Daniel, *The Nation That Refused to Starve* (New York, 1960), p. 11.

north; and continued instability in the south all underscored the necessity of providing South Vietnam with a strong military force. Between 1955 and 1961, military assistance constituted more than 78 percent of the total American foreign aid program.

In early 1956, the United States assumed from France full responsibility for training the South Vietnamese Army, and the Military Assistance and Advisory Group (MAAG) in Saigon undertook a crash program to build it into an effective force. Limited by the Geneva Accords to a strength of 342 men, the MAAG was augmented by various subterfuges to 692. From 1955 to 1960, it was headed by Lieutenant General Samuel Williams, a spit-and-polish veteran of the two world wars and Korea whose insistence on rigid discipline and vicious tongue-lashings earned him the nickname "Hanging Sam" in the army.

The MAAG faced truly formidable obstacles. The United States inherited from France an army of more than 250,000 soldiers, poorly organized, trained, and equipped; lacking in national spirit; suffering from low morale; and deficient in officers and trained specialists such as engineers and artillerymen. The army's supply problems were compounded by the French, who took most of the best equipment with them and left behind tons of useless and antiquated material. The American advisers had to bridge profound language and cultural gaps. Despite good intentions, they often patronized the Vietnamese, sometimes even referring to them as "natives." "Probably the greatest single problem encountered by the MAAG," one of its officers wrote at the time, "is the continual task of assuring the Vietnamese that the United States is not a colonial power—an assurance that must be renewed on an individual basis by each new adviser."[31] From this weak foundation and in the face of serious practical difficulties, the MAAG was assigned the challenging mission of building an army capable of maintaining internal security and holding the line against an invasion from the north until outside forces could be brought in.

Under the MAAG's direction, the United States reorganized, equipped, and trained the South Vietnamese Army. It provided

---

[31]Judson J. Conner, "Teeth for the Free World Dragon," *Army Information Digest,* (November 1960 41; Ronald H. Spector, *Advice and Support: The Early Years, 1941–1960* (Washington, D.C., 1983), pp. 278–282.

roughly $85 million per year in military equipment, including uniforms, small arms, vehicles, tanks, and helicopters. It paid the salaries of officers and enlisted personnel, financed the construction of military installations, and underwrote the cost of training programs. The MAAG scaled down the army to a strength of 150,000 and organized it into mobile divisions capable of a dual mission. It launched an ambitious training program, based on American models, including a Command and General Staff College for senior officers, officer candidate schools, and specialized schools for noncoms. In 1960 alone, more than 1,600 Vietnamese soldiers participated in the Off-Shore Program, studying in the United States and other "free world" countries. Official spokespeople proclaimed by 1960 that the United States had achieved a "minor miracle," transforming what had been "little more than a marginal collection of armed men" into an efficient, modern army.[32]

As so often would happen in Vietnam, official rhetoric bore little resemblance to reality. The army still lacked sufficient officers in 1960, and General Williams later conceded that many of the officers holding key positions were of "marginal quality." As one of Williams's top assistants put it, "No one can make good . . . commanders by sending uneducated, poorly trained, and poorly equipped and motivated boys to Benning or Knox or Leavenworth or Quantico."[33] Diem's determination to maintain tight control over the army frustrated the MAAG's efforts to establish a smoothly functioning command system. The president personally ordered units into action, bypassing the Ministry of Defense and the General Staff. He chose safe rather than competent officers for critical posts. He promoted them on the basis of loyalty rather than merit and constantly shuffled the high command—"generals and colonels, it was said jokingly in Saigon, were the only first-class travelers in Vietnam."[34]

The basic problem was that the army was trained for the wrong mission. The MAAG would be sharply criticized for failing to prepare the South Vietnamese Army for dealing with guerrillas, but from the perspective of the mid-1950s its emphasis appears quite logical. Confronting the near-impossible task of building from

[32]Conner, "Teeth for the Free World Dragon," 33.
[33]Robert H. Whitlow, "The United States Military in South Vietnam, 1954–1960" (Master's thesis, University of Kentucky, 1972), p. 87.
[34]Jean Lacouture, *Vietnam between Two Truces* (New York, 1966), p. 117.

scratch an army capable of performing two quite diverse missions, the MAAG naturally leaned toward the conventional warfare with which it was most familiar. At least until 1958, moreover, the countryside was quiescent and Diem appeared firmly entrenched. Williams and most of his staff had served in Korea, and the seeming resemblance between the two situations inclined them to focus on the threat of invasion from the north. Also learning from experiences in Greece and the Philippines, they doubted that North Vietnam could mount an insurgency capable of threatening the south. The army was therefore trained, organized, and equipped to fight a conventional war, and its inadequacies were obvious only after South Vietnam was enveloped by a rural insurgency.

A paramilitary force, the Civil Guard, was to assist the army in maintaining internal security, but it was hampered from the outset by conflicts over organization and training. Advisers from Michigan State University sought a small group trained and equipped for police duties at the province and village level, while Diem, supported by Lansdale and the MAAG, preferred an auxiliary military force equipped with helicopters, armored cars, and bazookas and capable of small-scale military operations. Washington supported the Michigan State group and refused to furnish assistance for the Civil Guard until Diem acquiesced, but the guard never developed into an effective force. Diem used it as a dumping ground for inferior officers and in general gave it little support. The training provided by the Michigan State police experts, in Lansdale's words, left the guard "pathetically unready for the realities of the Vietnamese countryside. A squad of Civil Guard policemen, armed with whistles, nightsticks and 38 caliber revolvers, could hardly be expected to arrest a squad of guerrillas armed with submachine guns, rifles, grenades and mortars."[35]

The United States also pumped millions of dollars in foreign aid into the South Vietnamese economy between 1955 and 1960, the great bulk of it through the commercial-import program. Described by one zealous U.S. official as "the greatest invention since the wheel," this program was designed to make up South Vietnam's huge foreign exchange deficit while avoiding the runaway inflation that might have been set loose by a massive infusion of dollars into

[35]Lansdale, *Midst of Wars*, p. 353.

a vulnerable economy.[36] Vietnamese importers ordered from foreign export firms goods ranging from foodstuffs to automobiles, with Washington footing the bill. The importers paid for the goods in piasters, which then went into a "counterpart fund" held by the National Bank of Vietnam and were used by the government to cover operating expenses and finance development projects. From 1955 to 1959, the commercial-import program generated almost $1 billion in counterpart funds. The United States also furnished South Vietnam more than $127 million in direct economic assistance and more than $16 million in technical aid.

American aid brought significant results. The commercial-import program covered South Vietnam's foreign exchange deficit and, by making available large quantities of consumer goods, held inflation in check. U.S. money and technology helped repair the vast destruction from more than a decade of war, rebuilding highways, railroads, and canals and spurring a modest increase in agricultural productivity. Specialists from American land-grant colleges promoted new crops and established credit facilities for small farmers. Educators supervised the founding of schools and furnished textbooks. Public health experts provided drugs and medical supplies and assisted in training nurses and paramedics. A group of public administration specialists from Michigan State University instructed Vietnamese civil servants in skills ranging from typing to personnel management. Experts from MSU's school of law enforcement established a police academy to train what one brochure described as "Vietnam's finest," reorganized and updated the methods of the Vietnam Bureau of Investigation, and even helped the Saigon police install traffic lights and paint street lines to better handle growing traffic problems in the burgeoning metropolis.[37]

More than any other single factor, American aid enabled South Vietnam to survive the first few critical years after independence, and by the late 1950s the new nation appeared to be flourishing. In Saigon, one visitor reported, "the stores and market places are filled with consumer goods; the streets are filled with new motor scooters

[36]U.S. Senate, Committee on Foreign Relations, *Situation in Vietnam, Hearings, 1959* (Washington, D.C., 1959), p. 203.

[37]U.S. Operations Mission, *Building Economic Strength* (Washington, D.C., 1958), p. 75; John Ernst, *Forging a Fateful Alliance* (East Lansing, Mich., 1998), pp. 41–84.

and expensive automobiles; and in the upper-income residential areas new and pretentious housing is being built."[38] After conducting an investigation of the uses of American economic assistance, Democratic Senator Gale McGee of Wyoming proposed that South Vietnam be made a "showcase" for the foreign aid program, a place to which people from other countries could be brought to observe firsthand the "wholesome effects of our efforts to help other peoples help themselves."[39]

Appearances were again deceptive, for the American aid program had at best mixed results. The recipients were undoubtedly grateful for U.S. generosity, but they could not help but be suspicious as well. "After eighty years of ruthless exploitation by the French," one American observed, "many Vietnamese wonder why America is suddenly spending so much money in Vietnam." Americans working at the village level sought to promote their own values and culture, and they sometimes met indifference or even hostility among the Vietnamese. The villagers' reluctance to adopt American ways in turn frustrated the Americans and led them to question the Vietnamese work ethic.[40]

More important, although U.S. aid prevented an economic collapse and supported a high standard of living in Saigon, it did little to promote economic development or improve conditions in the villages where more than 90 percent of South Vietnam's population lived. From 1955 to 1959, military aid was four times greater than economic and technical assistance, and of the nearly $1 billion in counterpart funds, more than 78 percent went for military purposes. Such was the preoccupation with "security" among Vietnamese and Americans alike that those interested in other projects found it expedient to justify them in terms of defense. Saigon and Washington insisted that the continuing presence of serious external and internal threats allowed them no choice, but the heavy em-

[38]Milton C. Taylor, "South Vietnam: Lavish Aid, Limited Progress," *Pacific Affairs* 34 (1961), 242.
[39]Senate, *Hearings, 1959*, p. 369.
[40]MacAlister report to International Rescue Committee, n.d., document #4084, Donovan Papers; Pergande, "Private Voluntary Aid," p. 152.
[41]U.S. Senate, Committee on Foreign Relations, *United States Aid Program in Vietnam, Report, February 26, 1960* (Washington, D.C., 1960), p. 8.

phasis on military aid left little money for long-range economic development. The military program was the "tail that wags the dog," a Senate committee pointed out in 1960.[41]

The commercial-import program also contained built-in weaknesses. It was enormously wasteful, importers frequently ordered far more than could be consumed, and it created abundant opportunities for fast profits. The most serious weakness was that it financed an artificially high standard of living while contributing little to development. As late as 1957, about two-thirds of the imports consisted of consumer goods, and much of the wealth was drained off in conspicuous consumption rather than going into industry or agriculture. Diem stubbornly resisted American attempts to reduce the proportion of consumer goods, arguing that a lowering of living standards would create domestic unrest. The United States made some changes on its own, dropping from the list such obvious luxury items as record players and water skis and reducing consumer goods to about one-third of the total, but with little effect. Robert Scigliano concluded in 1963 that the commercial-import program had been a "large-scale relief project" that had not promoted "significant economic development in Vietnam."[42]

In spending the small percentage of funds allotted to development, Americans and Vietnamese frequently found themselves at odds. The United States insisted that industrial development be based on private enterprise and until the early 1960s refused to provide funds for state-owned industries. Diem and his entourage shared the mandarin's contempt for business and the nationalist's distrust of foreign capital. They denounced American attitudes as "medieval and retrograde" and insisted that they must have government ownership of major industries, at least at the start. The result was a bitter stalemate that inhibited development.

The massive infusion of American aid thus kept South Vietnam alive, but it fostered dependency rather than laying the foundation for a genuine independence. Rice production doubled between 1955 and 1960, but much of the increase was taken up in increased domestic consumption, while gains in industrial productivity were insignificant. South Vietnam relied on a high level of imports to

---

[42]Robert Scigliano, *South Vietnam: Nation under Stress* (Boston, 1964), p. 125.

maintain its standard of living and on American money to pay for them. Vietnamese and Americans agreed that a cutback or termination of American assistance would bring economic and political collapse. Vietnam was the "prototype of the dependent economy," Milton Taylor wrote in 1961, "its level of national income as dependent on outside forces as was the case when the country was a French colony. . . . American aid has built a castle on sand."[43]

The basic problem of nation building was political. There was much talk about assisting the Vietnamese to construct an American-style democracy, and U.S. advisers helped draft a constitution that contained many of the trappings of Western democracies, including a president and legislature elected by popular vote and guarantees of basic political rights. In fact, the United States devoted little attention to political matters and, despite its massive foreign aid program, exerted very little influence. Some Americans naively assumed that Diem shared their political values; others were preoccupied with the security problems that seemed most urgent. Most probably shared Dulles's view that it was enough for Diem to be "competent, anti-Communist and vigorous" and that while representative government was a desirable long-range objective, it could not be accomplished overnight.[44] For whatever reason, the United States did little to promote democracy or even political reform until South Vietnam was swept by revolution.

In any event, political reform would have been lost on Diem, for whom democracy was alien in terms of experience and temperament. Inasmuch as he had a political philosophy, it was the vague concept of "personalism," a fusion of Western and Eastern ideas that Diem and his brother Nhu used as a rationalization for absolute state power, distrust of popular rule, and the belief that a small elite was responsible for defining the general welfare. Good government, Diem once asserted with typical verbosity, was not a collection of laws but the "simple and patient art of fusing in a harmonious synthesis the desireable diversity of conceptions and the inevitable complexity of reality."[45]

[43]Taylor, "South Vietnam," 256.
[44]Dulles news conference, May 7, 1955, Dulles Papers, Princeton, N.J., Box 99; Frederick Reinhardt oral history interview, ibid.
[45]Elbridge Durbrow to State Department, December 22, 1958, in Department of State, *Foreign Relations of the United States, 1958–1960* (Washington, D.C., 1986), 1: 112.

Diem's vague words only slightly obscured his authoritarian tendencies. His model was the Emperor Ming Mang, the nineteenth-century "reformer" who created an assembly of mandarins to approve his royal decrees. Diem's philosophy of government was expressed with uncharacteristic succinctness in a line he personally added to the constitution: "The President is vested with the leadership of the nation." He identified *his* principles with the general good and firmly believed that the people must be guided by the paternalistic hand of those who knew what was best for them. A deeply suspicious individual, Diem was convinced, as Bernard Fall has written, that "compromise has no place and opposition of any kind must of necessity be subversive and must be suppressed with all the vigor the system is capable of."[46]

To please his American advisers, Diem paid lip service to democracy, but in practice he assumed absolute powers. He personally dominated the executive branch of government, reserving to himself and his brothers, three of whom were appointed to a cabinet of six, all power of decision making. Unable or unwilling to delegate authority, he oversaw the operations of the entire government down to the most minute detail. Cabinet members or upper-level civil servants who expressed opposition were quickly appointed to ambassadorships abroad—or worse. The executive branch dominated the legislature, which, in any case, was virtually handpicked through careful manipulation of the electoral process. In the first years of its existence, the National Assembly initiated nothing important and pliantly approved everything the president submitted to it.

The Diem government might have survived its authoritarianism had it pursued enlightened policies, but its inattention to the needs of the people and ruthless suppression of dissent stirred a rising discontent that eventually brought its downfall. Diem's policies toward the villages—traditionally the backbone of Vietnamese society—demonstrated a singular lack of concern and near-callous irresponsibility. Lansdale persuaded the president to initiate a Civic Action Program to extend government services to the villages, but Diem took little interest in it, and as Lansdale later lamented, "it flopped."[47] At American insistence, the government

---

[46]Bernard Fall, *The Two Vietnams: A Political and Military Analysis* (New York, 1967), p. 237.
[47]Lansdale, *Midst of Wars*, p. 212.

instituted a land reformprogram, but it, too, was implemented half-heartedly and did little to meet the rising appetite for land among South Vietnam's rural population.

The only significant "reform" enacted by the government during the 1950s touched off massive resentment in the villages. In a misguided effort to centralize federal authority and curb Vietminh influence in the countryside, Diem abolished traditional local elections and began to appoint village and provincial officials. The villagers had enjoyed virtual autonomy for centuries and received the outsiders, Frances FitzGerald observes, "much as they might have received proconsuls from a conquering power."[48] The fears aroused by the mere presence of these officials were often heightened by their actions. Many of Diem's appointees were chosen on the basis of personal loyalty, and most were poorly trained for their tasks. Some used their positions for personal enrichment; province chiefs were known to have arrested wealthy villagers on trumped-up charges and then forced them to pay bribes for their release.

Diem's vigorous assault against political opponents spawned rising discontent in the cities and the countryside. Newspapers that criticized the government were promptly shut down, and Nhu's Vietnam Bureau of Investigation rooted out suspected subversives in a manner that would have made F.B.I director J. Edgar Hoover blanch. Using authority handed down in various presidential ordinances, the government herded into "reeducation centers" thousands of Vietnamese—Communists and non-Communists alike—who were alleged to be threats to public order. The program was originally aimed at Vietminh "stay-behinds," but it was extended to anyone who dared speak out against the government. The regime admitted to the incarceration of 20,000 people by 1956, and the campaign was subsequently intensified. The government "has tended to treat the population with suspicion or coerce it," an American intelligence report concluded in 1960, "and has been rewarded with an attitude of apathy or resentment."[49]

[48]FitzGerald, *Fire in the Lake*, p. 154.
[49]Special Report on Internal Security Situation in Saigon," March 7, 1960, *USVN*, Book 10, 1267–1280.

IMAGES AND REALITY

In a remarkable display of public-private collaboration, U.S. government officials and private organizations mounted in the 1950s an artful propaganda campaign extolling American good deeds in Indochina and lionizing Diem and South Vietnam. Urged on by his superiors and private citizens such as Cardinal Spellman, U.S. Navy doctor Tom Dooley embellished his best-selling book, *Deliver Us from Evil*, with horrific—and unsubstantiated—tales of Vietminh atrocities and exaggerated his own and America's good works in Passage to Freedom to build support for nation building and Diem. Hollywood producers, with the backing of the omnipresent Lansdale and the American Friends of Vietnam, imaginatively transformed Graham Greene's virulently anti-American novel, *The Quiet American*, into a passionately pro-American film starring war hero Audie Murphy, a film, Lansdale told Diem, that "would help win more friends for you and Vietnam in many places in the world where it is shown."[50]

In part no doubt as a result of such propaganda, Diem retained a highly favorable image in the United States until South Vietnam was engulfed by revolution in the early 1960s. It is possible that even those Americans close to the government were unaware until the end of the decade of the extent to which he had alienated his people. In the eyes of most Americans, moreover, his vigorous anticommunism more than compensated for his shortcomings. Apologists such as Professor Wesley Fishel of Michigan State University conceded that Diem had employed authoritarian methods but argued that Vietnam's lack of experience with democracy and the threat of communism left him no choice. Ambassador Elbridge Durbrow agreed that Diem's "somewhat authoritarian" government was compatible with U.S. interests and insisted that the United States "look with tolerance" on the government's efforts to develop a political system that

---

[50]Lansdale to Joseph Mankiewicz, March 17, 1956, and Lansdale to Diem, October 28, 1957, Edward Lansdale Papers, Hoover Institution Library, Stanford, Calif.; Diana Shaw, "The Temptation of Tom Dooley," *Los Angeles Times Magazine*, December 15, 1991, 43–45. Subsequently discharged from the Navy because he was suspected of being a homosexual, Dooley, again with the backing of Lansdale and the American Friends of Vietnam, was sent on a medical mission to Laos, where he gained fame as the "Schweitzer of Asia."

conformed to Vietnamese traditions. The American media focused on the stability brought to South Vietnam by the "tough little miracle man," and when Diem visited the United States in 1957, he was widely feted. The image persisted even after insurgency had spread across the country. "On his record," *Newsweek*'s Ernest Lindley exclaimed in 1959, "he must be rated as one of the ablest free Asian leaders. We can take pride in our support."[51]

THE ORIGINS OF INSURGENCY

At the very time Americans were extolling the "miracles" wrought by Diem, the revolution that would sweep him from power and provoke massive U.S. intervention was taking root. Washington later went to great lengths to prove that the Second Indochina War was the result of "aggression from the north," the determination of North Vietnam to impose communism on its southern neighbor. Interestingly, since 1975, government-sponsored Vietnamese histories have also inflated the northern role in the southern revolution, coming very close to the line advanced by the United States at the time. Critics of American policy, on the other hand, have insisted that the revolution sprang from indigenous roots in response to Diem's oppressiveness and grew in strength without significant support or direction from the north.

Much remains unclear about the origins of the revolution, but the truth appears far more complex than either of these extremes. It seems evident, as William Duiker has concluded, that the insurgency was a "genuine revolt" based in the south but "organized and directed from the North." Even this interpretation does not do full justice to the complexity of the issue, however. The Communist Lao Dong party, which directed the revolution, was a unified national party consisting of representatives from all regions, and both northerners and southerners contributed to the debates that led to Politburo decisions. Le Duan, a top party official—and a southerner—played a crucial role in decision making throughout the war. From the beginning to the end of the conflict, moreover, party members

---

[51]Durbrow to State Department, December 7, 1959, *FR, 1958–1960,* 1: 269; Ernest K. Lindley, "An Ally Worth Having," *Newsweek,* June 29, 1959, 31.
[52]William J. Duiker, *The Communist Road to Power in Vietnam* (Boulder, Colo., 1981), p. 198; Robert K. Brigham, *Guerrilla Diplomacy* (Ithaca, N.Y., 1998) pp. 10–11, 18.

differed in the emphasis to be put on their two goals: building socialism in the north and carrying out the revolution in the south. Sometimes the two existed in relative harmony, but at other times they were in conflict, creating profound regional tensions and sharp divisions within the party apparatus.[52]

In the years after Geneva, North Vietnam approached the issue of unification with great caution. Neither the Soviet Union nor China supported an aggressive policy. In any event, like Diem, Ho Chi Minh and his lieutenants faced massive problems of postwar reconstruction and nation building. Reports of a "bloodbath" in which as many as 500,000 people were executed following implementation of a land reform program have been greatly exaggerated.[53] Hanoi's heavy-handed measures did provoke widespread opposition, however. Between 3,000 and 15,000 dissidents may, in fact, have been executed, and resistance in Ho Chi Minh's own Nghe An province had to be suppressed by the army. Without abandoning its goal of unification, a preoccupied Hanoi ordered stay-behind units in the south to protect the party apparatus but to avoid violence and concentrate on political activity.

The result, according to Communist party historians, was "the darkest period" for the revolution in the south. The elections were not held, and the amnesty promised by Geneva was not granted. More important, Diem's anti-Communist campaigns were devastatingly successful. More than 2,000 suspected communists were executed, some by guillotine, and by 1957, party membership had fallen to precarious levels. Facing extinction, local leaders began to defend themselves, sometimes violating the party line.

Between 1957 and 1959, Hanoi gradually committed itself to the insurgency in the south. The leadership appears to have been bitterly divided between those who wanted to consolidate the revolution in the north and those who wanted to liberate the south. In December 1956, the factions compromised, agreeing that the north should continue to take priority but authorizing southern insurgents to use violence to defend themselves. In March 1957, Hanoi approved plans to modernize its own armed forces.

[53]The most detailed and convincing account is in Edwin E. Moïse, *Land Reform in China and Vietnam* (Chapel Hill, N.C., 1983), pp. 178–268.

More important decisions came in 1959. Recognizing that the revolutionaries in the south were in desperate straits and that Diem's oppressiveness had created a favorable atmosphere for revolution, the party authorized the resumption of armed struggle and took active measures to support it. With the watchword "absolute secrecy, absolute security," it established a special force, Group 559, to construct an infiltration route to move personnel and supplies into South Vietnam through Laos—the beginning of the fabled Ho Chi Minh trail—and began to send back to the south to assume leadership roles Vietminh who had come north after Geneva. The Third Party Congress of September 1960 formally approved the shift to armed struggle, assigning liberation of the south equal priority with consolidation in the north. In December 1960, at Hanoi's direction, southern revolutionaries founded the National Liberation Front (NLF), a broad-based organization led by Communists but designed to rally all those disaffected with Diem by promising sweeping reforms and the establishment of genuine independence. In all these steps, North Vietnam carefully concealed its own hand, hoping to overthrow Diem by what would appear an indigenous revolution without provoking U.S. intervention.

The result was a drastic intensification of revolutionary activity in the south. The level of violence increased sharply: in 1958, an estimated 700 government officials were assassinated; in 1960, 2,500. In 1959, the insurgents shifted from hit-and-run attacks to full-scale military operations against government-controlled villages and exposed units of the South Vietnamese Army. The intelligence and propaganda networks that had fallen into disuse after Geneva were reactivated, and vigorous campaigns of political agitation were launched in the villages. Largely as a result of Diem's misguided policies, the insurgents found a receptive audience—the peasants were like a "mound of straw ready to be ignited," a captured guerrilla later told an interrogator.[54] By the time the NLF was formally organized, the Vietcong (a derogatory term, applied to the guerrillas by the Diem regime, meaning "Vietnam Communist") had attracted thousands of adherents from among the rural population and had established a presence in countless villages.

---

[54]U.S. Congress, Senate, Subcommittee on Public Buildings and Grounds, *The Pentagon Papers (The Senator Gravel Edition)* (4 vols.; Boston, 1971), 1: 329. Hereafter cited as *Pentagon Papers (Gravel)*.

THE IMPENDING CRISIS

Diem's response to the insurgency heightened popular antagonism toward his government. He intensified the anti-Communist campaign in the villages and tightened controls in the cities, arresting scores of alleged dissidents. Once again demonstrating that he was out of touch with rural Vietnam, he launched in the summer of 1959 an ill-fated "agroville" program to combat the rising violence in the countryside. The intent was to relocate the peasantry in areas where the army could protect them from guerrilla terror and propaganda, and the government sought to make the program attractive by providing the new communities with schools, medical facilities, and electricity. But the peasants deeply resented the forced removal from their homes and lands, which contained the sacred tombs of their ancestors, and the government's provisions for their relocation added to their discontent. They were given only about $5.50, which did not cover the cost of the land they were required to purchase, and they were forced to work on community projects without compensation. The agroville program was eventually abandoned, but only after it had provoked enormous rural discontent with the government.

Throughout 1960, evidence of the government's fragility mounted. The insurgency grew unchecked in the countryside, and the level of violence increased sharply. In January 1960, at Trang Sup, a village northeast of Saigon, four insurgent companies destroyed a South Vietnamese Army headquarters and seized large stocks of weapons, leaving the army and its U.S. advisers in a state of shock. The regime's unpopularity in Saigon was highlighted in April when a group of non-Communist politicians, many of whom had served in Diem's cabinet, met at the Caravelle Hotel and issued a manifesto bitterly protesting the government's oppressiveness and calling for sweeping reforms. In November, Diem narrowly thwarted an attempted coup by three paratroop battalions presumed to be among the most loyal units of the army. American intelligence reports ominously warned that if present trends continued, the collapse of the regime was certain.

Belatedly perceiving the strength of the insurgency and the inability of the South Vietnamese government and armed forces to cope with it, the United States in 1960 shifted the emphasis of its military programs from conventional warfare to counterinsurgency.

U.S. military officials began work on a comprehensive plan to expand the army and Civil Guard and equip and train them for antiguerrilla operations. While this plan was being formulated, the mission in Saigon took piecemeal steps to assist the South Vietnamese. Training programs already in operation were reoriented. Special American teams were sent to train South Vietnamese Ranger Battalions, and U.S. advisers were placed at the regimental level to give on-the-spot advice and assess the capabilities and needs of individual units. Although the shift to counterinsurgency represented a tacit admission that the original advisory program had failed, it did not produce the sort of drastic changes required to defeat the guerrillas. It merely resulted in additional military aid and proposals for bureaucratic reorganization.[55]

In the meantime, civilian officials made gentle and largely unsuccessful attempts to persuade Diem to change his ways. Many Americans, including Ambassador Elbridge Durbrow, feared that unless the president reformed his government and mobilized popular support, the insurgency would overwhelm South Vietnam. In October, Durbrow secured Washington's permission to broach the question directly to Diem. He tactfully urged the president to broaden his government by appointing a new cabinet, relax controls on the press and civil liberties, and pacify the rural population by restoring village elections and making credit easily available. Diem responded noncommittally that the proposals conformed with his own ideas but that it would be "most difficult" to implement them while the government faced internal rebellion.[56] Over the next few weeks, he tightened the controls, clamping down on the army and arresting the politicians who had issued the Caravelle Manifesto.

By the end of the year, Americans in Saigon were thoroughly alarmed by the impending crisis and deeply divided over how to combat it. Durbrow warned Washington that the Saigon government was in "serious danger" and that "prompt and even drastic action" was required to save it. In return for additional military aid, he advised, the United States should require Diem to institute

---

[55]Spector, *Advice and Support,* p. 372.
[56]Durbrow memorandum, October 15, 1960, *USVN,* Book 10, 1318.
[57]Durbrow to State Department, December 5, 1960, ibid., 1334–1336.

sweeping reforms.[57] The U.S. military mission in Saigon firmly resisted Durbrow's proposals. The MAAG's major concern was to develop an effective military response to the insurgency, and it feared that insistence on "democratic" reform would distract attention from the war and undercut Diem during a critical period. The debate became increasingly bitter, and meetings at the embassy, in the words of a participant, were "barely civil."[58]

Although the experiment in nation building was in obvious jeopardy by the end of the year, the Eisenhower administration did not resolve the debate in Saigon or take any major steps to salvage its huge investment. Throughout much of 1960, attention was focused elsewhere. A flare-up over divided Berlin sharpened Cold War tensions in Europe, and the Soviet shooting down of an American U-2 spy plane and torpedoing of a summit meeting in Paris provoked a major crisis. The emergence in neighboring Cuba of a revolutionary government headed by Fidel Castro and the establishment of close ties between Cuba and the Soviet Union aroused fears of Communist intrusion in America's backyard. The deterioration in South Vietnam was gradual, and a sense of crisis did not develop until late in the year, by which time Eisenhower was already planning to transfer power to the newly elected Democratic administration of John F. Kennedy.

Even then, Laos, rather than South Vietnam, seemed the most urgent problem in Indochina. A mildly pro-Western government had assumed power after Geneva and was given lavish American support, but when it attempted to reach an accommodation with the Pathet Lao insurgents who had fought with the Vietminh, the United States instigated a right-wing coup. The American-sponsored government launched an ambitious military campaign against the Pathet Lao, but it achieved little success and in 1960 was overthrown by a group of so-called neutralists. Rejecting a compromise, the Eisenhower administration firmly supported its client government and forced the neutralists into an uneasy alliance with the Pathet Lao. By the end of the year, North Vietnam and the Soviet Union had begun to furnish substantial support for the anti-American forces, and intensification of the civil war seemed certain.

[58]William Colby, *Honorable Men* (New York, 1978), p. 160.

In the twilight of his presidency, Eisenhower was deeply concerned about Laos and even pondered U.S. military intervention. Referring to Laos as the "cork in the bottle" whose removal could threaten all of Southeast Asia, the president, as early as September 1959, had grimly warned that it might "develop into another Korea."[59] At a meeting in late 1960, he advised that "we cannot let Laos fall to the Communists, even if we have to fight—with our allies or without them." In contrast to what has often been alleged, he seems *not* to have recommended unilateral U.S. intervention to Kennedy in a transition briefing on January 19, 1961, but the possibility of such intervention was discussed. Compared with Laos, South Vietnam seemed to be a "back-burner" problem and was not even mentioned during the January briefing on Southeast Asia.[60]

Between 1954 and 1961, the United States came full circle in Vietnam. In the aftermath of Geneva, Eisenhower and Dulles confronted a nearly hopeless situation in southern Vietnam. Some U.S. officials advised abandoning the area, and the administration briefly considered replacing Ngo Dinh Diem. When Diem unexpectedly prevailed over his domestic foes, however, the United States assumed from France the burden of nation building and committed itself firmly to his regime. Through the rest of the decade it poured huge sums of money and great effort into constructing in the southern part of Vietnam a bulwark against further Communist expansion in Southeast Asia.

Lacking knowledge of Vietnamese history and culture, Americans failed to comprehend the perhaps insuperable difficulties of nation building in an area with only the most fragile basis for nationhood. The ambitious programs developed in the 1950s papered over rather than corrected South Vietnam's problems. To have constructed a viable nation in southern Vietnam, moreover, would have required the most enlightened, imaginative, and determined Viet-

---

[59]Gordon Gray memorandum, September 14, 1959, Eisenhower Papers, "Cleanup" File, Box 5.

[60]The basis for the allegation was the Clark Clifford memorandum of conversation, January 19, 1961, *Pentagon Papers (Gravel)*, 2: 635–637. For a corrective, see Fred I. Greenstein and Richard H. Immerman, "What Did Eisenhower Tell Kennedy about Indochina? The Politics of Misperception," *Journal of American History* 79 (September 1992): 568–587.

[61]Dulles news conference, March 1, 1955, Dulles Papers, Princeton, N.J., Box 99.

namese leadership, an ingredient the United States could not provide. Ngo Dinh Diem may well have been the "best available man," as Dulles described him, and the United States pinned its hopes exclusively on him and helped him survive the tumultuous years 1954 and 1955.[61] But Diem lacked the qualities necessary for the formidable challenge of nation building, and by 1960 he faced a potent internal opposition supported by North Vietnam that he, like the French before him, seemed increasingly incapable of handling.

Through luck as much as anything else, the Eisenhower administration kept the Diem regime afloat for six years. Ironically, however, its limited success, exaggerated for public relations purposes, led ultimately to disastrous failure. Throughout the second half of the decade, the administration publicly proclaimed miraculous success where little existed and applauded South Vietnam's stability while producing an almost totally dependent regime that consumed millions of U.S. dollars. Thus, historian David Anderson has concluded, "ignorance and confidence bred an illusion of success that trapped Eisenhower and subsequent US presidents in a frustrating and futile effort to define and defend US interests in Vietnam."[62]

The quirks of the electoral calendar spared Eisenhower from facing the ultimate failure of his policies in Vietnam. Within a short time after taking office, however, John F. Kennedy would have to choose between abandoning what he had called "our offspring" or significantly increasing the American commitment.

---

[62]Anderson, *Trapped by Success,* p. ix.

The Self-Immolation of Thich Quang Duc
This classic 1963 photo of the immolation of
Buddhist monk Thich Quang Duc in the streets
of Saigon brought home to Americans the depth
of Vietnamese discontent with the Diem regime,
and it aroused grave concern among Kennedy
advisers and the public about the nation's
growing entanglement in Vietnam.
AP/Wide World Photos

CHAPTER 3

Limited Partnership

Kennedy and Diem, 1961–1963

"Our problems are critical," John F. Kennedy warned the nation in January 1961. "The tide is unfavorable. The news will be worse before it is better."[1] It was a theme Kennedy had sounded throughout the 1960 campaign, and it set the tone for the first years of his administration. In 1961, the world did appear to be entering the most perilous stage in its history. The struggle of hundreds of new nations to break from their colonial past and establish modern institutions unleashed chaos across much of the globe. The rhetoric and actions of the erratic Soviet Premier Nikita Khrushchev suggested a new Communist boldness, even recklessness, and a determination to exploit the prevailing instability. Soviet-American confrontation broadened and intensified in the late 1950s, and the development of awesome new weapons added an especially frightful dimension. Over the long haul, nationalism proved a more powerful force than communism or democratic capitalism, and within two years the eruption of the Sino-Soviet split would starkly expose the myth of a monolithic Communist "bloc." In 1961, however, the fate of the world appeared to hang in the balance, and Kennedy took office certain that America's survival depended on its capacity to defend "free" institutions. Should it falter, he warned, "the whole world, in my opinion, would inevitably begin to move toward the Communist bloc."[2]

[1]John F. Kennedy, State of the Union Address, January 30, 1961, *John F. Kennedy: Public Papers, 1961* (Washington, D.C., 1962), p. 27.
[2]Quoted in Seyom Brown, *The Faces of Power* (New York, 1969), p. 217.

THE NEW FRONTIER AND THE COLD WAR

Calling upon all Americans to become the "watchmen on the walls of freedom" and promising to assert firm, vigorous leadership, Kennedy pledged his administration to meet the perils of the new era. He gathered about him a youthful, energetic corps of advisers from the top positions in academia and industry, activists who shared his commitment to "get the country moving again." The New Frontiersmen accepted without question the basic assumptions of the containment policy, but they also believed they must take the initiative in meeting the Communist threat rather than simply reacting to it.[3] Coming to political maturity during World War II, they were alarmed by the danger of another global holocaust, but they were also exhilarated by the challenge of leading the nation through perilous times. They shared a deep sense of duty to their country and a Wilsonian view that destiny had singled out the United States to defend and spread the democratic ideal. Pragmatic centrists, they believed that no problem was without solution, and they were self-confident to the point of arrogance.[4]

Kennedy and his advisers also recognized that domestic politics demanded a firm and successful foreign policy. During the campaign of 1960, the senator from Massachusetts in strident tones had accused Eisenhower of indecisiveness and promised to regain the initiative in the Cold War. Having won the most narrow of electoral victories, he was keenly aware of his vulnerability. Especially in his first two years, he kept a wary eye on his domestic flank, and he was ever sensitive to Republican charges of weakness or appeasement.

The Kennedy administration set out at once to meet the challenges of the Cold War. The president ordered a massive buildup of nuclear weapons and long-range missiles to establish a credible deterrent to Soviet nuclear power. Persuaded that Eisenhower's heavy reliance on nuclear weapons had left the United States muscle-bound in many diplomatic situations, Kennedy also expanded and modernized the nation's conventional military forces

[3]Henry Fairlie, *The Kennedy Promise* (New York, 1973), p. 72.
[4]Thomas G. Paterson, "Bearing the Burden: A Critical Look at JFK's Foreign Policy," *Virginia Quarterly Review* 54 (Spring 1978): 197.

to permit a "flexible response" to various types and levels of aggression. Certain that the emerging nations would be the "principal battleground in which the forces of freedom and Communism [would] compete," the administration devoted much attention to developing an effective response to guerrilla warfare—"an international disease" the United States must learn to "destroy."[5] Kennedy took a keen personal interest in the theory, tactics, and weapons of counterinsurgency warfare and covert operations, encouraging his advisers to read the writings of revolutionaries such as Mao Tse-tung and Che Guevara and pushing the military services to develop means to combat their tactics. He also felt that America had to strike at the source of the disease, however, and pressed for the creation of economic and technical assistance programs to eliminate the conditions in which communism flourished and to channel revolutionary forces along democratic paths.

Vietnam stands as the most tragic legacy of the global activism of the Kennedy era. The president had long taken a close personal interest in Vietnam—once labeling it the "cornerstone of the Free World in Southeast Asia." In his eyes and those of many of his advisers, South Vietnam was a test case of America's determination to uphold its commitments in a menacing world and its capacity to meet the new challenges posed by guerrilla warfare in the emerging nations. He had joined in the attacks on Truman for "losing" China, and he was extremely sensitive to the political damage that could come from the loss of additional Asian real estate. Thus he was even less willing than Truman and Eisenhower to permit the fall of Vietnam to communism.

Inheriting from Eisenhower an increasingly dangerous if still limited commitment, he plunged deeper into the morass. Kennedy did not eagerly take up the burden in Vietnam, and his actions there contrast sharply with his rhetoric. In settling the major policy issues, he was cautious rather than bold, hesitant rather than decisive, and improvisational rather than carefully calculating. He delayed making a firm commitment for nearly a year and then acted only because the shaky Diem government appeared on the verge of collapse. Wary of the domestic and international consequences of a negotiated settlement but unwilling to risk full-scale involvement, he chose a cautious

[5]John McCloy and Walt W. Rostow quoted in Fairlie, *Kennedy Promise*, pp. 132, 264.

middle course, expanding the American role while trying to keep it limited. In the short run, such a policy offered numerous advantages, but over the long run it was delusive and dangerous. It encouraged Diem to continue on his self-destructive path while leading Americans to believe they could secure a favorable outcome without paying a heavy price. It significantly narrowed the choices, making extrication more difficult and creating a self-supporting argument for a larger and more dangerous commitment.

YEAR OF CRISES

Throughout the presidential campaign, Kennedy had stressed the perils the nation confronted, but he appears unprepared for the severity of the problems he inherited. Khrushchev's threat to resolve the status of divided Berlin on his own terms held out the possibility of a direct superpower confrontation. In January 1961, the Soviet premier delivered a seemingly militant speech avowing his support for wars of national liberation. In fact, the statement defied Kremlin hard-liners and the more aggressive Chinese by renouncing conventional war, and it may even have been intended to reassure the West. To the untutored ears of the inexperienced Kennedy administration, however, it appeared a virtual declaration of war, and stepped-up Soviet aid to Castro's Cuba and insurgents in the Congo and Laos seemed to confirm the magnitude of the threat. Such was the siege mentality that gripped the White House in early 1961 that Kennedy on one occasion greeted his advisers by grimly asking, "What's gone against us today?"[6]

Vietnam was not regarded as a major trouble spot in the administration's first hundred days. Eisenhower had not even mentioned it in his briefings, and it was only in January, after reading a gloomy report by Lansdale, that Kennedy learned of the steady growth of the insurgency and the increasing problems with Diem. Lansdale predicted a large-scale insurgent offensive before the end of the year, but he concluded optimistically that a "major American effort" could frustrate the Communist drive for power. Persuaded as Truman and

---

[6]Quoted in Walt Whitman Rostow, *The Diffusion of Power: An Essay in Recent History* (New York, 1972), p. 170.

Eisenhower before him that Vietnam was vital to America's global interests, Kennedy routinely approved an additional $42 million to support an expansion of the South Vietnamese Army.[7]

By the end of April, Kennedy's staff was again closely watching Vietnam. Acting on Ambassador Durbrow's advice, the president had conditioned the assistance granted in January on the institution of military and political reforms. But Diem had balked, and after three months the aid program remained stalled and the war languished.

At the same time, major foreign policy setbacks in Cuba and Laos appeared to increase the importance of Vietnam. A clandestine effort to overthrow Castro ended in disaster at the Bay of Pigs, leaving Kennedy in a state of acute shock and his administration profoundly shaken. After the Bay of Pigs, Kennedy was suspicious of the Joint Chiefs of Staff (JCS) and the intelligence community; he therefore rejected various proposals to put troops into Laos to stave off the impending defeat of the American-sponsored government. The military warned that protecting U.S. troops sent to Laos against possible Chinese or North Vietnamese countermoves might require extreme measures, even the use of nuclear weapons. The country was landlocked, a poor choice for intervention from a logistic standpoint, and many of Kennedy's advisers shared the view of Ambassador to India John Kenneth Galbraith that as a "military ally the entire Laos nation is clearly inferior to a battalion of conscientious objectors from World War I."[8] Moreover, as Kennedy himself repeatedly pointed out, it would be difficult to explain to the American public why he sent troops to remote Laos when he had refused to send them to nearby Cuba. In late April, the president concluded that a negotiated settlement was the best he could get in Laos, and the United States agreed to participate in a peace conference at Geneva.

More than anything else, the decision to negotiate in Laos led the administration to reevaluate its policy in Vietnam. Along with

[7]McGeorge Bundy to Rostow, January 30, 1961, John F. Kennedy Papers, National Security File, Box 192, John F. Kennedy Library, Boston, Mass.
[8]Galbraith to Kennedy, May 10, 1961, Kennedy Papers, Office File, Box 29. For Kennedy's Laos decisions, see Edmund F. Wehrle, " 'A Good, Bad Deal': John F. Kennedy, W. Averell Harriman, and the Neutralization of Laos, 1961–1962," *Pacific Historical Review* 67 (1998): 349–359 and Ben Weber, "Trapped by Ideological Ghosts: John F. Kennedy, Averell Harriman and the Laos Crisis of 1961 to 1963," (Master's Thesis, University of Kentucky, 2000).

its refusal to send U.S. aircraft or troops to salvage the Bay of Pigs operation, its unwillingness to intervene militarily in Laos appeared to increase the symbolic importance of taking firm stands elsewhere. The administration had captured the attention of the nation with its self-conscious activism, but in its first months it had little to show for it. "At this point we are like the Harlem Globetrotters," National Security Adviser McGeorge Bundy conceded, "passing forward, behind, sidewise, and underneath. But nobody has made a basket yet."[9] Kennedy confided to *New York Times* columnist Arthur Krock that he had to make certain that "Khrushchev doesn't misunderstand Cuba, Laos, etc. to indicate that the United States is in a yielding mood on such matters as Berlin."[10] Moreover, with the outcome of the Laos negotiations uncertain, it seemed urgent to prepare a fallback position in Southeast Asia, and Vietnam seemed a better place than Laos to make a stand.

Despite its growing concern with Vietnam, the administration did not institute major policy changes or drastically expand American commitments in the spring of 1961. The president authorized a modest increase of 100 advisers in the Military Assistance and Advisory Group (MAAG) and dispatched to Vietnam 400 Special Forces troops to train the Vietnamese in counterinsurgency techniques. Convinced in light of the Laos negotiations that Diem had to be handled with special care, Kennedy recalled Durbrow, the foremost advocate of hard bargaining tactics, and sent Vice President Lyndon B. Johnson to Saigon to give personal assurances of American support. To back up its diplomacy without provoking domestic or international concern, the administration launched covert warfare in Indochina. The United States sent clandestine teams of South Vietnamese across the seventeenth parallel to attack enemy supply lines, sabotage military and civilian targets, and agitate against the Hanoi regime. At the same time, the CIA initiated its "secret war" in Laos, arming some 9,000 Hmong tribespeople for actions against the Ho Chi Minh trail in what would become one of the largest paramilitary operations ever undertaken.[11]

[9]Fairlie, *Kennedy Promise*, p. 180.

[10]Krock memorandum of conversation with Kennedy, May 5, 1961, Arthur Krock Papers, Seeley G. Mudd Manuscript Library, Princeton, N.J., Box 59.

[11]For the beginnings of the Laos secret war, see Timothy N. Castle, *At War in the Shadow of Vietnam* (New York, 1993), especially pp. 39–44; and Jane Hamilton-Merritt, *Tragic Mountains* (Bloomington, Ind., 1993), pp. 70–112. See also Richard H. Shultz, Jr., *The Secret War Against Hanoi* (New York, 1999).

The reappraisal of the spring of 1961 was more important for the questions raised than for the solutions provided. The administration's decisions reflected, in the words of White House adviser Walt W. Rostow, a calculated policy of "buying time with limited commitments of additional American resources."[12] But many officials feared that this policy might not be enough, and a task force appointed by Kennedy to review American options began to consider the more drastic measures that might be required if the Laos negotiations broke down or the Communists launched a major offensive in Vietnam. Among other actions, the task force openly raised the possibility of sending, for the first time since 1954, American combat forces to Vietnam, and it also discussed air and naval operations against North Vietnam.

While the administration studied various choices, pressures mounted for expanded American involvement in Vietnam. After a whirlwind trip through East Asia with a major stopover in Saigon, Johnson reported that the decision to negotiate in Laos had shaken Diem's confidence in the United States and warned that if a further decline in morale was to be arrested, "deeds must follow words— soon."[13] After Johnson's visit, Diem himself requested additional aid. He displayed no interest in U.S. combat troops when the vice president discreetly raised the issue. Fiercely independent and keenly aware of the rising opposition to his regime, Diem apparently feared that the introduction of large numbers of American troops would not only give the National Liberation Front (NLF) a powerful rallying cry but also give the non-Communist opposition critical leverage. Shortly after Johnson departed Saigon, however, Diem warned Kennedy that the situation in Vietnam had become "very much more perilous" and requested sufficient additional American aid and advisers to expand his army by 100,000 troops.[14]

The Cold War intensified in the summer of 1961. During a stormy summit meeting in Vienna in June, Khrushchev again affirmed the Soviet commitment to wars of liberation, reinforcing the administration's fears and its inclination to respond somewhere. He "just beat hell out of me," Kennedy remarked. "If he thinks I'm

[12]Rostow, *Diffusion of Power*, p. 270.
[13]Johnson to Kennedy, May 23, 1961, Kennedy Papers, Office File, Box 30.
[14]U.S. Congress, Senate, Subcommittee on Public Buildings and Grounds, *The Pentagon Papers (Senator Gravel Edition)* (4 vols.; Boston, 1971), 2: 60. Hereafter cited as *Pentagon Papers (Gravel)*.

inexperienced and have no guts . . . we won't get anywhere with him. So we have to act."[15] In August, under cover of darkness, the Soviets constructed a steel and concrete wall separating West Berlin from the eastern zone, confronting an already beleagured Kennedy administration with yet another crisis.

THE TAYLOR-ROSTOW MISSION

In the supercharged atmosphere of the summer of 1961, some of Kennedy's advisers pressed for escalation in Vietnam. Rostow had long advocated the employment of such "unexploited counterguerrilla assets" as helicopters and the newly created Green Berets. "It is somehow wrong to be developing these capabilities but not applying them in a crucial theater," he advised Kennedy. "In Knute Rockne's old phrase, we are not saving them for the junior prom." The economist and former MIT professor compared the summer of 1961 to the year 1942, when the Allies had suffered defeats across the globe, warning Kennedy that "to turn the tide" the United States must "win" in Vietnam. If Vietnam could be held, Thailand, Laos, and Cambodia could be saved, and "we shall have demonstrated that the Communist technique of guerrilla warfare can be dealt with."[16]

Preoccupied with more urgent matters such as Berlin, Kennedy fended off his more belligerent advisers, approving only small additional increments of aid until a dramatic worsening of conditions in the fall of 1961 compelled him to act. Infiltration into South Vietnam doubled to nearly 4,000 in 1961. The NLF drastically stepped up operations in September and for a brief period even seized a provincial capital just fifty-five miles from Saigon. Intelligence analysts reported a substantial increase in the size of regular guerrilla forces. The journalist Theodore H. White noted a "political breakdown of formidable proportions" in South Vietnam,[17] and in September, Diem urgently requested additional economic assistance. By early October, both the JCS and the National Security Council

---

[15]Michael R. Beschloss, *The Crisis Years* (New York, 1991), p. 225.
[16]Rostow to Kennedy, March 29, 1961, Kennedy Papers, National Security File, Box 192, and June 17, 1961, Kennedy Papers, Office File, Box 65.
[17]Quoted in *Pentagon Papers (Gravel)*, 2: 70.

(NSC) were proposing the introduction of sizable American combat forces into Vietnam.

Kennedy remained cautious. He revealed to Krock a profound reluctance to send American troops to the Asian mainland. He expressed grave doubts that the United States should interfere in "civil disturbances caused by guerrillas," adding that "it was hard to prove that this wasn't largely the situation in Vietnam."[18] Increasingly concerned by the military and political deterioration in South Vietnam but fearful of expanding the American commitment, he dispatched Rostow and his personal military adviser, General Maxwell D. Taylor, to Vietnam to assess conditions firsthand and weigh the need for U.S. forces.

Taylor and Rostow confirmed the pessimistic reports that had been coming out of Saigon for the past month. The South Vietnamese Army was afflicted with a "defensive outlook." The Diem government was disorganized, inefficient, and increasingly unpopular. The basic problem was a "deep and pervasive crisis of confidence and a serious loss in national morale" stemming from developments in Laos, the intensification of guerrilla activity, and a devastating flood in the Mekong Delta. "No one felt the situation was hopeless," Taylor later recalled, but all agreed that it was "serious" and demanded "urgent measures."[19]

Taylor and Rostow recommended a significant expansion of American aid to arrest the deterioration in South Vietnam. They emphasized that the Vietnamese themselves must win the war; but they also concluded that the provision of American equipment and skilled American advisers working closely with the government at all levels could result in a "much better, aggressive, more confident performance from the Vietnamese military and civilian establishment."[20] Highly trained advisory groups, strategically placed throughout the South Vietnamese bureaucracy, could help identify and correct major political, economic, and military problems. Improved training for the Civil Guard and Village Self-Defense Corps would free the army for offensive operations, and equipment such as helicopters would give it the mobility to fight more effectively.

[18]Krock memorandum of conversation with Kennedy, October 11, 1961, Krock Papers, Box 59.
[19]Maxwell D. Taylor, *Swords and Ploughshares* (New York, 1972), p. 241.
[20]Rostow, *Diffusion of Power*, p. 275.

Taylor and Rostow also advocated what they called a "limited partnership" with the South Vietnamese government, a middle ground
between "formalized advice on the one hand" and "trying to run
the war on the other."[21]

The most novel—and ultimately most controversial—of the
proposals was to send an 8,000-person "logistic task force" of
American soldiers, comprising engineers, medical groups, and the
infantry to support them. The ostensible purpose was to assist in
repairing the massive flood damage in the Mekong Delta, but Taylor had other, more important motives in mind. Diem continued to
resist the introduction of U.S. combat troops, but many government
officials and many Americans in Saigon believed that troops were
desperately needed. Taylor himself felt a "pressing need to do
something to restore Vietnamese morale and to shore up confidence in the United States." The task force would serve as a "visible
symbol of the seriousness of American intentions," he advised
Kennedy, and would constitute an invaluable military reserve
should the situation in South Vietnam suddenly worsen.[22] The humanitarian purpose of the force would provide a convenient pretext for its introduction into Vietnam, and it could be removed
without embarrassment when its job was completed. Taylor and
Rostow emphasized that their proposals constituted minimum
steps. If these plans were not enough, the United States might have
to dispatch combat troops or launch offensive operations against
North Vietnam.

The proposal for a flood relief force aroused especially heated
discussion among Kennedy's advisers. Some feared that the introduction of combat troops in any form might jeopardize the Laos negotiations or provoke escalation in Vietnam. Others questioned
whether such a force would be large enough or, given its announced purpose of flood relief, capable of restoring morale.
Should it come under attack, the United States would face the more
difficult choice of supporting it with additional forces or withdrawing it altogether. "If we commit 6–8,000 troops and then pull them
out when the going gets rough we will be finished in Vietnam and

[21]Taylor to Kennedy, November 3, 1961, in Department of State, *Foreign Relations of
the United States, 1961–1963* (Washington, D.C., 1988), 1: 493. Hereafter cited as *FR*
with date and volume number.
[22]Taylor, *Swords and Ploughshares*, p. 239.

probably all of Southeast Asia," one NSC staffer warned.[23] There was general unhappiness with the "half-in, half-out" nature of the proposal. Top State Department officials expressed major reservations about committing troops in any form. Secretary of Defense Robert McNamara, the JCS, and McGeorge Bundy used the Taylor proposal to develop more far-reaching recommendations, urging Kennedy to make an unequivocal commitment to prevent the fall of South Vietnam and then be prepared to introduce large-scale U.S. combat forces "if that should become necessary for success."[24]

While the Taylor-Rostow report was circulating in Washington, Undersecretary of State Chester Bowles and the veteran diplomat W. Averell Harriman, the chief American negotiator on Laos, promoted a very different course. Harriman expressed grave doubt that Diem's "repressive, dictatorial and unpopular regime" could survive under any circumstances and warned that the United States should not "stake its prestige in Vietnam." Bowles admonished that the United States was "headed full blast up a dead end street." The two men thus pressed Kennedy to defer any major commitment to Diem. If the Laos negotiations proceeded smoothly, the United States could then expand the conference to include Vietnam and seek an overall settlement based on the 1954 Geneva agreements.[25] The Taylor report for the first time since 1954 posed a clear-cut choice between a major escalation of the conflict and possible extrication from Vietnam.

Faced with this difficult choice, Kennedy, in a way that would become institutionalized, opted for a cautious, middle-of-the-road approach. He flatly rejected a negotiated settlement. The administration had vowed to wage the Cold War vigorously, but in its first months it had suffered apparent setbacks in Cuba, Laos, and Berlin. Throughout the year, Republicans and right-wing Democrats had charged it with weakness, and Kennedy feared that a decision to

[23]Robert Johnson to Bundy, October 31, 1961, Kennedy Papers, National Security File, Box 194.
[24]Dean Rusk and Robert McNamara to Kennedy, November 11, 1961, *Pentagon Papers (Gravel)*, 2: 110–116.
[25]Harriman to Kennedy, November 11, 1961, Kennedy Papers, National Security File, Box 195; Chester Bowles, *Promises to Keep* (New York, 1971), p. 409; Stephen Pelz, "John F. Kennedy's 1961 Vietnam War Decisions," *Journal of Strategic Studies* 4 (December 1981): 378.

negotiate on Vietnam would unleash domestic political attacks as rancorous and destructive as those after the fall of China in 1949.

The president was also concerned about the international implications. Administration strategists felt that in a divided and dangerous world the United States must establish the credibility of its commitments. Should it appear weak, its allies would lose faith and its enemies would be emboldened to further aggression, a process that could leave the awful choice of a complete erosion of America's world position or nuclear war. By late 1961, Kennedy and many of his advisers were convinced that they must prove their toughness to Khrushchev. "That son of a bitch won't pay any attention to words," the president remarked during the Berlin crisis. "He has to see you move."[26]

Although determined to appear tough, Kennedy firmly resisted the proposal to send combat troops. He questioned the psychological value of Taylor's flood relief force, and he speculated—prophetically, as it turned out—that the commitment of some men would only lead to requests for more. "The troops will march in; the bands will play; the crowds will cheer," he told Arthur M. Schlesinger, Jr., "and in four days everyone will have forgotten. Then we will be told we have to send in more troops. It's like taking a drink. The effect wears off, and you have to take another."[27] He also rejected McNamara's proposal for a major verbal commitment to prevent the fall of South Vietnam, noting that a commitment without troops could bring the worst of both worlds. He expressed deep concern about taking on simultaneously major obligations in Europe and Southeast Asia. He was especially bothered by the prospect of direct involvement in a war whose origins were so "obscure" in an "area 10,000 miles away against 16,000 guerrillas with a native army of 200,000, where millions have been spent for years with no success." On several occasions, he expressed uncertainty that he could secure congressional and allied support to wage such a war.[28]

Carefully avoiding the extremes advocated by his advisers, Kennedy would go no further than approve Taylor's recommendations to increase significantly the volume of American assistance

[26]Quoted in Paterson, "Bearing the Burden," 206.
[27]Quoted in Arthur M. Schlesinger, Jr., *A Thousand Days* (Boston, 1965), p. 547.
[28]Notes on NSC meeting, November 15, 1961, *FR, 1961–1963,* 1: 607–608.

and the number of advisers in hopes this would arrest the military and political deterioration in South Vietnam. To oversee implementation of the new program, the administration created a formal military command and elevated the top military official to equal status with the ambassador. It took these steps in full recognition that it was violating the Geneva Accords of 1954, and on December 15 it released a "white paper" detailing North Vietnamese breaches of the Geneva agreements that justified its own response.[29]

In undertaking Taylor's "limited partnership" with South Vietnam, the administration at first took a hard line with Diem. American officials had long agreed that his repressive and inefficient government constituted a major obstacle to defeating the insurgency. Reluctant to commit American personnel, money, and prestige to a "losing horse," as Secretary of State Dean Rusk put it, the administration instructed the embassy in Saigon to inform Diem that approval of the new aid program would be contingent on specific promises to reorganize and reform the government and permit the United States a share in decision making.[30]

When the U.S. demands provoked an immediate crisis in Saigon, the administration quickly retreated. Diem angrily protested the small volume of money and equipment and lashed out at the proposals for a new relationship, bluntly informing Ambassador Frederick Nolting that South Vietnam "did not want to be a protectorate."[31] The administration responded firmly, holding up shipments of military equipment and instituting a quiet search for a possible replacement for Diem. Nolting strongly questioned the new policy, however, advising that a "cool and unhurried approach is our best chance of success."[32] And the State Department could identify no one who appeared capable of filling Diem's shoes. Convinced, as Kennedy put it, that "Diem is Diem and the best we've got," the administration backed down.[33] The new relationship was

[29]Department of State, *A Threat to the Peace: North Viet Nam's Effort to Conquer South Viet Nam* (Washington, D.C., 1961).

[30]Rusk to State Department, November 1, 1961, Kennedy Papers, National Security File, Box 194; *Pentagon Papers (Gravel)*, 2: 120.

[31]Nolting to State Department, November 18, 1961, Kennedy Papers, National Security File, Box 165.

[32]Nolting to State Department, November 29, 1961, Kennedy Papers, National Security File, Box 195.

[33]Quoted in Benjamin Bradlee, *Conversations with Kennedy* (New York, 1976), p. 59.

redefined to mean simply that one party would not take action without consulting the other, and the emphasis was shifted from reform to efficiency. The two governments agreed on an innocuous statement affirming these points, and the crisis passed.

Kennedy's decisions of 1961 mark yet another critical turning point in American involvement in Vietnam. Properly wary of deeper military involvement in a conflict he suspected might not be winnable, the president, primarily for political reasons, still refused to abandon the struggle. Rejecting the extremes of combat troops on the one hand and negotiations on the other, he settled for a limited commitment of aid and advisers. His caution was well placed, but his 1961 decisions increased direct American involvement and the commitment of U.S. prestige. He recognized from the start, moreover, that these limited steps might not be enough to save South Vietnam, and events would demonstrate that the commitments, once made, could not easily be kept limited. The new commitments marked a giant step toward America's assumption of responsibility for the war, a step symbolized by the creation of a formal military command.[34]

In instituting their new partnership, the United States and Diem entangled themselves more tightly in their fateful web. American frustration with Diem was understandable, but in searching for a more manageable replacement, U.S. officials arrogantly presumed to know what was best for South Vietnam. By assuming greater responsibility for the war, they undercut the nationalist claims on which Diem's success ultimately rested. Diem perceived that he could not defeat the insurgency and stay in power without U.S. support, but he recognized the dangers and tried desperately—and ultimately unsuccessfully—to avoid his ally's suffocating embrace. The U.S.–South Vietnam agreements of late 1961 thus opened the way for conflicts that would make a mockery of the word *partnership* and would have tragic consequences for all concerned.[35]

[34]Michael Cannon, "Raising the Stakes: The Taylor-Rostow Mission," *Journal of Strategic Studies* 12 (June 1989): 153–158.
[35]Kennedy sought to solidify the middle course in Vietnam and in other areas through what became known as the "Thanksgiving Day Massacre," in which the "dovish" Bowles was removed as undersecretary of state and the "hawkish" Rostow was sent to the State Department.

PROJECT BEEFUP

Their differences resolved for the moment, the United States and South Vietnam launched a two-pronged plan to contain the insurgency. Supported by a vast increase in American equipment and advisers, the South Vietnamese Army took the offensive against the guerrillas. At the same time, the Diem government adopted the so-called strategic hamlet program to gain the active participation of the rural population in the war against the NLF. The program has frequently been dismissed as the product of British or American influence, and Diem and Nhu did consult British counterinsurgency expert Sir Robert Thompson—in part to counter rising American power. But the program had deep indigenous roots and reflected an ambitious effort by the Saigon regime to revitalize rural South Vietnam and undermine the NLF. Peasants from scattered villages would be brought together into hamlets surrounded by moats and bamboo stake fences and guarded by military forces. The hamlets would not only protect the people against NLF terror but also provide the means to carry out a social and economic revolution based on local self-rule and self-sufficiency. The reinstitution of village elections, implementation of land reform, and building of schools and medical dispensaries would persuade villagers that life under the government offered more than under the insurgents. By restoring village autonomy, displacing the old elite, and encouraging economic development through self-help projects, the villagers would be bound together as a community, leaving the guerrillas a "foreign expeditionary corps facing a hostile population." Diem and Nhu envisioned an authentic nationalist revolution that would restore the villages to their traditional place in Vietnamese life. They hoped the strategic hamlet program would reduce their dependence on the United States. Their most grandiose vision saw it as a means to undermine North Vietnam and unify the country under their control.[36]

To support the counterinsurgency program, the United States, in what was called "Project Beefup," drastically expanded its role in Vietnam. The Military Assistance and Advisory Group was replaced

---

[36]See especially Philip E. Catton, "Counter-Insurgency and Nation Building: The Strategic Hamlet Programme in South Vietnam, 1961–1963," *The International History Review* 21 (December 1999): 918–940.

by an enlarged and reorganized Military Assistance Command, Vietnam (MACV), headed by General Paul D. Harkins. American military assistance more than doubled between 1961 and 1962 and included such major items as armored personnel carriers and more than 300 military aircraft. Kennedy authorized the use of defoliants to deny the guerrillas cover and secure major roads and the limited use of herbicides to destroy enemy food supplies.

The number of American "advisers" jumped from 3,205 in December 1961 to more than 9,000 by the end of 1962. Highly trained professionals, in many cases veterans of World War II and Korea, they epitomized the global commitment and can-do spirit of the Kennedy era. Their casual dress—brightly colored caps, shoulder holsters, and bandoliers—reflected their unusual mission. They stoically endured the harsh climate and the dysentery (promptly dubbed "Ho Chi Minh's revenge"), confident that they were not only defending Vietnam against a Communist takeover but also preparing themselves for the wars of the future. "It's as important for us to train as the Vietnamese," a helicopter pilot informed an American journalist.[37]

The advisers performed varied, ever-widening tasks. Special Forces units conducted Civic Action programs among the Montagnards of the Central Highlands. Helicopter pilots dropped detachments of troops from the Army of the Republic of Vietnam (ARVN) into battle zones deep in the swamplands and picked up the dead and wounded after engagements. Americans went with Vietnamese trainees on bombing and strafing missions and, when the Vietnamese ran short of pilots, flew the planes themselves. Army officers and enlisted personnel conducted expanded training programs for the ARVN and the Civil Guard, and advisers down to the battalion level fought with ARVN units on combat missions.

Initiating a process that would come to stigmatize the U.S. war in Vietnam as a whole, the Kennedy administration went to considerable lengths to deceive the American public about the extent and nature of its growing involvement. It refused to divulge the actual number of "advisers" sent to Vietnam and continued to insist that they were advisers long after they were actively engaged in combat. Elaborate schemes were devised to maintain that fiction. Low-ranking Viet-

---

[37]Quoted in Richard Tregaskis, *Vietnam Diary* (New York, 1963), p. 149.

namese enlisted men were placed in aircraft merely to provide cover for American pilots. Vietnamese pilots sat next to Americans so that combat casualties could be publicized as training accidents. Government spokespeople rigorously suppressed information about such actions as the bombing of civilians. Kennedy himself flatly denied at press conferences that American advisers were involved in combat. When the truth inevitably leaked out, the administration ordered officials in Saigon to tighten their control of the press in ways that would minimize the effects of harmful stories.[38]

Buoyed by the new weapons and American advisers, the ARVN launched major operations in the spring and summer of 1962, but it was never able to gain the initiative. Even with aircraft and sophisticated electronic equipment, it proved nearly impossible to locate enemy bases amid the dense forests and swampy paddies of South Vietnam. The very nature of an "air-phibious" operation—an air strike followed by the landing of troops—gave advance warning of an attack, often permitting the insurgents to slip away. "You have to land right on top of them or they disappear," a frustrated adviser complained, and one senior U.S. officer contemptuously dismissed helicopter operations as "rattle-assing around the country."[39] Government forces would often bomb and strafe large areas and land sizable detachments of troops with little result, and when they withdrew, the guerrillas reoccupied the region. The insurgents quickly adapted to the helicopters. Sometimes they would stand and fight, and they learned to bring down the slow, clumsy aircraft with small arms. On other occasions, they would lie in hiding until the helicopters had departed and then ambush the landing force.

While the ARVN and its U.S. advisers were chasing enemy main force units, the NLF expanded its grip on the villages. The intricate network of insurgency was tightly organized from top to bottom. Skilled propagandists, the guerrillas exploited local grievances to stir up class hatred and mobilize the peasantry against the government and behind their cause. They used the all-important issue of land to maximum advantage, lowering rents and distributing land to those without it. Local cadres were schooled to behave

[38]John M. Newman, *JFK and Vietnam* (New York, 1992), pp. 204–219; Richard Reeves, *President Kennedy* (New York, 1993), p. 280.
[39]Tregaskis, *Vietnam Diary,* p. 155; Malcolm W. Browne, *The New Face of War* (Indianapolis, 1968), p. 76.

properly toward the people, to be models of revolutionary virtue. At the same time, the NLF employed terror tactics to eliminate and intimidate South Vietnamese government officials, singling out the best and worst for brutal assassination and leaving a vacuum into which they could easily move. They dominated much of rural South Vietnam before the strategic hamlet program got underway; by late 1962 they had gained an estimated 300,000 members and a passive following of more than one million.[40]

Militarily, NLF units became increasingly bold and began to inflict heavy losses. As operations became more costly, ARVN commanders, apparently under orders from Diem, reverted to their old caution, relying more and more on airpower and refusing to risk their troops in battle.

The NLF's upper hand was dramatically revealed in a major battle in January 1963. An American adviser, the legendary Lt. Col. John Paul Vann, pressed his South Vietnamese division commander to attack three guerrilla companies near the village of Ap Bac. The South Vietnamese delayed for a day, giving the insurgents time to learn of the operation and prepare deadly defenses. Outnumbering enemy forces 10 to 1—the textbook ratio for success against guerrillas—the South Vietnamese planned a three-pronged assault against NLF positions. At the first signs of resistance, however, the attackers balked. One prong simply refused to attack. Other units failed to block enemy escape routes. The battle ended ingloriously, with the South Vietnamese firing on each other while the enemy slipped away. The vastly superior ARVN forces suffered 61 dead and 100 wounded, while the NLF left only three bodies behind. Thinking in entirely conventional terms, MACV claimed victory because the enemy had abandoned the field. Those on the scene and the reporters who covered the action knew better. Adviser Roger Hilsman informed Kennedy that it had been a "stunning defeat."[41]

The political implications of techniques employed in military operations increasingly disturbed some Americans. It was difficult to distinguish between insurgents and innocent civilians, and ARVN soldiers, their lives constantly under threat, were not in-

---

[40]Eric Bergerud, *The Dynamics of Defeat: The Vietnam War in Hau Nghia Province* (Boulder, Colo., 1991), 54–68, 82–84.
[41]The classic account is Neil Sheehan, *A Bright Shining Lie* (New York, 1988), pp. 212–265.

clined to make fine distinctions. Civilians, even women and children, were gunned down, giving the NLF a powerful propaganda weapon. The bombing and strafing of villages suspected of harboring guerrillas and the use of napalm and defoliants turned villagers against the government, and critics argued that they did more harm than good. American and South Vietnamese military officials insisted that air cover was essential to ground operations, however, and Diem and General Harkins vigorously promoted the use of napalm. It "really puts the fear of God into the Vietcong," the general exclaimed. "And that is what counts."[42]

The much ballyhooed strategic hamlet program also produced meager results. A similar plan had worked well in Malaya, where Malay villages were fortified against Chinese insurgents, but in Vietnam the hamlets were to be erected against Vietnamese, many of whom had lived among the villagers for years, and the issuance of more than seven million laminated identification cards proved a less than adequate safeguard against infiltration. In theory, the program was to avoid the massive relocation of peasants from sacred ancestral lands, the flaw of the ill-fated agroville plan, but in the delta region, where villagers lived in scattered settlements, the hamlets could not be established without displacement. The large-scale uprooting of the peasantry added to the discontent that had pervaded the rural population since Diem's ascent to power.

The plan was poorly implemented. South Vietnamese, U.S., and British officials had very different ideas about what should be done and often operated at cross-purposes. In contrast to the NLF, which worked patiently and with painstaking attention to detail, Diem and Nhu naively underestimated the difficulty of their task, seeking to do too much in too short a time. They established hamlets in areas where no real security existed, and the vulnerable settlements were quickly overrun or infiltrated by the NLF. Many of the hamlets lacked adequate defenses. In a visit to Vietnam in 1963, Hilsman encountered several spread over such large areas that a full division would have been required to defend them. "But the defenders," he recalled, "were only a few old men, armed with swords, a flintlock, and half a dozen American carbines."[43]

[42]Quoted in Roger Hilsman, *To Move a Nation* (New York, 1967), p. 442.
[43]Hilsman, *To Move a Nation*, p. 456.

In the hands of Diem and Nhu, moreover, the program did nothing to bind the people to the government. Land reform was implemented poorly, if at all, and many peasants were left landless. The United States allocated substantial funds for the institution of services in the hamlets, but inefficiency and corruption kept much of the money from its destination. The government lacked qualified people to staff the program, and many incompetent and corrupt officials represented it at the village level. They drove and coerced the villagers to achieve unrealistic goals, provoking resistance and flight to the NLF.[44]

The strategic hamlet program failed to achieve its goal of winning the war at the "rice roots." As a means of protecting the villagers from direct attack, it enjoyed some limited, short-term success, and among the Montagnards in the Central Highlands, where the United States assumed responsibility, it played a constructive role. By early 1963, however, even its most ardent supporters agreed that it was fundamentally flawed. In addition, the NLF, fearing that even limited government success would threaten its base among the rural population and leave its members as "fish on the chopping block," launched a systematic and effective campaign against key hamlets, creating specially trained units to destroy them by direct attack or infiltration.[45]

Some Kennedy advisers continued to insist that an effective counterinsurgency program required sweeping political reforms, but Diem stubbornly resisted. To appease his American "partners," he instituted token reforms such as the creation of a council of economic advisers. Instead of broadening his government, as the Americans urged, he retreated more and more into isolation, relying almost exclusively on Nhu, a frail and sinister man who tended toward paranoia and delusions of grandeur. The two men personally controlled military operations and directed the strategic hamlet program, and they brooked no interference from their American advisers. Nhu's wife, the beautiful, ambitious, and acid-tongued Dragon Lady (so

[44]Catton, "Counter-Insurgency and Nation-Building," 938–940.

[45]William J. Duiker, *The Communist Road to Power in Vietnam* (Boulder, Colo., 1981), p. 214. "Second Informal Appreciation of the Status of the Strategic Hamlet Program," September 1, 1963, Kennedy Papers, National Security File, Box 202. For a full and balanced discussion of the program, see Douglas S. Blaufarb, *The Counterinsurgency Era: U.S. Doctrines and Performance* (New York, 1977), pp. 89–127.

called after a popular cartoon character to whom she bore at least a faint resemblance), increasingly assumed the role of spokesperson for what by 1962 had become a narrow family oligarchy.

The suspicious and beleaguered Ngos tightened rather than relaxed the controls. The National Assembly pliantly passed laws prohibiting all types of public gatherings, weddings and funerals included, unless approved by the government in advance. The regime imposed on Americans as well as Vietnamese the most rigorous censorship. Diem angrily terminated the contract of the Michigan State University advisory group when several of its members, on returning to the United States, wrote articles that he branded "untrue, unfair, and tendentious."[46] The veteran *Newsweek* correspondent Francois Sully was expelled from Saigon for critical remarks about Madame Nhu.

OPTIMISM AND UNCERTAINTY

Throughout 1962, Vietnam remained an operational rather than a policy problem. Preoccupied with more pressing matters such as the Soviet military buildup in Cuba, top U.S. officials devoted little attention to Vietnam. Having decided the hard questions of policy in 1961, they did not consider fundamental changes in approach. Kennedy flatly rejected Rostow's proposal to put pressure on the Russians to stop the infiltration of soldiers and supplies from North Vietnam. He ignored Galbraith's warnings that the United States was becoming entrapped in a "long drawn out indecisive involvement" and might "bleed as the French did."[47]

As late as the end of 1962, a reappraisal appeared unnecessary, because both the embassy and military command in Saigon exuded optimism. To some extent, as Ambassador Nolting once conceded, their bullishness derived from a "whistle while we work" mentality that was necessary to sustain morale amid setbacks and frustration.[48] In time, however, they came to believe their own rhetoric. Their confidence was clearly misplaced, and they appeared at

---

[46]Wesley Fishel to John Hannah, February 17, 1962, Kennedy Papers, National Security File, Box 196.
[47]Galbraith to Kennedy, April 4, 1962, Kennedy Papers, National Security File, Box 196.
[48]Nolting to Harriman, November 19, 1962, *FR, 1961–1963*, 2: 738.

best fools, at worst dissemblers. But the flaws in the program were more apparent later than at the time. Strangers in an unfamiliar country, they depended for information on the South Vietnamese government, which produced impressive statistics to back claims of progress. Nolting and Harkins erred badly in accepting these figures at face value, but the conflict did not lend itself to easy analysis; they, like other observers, were impressed by the change of climate since 1961, when the Diem government had appeared on the verge of collapse. American policy was working, they argued, and with time and patience victory was attainable.

In late 1962, the American press corps in Saigon began to challenge the official optimism. Brash young correspondents such as David Halberstam of the *New York Times* and Neil Sheehan of *United Press International* did not question the importance of containing communism in Vietnam. Despite government efforts at obfuscation, however, they sniffed out the facts of growing U.S. involvement, and they argued, with increasing force, that the war was being lost. They denounced the Diem government as corrupt, repressive, and unpopular, the strategic hamlet program as a sham. They questioned official reports of military progress, arguing that government statistics were grossly inflated and that the ARVN was conducting "office-hours warfare," launching perfunctory operations during the day and returning to its bases in the evening. They insisted that the war could not be won as long as the United States persisted in its foolish policy of "sink or swim with Ngo Dinh Diem." The angry, defensive response of the embassy and the military command—"Get on the team!" a top military official demanded of one dissident journalist—only enraged the reporters and provoked charges that the government was deliberately deceiving the American people about the war.[49]

Other observers raised even more troublesome questions. Kennedy's old friend and former Senate colleague Mike Mansfield visited Vietnam at the president's request and returned in December 1962 with a highly pessimistic appraisal. In a formal, published statement, Mansfield noted that he could find little progress since his last visit in 1955. In a private report to Kennedy he was even

---

[49]The attitudes of the dissident journalists and their experiences are chronicled in David Halberstam, *The Making of a Quagmire* (New York, 1964). See also Clarence R. Wyatt, *Paper Soldiers* (New York, 1993), pp. 77–127.

more blunt, comparing the U.S. role with that of France during the First Indochina War and warning that the nation might be sucked into a large-scale and futile conflict. "It wasn't a pleasant picture I depicted for him," Mansfield later recalled.[50]

Mounting criticism of U.S. Vietnam policy aroused grave concern in Washington. The administration had attempted to keep its involvement under wraps, but the rising toll of American deaths and the critical newspaper reports raised troublesome questions. U.S. officials spent hours investigating the journalists' reports and answering their allegations, and Kennedy himself attempted unsuccessfully to get the *Times* to recall Halberstam. The president was stung by Mansfield's report, but he could not ignore the warnings of an old and valued friend, and he immediately dispatched Hilsman and Michael Forrestal, a member of the White House staff, on a fact-finding mission to Vietnam.

The Hilsman-Forrestal report of early 1963 struck a middle ground between the harsh criticism of the journalists and the rosy optimism of the embassy. The two men expressed serious reservations about the effectiveness of ARVN military operations, found flaws in the implementation of the strategic hamlet program, and conceded that Diem had become increasingly isolated from the people. They concluded that the United States and South Vietnam were "probably winning" but quickly added that the war would "probably last longer than we would like" and "cost more in terms of both lives and money than we had anticipated."[51] Despite a generally pessimistic appraisal and cautiously optimistic conclusions, Hilsman and Forrestal found U.S. policy sound in its conception and recommended only tactical changes to ensure more effective implementation. Their report reinforced doubts about the reliability of official estimates of progress but kept alive hopes that the United States might yet achieve its goals.

Throughout the spring of 1963, optimism and uncertainty coexisted uneasily in Saigon and Washington. The embassy and military command continued to exude confidence, and Harkins even informed a gathering of top officials in Honolulu in April that the war might be over by Christmas. Intelligence analyses were much more

---

[50]Mike Mansfield oral history interview, Kennedy Papers.
[51]Hilsman-Forrestal report, January 25, 1963, *FR, 1961–1963*, 3: 50–52.

cautious, warning that the military situation remained fragile and un-predictable. In the White House, in the lower echelons of the Washington bureaucracy, and among some Americans in Vietnam, there was a gnawing uncertainty about how the war was really going and severe doubt, if it was not going well, about which way to turn.

Growing evidence of Vietnamese-American tension compounded the uncertainty. The tension existed at all levels and was probably inevitable given the rapid U.S. buildup in Vietnam and the vastly different approaches of the two peoples. Restless and impatient, the Americans were eager to get on with the job and were frustrated by the inertia that pervaded the government and army of South Vietnam. They sought to bypass the central government and deal directly with the villagers, thus, in effect, taking control of the war. Their arrogance was frequently manifested, one U.S. adviser conceded, by an attitude of "Get out of my way, I'd rather do it my-self!" Proud and sensitive, having only recently emerged from Western rule, the Vietnamese bristled at the presumptuousness of the newcomers who sought to tell them how to run their country. "Daily friction leads to no more love left," a Saigon newspaper philosophized in the spring of 1963.[52]

Relations at the top levels grew particularly tense. The Americans urged "democratic" reforms to secure popular support, they said, but Diem perceived that such reforms would undermine rather than strengthen his regime. Trapped in the dilemma he had feared from the start, he recognized that the American presence, although necessary to hold the line against the NLF, had introduced another—perhaps pivotal—element into the already volatile mix, and he became more and more sensitive to American criticism. Diem and Nhu were increasingly troubled by the growing number of Americans and their apparent efforts to run the war. They protested infringements of Vietnamese sovereignty and fretted about a new colonialism. "All these soldiers," Diem complained to the French ambassador. "I never asked them to come here. They don't even have passports."[53] The growing uneasiness was clearly revealed in May 1963 when Nhu publicly questioned whether the United States knew what it was doing in Vietnam and proposed

---

[52]Chester Cooper, *The Lost Crusade: America in Vietnam* (New York, 1970), p. 207; Ellen Hammer, *A Death in November* (New York, 1987), p. 33.
[53]Quoted in Hammer, *Death in November*, p. 121.

that U.S. forces might be reduced by as many as 5,000 soldiers. Sometime in the early summer of 1963, Diem and Nhu began to explore with Hanoi the possibility of a settlement based on American withdrawal from Vietnam.

In this atmosphere of confusion and mounting conflict, the Kennedy administration also began to discuss the possibility of troop withdrawals. As early as mid-1962, Secretary of Defense McNamara had instituted planning for a phased withdrawal of U.S. forces on grounds that once their training function was completed, the South Vietnamese would be able to take over. Sir Robert Thompson had also proposed such a move in April 1963, advising the president that an announcement "out of the blue" of a 1,000-person reduction would reassure the American public and undercut the Communists' "best propaganda line" that the United States was running the war.[54] Kennedy was increasingly alarmed by the South Vietnamese reaction to U.S. involvement. "Those people hate us," he told a journalist. "They are going to throw our asses out of there at almost any point."[55] Increasingly nervous about the South Vietnamese but still worried about the potential political costs from the "loss" of Vietnam, the president told McNamara to begin planning for overt military actions against North Vietnam *and* for a phased withdrawal of U.S. troops from South Vietnam.

Some former Kennedy advisers have since argued that the president's interest in troop withdrawals confirmed his determination to avoid an open-ended commitment and even to extricate the United States from Vietnam. Hilsman and White House staffer Kenneth O'Donnell claimed that by the summer of 1963 Kennedy had recognized the futility of American involvement and was prepared to liquidate it as soon as he had been reelected. "If I tried to pull out completely now from Vietnam," he reportedly explained to Mansfield, "we would have another Joe McCarthy red scare on our hands." Historian John Newman has gone further, claiming that Kennedy knew that the reports of success were not true, was determined to get out of Vietnam even if it meant the war would be

[54]Memorandum of conversation at the White House, April 4, 1963, *FR, 1961–1963,* 3:198–200.
[55]Quoted in Reeves, *President Kennedy,* pp. 484–485.

lost, and had even drawn up a secret plan to disguise his intentions until he had been safely reelected.[56]

Such interpretations are at best highly speculative. From the outset, the idea of troop withdrawals was designed as a political ploy to appease the American public and reassure the South Vietnamese. The extent to which Kennedy was committed to withdrawal remains quite unclear, and there is not a shred of evidence to support the notion of a secret plan for extrication. Even if he had made such a commitment, it is a sad commentary on his leadership that he was willing to risk additional American lives in a cause he considered hopeless merely to ensure his reelection.

THE BUDDHIST CRISIS

At the very time Kennedy and Diem were having sober second thoughts about their fateful partnership, an upheaval among Buddhists in the major cities of South Vietnam suddenly introduced a dramatic new threat to the Diem regime and new complications for an already faltering American policy. The affair began on May 8, seemingly inadvertently, when government troops fired into crowds gathered in Hue to protest orders forbidding the display of flags on the anniversary of Buddha's birth. The May 8 incident stirred new and vigorous protest. Buddhist leaders accused the government of religious persecution and demanded complete religious freedom. Unable or unwilling to conciliate his new opponents, Diem heatedly denied the existence of persecution and blamed the disorders on the Vietcong. Diem's response stimulated additional protest. Buddhist priests conducted well-publicized hunger strikes, and meetings in Hue and Saigon drew large crowds. The uprising attained new proportions on June 11 when a monk immolated himself in front of large, shrieking crowds at a major intersection in downtown Saigon. Sensitive to the potential value of drawing international attention to their cause, the Buddhist leadership had tipped foreign correspondents to the event,

---

[56]Kenneth P. O'Donnell and David F. Powers, *"Johnny, We Hardly Knew Ye": Memories of John Fitzgerald Kennedy* (New York, 1973), p. 16; Newman, *JFK and Vietnam*, pp. 236–237, 321–325.

and an American photographer's candid and poignant picture of the monk engulfed in flames soon appeared in newspapers and on television screens across the world.

From that fiery moment in June 1963, the Buddhist protest emerged into a powerful, apparently deeply rooted political movement that threatened the very survival of the Diem government. Quiescent in periods of stability, the Buddhists throughout Vietnamese history had assumed a role of political and moral leadership in times of crisis. The immolation of the elderly monk was a "call to rebellion," Frances FitzGerald has written, and the disaffected urban population of South Vietnam responded.[57] Students in the universities and high schools, including some Catholics, joined in mass protests, and discontent quickly spread to the army. The government's response spurred additional anger. While Diem did nothing, Madame Nhu publicly and with seeming glee dismissed the immolations as "barbecues" and offered to furnish the gasoline and matches for more. By midsummer, South Vietnamese society appeared on the verge of disintegration.

The crisis brought consternation to a Washington already uneasy over its Vietnam policy. The administration was caught off guard by the protest, surprised by the response it touched off and shocked by the immolation of the monk. Fearing that these ominous new developments might undercut American support for the war and further endanger a counterinsurgency program many suspected was already failing, the administration frantically attempted to reconcile the two sides, sending numerous emissaries to talk with Buddhist leaders and pressing Diem to take conciliatory measures.

Such efforts produced meager results. The Americans could never really determine what the Buddhists wanted, and Diem and Nhu were obdurate. Diem defiantly proclaimed that he would not permit himself and his country to be humiliated, even if the Americans "trained their artillery on this palace." Nhu instructed the Americans that it was impossible to fight a war with a guilty conscience and appealed for an aid program without strings like the one provided during World War II, when the United States assisted Soviet dictator Joseph Stalin without approving his regime.[58] The

[57]Frances FitzGerald, *Fire in the Lake: The Vietnamese and the Americans in Vietnam* (Boston, 1972), p. 134.
[58]Embassy Saigon to State Department, June 24, 1963, *FR, 1961–1963*, 3: 413; memorandum of conversation, Nhu and Robert Manning, July 17, 1963, ibid., 500–501.

government would make no more than token concessions. The demonstrations and immolations continued; in all, seven monks met fiery deaths. While Madame Nhu and the government-controlled Saigon press issued shrill tirades against the Buddhists and the United States, Nhu's police carted off hundreds of protesters to South Vietnam's already bulging jails.

By the late summer, the Kennedy administration was increasingly troubled and deeply divided. The Buddhist mind remained "terra incognito," one Kennedy adviser later conceded, but most Americans agreed that Diem's response had been provocative.[59] The fear persisted that there was no real alternative to Diem and that a change in government might bring even greater chaos to South Vietnam. Some administration officials retained confidence in the president himself, blaming the problems on Nhu and his wife and arguing that the damage might yet be repaired if they could be removed. But others began to view the Buddhist crisis as symbolic of basic, incorrectable defects in the regime and concluded that the United States must face the possibility of a change.

An incident in late August clinched the issue as far as Diem's American opponents were concerned. Nolting's appointment as ambassador expired in the summer of 1963, and during his farewell visit, Diem had assured him, as a personal favor, that no further repressive measures would be taken against the Buddhists. But on August 21, Nhu's U.S.-trained Special Forces carried out massive raids in Hue, Saigon, and other cities, ransacking the pagodas and arresting more than 1,400 Buddhists. Whether Diem approved the raids in advance remains unclear, but in the eyes of most Americans, his subsequent refusal to disavow Nhu's actions placed the onus of responsibility squarely upon him. These latest actions, just days after the solemn pledges to Nolting, appeared to the anti-Diemists a "deliberate affront" that demanded a firm response. Since the Kennedy administration had taken office, consideration had been given to Diem's replacement. Americans assumed as a matter of course a right and, indeed, a duty to intervene in South Vietnamese affairs as they saw fit. "We could not sit still and be the puppets of Diem's anti-Buddhist policies," Roger Hilsman later recalled.[60]

---

[59]Cooper, *Lost Crusade*, p. 210.
[60]Hilsman, *To Move a Nation*, p. 482; Hilsman oral history interview, Kennedy Papers.

Within several days after the raid on the pagodas, moreover, a group of South Vietnamese Army generals opened secret contacts with the United States. The most recent incident made clear, they warned, that Nhu would stop at nothing. Reporting evidence that he was not only planning their execution but also discussing with Hanoi a deal that would sell out the independence of South Vietnam, the generals inquired how the United States might respond should they move against the government. The anti-Diem group in Washington was undoubtedly alarmed by the reports that Nhu was making overtures to Hanoi; the reports reinforced their conviction that something must be done. More important, perhaps, the generals' inquiries suggested that there was, after all, an alternative.

The generals' overtures arrived in Washington on a Saturday, when many top officials were out of town, and Hilsman, Forrestal, and Harriman seized the opportunity to execute what Taylor later described as an "egregious end run."[61] They prepared a tough, if somewhat ambiguous, cable instructing the newly appointed ambassador, Henry Cabot Lodge, Jr., to give Diem an opportunity to rid himself of Nhu but adding that if he refused, the United States must "face the possibility that Diem himself cannot be preserved." They also instructed Lodge to make clear to the generals that the United States would not continue to support Diem if he refused to cooperate and that it would provide them with "direct support in any interim period of breakdown of central government mechanism."[62] These last words left deliberately vague what the United States might do and under what circumstances, but the thrust of the message was unmistakable: if Diem remained obdurate, the United States was prepared to abandon him. The cable was cleared with Kennedy, then vacationing on Cape Cod, and the president's endorsement was apparently used to secure the acquiescence of responsible officials in the Defense Department.

Lodge wasted no time implementing his instructions. From the day he set foot in Saigon, he had concluded that a change of government was necessary. He shared Hilsman's outrage at the August 21 incident. He had no doubt, he later recalled, that the raid on the

---

[61]Taylor, *Swords and Ploughshares*, p. 292.
[62]Telegram, August 24, 1963, U.S. Congress, House Committee on Armed Services, *United States—Vietnam Relations, 1945–1967: A Study Prepared by the Department of Defense* (Washington, D.C., 1971), Book 12, 536–537.

pagodas "marked the beginning of the end of the Diem regime."[63] His convictions were reinforced by his first meeting with Diem. When he warned that the regime's handling of the Buddhists was endangering American support for South Vietnam, Diem gave him a long lecture on the difficulties of governing a nation with a "dearth of educated people." The embassy subsequently contacted the generals through a CIA agent—"so the official American hand would not show"—offering assurances of support should they succeed in overthrowing the government but warning that the United States would not assist them in undertaking a coup or "bail them out" if they got into trouble.[64]

By the time Kennedy met with his advisers on Monday, August 26, the United States had concluded that a change of government was necessary. The meeting was tense and marked by sometimes bitter exchanges. Taylor and McNamara protested that instructions for a basic change in policy had been sent to Lodge behind their backs. The president himself was furious with the way the change had been effected—"This shit has got to stop!" he exclaimed at one point. He was unhappy with the change itself, feeling, as one of his advisers later put it, "that he had been painted into a corner and . . . would have preferred to give an even more ambivalent answer to the generals."[65] Significantly, however, he did not retreat from the policy that had been established. In subsequent messages, he advised Lodge to proceed cautiously, but he reaffirmed the instructions of August 24 and gave the ambassador unusually broad discretion in their implementation. Lodge was authorized to repeat to the generals assurances that while the United States would not assist them in a coup, it would support a new government that appeared to have a good chance of success. And he was authorized to announce publicly, and at his own discretion, a reduction in American aid to Diem, the signal the generals had requested as an indication of U.S. support.

[63]Lodge oral history interview, Kennedy Papers.
[64]Forrestal to Kennedy, August 26, 1963, Kennedy Papers, Office File, Box 128; Neil Sheehan et al., *The Pentagon Papers as Published by the New York Times* (New York, 1971), pp. 195–196. Hereafter cited as *Pentagon Papers (NYT)*. See also memorandum, "Contacts with Vietnamese Generals," October 23, 1963, Lyndon B. Johnson Papers, Lyndon B. Johnson Library, Austin, Tex., DSDUF, Box 2.
[65]Reeves, *President Kennedy*, p. 567; Cooper, *Lost Crusade*, p. 212.

While American officials in Washington and Saigon nervously awaited the generals' response, the plans for a coup gradually became unraveled. The leaders of the plot were unable to secure the support of key army units in the Saigon area, and despite the assurances given by the CIA go-between, they remained uncertain of American support. On August 31, they informed Harkins that the coup had been called off. "There is neither the will nor the organization among the generals to accomplish anything," Lodge cabled Washington with obvious disappointment.[66]

NO TURNING BACK

Although the August plot came to nothing, it marked another major turning point in American policy in Vietnam. Many officials had grave reservations about the desirability, feasibility, and possible consequences of a coup, but the anti-Diemists were able to commit the administration to their point of view. By making such a commitment, the administration encouraged opponents of the regime and made difficult, if not impossible, any real reconciliation with Diem. As Lodge put it, the United States was "launched on a course from which there is no respectable turning back."[67]

The Diem regime remained defiant. Nhu sent his wife out of the country, perhaps as much out of concern for her personal safety as to appease the United States. But he stubbornly refused to resign, and Lodge described him as a "lost soul, a haunted man who is caught in a vicious circle. The Furies are after him." The monkish Diem sought to discredit the Buddhist protest by claiming that the pagodas had been turned into bordellos where obscene photographs had been discovered and virgins were being despoiled.[68] The regime made no effort to conciliate the Buddhists or the United States.

Over the next four weeks, the Kennedy administration heatedly debated the choices open to it. Hilsman and others argued that there was no chance of stabilizing South Vietnam as long as Nhu remained, and they warned that Nhu might already be committed

---

[66]Quoted in *Pentagon Papers (Gravel)*, 2: 240.
[67]Lodge to Rusk, August 29, 1963, ibid., 738.
[68]Lodge to Rusk, September 9, 1963, *FR, 1961–1963*, 4: 142; Lodge to Rusk, September 19, 1963, ibid., 259.

to a deal with Hanoi that would force the United States out of Vietnam. They concluded that the administration must therefore apply firm pressure on Diem, including aid cuts, to compel him to remove Nhu and adopt the changes in policy necessary to defeat the Vietcong. Others, such as Nolting, advocated a final attempt at reconciliation. The failure of the August coup made clear, they argued, that there was no real alternative to Diem. The president was unlikely to remove Nhu, even under the most severe American pressure, and cuts in aid would only hurt the war against the Vietcong, antagonize the South Vietnamese people, and further destabilize the country. There was still a chance, they concluded, that if the United States repaired its relations with the government, the war might be won.

A "fact-finding" mission to South Vietnam only added to the uncertainty. General Victor Krulak of the Defense Department played down the possibilities of a coup and advised that the war could be won if the United States firmly supported Diem. In contrast, Joseph Mendenhall of the State Department reported a "virtual breakdown of the civil government in Saigon," warned of a possible religious war between Catholics and Buddhists, and concluded that there was no chance of defeating the guerrillas unless, "as a minimum, Nhu withdrew or was removed from the government." "You two did visit the same country, didn't you?" Kennedy remarked with obvious exasperation.[69]

The administration by this time was more divided on Vietnam than it had been on any other issue. "My God, my government's coming apart," Kennedy exclaimed on one occasion.[70] Such was the confusion and perplexity that at one point, in a moment of frustration, Attorney General Robert Kennedy blurted out the ultimate question, wondering aloud whether any South Vietnamese government was capable of winning the war and whether the United States should not begin to extricate itself from an impossible tangle. The question was both appropriate and timely. The disarray in South Vietnam was reaching a point where both factions in the administration may have been right—the country could not be stabilized with or without Diem.

[69]Hilsman, *To Move a Nation*, p. 502.
[70]Quoted in Reeves, *President Kennedy*, p. 565.

Also, major international developments for the first time raised a glimmer of hope for a negotiated settlement. In the aftermath of the Cuban missile crisis of October 1962—the most frightening face-off of the Cold War—long-simmering tensions between the Soviet Union and China burst forth into open hostility, and Washington and Moscow took the first halting steps toward relaxing Cold War tensions. The new and more complex international environment of 1963 spurred talk of peace in Vietnam. At the very time the United States was probing the possibility of a coup against Diem, French president Charles de Gaulle took the initiative, proposing neutralization of South Vietnam based on a U.S. withdrawal and economic and cultural exchanges between north and south preliminary to a political settlement. Behind the scenes, French and Polish diplomats sounded out Saigon and Hanoi on the possibility of negotiations, rumors swirled about Saigon of a deal brokered by France, and Nhu dropped hints that a settlement with Hanoi would avert the Americanization of South Vietnam.

Kennedy did not reject de Gaulle's proposal out of hand, but he doubted it could work. After months of tortuous negotiations, an agreement on Laos had been signed in July 1962, but it had broken down within less than a year. The North Vietnamese quickly resumed using Laos as a supply route, and Pathet Lao guerrillas mounted military operations against the neutralist government. Unable to control either, the Soviet Union washed its hands of the arrangement it had helped negotiate. Far from offering a model for neutralization of Vietnam, the Laos agreement confirmed to Americans the limits of negotiations.

Kennedy and his advisers had other reasons to be skeptical of de Gaulle's proposals. They suspected that he might be motivated by anti-Americanism. They especially feared that, given South Vietnam's present weakness, neutralization would quickly lead to unification under North Vietnamese domination. Kennedy told Laotian leader Souvanna Phouma that the United States would consider neutralization if "conditions indicated that it would be successful," but, he added, "the necessary ingredients seemed to be lacking." General de Gaulle's proposals were "fine" for "the future" but did not seem realistic "for the present."[71]

<hr>

[71]Quoted in David Kaiser, *American Tragedy: Kennedy, Johnson, and the Origins of the Vietnam War* (Cambridge, Mass., 2000), pp. 357–358.

In any event, there seemed no urgency. There was no firm proposal on the table and therefore no need for immediate action. Despite Robert Kennedy's exasperated question, most Americans were not yet persuaded that the war could not somehow be won. To Kennedy the middle ground still seemed open, and the "safe course, in his view, was to stay the course," at least until he could be reelected, even if it required overthrowing Diem.[72] The chief result of the talk of negotiations was to confirm U.S. suspicions of Nhu and to sharpen the desire to get rid of him.

Perhaps, as Robert McNamara and others have since suggested, de Gaulle's proposals for neutralization presented an opportunity, maybe even the last good chance, to avoid a long and bloody war.[73] Such an outcome has much to commend it in retrospect, but the obstacles to its realization at the time were enormous. Nhu seems to have expressed vague interest in negotiations only as a means to gain leverage against the United States, and Hanoi made some positive, if faint, noises only to drive a deeper wedge between Saigon and Washington. There are no indications that either side was serious about negotiating, and given their past hostility they would have had to bridge a huge chasm. In any event, the United States was not the least disposed at this time to move toward neutralization. Robert Kennedy's question was not raised again. The administration drifted along, divided against itself, uncertain of its direction, in truth rushing headlong toward a coup.

THE OVERTHROW OF NGO DINH DIEM

After more than a month of debate, Kennedy in early October settled on a short-run policy that, characteristically, split the difference between the two extremes promoted by his advisers. Still quite uncertain about what was going on in South Vietnam, he dispatched Taylor and McNamara to Saigon to get a first-hand appraisal of the military and political situation. Probably on the basis of discussions with Lodge, the two men quickly rejected any notion of conciliating

---

[72]Fredrik Logevall, *Choosing War: The Lost Chance for Peace and Escalation of War in Vietnam* (Berkeley, Calif., 1999), p. 42.
[73]Robert S. McNamara et al., *Argument without End: In Search of Answers to the Vietnam Tragedy* (New York, 1999), pp. 99–150.

Diem, arguing that it would merely reinforce his belief that he could bend the United States to his will. To assess the prospects of a coup, a tennis match was arranged between Taylor and General Duong Van Minh, one of the leaders of the August plot, at the Saigon Officers Club. Minh's "sole interest that afternoon seemed to be tennis," Taylor later recalled, and the Americans surmised that the generals had "little stomach" for another attempt to overthrow the government.[74] Taylor and McNamara therefore concluded that the only practicable course was to apply "selective pressures," including cuts in foreign aid, to the regime. Such an approach would probably not force Diem to remove Nhu, but it might at least persuade him to stop oppressing political dissenters. Generally optimistic about the progress of the counterinsurgency program, McNamara and Taylor concluded that if Diem could be brought around, the insurgency might be reduced to "something little more than organized banditry" by the end of 1965.[75]

Although it badly misjudged the actual conditions in South Vietnam, the Taylor-McNamara report formed the basis of subsequent U.S. policy. The relative quiet in the countryside in late 1963 resulted from a deliberate North Vietnamese–NLF attempt to encourage negotiations rather than from the effectiveness of the counterinsurgency program. Taylor and McNamara underestimated the prospects of a coup and overestimated the efficacy of applying pressure to Diem. Apparently seeing no other route to take, Kennedy approved their recommendations on October 5, and over the next few weeks, the administration gradually implemented the policy of "selective pressures." Lodge remained away from the presidential palace, insisting that Diem must come to him. In the meantime, the administration recalled the CIA station chief in Saigon, John Richardson, known among Vietnamese and Americans as a close friend of Nhu; cut off funds to Nhu's Special Forces; and suspended shipments of tobacco, rice, and milk under the commodity import program.

A number of Kennedy advisers later emphatically denied that these measures were designed to stimulate a coup, and in the most literal sense they were correct. The McNamara-Taylor report had

[74]Taylor, *Swords and Ploughshares*, p. 297.
[75]Taylor-McNamara Report, October 2, 1963, *Pentagon Papers (Gravel)*, 2: 751–766.

explicitly rejected encouragement of a coup, and the aid cuts were designed to pressure Diem. The administration was not as innocent as some of its defenders have maintained, however. Hilsman later conceded that "some of the things that we did encouraged the coup, some we intended as pressure on Diem, although we knew it [*sic*] would encourage a coup."[76] Kennedy and his advisers would have been naive indeed if they did not recognize that the recall of Richardson, whom the generals had feared would tip off the August plot, and the cuts in aid, the very signal of support the generals had requested earlier, would influence Diem's opponents. And the timing is significant. The aid cuts were instituted after the generals had once again inquired how the United States would respond to a coup. The measures taken during October encouraged the generals to step up their planning and seek further assurances from the United States.

Once aware that the generals were again planning a coup, the administration did nothing to discourage them. The response to their inquiry was sufficiently vague to salve the consciences of those who preferred a coup but hesitated to accept direct responsibility for it and to satisfy the reservations of those who remained wary of dumping Diem. But the instructions offered the assurances the generals sought. Lodge was authorized to inform the plotters that although the United States did not "wish to stimulate a coup," it would not "thwart a change of government or deny economic and military assistance to a new regime if it appeared capable of increasing [the] effectiveness of the military effort, ensuring popular support to win [the] war and improving working relations with the U.S."[77]

With his administration sharply divided to the very end, Kennedy stuck by his compromise policy. Harriman, Hilsman, and others felt that Diem should go. Vice President Johnson, top CIA and Pentagon officials, and Harkins continued to insist that there was no real alternative and that Diem's removal would bring chaos to South Vietnam. They also felt, as Harkins put it, that it was "incongruous" after nine years of supporting Diem "to get him down, kick him around and get rid of him."[78] Kennedy himself vacillated, adhering to the policy of not overtly supporting a coup but not discouraging

[76]Hilsman oral history interview, Kennedy Papers.
[77]CIA to Lodge, October 6, 1963, *Pentagon Papers (Gravel)*, 2: 769.
[78]Quoted in ibid., 785.

one either. In this case, however, not to decide was to decide, and by leaving matters in the hands of Lodge, whose views were well known, the president virtually ensured the outcome. The major fear among Kennedy and some of his advisers in the anxious days of late October seems to have been that the coup might fail, provoking Diem, in Robert Kennedy's words, to "tell us to get the hell out of the country" and sending U. S. policy in Vietnam and indeed Southeast Asia "down the road to disaster." A successful coup, others warned, might impede prosecution of the war. Although he sought evidence that a coup could succeed, Kennedy seemed content to leave in Lodge's hands a decision whether to call it off or delay it.[79]

Throughout the last week of October, Saigon was gripped with tension and deluged with rumors as the various actors played out their complicated—and ultimately tragic—drama. Determined to avoid the mistakes of 1960 and August 1963, the generals lined up their forces with the closest attention to every detail. Keenly aware that the "elephants were crashing in the jungle," Nhu concocted an elaborate scheme to keep himself and his brother in power by staging a fake coup and using it as an excuse for eliminating suspected opponents. To complicate matters still further, in the last hours before the real coup, Diem suddenly turned conciliatory, inquiring of Lodge at their last meeting what the United States wanted of him. Whether he was merely trying to buy time or had concluded that he must place himself in the hands of his ally is unclear. In any event, his apparent concession came too late.

While Diem was talking with Lodge in the early afternoon of November 1, the generals seized key military installations and communications systems in Saigon, secured the surrender of Nhu's Special Forces, and demanded the resignation of Diem and Nhu. Defiant to the end, the brothers requested that the generals come to the palace for consultation, the ploy that had worked in 1960, and Diem phoned Lodge to determine the official American attitude toward the coup. Finding support nowhere, Diem and Nhu escaped through a secret underground passage to a Catholic church in the Chinese district, where they went to confession and received communion. They were subsequently captured and, despite promises of safe conduct, brutally

[79]Ken Hughes, "The Tale of the Tapes: JFK and the Fall of Diem," *The Boston Globe Magazine,* October 24, 1999, 14 ff.

murdered in the back of an armored personnel carrier. Diem was buried in an unmarked grave in a cemetery next to the house of the U.S. ambassador.

Throughout the coup, the United States followed to the letter its promises "not to thwart a change of government." American officials later insisted that they knew nothing of the timing or exact plans for a coup. In fact, CIA agent Lucien Conein maintained close touch with the generals in the planning stages through clandestine meetings at a dentist's office, and he had telephone contact with them while the coup was taking place. The United States refused even to intervene to ensure the personal safety of Diem and Nhu. Kennedy did send an old crony to try to persuade Diem to get rid of Nhu and seek refuge in the embassy. When Diem refused, however, the administration all but abandoned him. Lodge was considerably less than candid in the telephone conversation with Diem when he pretended ignorance of Washington's attitudes. During the last pathetic phone call, he offered to help, but he then went off to bed, leaving matters in the hands of the coup forces. Perhaps he accepted at face value the generals' pledges to spare Diem and Nhu, or he may have feared that any action taken on behalf of the brothers would be interpreted as a violation of the earlier U.S. assurances not to interfere.

The news of the coup and the bloody deaths of the Ngos evoked mixed reactions. In Saigon, jubilant crowds smashed statues of Diem, danced in the streets, and covered ARVN soldiers with garlands of flowers. "Every Vietnamese has a grin on his face today," Lodge excitedly informed Washington. In the ancient Vietnamese tradition, the mandate of heaven had passed. Among Americans there was a sense of relief and satisfaction. Lodge, the primary architect, hailed the coup as a "remarkably able performance in all respects." Some Washington officials agreed and went to great lengths to distinguish this "acceptable" coup from the "unacceptable" military takeovers then sweeping Latin America. Lodge went further, extolling the coup as a "useful lesson" in the way people "on the side of freedom," with the help of the United States, could "clean their own house," eliminating the "autocrats" and "Colonel Blimps" as a way to prevent being taken over by communists.[80]

---

[80]Lodge to State Department, November 2, 1963, *FR, 1961–1963*, 4: 526; Memorandum for record of White House meeting, November 1, 1963, *FR, 1961–1963*, 4: 518; Lodge to State Department, November 3, 1963, ibid., 546–548; Lodge to State Department, November 6, 1963, ibid., 577–578.

The deaths of Diem and Nhu were unsettling. The generals first attributed them to "accidental suicide," but photographs of the two mutilated bodies, hands tied behind their backs, made clear, as McGeorge Bundy sarcastically put it, that this was "not the preferred way to commit suicide." Some of Kennedy's advisers accepted the deaths as a matter of course. "Revolutions are rough. People get hurt," Hilsman told a reporter.[81] But Kennedy himself was deeply troubled. When he learned of the slaying of Diem and Nhu, Taylor later recalled, "he leaped to his feet and rushed from the room with a look of shock and dismay on his face which I had never seen before."[82] When someone justified the deaths on the grounds that the two men were tyrants, the president retorted that "they did the best they could for their country." People close to him found Kennedy more depressed than at any time since the Bay of Pigs and speculated that he realized that Vietnam had been his greatest foreign policy failure.[83]

Just three weeks later, Kennedy himself was assassinated in Dallas. His defenders, many of whom would become outspoken opponents of the war, would later argue that he was planning to extricate the United States from what he had concluded was a quagmire. Kennedy undoubtedly harbored deep-seated doubts about the prospects for success in South Vietnam, and he had adamantly opposed the commitment of U.S. combat troops. On Laos and other issues, he had shown flexibility, and he had grown demonstrably more secure in office. A good case can therefore be made that when faced with the collapse of South Vietnam in 1964–1965, he might have taken a close look at diplomatic solutions.[84] At the same time, there is no persuasive evidence that he was committed to withdrawal. He had resisted negotiations as firmly as he opposed combat troops. In a speech to be given on the day of his death, he conceded that commitments in Third World nations could be "painful, risky, and costly," but, he added, "we

---

[81]Memorandum of White House meeting, November 4, 1963, *FR, 1961–1963,* 4:555–556; Hilsman quoted in Marguerite Higgins, *Our Vietnam Nightmare* (New York, 1965), p. 225.

[82]Taylor, *Swords and Ploughshares,* p. 301.

[83]Reeves, *President Kennedy,* p. 651; Schlesinger, *A Thousand Days,* pp. 997–998.

[84]For arguments that Kennedy would have responded differently than Johnson, see Logevall, *Choosing War,* pp. 396–400; Lawrence Freedman, *Kennedy's Wars: Berlin, Cuba, Laos, and Vietnam* (New York, 2000), pp. 400–413; and Kaiser, *American Tragedy,* pp. 3–5, 121, 265.

Death of Ngo Dinh Diem
South Vietnamese president Ngo Dinh Diem and his brother Ngo Dinh
Nhu were murdered in the back of an armored personnel carrier on
November 1, 1963. The Kennedy administration knew that the
assassination had been ordered by the coup leader, General Duong Van
Minh, but concealed that fact to cover its own complicity in the affair. The
murder of Diem shocked President Kennedy and reinforced his concerns
about American involvement in South Vietnam. Less than a month later,
Kennedy himself was assassinated in Dallas, texas.
Hulton/Archive

dare not weary of the test." The plan for a phased withdrawal,
often cited as evidence of Kennedy's determination to get out of
Vietnam, was from the outset provisional and conditional and was
designed to meet many different pressures. Referring to that plan,
Hilsman reassured a worried South Vietnamese official on November 27 that the United States would "Keep in Viet-Nam whatever

[85]Herbert S. Parmet, *JFK: The Presidency of John F. Kennedy* (New York, 1984), p. 336;
State Department to Embassy Saigon, November 27, 1963, *FR, 1961–1963,* 4: 640.

forces are needed for victory."[85] The president seems not to have decided what to do when he was killed. Apparently convinced that the military situation was not going badly, he seems to have hoped that the problem might still resolve itself without drastic action on the part of the United States.

What Kennedy might have done can never be known for certain, of course, and his administration must be judged on what it actually did during its brief tenure. The president and most of his advisers uncritically accepted the assumption that a non-Communist South Vietnam was vital to America's global interests, and their rhetoric in fact strengthened the hold of that assumption. That the president never devoted his full attention to Vietnam, as his defenders claim, seems clear. He reacted to crises and improvised responses on a day-to-day basis, seldom examining the implications of his actions. Although apparently troubled by growing doubts, he refused, even after the problems with Diem had reached a crisis point, to face the hard questions. His cautious middle course significantly enlarged the American role and commitment in Vietnam. Like most of his advisers, he acted on the arrogant presumption that the United States knew best what was right for Vietnam. "In the name of the struggle against the Viet Cong," Ellen Hammer has written, the Americans "claimed the right to intervene as they chose" and overthrew the Diem government primarily because it resisted their advice.[86] With the coup, the United States assumed direct responsibility for the South Vietnamese government. Whatever his fears or his ultimate intentions, Kennedy bequeathed to his successor a problem eminently more dangerous than the one he had inherited.

[86]Hammer, *Death in November*, p. 211.

President Johnson and His Advisers at the LBJ Ranch, December 1964
Not eager for a wider war but unwilling to stand by and watch South
Vietnam fall, Johnson and his advisers charted in 1964 and 1965 the fateful
course that would lead to America's longest and most divisive war.
LBJ Library

CHAPTER 4

Enough, but Not Too Much

Johnson's Decisions for War, 1963–1965

Between November 1963 and July 1965, Lyndon Baines Johnson transformed a limited commitment to assist the South Vietnamese government into an open-ended commitment to preserve an independent, non-Communist South Vietnam. Johnson inherited from Kennedy a rapidly deteriorating situation in South Vietnam. Fearing that large-scale involvement might jeopardize his chances of election in 1964 and threaten his beloved Great Society domestic programs, he temporized for over a year, expanding American assistance and increasing the number of advisers in hopes that a beefed-up version of his predecessor's policy might somehow stave off disaster. South Vietnam's survival appeared more in doubt than ever after Johnson's reelection, however, and over the next nine months he made his fateful decisions, authorizing a sustained air offensive against North Vietnam and dispatching ground forces to stem the tide in the south. By July 1965, the United States was engaged in a major war on the Asian mainland.

A "BIG JUICY WORM"

In late 1963, North Vietnam and the National Liberation Front (NLF) significantly escalated the war. The overthrow of Diem had been at best a mixed blessing for Hanoi, eliminating a potentially dangerous anti-Communist leader but also removing the rallying point for opposition in South Vietnam. For a time the revolutionary spirit ebbed. Desertions from the NLF increased and recruitment stalled, and even where the government lost ground, the insurgents did not always gain. The NLF proposed to Diem's successor the possibility of negotiations, but its proposals were rebuffed and it saw no weakening of U.S. resolve. Determined to attain the goal that had eluded them in 1954, North Vietnamese leaders increasingly recognized that they could not succeed without a major commitment of their own resources. At the Central Committee's Ninth Plenum in December 1963, the party leadership agreed to instruct the NLF to step up its political agitation and military operations against the Saigon government. More important, Hanoi decided to expand infiltration of personnel and supplies into the south. The North Vietnamese at this point seem to have been unsure of Soviet support, and they recognized the possibility of war with the United States. In what turned out to be a colossal miscalculation, they gambled that rapid escalation might force the disintegration of South Vietnam, leaving the United States no choice but to withdraw.

For Johnson and the United States, the road to war was longer and more tortuous. After listening to Ambassador Lodge's gloomy assessment of the postcoup prospects of the Saigon regime on November 24, 1963, the new president claimed to feel like a catfish that had just "grabbed a big juicy worm with a right sharp hook in the middle of it." Johnson vowed to meet the Communist challenge, however, and insisted that he would not let Vietnam go the way China had gone in 1949. He instructed Lodge to "go back and tell those generals in Saigon that Lyndon Johnson intends to stand by our word." Two days later, National Security Council Action Memorandum (NSAM) 273 incorporated his pledge into policy, affirming that it was "the central objective of the United States" to assist the "people and Government" of South Vietnam "to win their contest against the externally directed and supported communist conspiracy."[1]

During the first three months of Johnson's presidency, the situation in South Vietnam steadily worsened. Some Americans had assumed that the removal of Diem and Nhu would restore domestic harmony and promote political unity, but the effect was quite the opposite. Diem had systematically destroyed the opposition, and his death left a gaping political vacuum. Buddhists and Catholics

[1]Bill Moyers, "Flashbacks," *Newsweek,* February 10, 1975, 76; U.S. Congress, Senate, Subcommittee on Public Buildings and Grounds, *The Pentagon Papers (The Senator Gravel Edition)* (4 vols.; Boston, 1971), 3: 17–20. Hereafter cited as *Pentagon Papers (Gravel).*

constituted the most coherent groups in the cities, but their hatred of each other was implacable, and neither group represented a viable political force. The Buddhists were splintered into a bewildering array of factions. Although tightly disciplined, the Catholics had no political program or mass appeal. The coup released long pent-up forces, and in the months that followed new groups proliferated, but they were leaderless and hopelessly fragmented.

In the countryside, decay was also the norm. The removal of Diemist controls over information made clear that the statistics compiled by the government to demonstrate progress had been grossly in error. The insurgents controlled more people and territory than had been assumed. The strategic hamlet program was in shambles, many of the key hamlets in the critical Mekong Delta having been torn down either by guerrillas or by their own occupants. The situation was "very disturbing," McNamara warned Johnson in late December, and unless the trend could be reversed within the next few months, South Vietnam might be lost.[2]

The junta that assumed power after the coup did little to arrest the decline. It inherited a bureaucratic structure atrophied by "dry rot and lassitude."[3] The twelve army officers who formed the Military Revolutionary Council had been educated in France and spent most of their careers in French service. They lacked experience, had no program, and found little support among the various groups who had opposed Diem. Suspicious of each other and of competing factions within the army, uncertain about which way to move, they isolated themselves in their headquarters near Saigon's Tan Son Nhut Airport and did little. The few actions they took merely added to the confusion. The removal of Diem's province chiefs brought paralysis to local administration, and Harkins was alarmed by the junta's efforts to limit the role of U.S. advisers.

On January 29, 1964, a group of younger officers headed by General Nguyen Khanh overthrew the divided, ineffectual junta. Khanh appears to have doubted, with good reason, the capacity of the junta to govern, and he justified the coup by claiming that several members of the council had secretly endorsed de Gaulle's

[2]Robert McNamara to Johnson, December 21, 1963, Declassified Documents Reference System (R)88E. Hereafter cited as DDRS.

[3]Henry Cabot Lodge to Johnson, January 1, 1964, in Department of State, *Foreign Relations of the United States, 1964–1968* (Washington, D.C., 1992), 1: 1. Hereafter cited as *FR* with date and volume number.

proposals for a neutral South Vietnam. No evidence has ever been produced to support that claim, however, and it seems clear that the general resented being shunted aside by the junta and acted primarily out of personal ambition. The United States was complicit in the coup. Harkins and his aides were disturbed by the junta's lack of aggressiveness and its independence, and they seem to have welcomed and even encouraged Khanh's scheme. At the very least, the United States knew of the coup plot and did nothing to stop it.[4]

The coup reinforced Washington's growing doubts about its client state. Devious, opportunistic, and ambitious, Khanh in a notably checkered career had supported the Vietminh and the French and had worked for and against Diem, and his reliability must have been suspect. Putting the best face on a bad situation, some Americans comforted themselves that he was an able military commander and that, at least in contrast to Diem and the junta, he was "our boy." Lodge speculated that one-man rule might be preferable to a divided junta, and he was encouraged by Khanh's pledges to act decisively. Nothing would please the United States more, he informed the general, than "the sight of an oriental chief of state who wanted to go fast and did not hesitate to kick people in the rear end." Khanh's response—he hoped he would "pick the right rear ends to kick"—could not have offered much reassurance, however, and Lodge conceded that it would be premature to predict a long life for the new government.[5] The United States quickly recognized Khanh, but with little enthusiasm and even less confidence.

The Khanh government faced truly staggering problems. Military operations and the strategic hamlet program had come to a complete standstill. The government's authority was nonexistent throughout much of the countryside, and near anarchy prevailed in the cities. In Saigon the "atmosphere fairly smelled of discontent," General William Westmoreland later recalled, with "workers on strike, students demonstrating, the local press pursuing a persistent campaign of criticism of the new government."[6] As NLF incidents increased in number and boldness, the capital took on all the appearances of an armed camp. Government buildings, stores, and even

---

[4]Fredrik Logevall, *Choosing War: The Lost Chance for Peace and the Escalation of War in Vietnam* (Berkeley, Calif., 1999), pp. 99–102.
[5]Ibid., p. 102; Lodge to Secretary to State, February 5, 1964, DDRS (75) 215A.

cafés were surrounded by barbed wire, while soldiers stood guard in concrete sentry boxes reinforced with sandbags. Khanh himself took up residence in a house on the Saigon River, where he could flee by boat if necessary. American intelligence warned that unless the new government took charge immediately and dealt with its problems effectively, South Vietnam had, "at best, an even chance of withstanding the insurgency menace during the next few weeks or months."[7]

VIETNAM, THE GREAT SOCIETY, AND WORLD ORDER

To Lyndon Baines Johnson and the advisers around him, the crisis of early 1964 could not have been less welcome. Johnson had assumed office in a moment of great national tragedy, and he set as his first task conducting an orderly transition and restoring national calm. He attached great importance to passage of Kennedy's legislative agenda, long stalemated in Congress, both as a memorial to the fallen leader and as a springboard to launch his own reform program and campaign for election in his own right. From this standpoint, the emergence of a crisis in Vietnam could only be regarded as an intrusion.

But it was an intrusion that had to be handled effectively. From the outset, Johnson personalized the struggle in Vietnam. The new president was an extraordinarily complex individual. A physically imposing man, he had an ego and ambitions the size of his native Texas. A remarkably adroit politician, brilliant legislator, and highly successful Senate majority leader, he was a driven man, prodigiously energetic, single-minded, manipulative, often overbearing. At the same time, he could be generous, warm, and compassionate toward other people, and he was fiercely loyal to those who stood by him. "He had as many sides to him as a kaleidoscope," Dean Acheson once observed, an "unbelievable combination of sensitivity and coarseness, of understanding and obtuseness."[8] Despite his considerable accomplishments, Johnson remained profoundly insecure, especially in the area of foreign policy, and he viewed the emerging

---

[6]William C. Westmoreland, *A Soldier Reports* (Garden City, N.Y., 1976), p. 63.
[7]Quoted in *Pentagon Papers (Gravel)*, 3: 42.
[8]Quoted in Clark Clifford with Richard Holbrooke, *Counsel to the President: A Memoir* (New York, 1991), p. 386.

crisis in Vietnam as a crucial test of strength for his personal prestige, his authority as president of the United States and leader of the Free World, indeed for his manhood.

Recognizing his foreign policy inexperience, he retained and relied heavily on Kennedy's advisers. Secretary of State Dean Rusk, Secretary of Defense Robert McNamara, and National Security Adviser McGeorge Bundy had all played prominent roles in shaping Kennedy's Vietnam policy, and they also had a deep personal stake in upholding it. Indeed, they felt very strongly that expansion of the American commitment since 1961 had itself significantly increased the importance of holding the line there.

Johnson linked Vietnam inextricably to his domestic political fortunes. He saw the American commitment there as a vital part of the Kennedy program that he was sworn to uphold. He had been at the center of the political bloodletting that had followed the fall of China in 1949, and he was certain that the "loss" of Vietnam would produce an even more explosive upheaval, a "mean and destructive debate," he later commented, "that would shatter my Presidency, kill my administration, and damage our democracy."[9] Early in his presidency, he set out to create what he called the Great Society, the most ambitious legislative program of domestic reforms since Franklin Roosevelt's New Deal. He also tied Vietnam to the realization of these goals, fearing that if he showed weakness southern conservatives who opposed his domestic programs, especially his commitment to racial equality, would attack him with a vengeance. "If I don't go in now and they show later that I should have," he predicted, "then they'll . . . push Vietnam up my ass every time."[10]

In the eyes of Johnson and his key advisers, Vietnam also continued to be vital to America's larger foreign policy goals. Policy makers had begun to perceive by 1964 the extent to which major changes in world politics were challenging long-standing Cold War assumptions. In particular, open squabbling between the Soviet Union and China undermined the most basic assumption that in Vietnam as elsewhere the United States confronted a monolithic communism united in its drive for world domination.

[9]Doris Kearns, *Lyndon Johnson and the American Dream* (New York, 1976), p. 252.
[10]Brian VanDeMark, *Into the Quagmire* (New York, 1991), pp. xv, 60.
[11]Memorandum of conversation, Rusk and French ambassador, July 1, 1964, DDRS (75) 105A.

Most foreign policy experts still believed, however, that it was essential to hold the line in Vietnam. The ethos of the Cold War, by this time deeply engrained, put a premium on toughness and viewed compromise as a sign of weakness, retreat as a sign of cowardice. The United States must continue to display to the major Communist powers its certainty of purpose and strength of will. A firm stand in Vietnam would discourage any Soviet tendencies toward adventurism and encourage the nascent trend toward détente with the United States. It was especially important to continue to contain the presumably more aggressive and reckless Chinese. Policy makers also believed that the way the United States responded to "Communist provocations" in Vietnam would have "profound consequences everywhere." If the United States did not protect Vietnam, Secretary of State Rusk insisted, its "guarantees with regard to Berlin would lose their credibility."[11] Turbulence in the Third World, especially in Southeast Asia and the Western Hemisphere, appeared to pose serious dangers to American credibility and world order, and firmness in Vietnam would help ensure stability in a strife-torn world by demonstrating that violent challenges to the status quo would be resisted.

Some Americans, Johnson included, had grown increasingly concerned about Vietnam by this time. Some questioned whether it was important enough to justify a major war. Many others worried that the situation might be hopeless—"It's just the biggest damned mess I ever saw," Johnson himself conceded. Some key senators quietly began urging the president to disengage the United States from a situation that seemed to be spiraling out of control. Johnson himself was keenly aware of the pitfalls of escalation. "It's damned easy to get in a war," he admitted to his friend and political mentor Senator Richard Russell of Georgia, "but it's gonna be awfully hard to extricate yourself if you get in."[12]

Despite such concerns, Johnson and his advisers chose to stay the course. A man of action rather than reflection, the president did not subject an increasingly dangerous situation to searching reappraisal. He dismissed out of hand the idea of an American withdrawal from Vietnam, and he rejected without serious consideration

[12]Johnson phone conversation with McGeorge Bundy, May 27, 1964, in Michael R. Beschloss, *Taking Charge: The Johnson White House Tapes* (New York, 1998), pp. 370–373.

the neutralization scheme proposed by de Gaulle and endorsed by Senate Majority Leader Mike Mansfield and the columnist Walter Lippman. Johnson had made Vietnam a touchstone for his presidency, and he could not bear the prospect of failure. He took the image of falling dominoes seriously. Obsessed with appearing weak, he could not accept the idea of being president the first time "we've ever turned tail and been shoved out of a place." He did not like the fact that the United States was bogged down in Vietnam. But it was there, he concluded, and "we've got to conduct ourselves like men."[13]

MORE OF THE SAME

Despite his concern for Vietnam, the president was not prepared to employ American military power on a large scale in early 1964. Like Kennedy and Eisenhower before him, he had no enthusiasm for a massive engagement of American forces on the Asian mainland. Moreover, he and his advisers feared that Americanization of the war would further undercut the self-reliance of the Vietnamese. The introduction of large-scale American forces in Vietnam would provoke much hostile propaganda throughout the world. Most important, it might cause major disruptions at home, threatening Johnson's legislative program and his campaign for the presidency. He therefore turned down proposals developed by the Joint Chiefs of Staff (JCS) for air and ground operations against North Vietnam.

After a major policy review in mid-March, the president concluded that the "only realistic alternative" was "to do more of the same and do it more efficiently."[14] NSAM 288, approved March 17, did state U.S. objectives in more sweeping terms, emphasizing as the essential goal the preservation of an independent, non-Communist South Vietnam. The administration still hoped that its program of military and economic assistance would be workable, however, and at this point merely attempted to make it more effective. Aware that the most urgent problem was the weakness of the South Vietnamese government, Washington publicly affirmed its support for Khanh and privately advised the U.S. mission to do everything possible to avert further coups. NSAM 288 also called for a national mobiliza-

---

[13]Phone conversation with Richard Russell, June 11, 1964, ibid., p. 403.
[14]Kearns, *Johnson*, p. 196.

tion plan to put South Vietnam on a war footing and for significantly increasing the size of its armed forces. The president appointed General William Westmoreland, a paratrooper and veteran of World War II and Korea, to replace the ineffectual and perennially optimistic Harkins. Over the next nine months, the United States increased its "advisers" from 16,300 to 23,300 and expanded its economic assistance by $50 million. "As far as I am concerned," Johnson advised Lodge in April, "you must have whatever you need to help the Vietnamese do the job, and I assure you that I will act at once to eliminate obstacles or restraints wherever they may appear."[15]

Although the administration did little more than reaffirm existing policy in the spring of 1964, its attention was shifting increasingly toward North Vietnam. The change reflected a growing American concern over the infiltration of people and supplies from the north and mounting frustration with ground rules that permitted Hanoi to support the insurgency with impunity. Some U.S. officials seem also to have concluded that action against the north might somehow compensate for the lack of progress in the south. Others wished to signal Hanoi that it would pay a high price for its continued intervention. Although covert operations in North Vietnam had been notably unsuccessful, they were expanded in early 1964 to include intelligence overflights, the dropping of propaganda leaflets, and OPLAN 34A commando raids conducted by South Vietnamese guerrillas along the North Vietnamese coast. The administration also intensified its planning to prepare U.S. forces for possible "border control" operations into Cambodia and Laos, "tit-for-tat" retaliatory bombing raids into North Vietnam, and a series of "graduated overt pressures" against North Vietnam, including air attacks against military and industrial targets. Firm warnings were delivered to Hanoi through Canadian intermediaries that continued support for the insurgency could bring great devastation to North Vietnam itself. At a National Security Council (NSC) meeting on March 17, top administration officials expressed confidence that increased military and economic aid would be enough to stem the tide in South Vietnam. They also agreed that failure of the program outlined in NSAM 288 might compel them to take the war to North Vietnam.[16]

[15]Johnson to Lodge, April 4, 1964, Johnson Papers, Lyndon Baines Johnson Library, Austin, Texas, National Security File, Country File: Vietnam, Box 3.
[16]Summary record of NSC meeting, March 17, 1964, Johnson Papers, National Security File, NSC Meetings File, Box 1.

The spring 1964 program, like those before it, produced meager results. Under U.S. supervision, Khanh developed ambitious plans for bringing the government down to the village level, but there was a vast gap between planning and implementation. By some estimates, the NLF controlled more than 40 percent of the territory and more than 50 percent of the population, and in many areas it was so firmly entrenched that it could not be dislodged except by massive force. Where it could function freely, the government was hampered by a shortage of skilled officials and by what one American described as "outmoded concepts, directives and practices, bureaucratic constipation, [and] insufficient on-the-spot resources."[17] As a result of spiraling desertion rates, the strength of the Army of the Republic of Vietnam (ARVN) remained well below the figure authorized before the projected increase. The army won a few minor engagements in the early summer, but it was never able to gain the initiative. American officials publicly praised Khanh's "able and energetic leadership," and Khanh dutifully followed American suggestions for gaining popular support, visiting numerous villages and cities and even making a series of "fireside chats."

But while a word from well-placed Americans could topple governments in Vietnam, it could not create stability, and mere speeches were inadequate to bring together South Vietnam's disparate political forces. Catholics and Buddhists mobilized against each other and agitated against a government neither trusted. After a period of quiescence, the students began to stir again. The government itself was rent by internal dissension, and a coup plot in July failed only because the United States made known its opposition. Maxwell Taylor, who replaced Lodge as ambassador in midsummer, reported in August that "the best thing that can be said about Khanh's government is that it has lasted six months and has about a 50-50 chance of lasting out the year."[18]

In the meantime, Hanoi responded defiantly to American warnings. There is no reason to suppose that the North Vietnamese leaders wanted war with the United States. Rather, they seem to have hoped that intensification of aid to the NLF would topple the South Vietnamese government, leaving the United States no choice

[17]William Colby memorandum, May 11, 1964, Johnson Papers, National Security File, Country File: Vietnam, Box 3.
[18]Quoted in *Pentagon Papers (Gravel)*, 3:82.

but to abandon its ally. They may have dismissed the various U.S. "signals" as bluff. In any event, they were not prepared to abandon their long-sought goal in the face of American threats. In the spring and summer of 1964, North Vietnam mobilized its own forces for war, intensified transformation of the Ho Chi Minh Trail into a modern logistical network capable of handling large trucks, and began to prepare units of its own regular army for infiltration into South Vietnam intact. Premier Pham Van Dong bluntly informed Canadian Blair Seaborn in June that the stakes were as high for North Vietnam as for the United States and that the NLF and its supporters were prepared to endure regardless of the cost. If the United States insisted on war, he concluded with a ringing declaration, "We shall win!"[19]

Under these circumstances, Americans increasingly looked north for a solution they could not find in the south. Alarmed by the persistent lack of progress in South Vietnam, annoyed by Hanoi's defiant response, and fearful that the North Vietnamese might seek to exploit the administration's presumed immobility in an election year, some of Johnson's advisers by midsummer 1964 had developed a full "scenario" of graduated overt pressures against the north, according to which the president, after securing a congressional resolution, would authorize air strikes against selected North Vietnamese targets. Rusk and McNamara finally rejected the program for fear that it would "raise a whole series of disagreeable questions" that might jeopardize passage of the administration's civil rights legislation, but the proposals indicate the drift of official attitudes during this period.[20]

TONKIN GULF

The administration implemented much of the proposed "scenario" in early August in response to a series of still controversial events

---

[19]George C. Herring (ed.), *The Secret Diplomacy of the Vietnam War: The Negotiating Volumes of the Pentagon Papers* (Austin, Tex., 1983), p. 8.
[20]McNamara-Rusk memorandum, June 11, 1964, Johnson Papers, National Security File, Country File: Vietnam, Box 4. For a full discussion of these events see Andrew L. Johns, "Opening Pandora's Box: The Genesis and Evolution of the 1964 Congressional Resolution on Vietnam," *The Journal of American-East Asian Relations,* 6 (Summer–Fall 1977): 186–201.

in the Gulf of Tonkin. As part of the DeSoto Patrols that carried out electronic espionage off the coast of North Vietnam, the destroyer *USS Maddox* on the afternoon of August 2 encountered a group of North Vietnamese torpedo boats. South Vietnamese gunboats involved in OPLAN 34A operations had bombarded the nearby island of Hon Me the preceding evening, and the North Vietnamese, perhaps assuming that the *Maddox* had been supporting the covert attacks, closed in on the destroyer. In a brief and frenzied engagement, the *Maddox* opened fire, the patrol boats launched torpedoes, and aircraft from the *USS Ticonderoga* joined the fighting. The torpedo boats were driven away; one was badly damaged.

Johnson was reportedly enraged when he learned of the encounter, but no retaliation was ordered. "The other side got a sting out of this," Rusk remarked. "If they do it again, they'll get another sting."[21] To avoid any appearance of weakness and to assert traditional claims to freedom of the seas, the Navy ordered the *Maddox* to resume operations in the Gulf of Tonkin and sent the destroyer *C. Turner Joy* to support it. The United States may not have been seeking to provoke another attack, but it did not go out of its way to avoid one either. The administration kept the destroyers close to North Vietnamese shores, where they were vulnerable to attack. Eager for "open season" on a nation already looked upon as the enemy, responsible military officials in the area were choosing targets for retaliatory raids before reports of a second attack began to come in.

On the night of August 4, while operating in heavy seas some sixty miles off the North Vietnamese coast, the *Maddox* and *Turner Joy* suddenly reported being under attack. The initial reports were based on sonar and radar contacts, both of which were admittedly unreliable under the adverse weather conditions, and on sightings of torpedoes and enemy searchlights on a night one seaman described as "darker than the hubs of Hell." The captain of the *Maddox* later conceded that evidence of an attack was less than conclusive. North Vietnamese gunboats may have been operating in the area, but no evidence has ever been produced to demonstrate that they committed hostile acts and it now seems certain that no second attack took place.

---

[21]Quoted in John Galloway, *The Gulf of Tonkin Resolution* (Rutherford, N.J., 1970), p. 52. The authoritative study is Edwin E. Moïse, *Tonkin Gulf and the Escalation of the Vietnam War* (Chapel Hill, N.C., 1996).

Washington was poised to strike back. Reports of an impending attack began to arrive in the capital early on the morning of August 4, and the Joint Chiefs immediately insisted that the United States must "clobber" the attackers. Throughout the morning, while the destroyers reported being under continuous attack, the JCS worked out a series of retaliatory options ranging from limited air strikes against North Vietnamese naval installations to mining of parts of the coastline. When the president met with his advisers in the early afternoon, there seemed no doubt that an attack had taken place. The CIA pointed out quite logically that the North Vietnamese might be responding out of "pride" and defensively to the commando raids on their territory. But the administration concluded that Hanoi was trying to make the United States appear to be a "paper tiger," and Rusk denounced the attack as "an act of war." Determined to prove their toughness, Johnson and his advisers agreed, as McNamara put it, that "we cannot sit still as a nation and let them attack us on the high seas and get away with it." They quickly decided on a "firm, swift retaliatory [air] strike" against North Vietnamese torpedo boat bases.[22]

Although serious questions were subsequently raised about the alleged attacks, the administration stuck by its decision. "FLASH" messages from the *Maddox* indicated that "freak weather effects" on the radar and sonar, as well as "overeager" sonarmen, may have accounted for many of the reported torpedo attacks and enemy contacts. Contradicting earlier messages, the commander of the *Maddox* also admitted that there had been no "visual sightings" and that a "complete evaluation" of all the evidence should be made before retaliation was ordered. McNamara postponed the air strike temporarily to make "damned sure that the attacks had taken place." By late afternoon, however, he was convinced, on the basis of evidence that now appears suspect. Ignoring the belated uncertainty of the men on the scene, the secretary of defense accepted at face value the judgment of the commander in chief of the Pacific fleet, Admiral U.S. Grant Sharp, in Honolulu, whose certainty was based on the

[22]"Chronology of Events, Tuesday, August 4 and Wednesday, August 5, 1964, Tonkin Gulf Strike," Johnson Papers, National Security File, Country File: Vietnam, Box 18; summary notes of 538th NSC meeting, August 4, 1964, Johnson Papers, National Security File, NSC Meetings File, Box 1; Rusk to Taylor, August 8, 1964, DDRS(75)845-H.

first reports from the *Maddox* and intercepts of North Vietnamese messages indicating that two patrol boats had been "sacrificed."[23]

McNamara and his military advisers did not knowingly lie about the alleged attacks, but they were obviously in a mood to retaliate, and they seem to have selected from the available evidence those parts that confirmed what they wanted to believe. Accepting McNamara's conclusions without question, Johnson in the late afternoon authorized retaliatory air strikes against North Vietnamese torpedo boat bases and nearby oil storage dumps. Described by the Joint Chiefs as a "pretty good effort," the strikes destroyed or damaged twenty-five patrol boats and 90 percent of the oil storage facilities at Vinh.[24]

The president also seized a golden opportunity to secure passage of a congressional resolution authorizing him to take "all necessary measures to repel any armed attacks against the forces of the United States and to prevent further aggression." His purpose was to indicate to Hanoi that the nation was united in its determination to stand firm in South Vietnam. The resolution also served immediate domestic political needs. The show of force and the appeal for national support permitted him to disarm his Republican challenger, Senator Barry Goldwater (a Republican from Arizona), who had vigorously urged escalation of the war, and to demonstrate that he could be firm in defending American interests without recklessly expanding the war. In presenting its case, however, the administration deliberately deceived Congress and the American people. Nothing was said about the covert raids. Official reports indicated that the *Maddox* was engaged in routine patrols in international waters. The incidents were portrayed as "deliberate attacks" and "open aggression on the high seas."

---

[23]McNamara later referred to the intercepts as "unimpeachable evidence" that the second attack actually took place, but they are considerably less than that. The government has refused numerous requests to declassify the messages, but intelligence experts who have seen them have concluded that because of the time differences involved, they could not refer to a second attack and most probably were after-action reports on the first attack. See William Conrad Gibbons, *The U.S. Government and the Vietnam War: Executive and Legislative Roles and Relationships,* Part 2: 1961–1964 (Princeton, 1986), pp. 292, 298–299.

[24]"Chronology of Events," Johnson Papers, National Security File, Country File: Vietnam, Box 18; "Transcripts of Telephone Conversations, 4–5 August," Johnson Papers, National Security File, Country File: Vietnam, Box 228.

Congress responded quickly and pliantly. Senator Wayne Morse (a Democrat from Oregon) raised some embarrassing questions about the OPLAN34A raids and the mission of the American destroyers. Senator Ernest Gruening (a Democrat from Alaska) attacked the resolution as a "predated declaration of war," and Senator Gaylord Nelson (a Democrat from Wisconsin) attempted to limit the grant of authority to the executive branch. During a period when America's national interests seemed constantly in peril, however, Congress had grown accustomed to approving presidential initiatives without serious question, and the crisis atmosphere seemed to leave no time for debate. "The American flag has been fired upon," Representative Ross Adair (a Republican from Indiana) exclaimed. "We will not and cannot tolerate such things."[25] The Senate debated the resolution less than ten hours, during much of which time the chamber was less than one-third full. By his own admission more concerned with the challenge posed by Goldwater than with giving a blank check to Johnson, Senator J. William Fulbright (a Democrat from Arkansas) carefully shepherded the resolution through, choking off debate and amendments. The vote in the Senate was an overwhelming 88 to 2; only Morse and Gruening dissented. Consideration in the House was even more perfunctory, passage taking a mere forty minutes and the vote unanimous.

From a domestic political standpoint, Johnson's handling of the Tonkin Gulf incident was masterly. His firm but restrained response to the alleged North Vietnamese attacks won broad popular support, his rating in the Louis Harris poll skyrocketing from 42 to 72 percent overnight. He effectively neutralized Goldwater on Vietnam, a fact that contributed to his overwhelming electoral victory in November. Moreover, this first formal congressional debate on Vietnam brought a near-unanimous endorsement of the president's policies and provided him an apparently solid foundation on which to construct future policy.

In time, Johnson would pay a heavy price for his easy victory. U.S. prestige was now publicly and more firmly committed not merely to defending South Vietnam but also to responding to North Vietnamese provocations. By attacking North Vietnamese targets, the president temporarily silenced his hawkish critics inside and outside of government, but in doing so he had broken a

---

[25]Quoted in Anthony Austin, *The President's War* (Philadelphia, 1971), p. 98.

long-standing barrier against taking the war to the north. The first steps having been taken, the next ones would be easier. Johnson's victory in Congress may have encouraged him to take the legislators lightly in making future policy decisions on Vietnam. And when the administration's case for reprisals later turned out to be less than overwhelming, many members of Congress correctly concluded that they had been deceived. The president's resounding domestic triumph brought enormous, if still hidden, costs.

Unknown to the United States, the Tonkin Gulf incident also raised the stakes on the other side. Rather than deterring North Vietnam, Johnson's forceful response led it to step up its efforts in the south. Encouraged by signs of continued deterioration in South Vietnam and persuaded that the United States was on the verge of expanding the war, Hanoi decided in September 1964 to send to the south the first units of its own regular army to support a push for victory before the spring of 1965. In yet another major miscalculation, the North Vietnamese hoped to accomplish their goal before the United States could intervene directly in the war, thus avoiding a major conflict with a great power. Shortly after, North Vietnamese leaders went to Moscow and Beijing to seek additional support. The Soviet Union was still cautious, but found itself under increasing pressure to do something or lose its leadership position to the Chinese. While urging the North Vietnamese to prepare for a long war, China was more forthcoming, mobilizing forces along its border with North Vietnam and significantly expanding its military and economic assistance.[26]

The Johnson administration did not follow up the Tonkin Gulf reprisals with additional attacks against North Vietnam. The president was not about to jeopardize his political fortunes by escalating the war. Having established his determination to defend American interests with force if necessary, he emphasized in the final months of the campaign his wish to limit American involvement if possible. "We seek no wider war," he stated in numerous speeches.

At the same time, political turmoil in South Vietnam made caution essential. Attempting to exploit the Tonkin Gulf affair to save his political skin, Khanh on August 6 assumed near-dictatorial powers and imposed severe restrictions on civil liberties. Thou-

[26]Ang Cheng Guan, "The Vietnam War, 1962–1964: The Vietnamese Communist Perspective," *Journal of Contemporary History* 35 (October 2000): 617; William J. Duiker, *Ho Chi Minh: A Life* (New York, 2000), pp. 540–542.

sands of Saigonese took to the streets, and when an angry mob forced Khanh to stand atop a tank and shout "Down with dictatorships," the humiliated general resigned. For days, near anarchy reigned: mobs rampaged through the streets, Buddhists and Catholics waged open warfare, and gangs of thugs fought and pillaged with hatchets and machetes. Behind the scenes, politicians and generals, Khanh included, jockeyed for power.

Under these circumstances, the administration refused to escalate the war. By early September, the Air Force and Marine Corps were vigorously pressing for extended air attacks against North Vietnam. Ambassador Taylor and others conceded that such steps would have to be taken in time, but they argued that it would be too risky to "overstrain the currently weakened GVN [Government of Vietnam] by drastic action in the immediate future." Johnson concurred, stating that he did not wish to "enter the patient in a 10-round bout, when he was in no shape to hold out for one round." While keeping other options open, the administration decided merely to continue its covert operations against North Vietnam and to be ready to respond to North Vietnamese provocations on a "tit for tat basis."[27] Johnson remained sufficiently concerned about the approaching election and the internal situation in South Vietnam that he refused to retaliate when NLF guerrillas on November 1 attacked the U.S. air base at Bien Hoa, killing four Americans and destroying five aircraft.

DECISIONS FOR WAR

Johnson's reluctance would soon change. Scholars now agree that late 1964, early 1965 was the pivotal period in his escalation of the Vietnam War.[28] During this time, the president fundamentally altered the U.S. commitment by initiating the regular bombing of North Vietnam and by sending the first U.S. ground combat troops to South Vietnam. Some of his advisers doubted that even these

---

[27]McGeorge Bundy memorandum for the record, September 14, 1964, Johnson Papers, National Security File, Country File: Vietnam, Box 6.

[28]See, for example, Logevall, *Choosing War*; David Kaiser, *American Tragedy: Kennedy, Johnson, and the Origins of the Vietnam War* (New York, 2000); and H. R. McMaster, *Dereliction of Duty: Lyndon Johnson, Robert McNamara, the Joint Chiefs of Staff, and the Lies That Led to Vietnam* (New York, 1997).

steps would be enough, but they believed that the United States, to maintain its international credibility, should do everything it could as the "good doctor" to save the ailing patient, South Vietnam. Johnson, Rusk, McGeorge Bundy, and McNamara seem to have hoped that by gradually increasing the bombing and injecting U.S. forces into the ground war they could coerce North Vietnam into abandoning the southern insurgency. This strategy of gradual escalation, which drew on the recent experience of the Cuban missile crisis, was based on the dubious assumption that North Vietnam would give up its goals rather than risk complete destruction. The result for the United States was an irreversible commitment to a major war and Americanization of the conflict in South Vietnam.

Johnson was not forced into war by the exigencies of domestic or international politics. Public opinion in late 1964 was apathetic and permissive. Growing numbers of Americans opposed a major war, and while there was also opposition to withdrawal, the public would likely have gone along with a skillfully executed disengagement. Although some leading political figures and major newspapers endorsed drastic escalation, many others by early 1965 had become increasingly concerned with the prospect of war and favored deescalation and a negotiated settlement. Johnson's political position was as strong as it would ever be. He had just won an overwhelming electoral victory and had firm control of Congress. The administration often maintained that it was in Vietnam to prove its reliability to its allies. In fact, America's major allies doubted the importance of Vietnam and were even more skeptical that the United States could succeed there with military force. When the administration in the spring of 1964 launched a "many flags" campaign to get support from its allies, only Australia enthusiastically agreed to provide troops.[29]

The administration chose war for other reasons. A resolute Cold Warrior, Secretary of State Rusk believed that the United States must stand firm in Vietnam to contain an aggressively expansionist China. Johnson shared Rusk's concern and feared even more the political backlash from right-wing Republicans and southern Democrats should he falter in Vietnam. For the president, the Great Society remained the highest priority, and he continued to worry that a retreat on Vietnam would jeopardize his cherished do-

[29]Logevall, *Choosing War*, pp. 275–279, 304–305.

mestic goals. For personal reasons, he also found the possibility of failure intolerable.

Another leader might also have gone to war in these circumstances, but the way the United States went to war in early 1965—"by stealth"—bore the distinctive LBJ brand.[30] This approach was partly a result of personality and modus operandi. A cloakroom operator rather than master of debate, the former Senate majority leader did not like open discussion and freewheeling debate. His ego and insecurity led him to personalize dissent and opposition. He was determined to keep control in his own hands, and he also feared that a potentially divisive debate on Vietnam would distract attention from the domestic issues he wished to focus on. Thus, while taking major steps toward war, Johnson carefully and skillfully silenced public discussion and obscured the significance of what he was doing. By stressing the continuity of his policies and emphasizing that he was giving equal attention to military measures *and* negotiations, he persuaded both "hawks" and "doves" that he was moving in their direction. By deceit and obfuscation, he brilliantly mobilized a consensus behind his policies while blurring what these policies actually were.

The process began even before the election. On November 2, the day before Americans went to the polls, Johnson authorized intensive planning for future action in Vietnam, a "crucial step in the country's entry into a new war."[31] By the end of that month, a firm consensus had emerged among the president's advisers that the United States must soon undertake a carefully orchestrated bombing attack against North Vietnam. U.S. officials disagreed among themselves on the reasons for the bombing, some viewing it as a way of boosting morale in South Vietnam, others as a means of reducing infiltration from the north, and still others as a weapon to force Hanoi to stop supporting the insurgency. They also disagreed on the type of bombing campaign. The military pressed for a "fast and full squeeze"—massive attacks against major industries and military targets. Civilians advocated a "slow squeeze," a graduated series of attacks beginning with infiltration routes in Laos and slowly extending to North Vietnam. Despite warnings from intelligence sources that bombing would not decisively affect the war in

[30]Ibid., pp. 273, 314–315.
[31]Kaiser, *American Tragedy*, p. 355.

the south, most of Johnson's advisers endorsed the use of airpower in some form.

Only Undersecretary of State George Ball vigorously dissented. An experienced diplomat who as counsel to the French embassy had observed firsthand that nation's defeat in Indochina, Ball insisted that airpower would not solve the American dilemma in Vietnam. He doubted it would either improve morale in the south or compel Hanoi to give in. He also warned that in response to U.S. escalation North Vietnam might pour its virtually unlimited human resources into the struggle and China might intervene. Most important, after the process of escalation had been initiated, the United States could not be sure of controlling events. "Once on the tiger's back," Ball concluded, "we cannot be sure of picking the place to dismount."[32]

Ball's argument had little impact in Washington, and by the end of November Johnson's senior advisers had formulated concrete proposals for the use of American military power. Rejecting the more extreme program of the JCS, the advisers advocated a two-phase plan of gradually intensifying air attacks. The first phase, to last roughly a month, consisted of limited bombing raids against infiltration routes in Laos, along with reprisal strikes against North Vietnamese targets in response to any provocation. In the meantime, Taylor would use the promise of air attacks against North Vietnam to persuade the South Vietnamese to put their house in order. Once an acceptable level of stability had been attained, the United States would move into phase two, a large-scale air offensive against North Vietnam lasting from two to six months, to be followed if necessary by a naval blockade.

Johnson approved the program in December, a "momentous decision," historian Fredrick Logevall has emphasized, perhaps the most important of the war.[33] On December 1, the president approved immediate initiation of phase one bombing operations in Laos. Still reluctant to move too far too fast, he subsequently approved in principle the launching of retaliatory strikes and phase two bombing operations when the situation warranted. Those operations required a substantial deployment of ground combat forces, and the president also endorsed this highly significant measure.

[32]George W. Ball, *The Past Has Another Pattern* (New York, 1982), pp. 380–385.
[33]Logevall, *Choosing War*, pp. 270–273.

In approving what amounted to decisions for war, Johnson demanded absolute secrecy, covering his tracks so skillfully that he deceived his contemporaries and misled a generation of historians. Recognizing that even with his huge electoral mandate he would have only a brief honeymoon period to achieve his ambitious legislative goals, he was unwilling to permit the war to thwart his Great Society. If he had to go to war, he would do everything possible to obscure and conceal it. He made it a matter of "highest importance" that the December decisions be kept from the public. Speaking figuratively but firmly, he threatened to "shoot at sunrise" anyone who leaked sensitive information about the war.[34]

For the same reasons, he continued to move cautiously for more than a month. He was loathe to escalate too rapidly in view of his campaign assurances of no wider war. South Vietnam was still in turmoil, and he refused to send U.S. troops when the South Vietnamese were "acting as they are." He and his advisers also feared that U.S. reprisals might provoke further NLF attacks at a time when South Vietnam was "too shaky" to withstand a "major assault." He thus instructed Taylor to do everything possible to get the South Vietnamese to pull together. He refused even to retaliate when, on Christmas Eve, the NLF bombed a U.S. officers' quarters at the Brinks Hotel in Saigon, killing two Americans and injuring thirty-eight.[35]

ROLLING THUNDER

By the end of January, the president could delay no longer. One of the major arguments against escalation—the weakness of South Vietnam—had become the most compelling argument for it. After Khanh's resignation, a civilian government had been formed, but it could not consolidate its position. Upon returning to Saigon, Taylor informed South Vietnam's leaders that the United States would escalate the war if they could stabilize the government. The answer came immediately when Vice Air Marshal Nguyen Cao Ky and General Nguyen Chanh Thi executed yet another coup. Outraged, Taylor lectured the young officers as a drill instructor might talk to

---

[34]Kaiser, *American Tragedy,* p. 379; McMaster, *Dereliction of Duty,* p. 195.
[35]Meeting on Vietnam, December 1, 1964, Johnson Papers, Meeting Notes File, Box 1; Lyndon B. Johnson, *The Vantage Point* (New York, 1971), p. 121.

recruits. Perhaps something was wrong with his French, he snarled sarcastically, because his listeners had obviously not understood him. "Now you have made a real mess," he added angrily. "We cannot carry you forever if you do things like this."[36]

The harsh reprimand produced some "shame-faced grins," Taylor recalled, but no results.[37] The military finally agreed to co-operate with civilian politicians to form a new government, but Buddhist leaders refused to participate and launched a new round of demonstrations, hunger strikes, and immolations that took on increasingly anti-American tones. Protesters publicly demanded Taylor's resignation, and 5,000 students sacked the U.S. Information Service library in Hue. Rumors of coup plots abounded, and U.S. officials began to fear that a new government could emerge from the chaos and negotiate with the enemy on the basis of a U.S. withdrawal. In the meantime, NLF regular forces decimated two elite South Vietnamese units in major battles. Combined with reports that North Vietnamese regular units were now entering the south, the defeats aroused growing fear that the enemy had decided to launch an all-out attack that South Vietnam could not withstand.

By the end of January, most of Johnson's advisers agreed that the threat to the south and the ominous military danger required the United States to bomb the north. Throughout the month, Taylor bombarded Washington with warnings that failure to take drastic action could only lead to "disastrous defeat."[38] In his famous "fork in the road" memorandum of January 26, an "explosive" document as McNamara later recalled, McGeorge Bundy set out to end the indecision and delay. Speaking in "apocalyptic" language, he warned like Taylor that continuation of existing policy would lead to "disastrous defeat." The choice, he advised, was between using U.S. military power to change communist policy or trying to negotiate a way out. Favoring the more aggressive option, he pushed for implementation of retaliatory air strikes at the first opportunity followed by phase two bombing operations.[39]

[36]Quoted in Neil Sheehan et al., *The Pentagon Papers as Published by the New York Times* (New York, 1971), pp. 371–381. Hereafter cited as *Pentagon Papers (NYT)*.
[37]Maxwell D. Taylor, *Swords and Ploughshares* (New York, 1972), p. 330.
[38]Kaiser, *American Tragedy*, pp. 387–391.
[39]Ibid., pp. 392–393; Logevall, *Choosing War*, p. 317.

Undoubtedly with great reluctance but with also with firm resignation, Johnson concurred. "Stable government or no stable government we'll do what we have to do," he vowed. It was the decisive moment—Johnson moving to implement the program he had approved in principle in December. He dispatched Bundy to Saigon to see what further military action should be taken. Recognizing that a pretext for escalation would be useful, he resumed DeSoto Patrols in the Gulf of Tonkin.[40]

The awaited incident came on land instead of at sea. On February 7, NLF units attacked a U.S. Army barracks in Pleiku and a nearby helicopter base, killing nine Americans and destroying five aircraft. That evening, after a meeting of less than two hours, the administration decided to strike back. Only Senator Mansfield dissented, arguing that the United States might provoke Chinese intervention, but Johnson brusquely dismissed Mansfield's argument. "We have kept our guns over the mantel and our shells in the cupboard for a long time now," he exclaimed with obvious impatience. "I can't ask our American soldiers out there to continue to fight with one hand behind their backs."[41] The president ordered the immediate implementation of FLAMING DART, a plan of reprisal strikes already drawn up by the JCS. Later that day and again the following day American aircraft struck North Vietnamese military installations just across the sixteenth parallel. When, on February 10, the NLF attacked an American enlisted men's quarters at Qui Nhon, the president ordered another, even heavier series of air strikes.

Within less than forty-eight hours, the administration had moved from reprisals to a continuing, graduated program of air attacks against North Vietnam. Bundy returned from South Vietnam the day after the Pleiku raids and warned that "without new U.S. action defeat appears inevitable—probably not in a matter of weeks or perhaps even months, but within the next year or so." He and John McNaughton, who had accompanied him to Vietnam, urged the immediate implementation of a policy of "sustained reprisal" against the north. McNaughton conceded the risks but argued that "measured against the cost of defeat" the program would be "cheap," and even if it failed to turn the tide, "the value of the

---

[40]Kaiser, *American Tragedy*, p. 392.
[41]Johnson, *Vantage Point*, p. 125.

effort" would "exceed the costs."[42] The next day, apparently without extended debate, the administration initiated ROLLING THUNDER, the program of gradually intensified air attacks Bundy and Mc-Naughton had advocated.

The administration deceived the American public in explaining the reasons for and significance of its decision. Spokesmen from the president down justified the air strikes as a response to the Pleiku attack and emphatically denied any change of policy. It is abundantly clear, however, that Pleiku was the pretext for rather than the cause of the February decision. The possibility of a South Vietnamese collapse appeared to demand the adoption of a policy some Americans had been advocating for more than two months. It was, therefore, simply a matter of finding the right opportunity to justify measures to which the administration was already committed. Pleiku provided such an opportunity, although it could as easily have been something else. "Pleikus are like streetcars," McGeorge Bundy later remarked, by which he meant that if you missed one, another would be along shortly.[43] Despite the administration's disclaimers, the February decisions marked an important watershed in the war. The initiation of regular bombing attacks advanced well beyond the limited tit-for-tat reprisal strikes of Tonkin Gulf and provided a built-in argument for further escalation should that become necessary.

Indeed, almost as soon as the bombing program got under way, there were pressures to expand it. The initial attacks achieved meager results, provoking Taylor to complain that ROLLING THUNDER had constituted but a "few isolated thunder claps" and to call for a "mounting crescendo" of air strikes against North Vietnam.[44] Intelligence reports ominously warned that the military situation in South Vietnam was steadily deteriorating and that at the present rate the government might soon be reduced to a series of islands surrounding the provincial capitals. From the outset, Johnson had insisted on maintaining tight personal control over the air war— "they can't even bomb an outhouse without my approval," he is said to have boasted.[45] But in response to these urgent warnings,

[42]Ibid., pp. 127–128.
[43]Quoted in Anthony Lake (ed.), *The Vietnam Legacy* (New York, 1976), p. 183.
[44]*Pentagon Papers (Gravel)*, 3: 335.
[45]Westmoreland, *Soldier Reports*, p. 119.

the president permitted gradual expansion of the bombing and re-laxation of the restrictions under which it was carried out. The use of napalm was authorized to ensure greater destructiveness, and pilots were permitted to strike alternative targets without prior au-thorization if the original targets were inaccessible. In April, Ameri-can and South Vietnamese pilots flew a total of 3,600 sorties against North Vietnamese targets. The air war quickly grew from a spo-radic, halting effort into a regular, determined program.

GROUND TROOPS, ENCLAVES, AND PEACE MOVES

The expanded air war also provided the pretext for the introduc-tion of U.S. ground combat forces into Vietnam. Anticipating retal-iatory attacks for ROLLING THUNDER, General Westmoreland in late February urgently requested two Marine landing teams to protect the air base at Da Nang. Although he conceded the importance of protecting the base, Taylor expressed grave concern about the long-range implications of Westmoreland's request. He questioned whether American combat forces were adequately trained for guer-rilla warfare in the Asian jungles and warned that the introduction of such forces would encourage the ARVN to pass military respon-sibility to the United States. Most important, the introduction of even small numbers of combat troops with a specific and limited mission would violate a ground rule the United States had rigor-ously adhered to since the beginning of the Indochina wars. Once the first step had been taken, it would be "very difficult to hold [the] line."[46]

Taylor's objections were in many ways prophetic, but they were ignored. The president months before had approved in princi-ple the introduction of ground combat forces. The need appears to have been so pressing and immediate, the commitment so small, that the decision was made routinely, with little discussion of its long-range consequences. After less than a week of apparently per-functory debate, the president approved Westmoreland's request, and on March 8, two battalions of Marines, fitted out in full battle regalia, with tanks and 8-inch howitzers, splashed ashore near

[46]*Pentagon Papers (Gravel)*, 3: 418.

Marines Land at Da Nang
Shortly after 9:00 A.M. on March 8, 1965, Marines from the 3rd Battalion,
9th Marine Expeditionary Force, splashed ashore in rough seas at Da Nang.
They were the first U.S ground combat troops sent to Vietnam. With their
arrival, the United States crossed a major threshold in its escalation of the
war. The Marines were originally "tasked" to guard the air base at Da Nang.
But in less than a month, President Lyndon Johnson secretly authorized them
to move out and engage NLF and North Vietnamese soldiers in combat.
AP/Wide World Photos

Da Nang, where they were welcomed by South Vietnamese officials and by pretty Vietnamese girls passing out leis of flowers. It
was an ironically happy beginning for what would be a wrenching
experience for the two nations.

As Taylor had predicted, once the first step had been taken,
it was very difficult to hold the line. Alarmed by the slow pace
of the ARVN buildup and fearful of a major enemy offensive in
the Central Highlands, Westmoreland concluded by mid-March
that if the United States was to avert disaster in Vietnam, there
was "no solution . . . other than to put our own finger in the
dike."[47] He therefore advocated the immediate commitment of
two U.S. Army divisions, one to the highlands, the other to the
Saigon area. The Joint Chiefs forcefully endorsed Westmore-

[47]Westmoreland, *Soldier Reports,* p. 126.

land's request. Long impatient with the administration's caution and eager to assume full responsibility for the war, they even went beyond Westmoreland, pressing for the deployment of as many as three divisions to be used in offensive operations against the enemy.

The administration now found itself on what McNaughton called "the horns of a trilemma." The options of withdrawal and a massive air war against North Vietnam had been firmly rejected. It was apparent by mid-March, however, that the limited bombing campaign undertaken in February would not produce immediate results, and Westmoreland's urgent warnings raised fears that further inaction might lead to a South Vietnamese collapse. Many administration officials therefore reluctantly concluded that they must introduce American ground forces into Vietnam. They fully appreciated, on the other hand, the possible domestic political consequences of the sort of commitment Westmoreland proposed. And Taylor ominously warned that to place major increments of American forces in the highlands would invite heavy losses, even an American Dien Bien Phu.

The administration resolved its "trilemma" with a compromise, rejecting the military proposals but still approving a significant commitment of ground forces and an enlargement of their mission. At a conference in Honolulu in late April, McNamara, Taylor, and the Joint Chiefs agreed on a hastily improvised strategy to "break the will of the DRV/VC [Democratic Republic of Vietnam/Vietcong] by depriving them of victory." The bombing would be maintained at its "present tempo" for six months to a year. But the conferees agreed, as McNamara put it, that bombing "would not do the job alone."[48] They therefore decided that some 40,000 additional U.S. ground combat forces should be sent to Vietnam.

These forces were not to be used in the highlands or given an unrestricted mission, as Westmoreland and the Joint Chiefs had advocated, but would be used in the more cautious "enclave strategy" devised by Taylor. Deployed around the major U.S. bases, their backs to the sea, they would be authorized to undertake operations within fifty miles of their base areas. The administration hoped this limited commitment would deny the enemy a knockout blow, thus allowing time for the South Vietnamese buildup and for the bombing to take

[48]McNamara to Johnson, April 21, 1965, Johnson Papers, National Security File, Country File: Vietnam, Box 13.

its toll. Although the April decisions stopped short of the commitment urged by the military, they advanced well beyond the original objective of base security and marked a major step toward large-scale involvement in the ground war. The new strategy shifted emphasis from the air war against North Vietnam to the war in the south, and by adopting it, the administration at least tacitly committed itself to expand its forces as the military situation required.

By this time Johnson recognized that achievement of U.S. objectives in Vietnam would require a sustained and costly commitment, but he continued to refuse to submit his policies to public or congressional debate. Many administration officials shared a view widely accepted at the height of the Cold War that foreign policy issues were too complex and too important to be left to an indifferent and ignorant public and a divided and unwieldy Congress. Johnson seems to have feared that a declaration of war might trigger a Chinese or Soviet response or increase domestic pressures for an unlimited conflict in Vietnam. He particularly feared, as he later put it, that a congressional debate on "that bitch of a war" would destroy "the woman I really loved—the Great Society."[49] The president's unparalleled knowledge of Congress and his confidence in his renowned powers of persuasion encouraged him to believe that he could expand the war without provoking a backlash, and the repeated deference of the Congress to executive initiatives gave him no reason to anticipate a major challenge.

Johnson thus took the nation into war in Vietnam by indirection and dissimulation. The bombing was publicly justified as a response to the Pleiku attack and the broader pattern of North Vietnamese "aggression" rather than as a desperate attempt to halt the military and political deterioration in South Vietnam. The administration never publicly acknowledged the shift from reprisals to "sustained pressures." The dispatch of ground troops was explained solely in terms of the need to protect U.S. military installations, and not until June, when it crept out by accident in a press release, did spokespeople concede that American troops could undertake offensive operations.

Although the administration effectively concealed the direction of its policy, the obvious expansion of the war, particularly the bombing, attracted growing criticism. White House mail ran heav-

[49]Quoted in Kearns, *Johnson*, p. 251.

ily against the bombing. A few newspapers joined the *New York Times* in warning of the cost of "lives lost, blood spilt and treasure wasted, of fighting a war on a jungle front 7,000 miles from the coast of California." Prominent Democratic senators such as Frank Church, Mike Mansfield, and George McGovern urged the president to search for a negotiated settlement. Professors at the University of Michigan, Harvard, and Syracuse conducted all-night teach-ins; students on various campuses held small protest meetings and distributed petitions against the bombing; and on April 17, in a portent of things to come, 20,000 students gathered in Washington to march in protest against the war.

Escalation also aroused widespread criticism abroad and brought forth, even from some of America's staunchest allies, appeals for restraint. United Nations Secretary General U Thant of Burma had been trying for months to arrange private talks between the United States and North Vietnam, and when the administration ignored his overtures and initiated the bombing, he publicly charged that Washington was withholding the truth from the American people. In early April, seventeen nonaligned nations issued an "urgent appeal" for negotiations without precondition. Great Britain, as cochair of the Geneva Conference, called upon the parties to the conflict to state their terms for a settlement. In a move that infuriated Johnson, Canadian Prime Minister Lester Pearson, speaking on American soil, appealed to Washington to stop the bombing and work for a peaceful settlement.

The administration quickly responded to its critics. White House aides organized "Target: College Campuses," sending their "best young troops" to speak at universities and bringing professors and student leaders to Washington for "seminars."[50] The president invited dissident members of Congress and newspaper editors and representatives of foreign governments in for sessions that sometimes lasted for three hours, vigorously defending his policies and reminding his visitors of past favors. Administration spokespeople publicly replied to critics, revealing from the start an abrasiveness and arrogance that would steadily widen the gap between Washington and opponents of the war. Addressing the American Society for International Law, Rusk expressed incredulity at the

---

[50]Jack Valenti to McGeorge Bundy, April 23, 1965, Johnson Papers, National Security File, Country File: Vietnam, Box 13.

"stubborn disregard of plain facts by men who are supposed to be helping our young to learn . . . how to think."[51]

The administration also sought to disarm its critics by several dramatic peace initiatives. In a speech at Johns Hopkins University on April 7, Johnson affirmed that the United States was prepared to enter into "unconditional discussions" and even dangled before Hanoi the offer of a billion-dollar economic development program for the Mekong River Valley region, a program "on a scale even to dwarf our TVA."[52] In early May, the president, with considerable reluctance, approved a five-day bombing pause, accompanied by private messages to Hanoi indicating that a diminution of North Vietnamese and NLF military activity could lead to a scaling down of U.S. air attacks.

The president was unquestionably sincere in his desire for peace, but the spring 1965 initiatives were designed primarily to silence domestic and international critics rather than set in motion determined efforts to find a peace settlement. Despite Johnson's offer to participate in "unconditional discussions," the United States had no real desire to begin serious negotiations at a time when its bargaining position was so weak. Indeed, it had not even begun internal discussions to formulate a program for negotiations. The president made clear in his Johns Hopkins speech, moreover, that the United States would not compromise its fundamental objective of an independent South Vietnam, which, by implication, meant a non-Communist South Vietnam. And U.S. officials were certain that the North Vietnamese would not negotiate on this basis.

As expected, the peace moves brought the two nations no closer to negotiations. No more inclined than the United States to make concessions under duress, Hanoi denounced the bombing pause as a "worn-out trick of deceit and threat" and refused to curb its military activities. The extent to which North Vietnam was willing to negotiate at this point is unclear, but in any event the United States offered little inducement. On April 8, Pham Van Dong did release a four-point program. In theory at least, much of it did not conflict with basic U.S. objectives, and some officials urged further contacts to explore Hanoi's position. But the president and his top advisers interpreted the statement that a settlement must be in "ac-

[51]Quoted in *Time*, April 30, 1965, 29.
[52]*Public Papers of the Presidents of the United States, Lyndon B. Johnson, 1965* (Washington, D.C., 1966), 1: 394–399.

cordance with the program of the National Liberation Front" as only a thinly disguised cover for Communist domination of South Vietnam and saw no reason to discuss it further.

The peace moves did help still domestic and foreign criticism, at least temporarily, and the administration used the respite to solidify congressional support. On May 4, Johnson requested $700 million for military operations in Vietnam and made clear that he would regard a vote for the appropriation as an endorsement of his policies. The basic decisions had already been made, of course, and the president did nothing to clarify the policy he was actually pursuing. It was very difficult for the legislators to vote against funds for troops in the field, and Congress approved the request quickly and without dissent. Johnson would later cite this vote, along with the Tonkin Gulf Resolution, to counter those critics who said he had not given Congress an opportunity to pass on his Vietnam policy.

CULMINATION

In the three months after the May bombing pause, the Johnson administration took the final steps toward an open-ended commitment to war. Despite the bombing, continued increases in aid, and the infusion of ground forces, the military situation deteriorated drastically. At this most critical phase of the war, the ARVN was on the verge of disintegration. The desertion rate among draftees in training centers ran as high as 50 percent. Discouraged by the failure of the bombing and increasingly inclined to "let the Americans do it," the officer corps became even more cautious, and the high command was "close to anarchy" from internal squabbling and intrigue.[53] Bolstered by as many as four regiments of North Vietnamese regulars, the NLF took the offensive in May and in major engagements in the highlands and just north of Saigon mauled ARVN forces. The defeats increased Westmoreland's already pronounced doubts about the ARVN's capabilities, and the heavy losses completely upset his plans for building it up. By the end of May, he concluded that major increments of U.S. forces would be required to avert defeat.

---

[53]William Depuy memorandum for the record, March 9, 1965, and memorandum to Westmoreland, April 13, 1965, William Depuy Papers, U.S. Army Military History Institute, Carlisle Barracks, Pa., Folder D(65).

The political situation showed no signs of improvement. Khanh had continued to play a dominant role after his resignation in August 1964, resuming the premiership for a brief period and then taking command of the armed forces. After more than a year at or near the center of power, during which he had sharply exacerbated the divisions in South Vietnam, the embattled general finally withdrew in February 1965 and to the relief of the Americans accepted an appointment as "roving ambassador." Following an impossibly confusing series of coups and countercoups, a civilian government was formed by Phan Huy Quat, and relative quiet prevailed for a time. When Quat shook up his cabinet in May, however, the so-called Young Turks, Vice Air Marshal Ky and General Nguyen Van Thieu, finally emerged from the shadows, dissolving the government and assuming power.

The new government, the fifth since the death of Diem, would survive far longer than any of its predecessors, but at the outset its future seemed uncertain. Thieu, who assumed command of the armed forces, was respected by the Americans as a capable military leader, and Taylor regarded him as a man of "considerable poise and judgment."[54] The prime minister, Ky, was another matter entirely. Customarily attired in a flashy flying suit with a bright purple scarf and an ivory-handled pistol hanging ostentatiously on his hip, the flamboyant, mustachioed air marshal had a well-earned reputation for "drinking, gambling and chasing women," as well as for speaking out of turn and using the air force for personal political intrigue.[55] The Americans found it hard to take Ky seriously and saw little cause for optimism in his rise to power. The Ky-Thieu directorate "seemed to all of us the bottom of the barrel, absolutely the bottom of the barrel," assistant secretary of state William Bundy later recalled.[56]

Under these circumstances, Johnson's advisers again began pressing for vigorous action to stave off certain defeat. Long frustrated by the restrictions on the bombing, Westmoreland, the Joint Chiefs, and Walt Rostow of the State Department urged intensification of the air war. The present level of bombing, they contended, was merely inconveniencing Hanoi, and U.S. restraint had allowed

[54]Taylor, *Swords and Ploughshares*, p. 345.
[55]CIA memorandum, October 8, 1964, Johnson Papers, National Security File, Country File: Vietnam, Box 7.
[56]William Bundy oral history interview, Johnson Papers.

it to strengthen its offensive and defensive capabilities. Rostow, in particular, argued that victory could be attained if the United States would strike North Vietnam's industrial base.

At the same time, Westmoreland and the Joint Chiefs advocated a drastic expansion of American ground forces and the adoption of an offensive strategy. More certain than ever that South Vietnam lacked sufficient military strength to hold the line on its own, Westmoreland, with the support of the Joint Chiefs, requested an additional 150,000 U.S. troops in early June. Traditionalists in their attitude toward the use of military power, Westmoreland and the Joint Chiefs had opposed the enclave approach from the start and now insisted on an aggressive, offensive strategy. "You must take the fight to the enemy," General Earle Wheeler, the JCS chairman, affirmed. "No one ever won a battle sitting on his ass."[57] Indeed, by the summer of 1965, even Taylor conceded, as he later put it, that "the strength of the enemy offensive had completely overcome my former reluctance to use American ground troops in general combat."[58]

Only George Ball and Washington attorney Clark Clifford, a frequent personal adviser to Johnson, vigorously opposed a major commitment of U.S. ground forces. Ball expressed profound doubt that the United States could defeat the enemy "or even force them to the conference table on our terms, no matter how many hundred thousand white, foreign (U.S.) troops we deploy." He warned that approval of Westmoreland's proposals would lead to a "protracted war involving an open-ended commitment of U.S. forces, mounting U.S. casualties, no assurances of a satisfactory solution, and a serious danger of escalation at the end of the road." Once the United States was committed, there could be no turning back. "Our involvement will be so great that we cannot—without national humiliation—stop short of achieving our complete objectives." Clifford concurred, urging the president to keep U.S. forces to a minimum and probe "every serious avenue leading to a possible settlement." "It won't be what we want," he concluded, "but we can learn to live with it."[59]

[57]Henry Graff, *The Tuesday Cabinet* (Englewood Cliffs, N.J., 1970), p. 138.
[58]Taylor, *Swords and Ploughshares*, p. 347.
[59]Ball to Johnson, July 1, 1965, in Sheehan et al., *Pentagon Papers (NYT)*, pp. 449–454; Clifford to Johnson, May 17, 1965, Johnson Papers, National Security File, Country File: Vietnam, Box 16.

The clinching argument for a decision already virtually made was provided by McNamara after another whirlwind visit to Saigon in early July. The secretary of defense underscored the pessimistic reports from Westmoreland and Taylor and warned that to continue "holding on and playing for the breaks" would only defer the choice between escalation and withdrawal, perhaps until it was "too late to do any good." McNamara conceded that the expansion of American involvement would make a later decision to withdraw "even more difficult and costly than would be the case today." On the other hand, it might "stave off defeat in the short run and offer a good chance of producing a favorable settlement in the longer run." The secretary recommended the gradual deployment of an additional 100,000 combat forces.[60]

In late July, Johnson made his fateful decisions, setting the United States on a course from which it would not deviate for nearly three years and opening the way for eight years of bloody warfare in Vietnam. The president did not approve the all-out bombing campaign urged by Westmoreland and the Joint Chiefs. He and his civilian advisers continued to fear that a direct, full-scale attack on North Vietnam might provoke Chinese intervention. They also felt that the industrial base around Hanoi was a major trump card for the United States. The threat of its destruction might thus be more useful than destruction itself. The administration approved Westmoreland's request to use B-52s for saturation bombing in South Vietnam and permitted a gradual intensification of the bombing of North Vietnam. Sorties increased from 3,600 in April to 4,800 in June and would continue to grow thereafter. Johnson kept tight control over the bombing, personally approving the targets and restricting attacks to the area south of the twentieth parallel.

At the same time, the president authorized a major commitment of ground forces and a new strategy for their deployment. Determined to prevail in Vietnam and increasingly alarmed by the reports of military and political decline, he authorized in July the immediate deployment of 50,000 troops to South Vietnam. Recognizing that this would not be enough, he privately agreed to commit another 50,000 before the end of the year and, implicitly at least, committed himself to furnish whatever additional forces

---

[60]Johnson, *Vantage Point,* pp. 145–146.

might be needed later. Johnson also authorized Westmoreland to "commit U.S. troops to combat independent of or in conjunction with GVN forces in any situation when . . . their use is necessary to strengthen the relative position of GVN forces."[61] These decisions mark the culmination of a process initiated in December 1964. In July 1965, the president made an open-ended commitment to employ American military forces as the situation demanded. And by giving Westmoreland a free hand, he cleared the way for the United States to assume the burden of fighting in South Vietnam.

Significantly, in making these decisions, the Johnson administration all but ignored the object of its concern, its South Vietnamese ally. The Saigon government was not consulted on the decisions to bomb North Vietnam and introduce major increments of U.S. combat forces. The most that was done was to brief its leaders on the steps being taken and request their concurrence. Former ambassador Bui Diem later noted the absence of communication between allies, the "unself-conscious arrogance" of the Americans, and the impotence of the South Vietnamese, who acquiesced in the Americanization of the war against their better judgment and despite the fact that they had just emerged from years of foreign domination. "The Americans came in like bulldozers," Bui Diem observed, "and the South Vietnamese followed their lead without a word of dissent, for the most part without a thought of dissent."[62]

The president also refused to inform his own people. Some U.S. officials implored him to place the July decisions squarely before the nation. The JCS pressed for mobilization of the reserves and calling up the National Guard to make clear, as Wheeler later put it, that the United States was not becoming engaged in "some two-penny military adventure."[63] McNamara was sufficiently concerned about the domestic political implications to urge Johnson to declare a state of national emergency and ask Congress for an increase in taxes—in short, without seeking a declaration of war, to put the nation on a war footing. Johnson himself apparently toyed with the idea of securing another congressional resolution explicitly endorsing his policies. Some of his advisers proposed a "full scenario" of actions to explain the war to the public and promote public support. "How

[61]Sheehan et al., *Pentagon Papers (NYT)*, p. 412.
[62]Bui Diem with David Chanoff, *In the Jaws of History* (Boston, 1987), pp. 127, 153.
[63]Earle Wheeler oral history interview, Johnson Papers.

do you send young men there in great numbers without telling why?" former ambassador Henry Cabot Lodge, Jr., asked.[64]

After extensive deliberation, the president rejected all such steps. His attorney general assured him that he had the power to commit forces without going to Congress.[65] He continued to fear that anything resembling a declaration of war might provoke the Soviet Union and China. Most important, his civil rights and medicare bills were then at crucial stages in the legislative process, and congressional approval was pending on numerous other proposals. Johnson was determined to establish his place in history through the achievement of sweeping domestic reforms, and he feared that seeking from Congress authority to wage war in Vietnam would destroy his dreams of a Great Society at home. He thus informed his staff that he wished the decisions implemented in a "low-keyed manner in order (a) to avoid an abrupt challenge to the Communists, and (b) to avoid undue concern and excitement in the Congress and in domestic public opinion."[66]

To avoid undue excitement, the president continued to deceive the nation as to the significance of the steps he was taking. To make his decisions more palatable to potential waverers, he and his aides issued dire warnings that failure to act decisively would result in playing into the hands of those who wanted to take drastic measures, the "Goldwater crowd," who were "more numerous, more powerful and more dangerous than the fleabite professors."[67] To appease skeptics such as Mansfield, Johnson implied that he would give equal priority to seeking a diplomatic settlement, without divulging his certainty that such efforts were doomed to failure. Although he had approved the immediate deployment of 100,000 troops followed by another 100,000 in 1966, he revealed publicly only that he was sending 50,000, and he made the move as painless as possible by refusing to call up the reserves and increase taxes. He announced his decision on July 28 at a noon press conference instead of at prime time and lumped it in with other items in a way that obscured its significance. He continued to deny that he had authorized any change in policy and did not give

---

[64]Quoted in VanDeMark, *Into the Quagmire*, p. 207.
[65]Nicholas Katzenbach to Johnson, June 10, 1965, Johnson Papers, National Security File, Country File: Vietnam, Box 17.
[66]Benjamin Read memorandum, July 23, 1965, Johnson Papers, National Security File, Country File: Vietnam, Box 16.
[67]McGeorge Bundy to Johnson, July 14, 1965, Johnson Papers, Diary Backup File, Box 19.

a clear indication—even in the sense that he understood it at the time—of what lay ahead. His tactics reflected his continuing determination to achieve his goals in Vietnam without sacrificing the Great Society and his certainty that he could accomplish both tasks at once.

The July decisions represented the culmination of a year and a half of agonizing over America's Vietnam policy and stemmed logically from the administration's refusal to accept the consequences of withdrawal. Johnson especially feared the domestic consequences of failure in Vietnam. He and his top advisers also believed that to withdraw from Vietnam would encourage disorder throughout the world and drastically weaken American influence. Men of action and achievement, leaders of a nation with an unbroken record of success, they were unwilling to face the prospect of failure. If the United States pulled out of Vietnam, Johnson warned on one occasion, "it might as well give up everywhere else—pull out of Berlin, Japan, South America."[68]

In making the July commitments, the administration saw itself moving cautiously between the extremes of withdrawal and total war; it sought, in Johnson's words, to do "what will be enough, but not too much." The president and his advisers did not seek the defeat of North Vietnam. They did not "speak of conquest on the battlefield . . . as men from time immemorial had talked of victory," the historian Henry Graff recorded. They sought rather to inflict sufficient pain to compel the enemy to negotiate on terms acceptable to the United States—in Johnson's Texas metaphor, to apply sufficient force until the enemy "sobers up and unloads his pistol."[69]

Displaying the consummate political skill that had become his trademark, Johnson in the last week of July molded a consensus for his Vietnam policy. He appears to have been committed from the outset to take steps that would give the United States "the maximum protection at the least cost."[70] During the week of July 21–28, however, he gave the JCS and Ball their days in court, listening carefully to their arguments and raising numerous probing questions before rejecting their proposals for large-scale escalation and

[68]John D. Pomfret memorandum of conversation with Johnson, June 24, 1965, Arthur Krock Papers, Seeley G. Mudd Manuscript Library, Princeton, N.J., Box 59.
[69]Graff, *Tuesday Cabinet*, pp. 54, 59.
[70]Summary notes of National Security Council meeting, June 11, 1965, Johnson Papers, National Security File, NSC Meetings, Box 1.

withdrawal.[71] In meetings with the congressional leadership, he promised conservatives to hold the line in Vietnam, while reassuring liberals that he would not permit the war to get out of hand. "I'm going up old Ho Chi Minh's leg an inch at a time," he told Senator George McGovern.[72] Johnson's middle course probably reflected the aspirations of the American public and Congress, and the president went to war with support that appeared to be solid.

As Johnson himself had predicted, getting into war would be much easier than getting out. The administration's decisions of 1964 and 1965 were based on two fatal miscalculations. In seeking to do what would be "enough but not too much," the president and his advisers never analyzed with any real precision how much would be enough. When Ball warned that it might take as many as a half million troops, McNamara dismissed the figure as "outrageous."[73] JCS estimates of the forces needed and time required turned out to be not far off the mark. But the president devoted his energy to neutralizing the military politically rather than seeking their views, and the Joint Chiefs hesitated to press on him the truth as they saw it for fear it might deter him from war. They hoped, once they got a foot in the door, to chip away at the presidential restrictions until they got the type of war they wanted. The decisions of December 1964 through July 1965 also took place in a strategic vacuum, scant consideration being given to a precise formulation of goals and how U.S. power might best be used to achieve them.[74] Leaders of the most powerful nation in the history of the world, many U.S. officials could not conceive that a small, backward country could stand up against them. It would be like a Congressional filibuster, Johnson once speculated, "enormous resistance at first, then a steady whittling away, then Ho [Chi Minh] hurrying to get it over with."[75]

Miscalculating the costs that the United States would incur, the administration could not help but overestimate the willingness of

[71]Larry Berman, *Planning a Tragedy: The Americanization of the War in Vietnam* (New York, 1982), pp. 128–129.

[72]George McGovern, *Grassroots* (New York, 1977), pp. 104–105.

[73]Benjamin Read oral history interview, Johnson Papers.

[74]McMaster, *Dereliction of Duty*, pp. 257, 261, 275, 301.

[75]Kearns, *Johnson*, p. 266.

the nation to pay. On July 27, 1965, Mansfield penned a long, eloquent, and prophetic warning to his old friend and political mentor. He advised Johnson that Congress and the nation supported him because he was president, not because they understood or were deeply committed to his policy in Vietnam, and that there lingered beneath the surface a confusion and uncertainty that could in time explode into outright opposition.[76] Mansfield correctly perceived the flimsiness of Johnson's backing. As long as U.S. objectives could be obtained at minimal cost, Americans were willing to stay in Vietnam. When the war turned out to last much longer and cost much more than had been anticipated, however, the president's support would wither away, and the advocates of escalation and withdrawal he had parried so skillfully in July 1965 would turn on him.

Johnson disregarded Mansfield's admonitions. After months of uncertainty, he had set his course. In July 1965, quietly and without fanfare, he launched the United States on what would become its longest, most frustrating, and most divisive war. The nation responded with a sense of relief that the steps taken were not more costly and drastic. Reflecting the mood of the moment, *Newsweek* noted the absence of "hot tides of national anger" and remarked on the "strange, almost passionless war" the United States was waging in Vietnam. "There are no songs written about it," the magazine concluded, "and the chances that any will seem remote," a prophecy that turned out to be tragically off the mark.[77]

---

[76]Mansfield to Johnson, July 27, 1965, Johnson Papers, National Security File, National Security Council Histories: Deployment of Major U.S. Forces to Vietnam, July 1965, Box 40.
[77]*Newsweek*, August 9, 1965, 17–18.

President Johnson
The commander-in-chief has just listened to a
tape sent from Vietnam by his son-in-law
Charles Robb decribing an ambush in which
G.I.s were killed. His growing distress at the
inconclusive and intractable war mirrored that
of the country in 1967.
LBJ Library

CHAPTER 5

On the Tiger's Back

The United States at War, 1965–1967

While visiting the aircraft carrier *Ranger* off the coast of Vietnam in 1965, Robert Shaplen overheard a fellow journalist remark: "They just ought to show this ship to the Vietcong—that would make them give up."[1] From Lyndon Johnson in the White House to the GI in the field, the United States went to war in 1965 in much this frame of mind. The president had staked everything on the unexamined assumption that the enemy could be quickly brought to bay by the application of American military might. The first combat troops to enter Vietnam shared similar views. When "we marched into the rice paddies on that damp March afternoon," Marine Lieutenant Philip Caputo later wrote, "we carried, along with our packs and rifles, the implicit conviction that the Viet Cong would be quickly beaten."[2]

Although by no means unique to the Vietnam War, this optimism does much to explain the form that American participation took. The United States never developed a strategy appropriate for the war it was fighting, in part because it assumed that the mere application of its vast military power would be sufficient. The failure of one level of force led to the next and then the next, until the war attained a degree of destructiveness no one would have thought possible in 1965. Most important, the optimism with which the nation went to war more than anything else accounts for the great frustration that subsequently developed in and out of government.

---

[1]Robert Shaplen, *The Lost Revolution: The U.S. in Vietnam, 1946–1966* (New York, 1966), p. 186.
[2]Philip Caputo, *A Rumor of War* (New York, 1977), p. xii.

Failure never comes easily, but it comes especially hard when success is anticipated at little cost.

Within two years, the optimism of 1965 had given way to deep and painful frustration. By 1967, the United States had nearly a half million combat troops in Vietnam. It had dropped more bombs than in all theaters in World War II and was spending more than $2 billion per month on the war. Some American officials persuaded themselves that progress had been made, but the undeniable fact was that the war continued. Lyndon Johnson thus faced an agonizing dilemma. Unable to end the war by military means and unwilling to make the concessions necessary to secure a negotiated settlement, he discovered belatedly what George Ball had warned in 1964: "once on the tiger's back we cannot be sure of picking the place to dismount."

American strategy in Vietnam was improvised rather than carefully designed and contained numerous contradictions. The United States went to war in 1965 to prevent the collapse of South Vietnam, but it was never able to relate its tremendous military power to the fundamental task of establishing a viable government in Saigon. The administration insisted that the war must be kept limited—the Soviet Union and China must not be provoked to intervene—but the president counted on a quick and relatively painless victory to avert unrest at home. That these goals might not be compatible apparently never occurred to Johnson and his civilian advisers. The United States injected its military power directly into the struggle to cripple the insurgency and persuade North Vietnam to stop its "aggression." The administration vastly underestimated the enemy's capacity to resist, however, and did not confront the crucial question of what would be required to achieve its goals until it was bogged down in a bloody stalemate.

While the president and his civilian advisers set limits on the conduct of the war, they did not provide firm strategic guidelines for the use of American power. Left on its own, the military fought the conventional war for which it was prepared without reference to the peculiar conditions in Vietnam. Westmoreland and the Joint Chiefs chafed under the restraints imposed by the civilians. Sensitive to General Douglas MacArthur's fate in Korea, however, they would not challenge the president directly or air their case in public. On the other hand, they refused to develop a strategy that accommodated the restrictions imposed by the White House; instead, they attempted to break the restrictions down one by one until they got what they wanted. The result was considerable ambiguity in purpose and method, growing civil-military tension, and a steady escalation that brought increasing costs and uncertain gain.[3]

ROLLING THUNDER

The United States relied heavily on bombing.[4] Airpower doctrine emphasized that the destruction of an enemy's war-making capacity would force that enemy to come to terms. The limited success of strategic bombing as applied on a large scale in World War II and on a more restricted scale in Korea raised serious questions about the validity of this assumption, and the conditions prevailing in Vietnam, a primitive country with few crucial targets, might have suggested even more questions. The air force and navy advanced unrealistic expectations about what airpower might accomplish, however, and clung to them long after experience had proven them unjustified. The civilian leadership accepted the military's arguments, at least to a point, because bombing was cheaper in lives lost and therefore more palatable at home, and because it seemed to offer a quick and comparatively easy solution to a complex problem. Initiated in early 1965 as much from the lack of alternatives as from anything else, the bombing of North Vietnam was expanded over the next two years in the vain hope that it would check infiltration into the south and force North Vietnam to the conference table.

The air war gradually assumed massive proportions. The president firmly resisted the Joint Chiefs' proposal for a knockout blow, but as each phase of the bombing failed to produce results, he expanded the list of targets and the number of strikes. Sorties against North Vietnam increased from 25,000 in 1965 to 79,000 in 1966 and 108,000 in 1967; bomb tonnage increased from 63,000 to 136,000 to 226,000. Throughout 1965, ROLLING THUNDER concentrated on military bases, supply depots, and infiltration routes in the southern

---

[3]George C. Herring, *LBJ and Vietnam: A Different Kind of War* (Austin, Tex., 1994), pp. 26–62.

[4]The best analyses of the air war are Mark Clodfelter, *The Limits of Air Power: The American Bombing of North Vietnam* (New York, 1989), and Earl H. Tilford, Jr., *Setup: What the Air Force Did in Vietnam and Why* (Maxwell Air Force Base, Ala., 1991).

part of the country. From early 1966 on, air strikes were increasingly directed against the North Vietnamese industrial and transportation systems and moved steadily northward. In the summer of 1966, Johnson authorized massive strikes against petroleum storage facilities and transportation networks. A year later, he permitted attacks on steel factories, power plants, and other targets around Hanoi and Haiphong as well as on previously restricted areas along the Chinese border.

The bombing inflicted an estimated $600 million damage on a nation still struggling to develop a viable, modern economy. The air attacks crippled North Vietnam's industrial productivity and disrupted its agriculture. Some cities were virtually leveled, others severely damaged. Giant B-52s, carrying payloads of 58,000 pounds, relentlessly attacked the areas leading to the Ho Chi Minh Trail, leaving the countryside scarred with huge craters and littered with debris. The bombing was not directed against the civilian population, and the administration publicly maintained that civilian casualties were minimal. But the CIA estimated that in 1967 total casualties ran as high as 2,800 per month and admitted that these figures were heavily weighted with civilians; McNamara privately conceded that civilian casualties were as high as 1,000 per month during periods of intensive bombing. A British diplomat later recalled that by the fall of 1967 there were signs among the civilian population of the major cities of widespread malnutrition and declining morale.[5]

The manner in which airpower was used in Vietnam virtually ensured that it would not achieve its objectives, however. Whether, as the Joint Chiefs argued, a massive, unrestricted air war would have worked remains much in doubt. In fact, the United States had destroyed most major targets by 1967 with no demonstrable effect on the war. Nevertheless, the administration's gradualist approach gave Hanoi time to construct an air defense system, protect its vital resources, and develop alternative modes of transportation. Gradualism encouraged the North Vietnamese to persist despite the damage inflicted upon them.

North Vietnam demonstrated great ingenuity and dogged perseverance in coping with the bombing. Civilians were evacuated

[5]Raphael Littauer and Norman Uphoff (eds.), *The Air War in Indochina* (Boston, 1972), pp. 39–43. For a firsthand account of the impact of the bombing, see John Colvin, "Hanoi in My Time," *Washington Quarterly* (Spring 1981): 138–154.

Ho Chi Minh Trail
This picture, taken by a Vietnamese photojournalist killed in the war, vividly illustrates the challenges of the Ho Chi Minh Trail. This main artery of North Vietnamese support for the southern insurgency wound more than 600 miles over rugged territory to delivery points in South Vietnam, and those who traversed it faced many dangers. For much of the war, the bicycle was an essential means to convey supplies along the trail. Properly loaded, it could carry as much as 500 pounds, and it has earned a special place of honor in the military museum in Hanoi.
Photo by Nguyen Luong Nam (courtesy: Requiem Photo Project)

from the cities and dispersed across the countryside; industries and storage facilities were scattered and in many cases concealed in caves and under the ground. The government claimed to have dug over 30,000 miles of tunnels, and in heavily bombed areas the people spent much of their lives underground. An estimated 500,000 North Vietnamese, many of them women and children, worked full-time repairing bridges and railroads, and piles of gravel were kept along the major roadways, enabling "Youth Shock Brigades" to fill craters within hours after the bombs fell. Concrete and steel bridges were replaced by ferries and pontoon bridges made of bamboo stalks, which were sunk during the day to avoid detection. Truck drivers covered vehicles with palm fronds and banana leaves and traveled at night, without headlights, guided only by white markers along the roads. B-52s blasted the narrow roads through the Mu Gia Pass leading to the Ho Chi Minh Trail, but to American amazement trucks moved back through within several days. "Caucasians cannot really imagine what ant labor can do," one American remarked with a mixture of frustration and admiration.[6]

Losses in military equipment, raw materials, and vehicles were more than offset by drastically increased aid from the Soviet Union and China. U.S. escalation did not force the two Communist rivals back into a close alliance, as George Ball had feared. Nevertheless, along with their increasingly heated rivalry, it permitted Hanoi to play one against the other to get increased aid and prevent either from securing predominant influence.

Until 1965, the Soviet Union had remained detached from the conflict, but the new leaders who overthrew premier Nikita Khrushchev in October 1964 took a much greater interest in Vietnam, and U.S. escalation presented challenges and opportunities they could not ignore. The bombing created a need for sophisticated military equipment that only the Soviets could provide, giving them a chance to wean North Vietnam from dependence on China. At a time when the Chinese were loudly proclaiming Soviet indifference to the fate of world revolution, the direct threat to a Communist state posed by U.S. escalation required the Russians to prove *their* credibility. The expanding war provided opportunities for the USSR to undermine U.S.

---

[6]Quoted in Townsend Hoopes, *The Limits of Intervention* (New York, 1970), p. 79. For North Vietnam's response to the air war, see Jon M. Van Dyke, *North Vietnam's Strategy for Survival* (Palo Alto, Calif., 1972).

prestige, tie down both of its major rivals, test its own weapons under combat conditions, and analyze the latest U.S. military hardware. The Soviets were nervous about escalation of the war and especially feared a nuclear confrontation like the 1962 Cuban missile crisis. They resented North Vietnam's stubborn independence, bemoaned the fact that their massive aid did not purchase commensurate influence with Hanoi, and complained of the way the North Vietnamese used their freighters in Haiphong harbor as shields against U.S. bombing. But the Russians steadily expanded their support. Up to January 1, 1968, they furnished more than 1.8 billion rubles in assistance to North Vietnam, 60 percent of which was for military aid that included such modern weapons as fighter planes, surface-to-air missiles (SAMs), and tanks. Three thousand Soviet technicians took direct part in the war effort, some of them manning antiaircraft batteries and SAM sites and actually shooting down U.S. aircraft.[7]

For China also, the war with the United States—especially the air war—presented challenges and opportunities. The Chinese had supported North Vietnam since the Geneva Conference, and at a time when they were asserting leadership of the world revolutionary movement, they could not help but view U.S. escalation as a "test case for 'true communism.' " They deemed the defense of North Vietnam essential to their own security, and by rallying his people to meet an external threat, party chairman Mao Zedong sought to mobilize support for his radicalization of China's domestic policies. Like the Soviets, the Chinese feared a confrontation with the United States. They therefore let it be known that should the United States invade North Vietnam they would send their own forces. They also made clear through words and deeds their full support for their ally. Under agreements worked out in 1964 and 1965, approximately 320,000 Chinese engineering and artillery troops helped the Vietnamese build new highways, railroads, and bridges to facilitate the transport of supplies from China and build manned antiaircraft positions to defend the existing network from American attack. The Chinese also provided huge quantities of vehicles, small arms and ammunition, uniforms and shoes, rice and other foodstuffs, even volleyball and table tennis equipment for the recreation of North Vietnamese troops.

---

[7]Ilya V. Gaiduk, "The Vietnam War and Soviet-American Relations, 1964–1973: New Russian Evidence," *Cold War International History Project Bulletin* (Winter 1995/1996): 232, 250–258.

In contrast to the First Indochina War, the wary Vietnamese did not permit their powerful northern neighbors to share in decision making, and as Vietnamese relations with the Soviet Union warmed those with China cooled. Overall, the Vietnamese developed into an art form the exploitation of divisions among their allies, and total assistance between 1965 and 1968 has been estimated at more than $2 billion. Chinese and Soviet aid helped counter U.S. air attacks, replaced equipment lost through the bombing, and freed North Vietnam to send more of its own troops to the South. Such aid played a crucial, perhaps even decisive, role in the outcome of the war.[8]

Other factors reduced the effectiveness of the bombing. Heavy rains and impenetrable fog forced curtailment of missions during the long monsoon season, from September to May. Pilots claimed to be able to bomb with "surgical" precision, but the weather and techniques that had not advanced much since World War II made for considerable inaccuracy, and many targets had to be bombed repeatedly before they were finally destroyed. As they came closer to Hanoi and Haiphong, American aircraft ran up against a deadly air defense system. Soviet SAMs and MiG fighters did not score a high kill rate, but they threw off bombing patterns and forced pilots down to altitudes where they confronted heavy flak and small-arms fire. One U.S. pilot described North Vietnam as the "center of hell with Hanoi as its hub."[9]

Despite the extensive damage inflicted on North Vietnam, the bombing did not achieve its goals. It absorbed a great deal of personnel and resources that might have been diverted to other military uses. It hampered the movement of troops and supplies to the south, and its proponents argued that infiltration would have been much greater without it. Official American estimates nevertheless conceded that infiltration increased from about 35,000 soldiers in 1965 to as many as 90,000 in 1967, even as the bombing grew heavier and more destructive. North Vietnamese Army (NVA) and National Liberation Front (NLF) troops required only 34 tons of supplies a day from outside South Vietnam, "a trickle too small for airpower to stop."[10] It is

---

[8]Jian Chen, "China's Involvement in the Vietnam War, 1964–1969," *China Quarterly* 142 (June 1995): 356–386; Zhang Xiaoming, "The Vietnam War, 1964–1969: A Chinese Perspective," *Journal of Military History* 60 (October 1996): 731–762.
[9]Quoted in Clodfelter, *Limits of Air Power*, pp. 131–132.
[10]Tilford, *Setup*, p. 113.

impossible to gauge with any accuracy the psychological impact of the bombing on North Vietnam, but it did not destroy Hanoi's determination to prevail, and it gave the leadership a powerful rallying cry to mobilize the civilian population in support of the war.

By 1967, the United States was paying a heavy price for no more than marginal gains. The cost in bombs of a B-52 mission ran to $30,000 per sortie. The direct cost of the air war, including operation of the aircraft, munitions, and replacement of planes, was estimated at more than $1.7 billion during 1965 and 1966, a period when aircraft losses exceeded 500. Overall, the United States between 1965 and 1968 lost 950 aircraft costing roughly $6 billion. According to one estimate, for each $1 of damage inflicted on North Vietnam, the United States spent $9.60. The costs cannot be measured in dollars alone, however. Captured U.S. fliers gave Hanoi hostages who would assume increasing importance in the stalemated war. The continued pounding of a small, backward country by the world's wealthiest and most advanced nation gave the North Vietnamese a propaganda advantage they exploited quite effectively. Opposition to the war at home increasingly focused on the bombing, which, in the eyes of many critics, was at best inefficient, at worst immoral.

SEARCH AND DESTROY

American ground operations in the south also escalated dramatically between 1965 and 1967. Even before he had significant numbers of combat forces at his disposal, Westmoreland had formulated the strategy he would employ until early 1968. It was a strategy of attrition, the major·objective of which was to locate and eliminate NLF and North Vietnamese regular units. Westmoreland has vigorously denied that he was motivated by any "Napoleonic impulse to maneuver units and hark to the sound of cannon," but "search and destroy," as his strategy came to be called, did reflect traditional U.S. Army doctrine. In Westmoreland's view, North Vietnam's decision to commit large units to the war left him no choice but to proceed along these lines. He did not have sufficient forces to police the entire country, nor was it enough simply to contain the enemy's main units. "They had to be pounded with artillery and bombs and eventually brought to battle on the ground if they were not forever to remain a threat." Once the enemy's regulars had been destroyed,

Westmoreland reasoned, the South Vietnamese government could stabilize its position and pacify the countryside, and the adversary would have to negotiate on terms acceptable to the United States.[11]

Westmoreland's aggressive strategy required steadily increasing commitments of personnel. To secure some of the needed troops and give international respectability to its commitment in Vietnam, the Johnson administration mounted a "many flags" campaign among its allies, pressing them to commit forces and dangling subsidies, arms packages, and trade deals as inducements. The president himself got into the act, warning allied diplomats in 1967 of a "brush fire" in their backyard. If "you're wise . . . ," he advised them, "you'll help me stamp it out before it reaches you. It will reach you," he concluded ominously, "before it reaches me."[12]

The results, from the U.S. perspective, were disappointing. America's European allies saw in a way the Johnson administration never did the dubiousness of its cause in Vietnam. They questioned whether the stakes were as high as the United States claimed, whether its credibility was really on the line. On the contrary, they feared that America might suffer more from a failed intervention than from a face-saving withdrawal. In any event, they doubted, given the weakness of South Vietnam, that even a massive injection of U.S. power could do more than delay an inevitable defeat. Except for France, America's major European allies did not openly oppose America's policy in Vietnam, but they adamantly refused, despite relentless U.S. pressure and Johnson's personal arm-twisting, to provide even the token military forces the administration requested.

Even in the Pacific region the results were disappointing. The most hawkish of the allies at the outset of the war, Australia sent 8,000 soldiers and paid for them itself. Although dependent on the United States for its very survival, South Korea drove a hard economic bargain for the 60,000 troops it provided. Others were reluctant to refuse but also uneager to make large commitments. New Zealand doubted that the United States could achieve its goals in Vietnam but recognized that U.S. departure from the region would leave a "strategic task of frightening dimensions." To appease Washington, Wellington sent an artillery battery as a token. Thai-

---

[11]William C. Westmoreland, *A Soldier Reports* (Garden City, N.Y., 1976), pp. 149–150.
[12]New Zealand embassy, Washington, to Ministry of External Affairs, November 3, 1967, EA 478/4/8, Records of the New Zealand Ministry of External Relations and Trade, Wellington, N.Z.

land also committed a small "volunteer" contingent; the Philippines an engineering battalion; and Nationalist China small, highly trained units for covert operations. As the war dragged on inconclusively and became more unpopular throughout the world, even the Pacific allies grew more reluctant to succumb to U.S. blandishments, pleading budgetary constraints and domestic politics as excuses. When Maxwell Taylor and Clark Clifford visited the region in 1967 seeking additional forces, they found allied leaders "friendly but usually cautious and defensive," talking more about what they had done in the past than about what they would do in the future. Allied forces in Vietnam peaked at around 71,000 in early 1969.[13]

The United States thus provided the bulk of the forces, and even before the 1965 buildup had been completed, Westmoreland requested sufficient additional troops to bring the total to 450,000 by the end of 1966. While the administration retained tight control over the air war, it gave its field commander broad discretion in developing and executing the ground strategy, and it saw no choice but to give him most of the troops he asked for. In June 1966, the president approved a force level of 431,000 to be reached by mid-1967. While these deployments were being approved, Westmoreland was developing requests for an increase to 542,000 troops by the end of 1967.

Furnished with thousands of fresh American troops and a massive arsenal of modern weaponry, Westmoreland took the war to the enemy. He accomplished what has properly been called a "logistical miracle," constructing virtually overnight the facilities to handle huge numbers of U.S. troops and enormous volumes of equipment. The Americans who fought in Vietnam were the best-fed, best-clothed, and best-equipped army the nation had ever sent to war.

In what Westmoreland described as the "most sophisticated war in history," the United States attempted to exploit its technological superiority to cope with the peculiar problems of a guerrilla war. To locate an ever-elusive enemy, the military used small, portable radar units and "people sniffers" that picked up the odor of human urine. IBM 1430 computers were programmed to predict likely times and places of enemy attacks. Herbicides were used on a wide scale and with devastating ecological consequences to deprive the guerrillas of natural cover. C-123 RANCHHAND crews, with

<hr />

[13]Clifford-Taylor report, August 5, 1967, Johnson Papers, Lyndon Baines Johnson Library, Austin, Texas, National Security File, Country File: Vietnam, Box 91.

Total U.S. Military Personnel in South Vietnam

Date	Army	Navy	Marine Corps	Air Force	Coast Guard	Total
31 Dec. 1960	800	15	2	68	—	About 900
31 Dec. 1961	2,100	100	5	1,000	—	3,205
30 June 1962	5,900	300	700	2,100	—	9,000
31 Dec. 1962	7,900	500	500	2,400	—	11,300
30 June 1963	10,200	600	600	4,000	—	15,400
31 Dec. 1963	10,100	800	800	4,600	—	16,300
30 June 1964	9,900	1,000	600	5,000	—	16,500
31 Dec. 1964	14,700	1,100	900	6,600	—	23,300
30 June 1965	27,300	3,800	18,100	10,700	—	59,900
31 Dec. 1965	116,800	8,400	38,200	20,600	300	184,300
30 June 1966	160,000	17,000	53,700	36,400	400	267,500
31 Dec. 1966	239,400	23,300	69,200	52,900	500	385,300
30 June 1967	285,700	28,500	78,400	55,700	500	448,800
31 Dec. 1967	319,500	31,700	78,000	55,900	500	485,600
30 June 1968	354,300	35,600	83,600	60,700	500	534,700
31 Dec. 1968	359,800	36,100	81,400	58,400	400	536,100
30 Apr. 1969	363,300	36,500	81,800	61,400	400	*543,400
30 June 1969	360,500	35,800	81,500	60,500	400	538,700
31 Dec. 1969	331,100	30,200	55,100	58,400	400	475,200
30 June 1970	298,600	25,700	39,900	50,500	200	414,900
31 Dec. 1970	249,600	16,700	25,100	43,100	100	334,600
30 June 1971	190,500	10,700	500	37,400	100	239,200
31 Dec. 1971	119,700	7,600	600	28,800	100	156,800
30 June 1972	31,800	2,200	1,400	11,500	100	47,000
31 Dec. 1972	13,800	1,500	1,200	7,600	100	24,200
30 June 1973	**	**	**	**	**	**

*Peak strength.
**Totals for all five services combined less than 250.
Source: U.S., Department of Defense, OASD (Comptroller), Directorate for Information Operations, March 19, 1974.

the sardonic motto "Only You Can Prevent Forests," sprayed more than 100 million pounds of chemicals such as Agent Orange over millions of acres of forests, destroying an estimated one-half of South Vietnam's timberlands and leaving horrendous human and ecological costs. C-47 transports were converted into terrifying gunships (called "Puff the Magic Dragon" after a popular folk song of the era) that could fire 18,000 rounds a minute.

The United States relied heavily on artillery and airpower to dislodge the enemy at minimal cost, and it waged a furious war against NLF and North Vietnamese base areas. "The solution in Vietnam is more bombs, more shells, more napalm . . . till the other side cracks and gives up," observed General William Depuy, one of the principal architects of "search and destroy."[14] From 1965 to 1967, South Vietnamese and U.S. airmen dropped over a million tons of bombs on South Vietnam, more than twice the tonnage dropped on the north. Retaliatory bombing was employed against some villages suspected of harboring guerrillas. Airpower was used to support forces in battle according to the "pile-on concept," in which U.S. troops encircled enemy units and called in the aircraft. "Blow the hell out of him and police up," one officer described it.[15] A much greater proportion of the air strikes comprised what was loosely called interdiction—massive, indiscriminate raids, primarily by B-52s, against enemy base areas and logistics networks. Entire areas of South Vietnam were designated Free Fire Zones, which could be pulverized without regard for the inhabitants.

North Vietnam matched U.S. escalation of the war. Although surprised by American willingness to fight for South Vietnam and keenly aware of the enormous cost of a full-scale war, Hanoi had invested so much in the struggle and was so deeply committed to its cause that it saw no choice but to meet the challenge. In late 1965, North Vietnamese leaders mobilized the entire nation to "foil the war of aggression of the U.S. imperialists." Recognizing that their very survival was at stake, the North Vietnamese developed a sophisticated strategy of *dau tranh* (struggle) that sought to closely integrate the military, political, and diplomatic dimensions of war in ways that promoted their cause. North Vietnamese and NLF

---

[14]Quoted in Daniel Ellsberg, *Papers on the War* (New York, 1972), p. 234.
[15]Quoted in Littauer and Uphoff, *Air War*, p. 52.

strategists often disagreed on how aggressively to pursue the war in the south and to what extent the North Vietnamese rear area should be put at risk. But they concurred that the South Vietnamese government and army and American public opinion were their enemies' most vulnerable points, and they attempted through intensive guerrilla and main unit operations to put maximum military pressure on the South Vietnamese and keep U.S. casualties high in hopes that Americans would weary of the war.

Infiltration into South Vietnam was crucial to victory, and the fabled Ho Chi Minh Trail was the key to infiltration. From the beginning of the American war, the North Vietnamese committed vast human and material resources to expanding and improving this vital lifeline. What had been a primitive footpath with elephants sometimes used as a mode of conveyance was transformed by the late 1960s into a complex and sophisticated network of arteries into South Vietnam, with some paved roads capable of handling heavy trucks and with rest stations at numerous points. Thousands of workers, including women and children, devoted much of their lives to keeping the roads open. For the porters and soldiers who went to South Vietnam, the trip remained arduous. Depending on the means of travel, the 600-mile trek could take from two weeks to six months and it was fraught with peril from deadly tigers and bears, from the terror of American B-52 bombing, and especially from the scourge of malaria. Many way stations soon had cemeteries that marked the danger. The bicycle remained a major mode of transportation, and as modified for use on the trail it could handle several hundred pounds of crucial supplies. During peak periods in the late 1960s, North Vietnam could move an estimated 400 tons of supplies per week and as many as 5,000 soldiers a month into South Vietnamese battle zones.

Throughout 1965 and 1966, the North Vietnamese and NLF attempted to keep the Americans off balance, thereby disrupting search-and-destroy operations. In 1967, they engaged U.S. forces in major actions around the demilitarized zone, giving themselves short supply lines and convenient sanctuary and hoping to draw the Americans away from the populated areas and leave the countryside vulnerable to the NLF. Tactically, the North Vietnamese relied on ambushes and hit-and-run operations and sought to "cling to the belts" of the Americans in close-quarter fighting to minimize the impact of their vastly superior firepower. Like their NLF counterparts, the North Vietnamese were capable fighters. "Damn, give

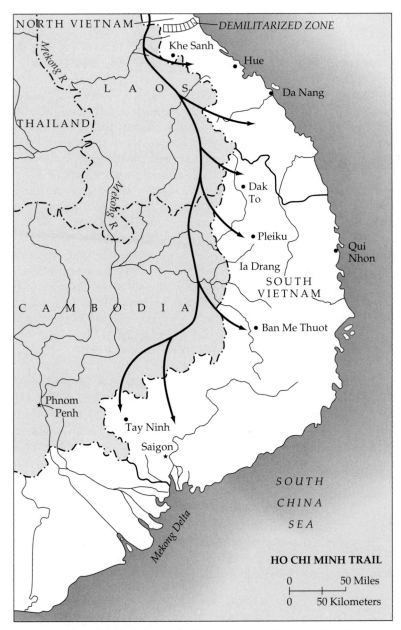

Map by Jeffrey L. Ward. Reprinted with permission of Simon & Schuster from
Our Vietnam—Nuoc Viet Ta: A History of the War: 1954–1975 by A. J.
Langguth, p. 397. Maps Copyright © 2000 by Jeffrey L. Ward.

me two hundred men that well disciplined and I'll capture this whole country," one U.S. adviser commented after a major battle in the Central Highlands in late 1965.[16]

During 1966 and 1967, intensive fighting took place across much of South Vietnam. Along the demilitarized zone, Marines and North Vietnamese regulars were dug in like the armies of World War I, pounding each other relentlessly with artillery. In the jungle areas, small American units probed for the hidden enemy in a manner comparable to the Pacific island campaigns of World War II. Increasingly, however, Westmoreland concentrated on large-scale search-and-destroy operations against enemy base areas. Operation CEDAR FALLS, a major campaign of early 1967, sent some 30,000 U.S. troops against the Iron Triangle, an NLF stronghold just north of Saigon. After B-52s saturated the area, American forces surrounded it, and helicopters dropped large numbers of specially trained combat troops into the villages. Following removal of the population, giant Rome plows with huge spikes on the front leveled the area, destroying what remained of the vegetation and leaving the guerrillas no place to hide. The region was then burned and bombed again to destroy the miles of underground tunnels dug by the insurgents.

It remains difficult to assess the results of U.S. ground operations from 1965 to 1967. American troops fought well, despite the miserable conditions under which the war was waged—dense jungles and deep swamps, fire ants and leeches, booby traps and ambushes, an elusive but deadly enemy. In those instances where main units were actually engaged, the Americans usually prevailed, and there was no place in South Vietnam where the enemy enjoyed security from U.S. firepower. It was clear by 1967 that the infusion of American forces had staved off what had appeared in 1965 to be certain defeat.

In a war without front lines and territorial objectives, where "attriting the enemy" was the major goal, the "body count" became the index of progress. Most authorities agree that the figures were notori-

---

[16]Quoted in the *New York Times*, October 28, 1965. William J. Duiker, *The Communist Road to Power in Vietnam* (Boulder, Colo., 1981), pp. 240–256, contains a persuasive assessment of North Vietnamese strategy. The story of the Ho Chi Minh Trail is well told in John Prados, *The Blood Road: The Ho Chi Minh Trail and the Vietnam War* (New York, 1999)

The Destruction of Ben Suc
The village of Ben Suc was a major NLF supply center in the notorious Iron Triangle northwest of Saigon. The NLF had dominated this area for years, and in 1967 the United States set out to save it by destroying it. More than 6,000 civilians were forcibly evacuated from Ben Suc, after which the village was bombed by B-52s for four days. Two Army divisions then moved in. Ben Suc ceased to exist, and *Time* magazine reported that "even a crow flying across the Triangle will have to carry lunch from now on." The NLF quickly returned to the Iron Triangle, however, and it became a staging area for the 1968 Tet Offensive.
Dick Swanson/TimePix

ously unreliable. The sheer destructiveness of combat made it difficult to produce an accurate count of enemy killed in action. It was impossible to distinguish between guerrillas and noncombatants, and in the heat of battle American "statisticians" made little effort. "If it's dead and Vietnamese, it's VC, was a rule of thumb in the bush," Philip Caputo has recalled.[17] Throughout the chain of command there was heavy pressure to produce favorable figures, and padding occurred at each level until by the time the numbers reached Washington, they bore little resemblance to reality. Even with an inflated

[17]Caputo, *Rumor of War*, p. xviii.

NLF Tunnel System
During the wars with France and the United States, the Vietminh and later
the National Liberation Front dug by hand thousands of miles of tunnels
that connected villages and linked staging areas to battle zones. Inside
these underground fortresses were supply depots, ordnance factories,
hospitals, printing presses, sleeping quarters, kitchens, and even theaters
for propaganda plays.

body count—and estimates of padding range as high as 30 percent—
it is clear that the United States inflicted huge losses on the enemy.
Official estimates placed the number as high as 220,000 by late 1967.
Largely on the basis of these figures, the American military command
insisted that the United States was winning the war.

As with the air war, the strategy of attrition had serious flaws.
It assumed that the United States could inflict intolerable losses on
the enemy while keeping its own within acceptable bounds, an assumption that flew in the face of past experience with land wars on
the Asian continent and the realities in Vietnam. An estimated
200,000 North Vietnamese reached draft age each year, and Hanoi
was able to replace its losses and match each American escalation.
Moreover, the conditions under which the war was fought permitted the enemy to control its casualties. The North Vietnamese and
NLF remained extraordinarily elusive and were generally able to
avoid contact when it suited them. They fought at times and places
of their own choosing and on ground favorable to them. If losses
reached unacceptable levels, they simply melted into the jungle or
retreated into sanctuaries in North Vietnam, Laos, and Cambodia.

The United States could thus gain no more than a stalemate. The
North Vietnamese and NLF had been hurt, in some cases badly, but
their main forces had not been destroyed. They retained the strategic

North and South Vietnam at War
From The Eye Witness History of the Vietnam War 1961–1975 *by George Esper, copyright © 1983 by Villard Books. Used by permission of Villard Books, a division of Random House.*

initiative and could strike sharply and quickly when and where they chose. Westmoreland did not have sufficient forces to wage war against the enemy's regulars and control the countryside. The NLF political structure thus remained largely untouched, and even in areas such as the Iron Triangle, when American forces moved on to fight elsewhere, the insurgents quietly slipped back in. It all added up to a "state of irresolution," Robert Shaplen observed in 1967.[18]

Skeptics increasingly questioned whether the progress made was not more than offset by the consequences of large-scale American military operations. In 1966 alone, unexploded American bombs and shells provided the guerrillas with enough explosives to kill as many as 1,000 people. The massive bombing and artillery fire disrupted the agriculture on which the South Vietnamese economy depended, produced huge civilian casualties, and drove millions of noncombatants into hastily constructed refugee camps or into the already overcrowded cities. American military operations further undermined the social fabric of an already fragile nation and alienated the people from a government that never had a firm base of popular support. "It was as if we were trying to build a house with a bulldozer and wrecking crane," one American official later observed.[19]

Americanization of the war also had a debilitating effect on the South Vietnamese Army. Westmoreland had called for American forces because he doubted the battle-worthiness of the Army of the Republic of Vietnam (ARVN), and once he had them, he relied primarily on them. During the period of American military preponderance, the ARVN was largely shunted aside, relegated to lesser operations and population control, chores its officers considered demeaning and took on with considerable reluctance. The sense of inferiority thus engendered did nothing to resolve the problems of morale and leadership that had always been the ARVN's curse. Much time and money were spent training and equipping the South Vietnamese from 1965 to 1967, but it was all in the American mold, preparing them to fight the kind of war the Americans were waging. The ARVN thus became more than ever dependent on the United States and was ill prepared to assume the burden of the fighting at some later, unspecified date.

The United States paid a heavy price for limited gains. In many operations vast quantities of firepower were expended, sometimes with negligible results. The ammunition costs of the war were "astronomical," Army Chief of Staff Harold Johnson later recalled, and some surveys revealed that as much as 85 percent of the ammuni-

---

[18]Robert Shaplen, *The Road from War: Vietnam, 1965–1970* (New York, 1970), p. 167.
[19]Stephen Young, quoted in W. Scott Thompson and Donaldson D. Frizzell, *The Lessons of Vietnam* (New York, 1977), p. 225.

tion used was unobserved fire, "a staggering volume."[20] Although the United States killed 700 guerrillas in the CEDAR FALLS operation, the enemy main force escaped. American casualties were small compared with Vietnamese, but the number killed in action rose to 13,500 by late 1967, and swelling draft calls and mounting casualties brought rising opposition to the war at home.

Thus, despite the impressive body count figures, it was clear to many observers by mid-1967 that the hopes of a quick and relatively inexpensive military victory had been misplaced. Each American blow "was like a sledgehammer on a floating cork," the journalist Malcolm Browne observed. "Somehow the cork refused to stay down."[21] By this point the United States had nearly 450,000 troops in Vietnam. Westmoreland conceded that even if his request for an additional 200,000 soldiers was granted, the war might go on for as long as two years. If not, he warned, it could last five years or even longer.

THE "OTHER WAR": NATION BUILDING AND PACIFICATION

While drastically expanding its military operations in Vietnam, the United States also grappled with what many had always regarded as the central problem—construction of a viable South Vietnamese nation. Ky surprised skeptics by surviving in office for more than six months. Persuaded that it finally had a solid foundation upon which to build, the administration in early 1966 decided to make clear its commitment and press Ky to reform his government. At a hastily arranged "summit" meeting in Honolulu, Johnson publicly embraced a somewhat embarrassed Ky, symbolizing the new commitment, and secured his agreement to a sweeping program of reform. The president left no doubt of the importance he attached to the pledges. The Honolulu communiqué was a "kind of bible," he declared. He would not be content with promises or "high-sounding words" but must have "coonskins on the wall."[22]

No sooner had Ky returned to Saigon than he faced a stiff internal challenge. Quiescent for nearly a year, the Buddhists viewed

[20]Harold Johnson oral history interview, U.S. Army Military History Institute, Carlisle Barracks, Pa.
[21]Malcolm W. Browne, *The New Face of War* (Indianapolis, Ind., 1968), p. ix.
[22]Transcript of Johnson briefing, February 8, 1966, Johnson Papers, National Security File, International Meetings File: Honolulu, Box 2.

Honolulu as a clear sign that Ky, with American support, would attempt to maintain absolute power, and again they took to the streets. As in 1963, the demonstrations began in Hue and were led by Buddhist monks, but they quickly spread to Saigon and drew together the many groups dissatisfied with the regime: students, labor unions, Catholics, and even factions within the army. The demonstrations took on an increasingly anti-American tone. Signs reading "END FOREIGN DOMINATION OF OUR COUNTRY" appeared in Hue and Da Nang. An angry mob burned the U.S. consulate in Hue, and fire fighters refused to extinguish the blaze.

The Buddhist crisis exposed the fragility of the Saigon government and the weakness of the U.S. position in Vietnam. The existence of a virtual civil war within an insurrection dampened the hopes that had begun to develop for Ky's government. The protesters advocated the holding of elections and the restoration of civilian government, goals to which the United States could hardly take exception. The State Department nevertheless feared that giving in to the Buddhists would "take us more rapidly than we had envisaged down a road with many pitfalls," and Rusk instructed the embassy to persuade moderate Buddhist leaders to drop their "unrealistic demands" because of the "grave danger of simply handing the country over to the Viet Cong."[23]

The conflict in I Corps, the northern military section of South Vietnam, almost forced a reassessment of U.S. policy. Although they attempted to remain neutral, the U.S. Marines stationed in the area came under fire several times from ARVN units sympathetic to the Buddhists and from those loyal to Ky, and on occasion the troops had to threaten to use force to defend themselves against one side or the other. The Marines naturally expressed "bitterness and disgust" that while they were putting their lives on the line to save South Vietnam, the South Vietnamese were fighting each other. When American "mediation" failed and the crisis worsened, some U.S. officials proposed abandoning Ky to save South Vietnam, and others began to seriously consider plans for a face-saving American withdrawal from South Vietnam. Acting without approval from Washington, the embattled Ky eventually solved the American dilemma and saved his own skin by dispatching 1,000

[23]Rusk to Embassy Saigon, March 16, 1966, Johnson Papers, National Security File, Country File: Vietnam, Box 28; Rusk to Embassy Saigon, April 5, 1966, Johnson Papers, National Security File, Country File: Vietnam, Box 29.

South Vietnamese marines to Da Nang to suppress the rebellion. The Buddhists gave way in the face of superior force and withdrew in sullen protest. Although annoyed by Ky's independence, the administration was relieved and more than satisfied with the outcome. The president "categorically thrust aside the withdrawal option," William Bundy recalled, and "we all relaxed."[24]

In the aftermath of the Buddhist crisis, Americans and Vietnamese struggled to live up to the lofty promises of Honolulu. From Washington's standpoint, pacification was a top-priority item. Improving the South Vietnamese standard of living was the one area of the war that struck a responsive chord in Johnson. A populist reformer at heart, he identified with the people of South Vietnam and deeply sympathized with their presumed desire for political freedom and economic progress. Like most of his colleagues, he believed it was necessary to win the support of the people to defeat the NLF, and he felt a keen personal need to endow the war with some higher purpose. He could wax eloquent about such topics as inoculation programs, educational reform, and the use of American expertise to teach the Vietnamese to raise larger hogs and grow more sweet potatoes. "Dammit," he exploded on one occasion, "we need to exhibit more compassion for these Vietnamese plain people. . . . We've got to see that the South Vietnamese government wins the battle . . . of crops and hearts and caring."[25] Under intensive prodding from Washington, the Americans and South Vietnamese devised an ambitious Revolutionary Development (RD) program, consciously imitative of NLF techniques, in which teams of fifty-nine people trained in propaganda and social services would go into the villages, live with the people, and carry out hundreds of tasks to build popular support for the government and undermine the guerrillas.

Revolutionary Development encountered many of the problems that had frustrated earlier pacification programs. The creaking Saigon bureaucracy and poor coordination between Americans and Vietnamese hampered administration of the plan. It was impossible to recruit sufficient participants in a country short of personnel, and less than half the cadres needed actually went into training. Candidates

[24]William Bundy oral history interview, Johnson Papers; Robert Topmiller, "Confrontation in Danang: III MAF and the Buddhist Struggle Movement in South Vietnam, 1966," *Journal of American–East Asian Relations* 6 (Summer–Fall 1997): 207–234.
[25]Jack Valenti, *A Very Human President* (New York, 1973), p. 133; Lady Bird Johnson, *A White House Diary* (New York, 1970), pp. 370–371.

were trained on a mass-production basis for a mere three months and in most cases were inadequately prepared for the formidable task that lay ahead. Once in the field, the RD teams were frustrated by local officials who regarded them as a threat. Funds promised for many projects never reached their destination. Having seen so many other programs come and go, the villagers greeted the arrivals with a mixture of apathy and caution. Because of the chronic personnel shortage, many cadres were often shifted to new areas before their work was completed, and any gains were quickly erased. Good performance by RD teams was sometimes undercut by the behavior of ARVN units that extorted taxes and fees from the villagers and stole chickens and pigs. When asked what would most help pacification in his area, one U.S. adviser responded: "Get the 22nd [ARVN] Division out of the province."[26]

The fundamental problem was the absence of security. The U.S. military was preoccupied with the shooting war and gave little attention to what became known as "the other war" (the term itself suggested the absence of coordination between pacification and military operations). In most cases the ARVN was incapable of providing security, and in some areas it was part of the problem. Sometimes, RD teams would make progress, only to have it nullified when American aircraft bombed their villages. Cadres were frequently sent into insecure areas, where they were harassed and terrorized by guerrillas. Many fled. Those who stayed and worked effectively with the people were often found with their throats slit. During a seven-month period in 1966, 3,015 RD personnel were murdered or kidnapped.[27]

Under these circumstances, pacification achieved little. Roads were repaired, schools built, and village elections held, but even on the basis of the highly inaccurate methods used to measure progress, the number of "pacified" villages increased by a mere 5 percent in the first year. To revive the program, Johnson placed it under the immediate authority of the U.S. military command in the spring of 1967, and Westmoreland persuaded a reluctant ARVN to commit the bulk of its forces to rural security. These changes would eventually

[26]Daniel Ellsberg memorandum, March 30, 1966, John P. Vann Papers, U.S. Army Military History Institute, Carlisle Barracks, Pa.

[27]Douglas A. Blaufarb, *The Counterinsurgency Era: U.S. Doctrines and Performance* (New York, 1977), pp. 205–242, contains a full discussion of the Revolutionary Development program.

produce better results, but at a time when the vast American military effort had attained nothing better than a stalemate, the failure of pacification was especially discouraging.

In at least one area, the two nations did live up to the goals of the Honolulu communiqué: a new constitution was drafted and national elections were held. The Americans did not presume that the export of democracy would solve South Vietnam's problems. On the contrary, many agreed with Lodge (who had returned for a second tour as ambassador) that the establishment of real democracy in a land with no Western democratic traditions was "clearly an impossible task," and some feared that a genuinely open political process would lead to chaos. The Americans nevertheless felt that a new constitution and elections would give South Vietnam a better image and might, in Lodge's words, "substitute a certain legitimacy for the hurly-burly of unending coups."[28]

The Ky regime dutifully followed American advice, but in a way that ensured its own perpetuation. Elections for a constituent assembly were so tightly circumscribed that the Buddhists boycotted them. The assembly met in early 1967 and turned out a polished document, based on American and French models and including a Bill of Rights. The government nevertheless insisted on a strong executive and on provisions permitting the president to assume near-dictatorial powers in an emergency, which could be declared at his discretion. Those branded Communists or "neutralist sympathizers" were disqualified from office. The president was to be elected by a plurality, ensuring that opposition candidates did not band together in a runoff.

Throughout the preelection maneuvering, the United States quietly but firmly supported the government's efforts to remain in power. The State Department expressed concern about the wholesale disqualification of opposition candidates, but Lodge prevailed with his argument that the "GVN [Government of Vietnam] should not be discouraged from taking moderate measures to prevent [the] elections from being used as a vehicle for a Communist takeover."[29] The most serious challenge came from bitter internal squabbling, which was resolved only under intense pressure from the United

[28]Henry Cabot Lodge, Jr., *The Storm Has Many Eyes* (New York, 1973), p. 215.
[29]U.S. Congress, Senate Subcommittee on Public Buildings and Grounds, *The Pentagon Papers (The Senator Gravel Edition)* (4 vols., Boston, 1971), 2:384.

States and after a long meeting, filled with histrionics, in which Ky tearfully gave way and agreed to run for the vice presidency on a ticket headed by General Thieu.

The September 1967 elections were neither as corrupt as critics charged nor as pure as Johnson claimed. The regime conducted them under conditions that made defeat unlikely, and there was evidence of considerable last-minute fraud. But the large turnout and the fact that elections had been held in the midst of war were cited by Americans as evidence of growing political maturity. What stands out in retrospect is the narrowness of the government's victory. The Thieu-Ky ticket won 35 percent of the vote, but Truong Dinh Dzu, an unknown lawyer who had run on a platform of negotiations with the NLF, won 17 percent. The elections may have provided the regime with a measure of respectability, but they also underscored its continued weakness. In a nation where political authority derived from the will of heaven and popular support was an obligation, the narrowness of the victory could only appear ludicrous. Many Vietnamese cynically regarded the entire process as "an American-directed performance with a Vietnamese cast."[30]

THE IMPACT OF AMERICANIZATION

While the United States and South Vietnam struggled to resolve old problems, Americanization of the war created new and equally formidable problems. Those Americans who visited South Vietnam for the first time were stunned by the sheer enormity of the U.S. effort, a huge, sprawling, many-faceted military-civilian apparatus, generally uncoordinated, in which all too frequently the various components worked against rather than in support of each other. By late 1967, the United States had almost a half million troops in Vietnam. The civilian side of the war also expanded to elephantine proportions, with an aid program of $625 million, which was one-fourth of the economic assistance given to the entire world, and 6,500 American civilians working in various capacities. Presidential speechwriter Harry McPherson spoke of the "colossal size of our effort." White House aide John Roche described the American presence as "just unbelievable," the "Holy Roman Empire going to

[30]Shaplen, *Road from War*, p. 151.

war," and observed sarcastically that cutting its size by two-thirds might increase its efficiency by 50 percent.[31]

One of the most serious—and most tragic—problems caused by Americanization of the war was the refugee problem. The expansion of American and enemy military operations drove an estimated four million South Vietnamese, roughly 25 percent of the population, from their native villages. Some drifted into the already teeming cities; others were herded into shabby refugee camps. The United States furnished the government with some $30 million a year for the care of the refugees, but much of the money never reached them. Resettlement programs were initiated from time to time, but the problem was so complex that it would have taxed the ingenuity of the most imaginative officials. In any event, nothing could have compensated the refugees for the loss of their homes and lands. A large portion of South Vietnam's population was left rootless and hostile, and the refugee camps became fertile breeding grounds for insurgent fifth columns.

The sudden infusion of a half million American troops, hundreds of civilian advisers, and billions of dollars had a profoundly disruptive effect on a weak and divided nation. The buildup was so rapid and so vast that it threatened to overwhelm South Vietnam. Saigon's ports were congested with ships and goods, and vessels awaiting unloading were backed up far out to sea. The city itself became a "thorough-going boom town," Shaplen remarked, its streets clogged with traffic, its restaurants "bursting with boisterous soldiers," its bars as "crowded as New York subway cars in the rush hour."[32] Signs of the American presence appeared everywhere. Vietnamese children wore Batman T-shirts. Long strips of seedy bars and brothels sprang up overnight around base areas—the one at Bien Hoa came to be known as Tijuana East. In a remote village near Da Nang, Caputo encountered houses made of discarded beer cans: "red and white Budweiser, gold Miller, cream and brown Schlitz, blue and gold Hamm's from the land of sky-blue waters."[33]

American spending had a devastating effect on the vulnerable South Vietnamese economy. Prices increased by as much as 170 percent during the first two years of the buildup. The United States

---

[31]Herring, *LBJ and Vietnam*, pp. 20–21.
[32]Shaplen, *Road from War*, pp. 20–21.
[33]Caputo, *Rumor of War*, p. 107.

eventually controlled the rate of inflation by paying its own soldiers in scrip and by flooding the country with consumer goods, but the corrective measures themselves had harmful side effects. Instead of using American aid to promote economic development, South Vietnamese importers bought watches, transistor radios, and motorbikes to sell to people employed by the United States. The vast influx of American goods destroyed South Vietnam's few native industries and made the economy even more dependent on continued outside aid. By 1967, much of the urban population was employed providing services for the Americans.

In the bonanza atmosphere, crime and corruption flourished. Corruption was not new to South Vietnam or unusual in a nation at war, but by 1966 it operated on an incredible scale. Government officials rented land to the United States at inflated prices; required bribes for driver's licenses, passports, visas, and work permits; extorted kickbacks for contracts to build and service facilities; and took part in the illicit importation of opium. The black market in scrip and dollars became a major enterprise. Import licenses for items in the commercial import program became licenses to steal. With the connivance of Americans, garbage trucks left PXs loaded with stolen goods to be sold on the black market. On Saigon's PX Alley, an open-air market covering two city blocks and made up of more than 100 stalls, purchasers could buy everything from hand grenades to Scotch whiskey at markups as high as 300 percent. Americans and Vietnamese reaped handsome profits from the illegal exchange of currencies. International swindlers and "monetary camp followers" quickly got into the act, and the currency-manipulation racket developed into a "massive financial international network" extending from Saigon to Wall Street, with connections to Swiss banks and Arab sheikhdoms. The pervasive corruption undermined the U.S. aid program and severely handicapped efforts to stabilize the economy of South Vietnam.[34]

American officials perceived the problem, but they could not find solutions. Ky candidly admitted that "most of the generals are corrupt. Most of the senior officials in the provinces are corrupt." But, he would add calmly, "corruption exists everywhere, and peo-

[34]*New York Times,* November 16, 1966; Abraham Ribicoff to Robert McLellan, January 15, 1969, and memorandum, January 15, 1970, Abraham Ribicoff Papers, Library of Congress, Washington, D.C., Box 432.

ple can live with some of it. You live with it in Chicago and New York."[35] The embassy pressed the government to remove officials known to be corrupt, but with little result. "You fight like hell to get someone removed and most times you fail and you just make it worse," a frustrated American explained to journalist David Halberstam. "And then on occasions you win, why hell, they give you someone just as bad."[36] The United States found to its chagrin that as its commitment increased, its leverage diminished. Concern with corruption and inefficiency was always balanced by fear that tough action might alienate the government or bring about its collapse. Lodge and Westmoreland were inclined to accept the situation and deal with other problems.

Tensions between Americans and South Vietnamese increased as the American presence grew. The two peoples approached each other with colossal ignorance. "My time in Vietnam is the memory of ignorance," one GI later conceded. "I didn't know the language. I knew nothing about the village community. I knew nothing about the aims of the people—whether they were for the war or against it."[37] Indeed, for many Americans, the elementary task of distinguishing friend from foe became a sometimes impossible challenge. "What we need is some . . . kind of litmus paper that turns red when it's near a communist," one U.S. officer, half seriously, half jokingly, told journalist Malcolm Browne.[38] The Vietnamese found American culture incomprehensible, and they knew little more about American history than some clichés about the Marshall Plan and anticommunism.

Although fighting in a common cause, the two peoples grew increasingly suspicious and resentful of each other. Because of chronic security leaks, the United States kept Vietnamese off its major bases, and NLF infiltration of the ARVN's top ranks compelled U.S. officers to keep from their Vietnamese counterparts the details of major military operations. The more the Americans assumed the burden of the fighting, the more they demeaned the martial abilities of their ally. "I wish the southern members of the clan would display the

[35]Harry McPherson to Johnson, June 13, 1967, Johnson Papers, McPherson File, Box 29.

[36]David Halberstam, "Return to Vietnam," *Harpers* 235 (December 1967): 52.

[37]Quoted in Clark Dougan and Stephen Weiss, *The American Experience in Vietnam* (New York, 1988), p. 62.

[38]Browne, *New Face of War,* p. 46.

fighting qualities of their northern brethren," a senior U.S. officer observed with obvious scorn.[39] The ARVN indeed became an object of ridicule, its mode of attack best depicted, according to a standard American joke, by the statue of a seated soldier in the National Military Cemetery. Vietnamese slowness to accept American methods exasperated U.S. advisers. "I am sure that if Saigon were left to fend for itself . . . in 20 years this place would be all rice paddies again," one American acidly observed.[40] The seeming indifference of many Vietnamese, while Americans were dying in the field, provoked growing resentment and hatred. The unerring ability of the villagers to avoid mines and booby traps that killed and maimed GIs led to charges of collusion with the enemy.

The Vietnamese attitude toward the foreigner was at best ambivalent. The Vietnamese undoubtedly appreciated American generosity, but they came to resent American ways of doing things. They complained that American soldiers "acted despicably" toward the villagers, tearing up roads and endangering the lives of noncombatants by reckless handling of vehicles and firearms. An ARVN major protested that Americans trusted only those Vietnamese who accepted without question their way of doing things and that they doled out their aid "in the same way as that given to beggars."[41] The Vietnamese recognized their need for U.S. help, and some were probably quite content to let the United States assume complete responsibility for the war. On the other hand, many Vietnamese resented the domineering manner of the Americans and came to consider the U.S. "occupation" a "demoralizing scourge," even theorizing that "if we could only get rid of the Americans, then we could worry about the Viet Cong." Thoughtful Vietnamese recognized that Americans were not "colonialists," Shaplen observed. But, he added, "there has evolved here a colonial ambiance that can sometimes be worse than colonialism itself."[42]

[39]General A. S. Collins to Edward F. Smith, November 15, 1966, A. S. Collins Papers, U.S. Army Military History Institute, Carlisle Barracks, Pa.

[40]Curtis Herrick diary, January 13, 1965, Curtis Herrick Papers, U.S. Army Military History Institute, Carlisle Barracks, Pa.

[41]Weekly Psyops Field Operation Report, December 2, 1967, Vann Papers, U.S. Army Military History Institute, Carlisle Barracks, Pa.

[42]Shaplen, Road from War, p. 154.

Progress in the critical area of nation building was thus even more limited than on the battlefield. To be sure, the government survived, and after the chronic instability of the Khanh era, that in itself appeared evidence of progress. Survival was primarily a result of the formidable American military presence, however, and did not reflect increased popular support or intrinsic strength. Returning to South Vietnam after an absence of several years, Halberstam was haunted by a sense of déjà vu. There were new faces, new programs, and an abundance of resources, and the Americans continued to speak optimistically. But the old problems persisted, and the "new" solutions appeared little more than recycled versions of old ones. "What finally struck me," he concluded, "was how little had really changed here."[43]

WAGING PEACE

The steady expansion of the war spurred strong international and domestic pressures for negotiations, but the military stalemate produced an equally firm diplomatic impasse. American officials later tallied as many as 2,000 attempts to initiate peace talks between 1965 and 1967. Neither side could afford to appear indifferent to such efforts, but neither was willing to make the concessions necessary to bring about negotiations. Although the North Vietnamese attempted to exploit the various peace initiatives for propaganda advantage, they counted on the American people to tire of the war, and they remained certain that they could achieve their goals if they persisted. Hanoi adamantly refused to negotiate without first securing major concessions from the United States. Johnson and his advisers could not ignore the various proposals for negotiations, but they doubted that anything would come of them and suspected, not without reason, that Hanoi was expressing interest merely to get the bombing stopped. Despite any firm evidence of results, the president remained confident at least until 1967 that North Vietnam would eventually bend to American pressure, and he feared that a conciliatory stance would undercut his strategy. To defuse international and domestic criticism, Johnson repeatedly insisted that he was ready to negotiate, but he refused to make the

[43]Halberstam, "Return to Vietnam," p. 50.

concessions Hanoi demanded. As each side invested more in the struggle, the likelihood of serious negotiations diminished.[44]

The positions of the two sides left little room for compromise. The North Vietnamese denounced American involvement in Vietnam as a blatant violation of the Geneva Accords, and as a precondition for negotiations, their Four Points required that the United States withdraw its troops, dismantle its bases, and stop all acts of war against their country. The internal affairs of South Vietnam must be resolved by the South Vietnamese themselves "in accordance with the program of the National Liberation Front." North Vietnam was apparently flexible in regard to the timing and mechanism for political change in the south, but on the fundamental issues it was adamant. The "puppet" Saigon regime must be replaced by a government representative of the "people" in which the front would play a prominent role. Hanoi made clear, moreover, that the "unity of our country is no more a matter for negotiations than our independence."[45]

The United States formally set forth its position in early 1966. "We put everything into the basket but the surrender of South Vietnam," Secretary of State Dean Rusk later claimed, but in fact the administration's "Fourteen Points" offered few concessions.[46] The United States indicated that it was willing to stop the bombing, but only after Hanoi took reciprocal steps of de-escalation. It would withdraw its troops from the south, but only after a satisfactory political settlement had been reached. The administration accepted the principle that the future of South Vietnam must be worked out by the South Vietnamese. At the same time, it made clear that it would not admit the NLF to the government—that would be like "putting the fox in a chicken coop," Vice President Hubert H. Humphrey asserted.[47] The Fourteen Points conceded merely that the views of the NLF "would have no difficulty being represented," and this only after Hanoi had "ceased its aggression." Beneath

[44]Allan E. Goodman, *The Lost Peace: America's Search for a Negotiated Settlement of the Vietnam War* (Stanford, Calif., 1978), pp. 23–60, contains a detailed and generally persuasive account of the 1965–1967 peace initiatives.
[45]Quoted in Gareth Porter, *A Peace Denied: The United States, Vietnam, and the Paris Agreements* (Bloomington, Ind., 1975), p. 29.
[46]Quoted in Chester Cooper, *The Lost Crusade: America in Vietnam* (New York, 1970), p. 294.
[47]Quoted in Henry Graff, *The Tuesday Cabinet* (Englewood Cliffs, N.J., 1970), p. 67.

these ambiguous words rested a firm determination to maintain an independent, non-Communist South Vietnam.

To silence domestic and international critics and test the diplomatic winds in Hanoi, the administration modified its position a bit in late 1966. Throughout the summer and fall, various third parties struggled to find a common ground for negotiations, and after a series of frenzied trips back and forth between Hanoi and Saigon, the Polish diplomat Januscz Lewandowski drafted a ten-point plan for settlement of the conflict. Johnson and his advisers were highly skeptical of the peace moves, which they dismissed as "Nobel Prize fever." They felt that the Lewandowski draft was vague on many critical points and that it gave away too much. The administration could not afford to appear intransigent, however, and it eventually accepted Lewandowski's proposals as a basis for negotiations with the qualification that "several specific points are subject to important differences of interpretation." Responding to Lewandowski's entreaties, the United States also advanced a two-track proposal to provide a face-saving way around Hanoi's opposition to mutual de-escalation. The United States would stop the air strikes in return for confidential assurance that North Vietnam would cease infiltration into key areas of South Vietnam within a reasonable period. Once Hanoi had acted, the United States would freeze its combat forces at existing levels and peace talks could begin.[48]

Code-named MARIGOLD, the Polish initiative ended in fiasco. A North Vietnamese diplomat has recently claimed to have been in Warsaw, awaiting a visit from the U.S. ambassador, but the extent to which North Vietnam had committed itself to the ten-point plan and was willing to compromise on the basic issues remains unclear. In any case, the initiative aborted. Several days before the scheduled opening of the talks, U.S. aircraft struck railroad yards within five miles of the center of Hanoi, causing heavy damage to residential areas and numerous civilian casualties. Frequently explained as the product of poor coordination within the American government—the right hand did not know what the left was doing—the bombing resulted from a conscious decision. Lodge, McNamara, and Undersecretary of State Nicholas Katzenbach all urged Johnson to refrain

[48]The most recent account is James G. Hershberg, *Who Murdered "Marigold"? New Evidence on the Mysterious Failure of Poland's Secret Initiative to Start U.S.–North Vietnamese Peace Talks, 1966.* (Washington, D.C., 2000).

from bombing near Hanoi during the most delicate stage of Lewandowski's diplomacy, but the president would have none of it. Like many other U.S. officials, he suspected that the entire arrangement was "phony," and he insisted that a bombing halt had not been a precondition for the Warsaw talks. Johnson's assessment of North Vietnamese intentions may have been correct, but the December bombings, which came after a long lull forced by bad weather, must have appeared to Hanoi to be a major escalation of the air war timed to coincide with the peace moves. The North Vietnamese had always insisted that they would not negotiate under threat and pressure, and they quickly broke off the contact. The Poles felt betrayed, and MARIGOLD withered.

In response to international and, in the case of the United States, domestic pressures, each side in 1967 inched cautiously away from the rigid positions assumed earlier. North Vietnam no longer insisted on acceptance of its Four Points, including a complete American military withdrawal, as a precondition for negotiations, demanding only that the bombing be ended without condition. Hanoi also relaxed its terms for a settlement, indicating, among other points, that reunification could take place over a long period of time. The United States retreated from its original position that North Vietnam must withdraw its forces from the south in return for cessation of the bombing, insisting merely that further infiltration must be stopped. Despite these concessions, the two nations remained far apart on the means of getting negotiations started. And although their bargaining positions had changed slightly, they had not abandoned their basic goals. Each had met with frustration and had incurred heavy losses on the battlefield, but each still retained hope that it could force the other to accept its terms. The two sides thus remained unwilling to compromise on the central issue—the future of South Vietnam. The story of the 1965–1967 peace initiatives, one scholar has concluded, marks "one of the most fruitless chapters in U.S. diplomacy."[49]

THE WAR AT HOME

By mid-1967, Johnson was snared in a trap he had unknowingly set for himself. His hopes of a quick and relatively painless victory had

[49]Goodman, *Lost Peace,* p. 24.

been frustrated. He was desperately anxious to end the war, but he had been unable to do so by force, and in the absence of a clear-cut military advantage or a stronger political position in South Vietnam, he would not do so by negotiation.

As the conflict increased in cost, moreover, he found himself caught in the midst of an increasingly angry and divisive debate, a veritable civil war that by 1967 seemed capable of wrecking his presidency and tearing the country apart. Dissent in wartime is a firmly established American tradition, of course, but Vietnam aroused more widespread and passionate opposition than any other U.S. war. It occurred in a time of social upheaval, when Americans were questioning their values and institutions as at few other periods in their history. It occurred in a time of generational strife. It occurred when the verities of the Cold War were coming into question. The war thus divided Americans as nothing since the debate on slavery a century earlier. It divided businesses, churches and campuses, neighbors and families. It set class against class. As the debate intensified, civilities were increasingly cast aside. Advocates of each side tried to shout the other down, denying basic rights of free speech. Argument was often accompanied by verbal abuse and even physical violence.

At one extreme were the hawks, largely right-wing Republicans and conservative Democrats, who viewed the conflict in Vietnam as an essential element in the global struggle with communism. Should the United States not hold the line, they argued, the Communists would be encouraged to further aggression, allies and neutrals would succumb to Communist pressures, and the United States would be left alone to face a powerful and merciless enemy. Strong nationalists who were certain of America's invincibility and deeply frustrated by the stalemate in Vietnam, the hawks viewed antiwar protest as treason, denounced the restraints imposed on the military, and demanded that the administration do what was necessary to attain victory. "Win or get out," Representative Mendel Rivers, a Democrat from South Carolina, advised President Johnson in early 1966.[50]

At the other extreme were the doves, a vast, sprawling, extremely heterogeneous and fractious group who opposed the war with increasing bitterness and force. The "movement" grew almost

---

[50]Notes on meeting with congressional leadership, January 25, 1966, Johnson Papers, Meeting Notes File, Box 1.

in proportion to the escalation of the conflict. It included such diverse individuals as the pediatrician Dr. Benjamin Spock, heavyweight boxing champion Muhammad Ali, actress Jane Fonda, author Norman Mailer, old-line pacifists such as A. J. Muste and new radicals such as Tom Hayden, civil rights leader Dr. Martin Luther King, Jr., and conservative Arkansas Senator J. William Fulbright. The doves constituted only a small percentage of the population, but they were an unusually visible and articulate group. Their attack on American foreign policy was vicious and unrelenting. In time, their movement became inextricably linked with the cultural revolution that swept the United States in the late 1960s and challenged the most basic of American values and institutions, leaving divisions that would last into the next century.

College students comprised the shock troops of the movement. Inspired by John Kennedy's idealism and appeals to service, schooled in the civil rights movement, and increasingly outraged by the war and the draft, a small but vocal and highly articulate group of students took the lead in 1965 in openly protesting the war. Brash, self-confident, often self-righteous, they proved skillful propagandists. They fused pop music with protest and in doing so "helped fix the minds of a generation." Only a minority of American college students opposed the war and an even smaller minority actively protested it. Spearheaded by organizations such as Students for a Democratic Society, however, these few students initiated and set the tone for the early antiwar protests, catching the government off guard and leaving it unsure how to respond. They raised public consciousness about the war. Through what has been called "offspring-lobbying," they exerted some influence on their elders. They continued to draw attention even as other groups assumed leadership of the movement.[51]

Although it defies precise categorization, the antiwar movement tended to group ideologically along three principal lines.[52] For pacifists such as Muste, who opposed all wars as immoral, Vietnam was but another phase of a lifelong crusade. For the burgeon-

---

[51]Rhodri Jeffreys-Jones, *Peace Now! American Society and the Ending of the Vietnam War* (New Haven, Conn., 1999), pp. 43–92.
[52]See Charles DeBenedetti with Charles Chatfield, *An American Ordeal: The Antiwar Movement of the Vietnam Era* (Syracuse, N.Y., 1990), and David W. Levy, *The Debate over Vietnam* (Baltimore, 1991), pp. 171–178.

ing radical movement of the 1960s, opposition to the war extended beyond questions of morality. Spawned by the civil rights movement, drawing its largest following among upper-middle-class youth on elite college campuses, the New Left joined older leftist organizations in viewing the war as a classic example of the way the American ruling class exploited helpless people to sustain a decadent capitalist system.[53]

Antiwar liberals far exceeded in numbers the pacifists and radicals. Although they did not generally question "the system," they increasingly challenged the war on legal, moral, and practical grounds. Liberals charged that U.S. escalation in Vietnam violated the 1954 Geneva Accords, the United Nations Charter, and the Constitution of the United States. Many liberal internationalists who had supported World War II, Korea, and the Cold War found Vietnam morally repugnant. By backing a corrupt, authoritarian government, they contended, the United States was betraying its own principles. The use of weapons such as cluster bombs, herbicides, and napalm violated basic standards of human behavior, and in the absence of any direct threat to American security, the devastation wreaked on North and South Vietnam was indefensible.

Many more liberals questioned the war on practical grounds. It was essentially an internal struggle among Vietnamese, they argued, whose connection with the Cold War was at best indirect. Liberals questioned the validity of the domino theory, especially after the Indonesian army in 1965 threw out the erratic Sukarno and crushed the Indonesian Communist party. They agreed that Vietnam was of no more than marginal significance to the security of the United States. Indeed, they insisted, the huge investment there was diverting attention from more urgent problems at home and abroad, damaging America's relations with its allies, and inhibiting the development of a more constructive relationship with the Soviet Union. The liberal critique quickly broadened into an indictment of American "globalism." The United States had fallen victim to the "arrogance of power," Fulbright claimed, and was showing "signs of that fatal presumption, that over-extension of power and mission, which brought ruin to ancient Athens, to Napoleonic France and to Nazi Germany."[54]

[53]Irwin Unger, *The Movement* (New York, 1974), pp. 35–93.
[54]Quoted in Thomas Powers, *Vietnam: The War at Home* (Boston, 1984), p. 118.

The various groups that made up the movement disagreed sharply on goals and methods. For some pacifists and liberals, terminating the war was an end in itself; for radicals, it was a means to the ultimate end—the overthrow of American capitalism. Many New Left radicals indeed feared that a premature end to the war might sap the revolutionary spirit and hinder achievement of their principal goal. Most liberals stopped short of advocating withdrawal from Vietnam, much less domestic revolution, proposing merely an end to the bombing, gradual de-escalation, and negotiations. Disagreement on methods was even sharper. Liberals generally preferred nonviolent protest and political action within the system and sought to exclude Communists from demonstrations. Radicals and some pacifists increasingly pressed for a shift from protest to resistance. Some openly advocated the use of violence to bring down a system that was itself violent.

Opposition to the war took many different forms. Fulbright conducted a series of nationally televised hearings, bringing before the viewing public such critics of administration policies as General James Gavin and diplomat George F. Kennan, the father of the containment policy. There were hundreds of acts of individual defiance. The folk singer Joan Baez refused to pay that portion of her income tax that went to the defense budget. Muhammad Ali declared himself a conscientious objector and refused induction orders. Three Army enlisted men—the Fort Hood Three—challenged the constitutionality of the conflict by refusing to fight in what they labeled an "unjust, immoral, and illegal war." Army Captain Howard Levy used the doctrine of individual responsibility set forth in the Nuremberg war crimes trials to justify his refusal to train medical teams for combat in Vietnam. Thousands of young Americans exploited legal loopholes, even mutilated themselves, to evade the draft; an estimated 30,000 fled to Canada, and some served jail sentences rather than go to Vietnam. Seven Americans adopted the method of protest of South Vietnam's Buddhists, publicly immolating themselves. Such was the case of the young Quaker Norman Morrison directly below McNamara's Pentagon office window in November 1965!

Antiwar rallies and demonstrations drew larger crowds in 1966 and 1967, and the participants became more outspoken in their opposition. Protesters marched daily around the White

House chanting "Hey, hey, LBJ, how many kids have you killed today?" and "Ho, Ho, Ho Chi Minh, NLF is going to win." Antiwar forces attempted lie-ins in front of troop trains, collected blood for the NLF, and tried to disrupt the work of draft boards, Army recruiters, and the Dow Chemical Company, producer of the napalm used in Vietnam.

The most dramatic act of protest came on October 21, 1967, with the March on the Pentagon, the culmination of Stop the Draft Week. A diverse group estimated at 100,000 including colorfully arrayed hippies and intellectuals such as Mailer, gathered at the Lincoln Memorial for songs of protest by performers such as Peter, Paul, and Mary and Phil Ochs and speeches proclaiming the beginning of "active resistance." As many as 35,000 protesters subsequently crossed the Potomac and advanced on the Pentagon. The demonstrators were unable to levitate the "nerve center of American imperialism" and exorcise its evil spirits, as radical Abbie Hoffman had promised, but a small group conducted a sit-in. Some carried NLF flags, others smoked marijuana, and a few put flowers in the barrels of the rifles of soldiers guarding the building. Soldiers were challenged to leave their posts. The demonstration ended that evening in violence when federal marshals moved in with clubs and tear gas and arrested nearly 700 demonstrators.[55]

The impact of the antiwar protests remains one of the most controversial issues raised by the war. The obvious manifestations of dissent in the United States undoubtedly encouraged Hanoi to hold out for victory, although there is nothing to suggest that the North Vietnamese would have been more compromising in the absence of the protests. Antiwar protest did not turn the American people against the war, as some critics have argued. The effectiveness of the movement was limited by the divisions within its own ranks. Public opinion polls made abundantly clear, moreover, that a majority of Americans found the antiwar movement, particularly its radical and hippie elements, more obnoxious than the war itself. In a perverse sort of way, the protest may even have strengthened support for a war that was not in itself popular. The impact of the movement was much

[55]Terry H. Anderson, *The Movement and the Sixties: Protest in America from Greensboro to Wounded Knee* (New York, 1995), pp. 178–179.

March on the Pentagon
This picture of an antiwar protestor placing a flower in the barrel of the
rifle of a soldier guarding the Pentagon was taken during the March on the
Pentagon in October, 1967, the largest antiwar demonstration to that time.
Bernie Boston Photography

more limited and subtle. It forced Vietnam into the public consciousness and challenged the rationale of the war and indeed of
a generation of Cold War foreign policies. It exposed error and
self-deception in the government's claims, encouraging distrust
of political authority. It limited Johnson's military options and
may have headed off any tendency toward more drastic escalation. Perhaps most important, the disturbances and divisions set
off by the antiwar movement caused fatigue and anxiety among
the policy makers and the public, thus eventually encouraging efforts to find a way out of the war.[56]

The majority of Americans rejected both the hawk and dove
positions, but as the war dragged on and the debate became more
divisive, public concern increased significantly. Expansion of the

[56]DeBenedetti and Chatfield, *American Ordeal,* pp. 387–408; Melvin Small, *Johnson,
Nixon, and the Doves* (New Brunswick, N.J., 1988), pp. 226–234. For a contrary view
see Adam Garfinkle's *Telltale Hearts: The Origins and Impact of the Vietnam Antiwar
Movement* (New York, 1995).

war in 1965 was followed by a surge of popular support—the usual rally-round-the-flag phenomenon. But the failure of escalation to produce any discernible progress and indications that more troops and higher taxes would be required to sustain a prolonged and perhaps inconclusive war combined to produce growing frustration and impatience.[57] If any bird symbolized the public disenchantment with Vietnam, opinion analyst Samuel Lubell observed, it was the albatross, with many Americans sharing a "fervent desire to shake free of an unwanted burden." The public mood was probably best expressed by a woman who told Lubell: "I want to get out but I don't want to give up."[58]

Support for the war dropped sharply during 1967. By the summer of that year, draft calls exceeded 30,000 per month, and more than 13,000 Americans had died in Vietnam. In early August, the president recommended a 10 percent surtax to cover the steadily increasing costs of the war. Polls taken shortly after indicated that for the first time a majority of Americans felt the United States had erred in intervening in Vietnam, and a substantial majority concluded that despite a growing investment, the United States was not "doing any better." Public approval of Johnson's handling of the war plummeted to 28 percent by October.

African Americans opposed the war in numbers much larger than the general population. At first supportive of U.S. involvement, they grew increasingly and understandably dubious about fighting for freedom in Vietnam when they did not have full freedom at home. Many came to view the war as a racial conflict whose goal was to oppress another people of color. They felt directly the mounting economic consequences of the war and, despite administration disclaimers, perceived that it was draining funds from government programs that benefited them. "The Great Society has been shot down on the battlefields of Vietnam," King lamented in 1967. African Americans correctly saw themselves as the primary victims of an inequitable selective service system that drafted their sons in disproportionate numbers

[57]Sidney Verba et al., "Public Opinion and the War in Vietnam," *American Political Science Review* 61 (June 1967): 317–333; John E. Mueller, "Trends in Popular Support for the Wars in Korea and Vietnam," ibid., 65 (June 1971): 358–375; and Peter W. Sperlich and William L. Lunch, "American Public Opinion and the War in Vietnam," *Western Political Quarterly* 32 (March 1979): 21–44.

[58]Samuel Lubell, *The Hidden Crisis in American Politics* (New York, 1971), pp. 254–260.

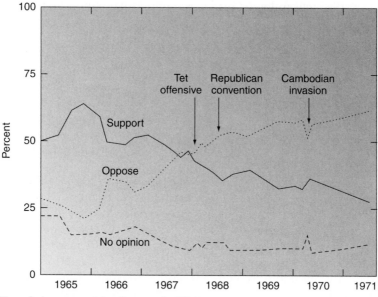

Trends in support for the war in Vietnam.
From John E. Mueller, War, Presidents, & Public Opinion, *p. 56. Copyright © 1985 University Press of America. Reprinted with permission of Rowman & Littlefield Publishers.*

and used them as cannon fodder. King's speech of April 4, 1967, publicly breaking with the administration over the war, was a signal of revolt. Blacks did not join the antiwar protests in large numbers, but their growing opposition damaged the administration politically, and their resistance to the draft and discontent within the military itself weakened the war effort.[59]

Waning public confidence was mirrored in the press and Congress. A number of major metropolitan dailies shifted from support of the war to opposition in 1967, and the influential Time-Life publications, fervently hawkish at the outset, began to raise serious questions about the administration's policies. Members of Congress found it impossible to vote against funds for American forces in the field and hesitated to challenge the president directly, but many who had firmly backed him at first came out openly against him.

[59]Jeffreys-Jones, *Peace Now,* pp. 94–117. The King quote is from p. 98.

Admitting that he had once been an "all-out hawk," Republican Senator Thruston B. Morton of Kentucky spoke for the converts when he complained that the United States had been "planted into a corner out there" and insisted that there would "have to be a change."[60] White House aides nervously warned of further defections in Congress and major electoral setbacks in 1968 in the absence of dramatic changes in the war.[61]

By late 1967, for many observers the war had become the most visible symbol of a malaise that afflicted all of American society. Not all would have agreed with Fulbright's assertion that the Great Society was a "sick society," but many did feel that the United States was going through a kind of national nervous breakdown. The "credibility gap"—the difference between what the administration said and what it did—had produced a pervasive distrust of government. Rioting in the cities, a spiraling crime rate, and noisy demonstrations in the streets suggested that violence abroad had produced violence at home. Increasingly divided against itself, the nation appeared on the verge of an internal crisis as severe as the Great Depression of the 1930s. Anxiety about the war had not translated into a firm consensus for escalation or withdrawal, but the public mood—tired, angry, and frustrated—posed perhaps a more serious threat to the administration than did the antiwar movement.

THE WAR IN WASHINGTON

The public debate on Vietnam was paralleled by increasingly sharp divisions within the government. Rejecting CIA estimates that played down the success of U.S. military operations, Westmoreland insisted that progress was being made and that the war could be won if the United States used its military power effectively. Although they had beaten down many of the restrictions on the bombing by 1967, the Joint Chiefs remained deeply dissatisfied with the conduct of the air war and angered by the president's continuing refusal to mobilize the reserves. Westmoreland had been

---

[60]For the shift of 1967, see Don Oberdorfer, *Tet!* (Garden City, N.Y., 1971), pp. 83–92, and Louis Harris, *The Anguish of Change* (New York, 1973), pp. 60–61.
[61]Walt Rostow to Johnson, August 1, 1967, Johnson Papers, Declassified and Sanitized Documents from Unprocessed Files (DSDUF), Box 2; Harry McPherson to Johnson, August 25, 1967, Johnson Papers, McPherson File, Box 32.

given considerable leeway in implementing ground operations, but he resented what he later described as "naive, gratuitous advice" from the "self-appointed field marshals" in the State and Defense Departments, and he was frustrated by restrictions that forbade him from going into enemy sanctuaries.[62]

Westmoreland and the Joint Chiefs joined forces in the spring of 1967 to seek a commitment to all-out war. Still confident that search and destroy could succeed, the field commander requested an additional 200,000 troops to step up ground operations against the enemy. The Joint Chiefs urged a limited mobilization of the reserves to secure the new increments. To deny the enemy its sanctuaries, the military pressed for intensive ground and air operations in Cambodia and Laos as well as for an amphibious "hook" across the demilitarized zone into North Vietnam. Conceding that the air war had reached the point of "target saturation," the Joint Chiefs nevertheless advocated intensified bombing of the Hanoi-Haiphong area and the mining of North Vietnamese ports. Presenting a united front, the military urged expansion of the war to force a North Vietnamese defeat.[63]

By the time the military presented its proposals, some of Johnson's civilian advisers were openly advocating the abandonment of policies they had come to regard as bankrupt. Throughout 1966, opposition to the war increased within the administration. Some internal critics, including Bill Moyers of the White House staff and George Ball, quietly resigned, feeling, as James Thomson later put it, "totally alienated from the policy, but helpless as to how to change it."[64] The opposition continued to grow and increasingly centered among the civilians in the Defense Department.

The major proponent of change by the spring of 1967 was, ironically, the secretary of defense, a man so closely associated with escalation that the war had once been called "McNamara's war." McNamara seems to have concluded as early as 1965 that the war could not be won in any meaningful sense. In the summer of 1966, he began to fear that the vast expansion of the war was endanger-

---

[62]Westmoreland, *A Soldier Reports*, p. 161.

[63]Westmoreland to Joint Chiefs of Staff, March 28, 1967, in Neil Sheehan et al., *The Pentagon Papers as Published by the New York Times* (New York, 1971), pp. 560–565, hereafter cited as *Pentagon Papers (NYT)*; Joint Chiefs of Staff to McNamara, April 20, 1967, ibid., pp. 565–567.

[64]James C. Thomson, "Getting Out and Speaking Out," *Foreign Policy* 13 (Winter 1973–1974), 57.

ing the global security position he had labored so diligently to construct since taking office in 1961. He was troubled by the destructiveness of the war, particularly the civilian casualties, and by the growing domestic opposition, brought home to him in public appearances when he had to shove his way through and shout down protesters. McNamara's reputation as a businessman and public servant had been based on his ability to attain maximum results at minimal cost. By early 1967, however, he was forced to admit that escalation of the war had not produced results in the major "end products—broken enemy morale and political effectiveness." The South Vietnamese government seemed no more stable than before; pacification had, "if anything, gone backward." The air war had brought heavy costs but limited results. "Ho Chi Minh is a tough old S.O.B.," McNamara conceded to his staff. "And he won't quit no matter how much bombing we do."[65] Moreover, the secretary of defense admitted that the bombing had cost the United States heavily in terms of domestic and world opinion. "The picture of the world's greatest superpower killing or seriously injuring 1,000 non-combatants a week, while trying to pound a tiny, backward nation into submission on an issue whose merits are hotly disputed, is not a pretty one," he advised Johnson in early 1967.[66] McNamara and his advisers were also disillusioned with the ground war in South Vietnam. Increases in U.S. troops had not produced correspondingly larger enemy losses, and there was nothing to indicate that further expansion of the war would place any real strains on North Vietnamese personnel.

Torn between disenchantment with the war and loyalty to his president, McNamara throughout 1967 quietly and somewhat hesitantly pressed for basic changes in policy. Arguing that major military targets in North Vietnam had already been destroyed, he proposed either an unconditional bombing halt or restriction of the bombing to the area south of the twentieth parallel. Such a move, he added, would appease critics of the war at home and might lead to serious negotiations. The secretary of defense also advocated a ceiling on troop levels and a shift from search and destroy to a more limited ground strategy based on providing security for the population of South Vietnam.

[65]Quoted in Henry Trewhitt, *McNamara* (New York, 1971), p. 235.
[66]McNamara to Johnson, May 19, 1967, in Sheehan et al., *Pentagon Papers (NYT)*, p. 580.

In somewhat ambiguous terms, he further proposed a scaling down of American political objectives. Inasmuch as the United States had gone to war to contain China, he argued, it had succeeded: the Communist defeat in Indonesia and rampant political turmoil within China itself suggested that trends in Asia were now running in favor of the United States. The administration might therefore adopt a more flexible bargaining position. It could still hope for an independent, non-Communist South Vietnam, but it should not obligate itself to "guarantee and insist upon these conditions." Obliquely at least, McNamara appears to have been suggesting that the United States modify its military strategy and diplomatic stance to find a face-saving way out of Vietnam.[67]

By the summer of 1967, Lyndon Johnson was a deeply troubled man, physically and emotionally exhausted, frustrated by his lack of success, torn between his advisers, uncertain which way to turn. He seems to have shared some of McNamara's reservations, and he flatly rejected the military proposals to expand the war. "Bomb, bomb, bomb, that's all you know," he complained to the Joint Chiefs on several occasions.[68] He was worried by the implications of Westmoreland's ground strategy and his request for more troops. "When we add divisions, can't the enemy add divisions?" he asked the general pointedly in April. "If so, where does it all end?"[69] He remained firmly opposed to mobilizing the reserves and expanding the war. He continued to fear a confrontation with the Soviet Union or China. "I am not going to spit in China's face," he insisted.[70]

Johnson could not accept McNamara's recommendations, however. He had gradually lost confidence in his secretary of defense, whose dovishness he incorrectly attributed to the pernicious influence of his archenemy Robert Kennedy. The relationship between Johnson and McNamara had so soured by late 1967 that the secretary gladly accepted an appointment to head the World Bank. Westmoreland continued to report steady progress, moreover, and the president was not ready to concede defeat. He would not consider a

---

[67]Ibid., pp. 584–585.

[68]Quoted in Lawrence J. Korb, *The Joint Chiefs of Staff: The First Twenty-Five Years* (Bloomington, Ind., 1976), p. 181.

[69]Excerpt from Johnson-Westmoreland conversation, April 20, 1967, in Sheehan et al., *Pentagon Papers (NYT)*, p. 567.

[70]Quoted in C. L. Sulzberger, *Seven Continents and Forty Years* (New York, 1977), p. 435.

return to the enclave strategy—"We can't hunker down like a jack-ass in a hailstorm," he said—or even a ceiling on the troop level.[71] Although he seems to have agreed that the bombing had accomplished nothing, he was not prepared to stop or even limit it. Denouncing McNamara's proposals as an "aerial Dien Bien Phu," the Joint Chiefs apparently contemplated resignation en masse if Johnson approved those proposals, and the hawkish Mississippi Senator John Stennis was planning an investigation into the conduct of the air war.[72] The president was not prepared to risk a confrontation with the hawks or a potentially explosive public debate on the bombing. Moreover, many of those to whom Johnson turned for advice argued strongly against McNamara's recommendations. Dean Rusk, Walt Rostow, Maxwell Taylor, Clark Clifford, and McGeorge Bundy all agreed that domestic critics would not be appeased by a bombing halt. Doves, like hawks, had "insatiable appetites," Bundy warned, and if concessions were made to them, they would merely demand more. "To stop the bombing today would give the Communists something for nothing," Bundy added, and would be seen by Hanoi as a sign of weakness.[73]

Johnson thus continued to hold the shrinking middle ground between the positions offered by his advisers. He rejected military proposals to expand the war and Westmoreland's request for 200,000 additional soldiers, approving an increase of only 55,000. No ceilings were set, however, and there was no reassessment of the search-and-destroy strategy. Johnson also turned down McNamara's proposals to limit or stop the bombing. Indeed, to placate the Joint Chiefs and congressional hawks, he significantly expanded the list of targets, authorizing strikes against bridges, railyards, and barracks within the Hanoi-Haiphong "donut" and formerly restricted areas along the Chinese border.

Johnson's decisions of 1967, even more than those of 1965, were improvisations that defied military logic and did not face, much less resolve, the contradictions in American strategy. The bombing was sustained not because anyone thought it would work but because Johnson deemed it necessary to pacify certain domestic factions and

[71]Ibid., p. 436.
[72]Korb, *Joint Chiefs of Staff*, p. 166.
[73]Bundy to Johnson, ca. May 4, 1967, in Sheehan et al., *Pentagon Papers (NYT)*, pp. 569–572.

because stopping it might be regarded as a sign of weakness. The president refused to give his field commander the troops he considered necessary to make his strategy work, but he did not confront the inconsistencies in the strategy itself.

The administration did modify its negotiating position in late 1967. The so-called San Antonio formula, first conveyed secretly to the North Vietnamese by the Harvard political scientist Henry Kissinger through French intermediaries and then announced publicly in September, backed away from a firm prior agreement on mutual de-escalation. The United States would stop the bombing "with the understanding" that this action would lead "promptly to productive discussions"; it would "assume" that North Vietnam would not "take advantage" of the cessation of air strikes. As later explained, this provision meant that Hanoi would not significantly increase the infiltration of soldiers and supplies across the sixteenth parallel.[74] The administration also indicated its willingness to admit the NLF to political participation in South Vietnam, a major step away from its earlier stance. This softening of the American bargaining position did not reflect the change of goals that McNamara had recommended, however. The commitment to the Thieu regime remained firm, and the willingness to deal with the NLF appears to have been based on a hope that it could be co-opted or defeated by political means.

By the end of the year, moreover, Johnson recognized that additional steps would be necessary to hold off disaster. After months of uncertainty, the administration finally concluded in the late summer that slow but steady progress was being made. Officials in Saigon optimistically reported that U.S. operations were keeping the enemy off balance and inflicting enormous losses. The NLF was encountering increasingly difficult problems in recruiting. The ARVN's desertion rate had declined noticeably, and the performance of some units in combat had improved. After months of floundering, pacification seemed to be getting off the ground. Even the generally pessimistic McNamara was moved to comment in July that "There is no military stalemate."[75]

---

[74]George C. Herring (ed.), *The Secret Diplomacy of the Vietnam War: The Negotiating Volumes of the Pentagon Papers* (Austin, Tex., 1983), pp. 538–544.
[75]Notes on meeting, July 12, 1967, Johnson Papers, Tom Johnson Notes on Meetings, Box 1.

By this time, however, the home front was obviously collapsing. The consensus Johnson had so carefully woven in 1964 was in tatters, the nation more divided than at any other time since the Civil War. Opposition in Congress, as well as inattention and mismanagement resulting at least partially from the administration's preoccupation with Vietnam, had brought his cherished Great Society programs to a standstill. The president himself was a man under siege in the White House; his popularity steadily waning, he was the target of vicious personal attacks. His top aides had to be brought surreptitiously into public forums to deliver speeches. "How are we going to win?" he asked plaintively at a top-level meeting in late 1967. Anticipating his dramatic March 31, 1968, decision, a despondent LBJ pondered not running for reelection.[76]

Johnson was alarmed by the position he found himself in, stung by his critics, and deeply hurt by the desertion of trusted aides. He angrily dismissed much of the criticism as unfair, and he repeatedly emphasized that his critics offered no alternatives. The harsher the criticism, the more he chose to disregard it by discrediting the source. Fulbright was a "frustrated old woman" because he had never been appointed secretary of state. Youthful dissenters had not lived through World War II. They would not "know a Communist if they tripped over one." The president cited with undisguised satisfaction an FBI report indicating that a large number of draft-card burners had spent time in mental institutions.[77]

He recognized that he could not ignore the opposition, however. From the beginning, he had perceived that "the weakest chink in our armor is public opinion." During the early years, he seems to have feared the hawks more than the doves, but by late 1967 he had changed his mind. "The major threat we have is from the doves," he told his advisers in September 1967.[78] Increasingly fearful that the war might be lost in the United States, he launched a two-pronged offensive to silence his most outspoken enemies and win public support for his policies.

---

[76]Notes on meetings, October 3, 16, 1967, Johnson Papers, Tom Johnson Notes on Meetings, Box 1.

[77]Quoted in Doris Kearns, *Lyndon Johnson and the American Dream* (New York, 1976), pp. 312–313; Graff, *Tuesday Cabinet*, pp. 99–100; notes on meeting with congressional leaders, October 31, 1967, Johnson Papers, Diary Backup.

[78]Jim Jones notes on meeting, September 5, 1967, Johnson Papers, Meeting Notes File, Box 2.

Mistakenly believing that the peace movement was turning the public against the war, he set out to destroy it. He instructed the CIA to institute a program of surveillance of antiwar leaders to prove his suspicions that they were Communists operating on orders from foreign governments. This program, later institutionalized as Operation CHAOS, violated the CIA's charter. It eventually led to the compilation of files on more than 7,000 Americans. Johnson repeatedly expressed his unwillingness to indulge in McCarthyite methods, but when the CIA was unable to prove the links he suspected, he leaked information to right-wing members of Congress that he had such proof, leaving it to them to issue public charges that the peace movement was "being cranked up in Hanoi." The war against the peace movement soon shifted from surveillance to harassment and disruption. Law enforcement agencies began to indict antiwar leaders like Dr. Spock for such action as counseling draft resistance. The FBI infiltrated the peace movement with the object of disrupting its work and causing its members to do things that would further discredit them in the eyes of the public.[79]

At the same time, Johnson mounted an intensive campaign to shore up popular support for the war. From behind the scenes, administration officials organized the Committee for Peace with Freedom in Vietnam, an ostensibly private organization headed by former Illinois Senator Paul Douglas, to mobilize the "silent center" in American politics. Johnson's advisers supplied to friendly senators, including some Republicans, information to help answer the charges of congressional doves. A Vietnam Information Group was set up in the White House to monitor public reactions to the war and deal with problems as soon as they surfaced.[80] Recognizing that the major obstacle he faced was the widespread perception that the war was a stalemate, the president ordered the embassy and military command in Saigon to "search urgently for occasions to present sound evidence of progress in Vietnam." U.S. officials dutifully responded, producing reams of statistics to show a steady rise in enemy body counts and the number of villages pacified, and publishing captured documents that supported these claims. The

---

[79]Charles DeBenedetti, "A CIA Analysis of the Anti-Vietnam War Movement: October 1967," *Peace and Change* 9 (Spring 1983): 31–35.
[80]See the extensive correspondence in Johnson Papers, Marvin Watson File, Box 32.

White House even arranged for influential citizens to go to Vietnam and observe the progress firsthand.[81]

As part of the public relations offensive, Westmoreland was brought home in November, ostensibly for top-level consultations but in fact to reassure a troubled nation. Upon arriving in Washington, he told reporters, "I am very, very encouraged. . . . We are making real progress." In a November 21 speech to the National Press Club, he offered a generally optimistic appraisal of the war, advising that although the enemy had not been defeated, it had been badly hurt. "We have reached an important point where the end begins to come into view," he concluded, and he even hinted that the United States might begin troop withdrawals within two years.[82]

Although his public relations offensive began to show immediate results, Johnson seems to have concluded by the end of the year that a change of strategy in Vietnam might also be necessary. Pressures for abandoning Westmoreland's search-and-destroy operations mounted throughout 1967. Increasingly disillusioned with the high cost and lack of results, McNamara's civilian advisers pressed for a shift to small-unit patrols that would be more "cost-effective" and would reduce U.S. casualties.[83] In his last major policy memorandum to Johnson, the secretary of defense proposed a study of military operations in the south to find ways to reduce U.S. casualties and force the South Vietnamese to assume a greater burden of the fighting. Recognizing that public disillusionment threatened not only success in Vietnam but also the internationalist foreign policy the nation had pursued since World War II, a group of leading "establishment" figures, meeting under the auspices of the Carnegie Endowment, proposed a "clear and hold" strategy that would stabilize the war at a "politically tolerable level" and save South Vietnam "without surrender and without risking a wider war."[84]

[81]Walt Rostow to Ellsworth Bunker, September 27, 1967, Johnson Papers, DSDUF, Box 4; Eugene Locke to Johnson, October 7, 1967, Johnson Papers, National Security File, Country File: Vietnam, Box 99.

[82]Quoted in Richard P. Stebbins, *The United States in World Affairs, 1967* (New York, 1968), p. 68.

[83]Depuy to Westmoreland, October 19, 1967, William Depuy Papers, U.S. Army Military History Institute, Carlisle Barracks, Pa., Folder WXYZ(67).

[84]Carnegie Endowment Proposals," December 5, 1967, Matthew B. Ridgway Papers, U.S. Army Military History Institute, Carlisle Barracks, Pa., Box 34A.

The major impetus for change came from the so-called Wise Men, a distinguished group of former government officials whom Johnson occasionally called upon for guidance. Admitting that he was "deeply concerned about the deterioration of public support," he appealed to them in early November to advise him on how to unite the country behind the war. The Wise Men generally endorsed existing policies. They did warn, however, that "endless inconclusive fighting" was "the most serious single cause of domestic disquiet." To counter this problem, they proposed adopting a ground strategy that would be less expensive in blood and treasure, and they advised shifting to the South Vietnamese greater responsibility for the fighting. Acting as a spokesman for the Wise Men, former presidential assistant McGeorge Bundy went a step further. Conceding that it was a serious matter to challenge the field commander in time of war, Bundy advised the president that since Vietnam had now become a critical issue at home, he had an obligation to do so. He urged Johnson to "visibly take command of a contest that is more political in its character than any other in our history except the Civil War" and to find a strategy that would be tolerable in cost to the American people for the five to ten years that might be required to stabilize the situation in Vietnam.[85] Johnson did not initiate a change in strategy before the end of the year. He did, however, privately commit himself to "review" the conduct of ground operations with an eye toward reducing U.S. casualties and transferring greater responsibility to the South Vietnamese.[86] Even before the Tet Offensive of 1968, he was moving in the direction of what would later be called Vietnamization.

Although he began to consider a change in strategy, Johnson did not reevaluate his essential goals in Vietnam. To take such a step would have been difficult for anyone as long as there was hope of eventual success. It would have been especially difficult for Lyndon Johnson. Enormously ambitious, he had set high goals for his presidency, and he was unwilling to abandon them even in the face of frustration and massive unrest at home. It was not a matter

[85]Jim Jones notes on meeting, November 2, 1967, Johnson Papers, Meeting Notes File, Box 2; Bundy to Johnson, November 10, 1967, Johnson Papers, Diary Backup, Box 81.
[86]Johnson memorandum for the record, December 18, 1967, in Lyndon B. Johnson, *The Vantage Point* (New York, 1971), pp. 600–601.

of courage, for by persisting in the face of declining popularity Johnson displayed courage as well as stubbornness. It was primarily a matter of pride. The president had not wanted the war in Vietnam, but once committed to it he had invested his personal prestige to a degree that made it impossible to back off. He chose to stay the course in 1967 for the same reasons he had gone to war in the first place—because he saw no alternative that did not require him to admit failure or defeat.

While quietly contemplating a change in strategy, Johnson publicly vowed to see the war through to a successful conclusion. "We are not going to yield," he stated repeatedly. "We are not going to shimmy. We are going to wind up with a peace with honor which all Americans seek." At a White House dinner for the prime minister of Singapore, the president expressed his commitment in different terms. "Mr. Prime Minister," he said, "you have a phrase in your part of the world that puts our determination very well. You call it 'riding the tiger.' You rode the tiger. We shall!" The words would take on a bitterly ironic ring in the climactic year 1968.[87]

---

[87]Quoted in Stebbins, *United States in World Affairs, 1967*, pp. 397–398.

Tet, 1968
This classic photo of the street execution of a Vietcong captive by the
Saigon police chief brought home to Americans the savagery of the battles
of Tet, and aroused growing concern about the type of government and
war they were supporting.
AP/Wide World Photos

CHAPTER 6

A Very Near Thing

The Tet Offensive and After, 1968

At 2:45 A.M. on January 30, 1968, a team of National Liberation Front (NLF) sappers blasted a large hole in the wall surrounding the U.S. embassy in Saigon and dashed into the courtyard of the compound. For the next six hours, the most important symbol of the American presence in Vietnam was the scene of one of the most dramatic episodes of the war. Unable to get through the heavy door at the main entrance of the embassy building, the attackers retreated to the courtyard and took cover behind large concrete flower pots, pounding the building with rockets and exchanging gunfire with a small detachment of military police. They held their positions until 9:15 A.M., when they were finally overpowered. All nineteen were killed or severely wounded.

The attack on the embassy was but a small part of the Tet Offensive, a massive, coordinated assault against the major urban areas of South Vietnam. In most other locales, the result was the same: the attackers were repulsed and incurred heavy losses. Later that morning, standing in the embassy courtyard amid the debris and fallen bodies in a scene one reporter described as a "butcher shop in Eden," Westmoreland rendered his initial assessment of Tet. The "well-laid plans" of the North Vietnamese and NLF had failed, he observed. "The enemy exposed himself by virtue of his strategy and he suffered heavy casualties." Although his comments brought moans of disbelief from the assembled journalists, from a short-term tactical standpoint Westmoreland

225

was correct: Tet represented a defeat for the enemy.[1] As Bernard Brodie has observed, however, the Tet Offensive was "probably unique in that the side that lost completely in the tactical sense came away with an overwhelming psychological and hence political victory."[2] Tet had a tremendous impact in the United States and ushered in a new phase of a seemingly endless war.

GENERAL OFFENSIVE, GENERAL UPRISING

During the summer of 1967, the North Vietnamese and NLF decided on a change in strategy, a "general offensive, general uprising" to achieve decisive victory. Some Americans have depicted the Tet Offensive as a last-gasp, desperation move, comparable to World War II's Battle of the Bulge, in which a beleaguered enemy attempted to snatch victory from the jaws of defeat. This description seems quite doubtful, although the decision to take the offensive probably did reflect growing concern with the heavy casualties in the south, the damage done by the U.S. bombing of North Vietnam, and the possible costs of a prolonged war of attrition with the United States. It may have been born of excessive optimism, a growing perception that the urban areas of South Vietnam were ripe for revolution and the United States was vulnerable.[3] It came after weeks of soul-searching and agonizing on the part of the politburo in Hanoi and heated debate between northerners and southerners on the aggressiveness with which to pursue the war in the south.

During the second half of 1967, the politburo began developing plans to implement the new strategy. To lure U.S. troops away from the major population centers and maintain heavy casualties, a

[1]Quoted in Don Oberdorfer, *Tet!* (Garden City, N.Y., 1973), p. 34. For a more recent analysis, see Marc Jason Gilbert and William Head, (eds.), *The Tet Offensive* (Westport, Conn., 1996).

[2]Bernard Brodie, "The Tet Offensive," in Noble Frankland and Christopher Dowling (eds.), *Decisive Battles of the Twentieth Century* (London, 1976), p. 321.

[3]This inference is confirmed in North Vietnamese sources. Ministry of Defense, Vietnam Institute of Military History, "Saigon-Gia Dinh Offensive Sector (1968)" (Hanoi, 1988), trans. by Robert J. Destatte, concludes among other observations that although a great victory was won at Tet the major goals were not achieved because they were unrealistic and because enemy strength was underestimated. My thanks to Dr. John Carland of the U.S. Army's Center of Military History for sharing this document with me.

number of large-scale diversionary attacks would be launched in remote areas. These attacks would be followed by coordinated guerrilla assaults against the major cities and towns of South Vietnam designed to rock the Saigon government to its foundations, ignite a "general uprising" among the population, and shake the will of the United States. Seeking maximum shock effect, the politburo even planned an attack on the U.S. embassy. "Let us say to the world that we can attack anywhere, in a place the United States could never expect," a southern leader proclaimed.[4] Simultaneously, new efforts would be made to open negotiations with the United States. The maximum aim was probably to force the collapse of South Vietnam and a U.S. withdrawal. At the very least, the politburo hoped through these coordinated actions to initiate a new phase of "fighting while negotiating" that would stop the bombing, bring about negotiations, weaken the Saigon regime, and exacerbate differences between the United States and South Vietnam. The politburo's ultimate objective would be a negotiated settlement providing for an American withdrawal and a coalition government controlled by the NLF.

Hanoi began executing its plan in late 1967. In October and November, North Vietnamese regulars attacked the Marine base at Con Thien, across the Laotian border, and the towns of Loc Ninh and Song Be near Saigon and Dak To in the Central Highlands. Shortly after, two North Vietnamese divisions laid siege to the Marine garrison at Khe Sanh near the Laotian border. In the meantime, crack NLF units moved into the cities and towns, accumulating supplies and laying final plans. To undermine the Saigon government, the insurgents encouraged the formation of a "popular front" of neutralists and attempted to entice government officials and troops to defect by offering generous pardons and positions in a coalition government. To spread dissension between the United States and Thieu, the front opened secret contacts with the U.S. embassy in Saigon and disseminated rumors of peace talks. Hanoi followed in December 1967 by stating categorically that it would negotiate if the United States stopped the bombing.

[4]Quoted in A. J. Langguth, *Our Vietnam: The War 1954–1975* (New York, 2000), p. 468. The fullest account of the decisions is Ang Chen Guan, "Decision-Making Leading to the Tet Offensive (1968)—The Vietnamese Perspective," *Journal of Contemporary History* 33 (July 1998): 341–353.

The first phase of the plan worked to perfection. Westmoreland quickly dispatched reinforcements to Con Thien, Loc Ninh, Song Be, and Dak To, in each case driving back the North Vietnamese and inflicting heavy losses but dispersing U.S. forces and leaving the cities vulnerable. By the end of 1967, moreover, the attention of Westmoreland, the president, and indeed much of the nation was riveted on Khe Sanh, which many Americans assumed was General Giap's play for a repetition of Dien Bien Phu. The press and television carried daily reports of the action. Insisting that the fortress be held at all costs, Johnson kept close watch on the battle with a terrain map in the White House war room. Westmoreland sent 6,000 soldiers to defend the garrison, and B-52s carried out the heaviest air raids in the history of warfare, eventually dropping more than 100,000 tons of explosives on a five-square-mile battlefield.

While the United States was preoccupied with Khe Sanh, the North Vietnamese and NLF prepared for the second phase of the operation. The offensive against the cities was timed to coincide with the beginning of Tet, the lunar new year and the most festive of Vietnamese holidays. Traditionally, at Tet, people returned to their native villages and engaged in a week of celebrations, renewing ties with family, honoring ancestors, indulging in meals, and shooting firecrackers. Throughout the war, both sides had observed a cease-fire during Tet, and Hanoi correctly assumed that South Vietnam would be relaxing and celebrating, with soldiers visiting their families and government officials away from their offices. While the Americans and South Vietnamese prepared for the holidays, NLF units readied themselves for the bloodiest battles of the war. Mingling with the heavy holiday traffic, guerrillas disguised as Army of the Republic of Vietnam (ARVN) soldiers or civilians moved into the cities and towns, some audaciously hitching rides on American vehicles. Weapons were smuggled in on vegetable carts and even in mock funeral processions. At Cu Chi in the Iron Triangle, recruits practiced getting inside a replica of the U.S. embassy grounds.

Within twenty-four hours after the beginning of Tet, January 30, 1968, the NLF launched a series of attacks extending from the demilitarized zone to the Ca Mau Peninsula on the southern tip of Vietnam. In all, they struck thirty-six of forty-four provincial capitals, five of the six major cities, sixty-four district capitals, and fifty hamlets. In addition to the daring raid on the embassy, NLF units assaulted Saigon's Tan Son Nhut Airport, the presidential palace, and the headquarters of South Vietnam's general staff. In Hue, 7,500 NLF and North Vietnamese troops stormed and eventually took control of the ancient Citadel, the interior town that had been the seat of the emperors of the Kingdom of Annam.

U.S.–SOUTH VIETNAMESE RESPONSE

The offensive caught the United States and South Vietnam off guard. American intelligence had picked up signs of intensive enemy activity in and around the cities and had even translated captured documents that, without giving dates, outlined the plan in some detail. The U.S. command was so preoccupied with Khe Sanh, however, that it viewed evidence pointing to the cities as a diversion to distract it from the main battlefield. As had happened so often before, the United States underestimated the capability of the enemy. The North Vietnamese appeared so bloodied by the campaigns of 1967 that the Americans could not conceive they could bounce back and deliver a blow of the magnitude of Tet. "Even had I known exactly what was to take place," Westmoreland's intelligence officer later conceded, "it was so preposterous that I probably would have been unable to sell it to anybody."[5]

Although taken by surprise, the United States and South Vietnam recovered quickly. The timing of the offensive was poorly coordinated, and premature attacks in some towns sounded a warning that enabled Westmoreland to get reinforcements to vulnerable areas. In addition, the NLF was slow to capitalize on its initial successes, giving the United States time to mount a strong defense. In Saigon, American and ARVN forces held off the initial attacks and within several days cleared the city, inflicting huge casualties, taking large numbers of prisoners, and forcing the remnants to melt into the countryside. Elsewhere the result was much the same. The ARVN fought better under pressure than any American would have dared predict, and the United States and South Vietnam used superior mobility and firepower to devastating advantage. The NLF launched a

---

[5]Quoted in William C. Westmoreland, *A Soldier Reports* (Garden City, N.Y., 1976), p. 321. For a full analysis of the U.S. intelligence failure at Tet, see James J. Wirtz, *The Tet Offensive: Intelligence Failure in War* (Ithaca, N.Y., 1991).

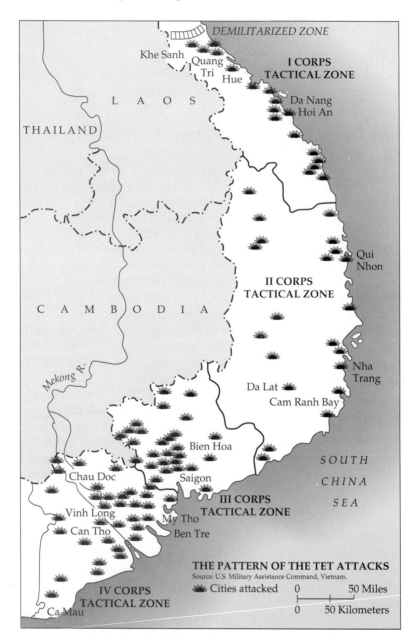

DEMILITARIZED ZONE

Khe Sanh
Quang
Tri
Hue

**I CORPS
TACTICAL ZONE**

Da Nang
Hoi An

L A O S

THAILAND

Qui
Nhon

**II CORPS
TACTICAL ZONE**

C A M B O D I A

Mekong R.

Nha
Trang

Da Lat
Cam Ranh Bay

Bien Hoa

Chau Doc
Saigon

SOUTH

CHINA

**III CORPS
TACTICAL ZONE**

SEA

Vinh Long
Can Tho

My Tho
Ben Tre

THE PATTERN OF THE TET ATTACKS
Source: U.S. Military Assistance Command, Vietnam.

Cities attacked   0   50 Miles

**IV CORPS
TACTICAL ZONE**

Ca Mau

0   50 Kilometers

Hue during the Tet Offensive
This picture shows U.S. Marines walking the streets of Hue after a fierce, month-long battle to regain control from the North Vietnamese and NLF. Once the imperial capital of Annam and a city of great beauty and charm, Hue was left after the 1968 Tet Offensive, in the words of one observer, "a shattered, stinking hulk, its streets choked with rubble and rotting bodies." *Getty Archive Photos*

second round of attacks on February 18, but these were confined largely to rocket and mortar barrages against U.S. and South Vietnamese military installations and steadily diminished in intensity.

Hue was the only exception to the general pattern. The liberation of that city took nearly three weeks, required heavy bombing and intensive artillery fire, and ranks among the bloodiest and most destructive battles of the war. The United States and South Vietnam lost an estimated 500 killed, while enemy killed in action have been estimated at as high as 5,000. The savage fighting caused huge numbers of civilian casualties and created an estimated 100,000 refugees. The bodies of 2,800 South Vietnamese were found in mass graves in and around Hue, the product of NLF and North

Vietnamese executions, and another 2,000 citizens were unaccounted for and presumed murdered.

It remains difficult to assess the impact of the battles of Tet. The North Vietnamese and NLF did not force the collapse of South Vietnam. They were unable to establish any firm positions in the urban areas, and the South Vietnamese people did not welcome them as "liberators." Their battle deaths have been estimated at as high as 40,000, and although this figure may be inflated, the losses were huge. The NLF bore the brunt of the fighting; its regular units were hurt badly and would take mouths to recover, and its political infrastructure suffered crippling losses.

If, in these terms, Tet represented a "defeat" for the enemy, it was still a costly "victory" for the United States and South Vietnam. ARVN forces had to withdraw from the countryside to defend the cities, and pacification incurred another major setback. The destruction within the cities heaped formidable new problems on a government that had shown limited capacity to deal with the routine. American and South Vietnamese losses did not approach those of the enemy, but they were still high: in the first two weeks of the Tet campaigns, the United States lost 1,100 killed in action and South Vietnam 2,300. An estimated 12,500 civilians were killed, and Tet created as many as one million new refugees. As with much of the war up to then, there was a great deal of destruction and suffering, but no clear-cut winner or loser.

CONFUSION AND UNCERTAINTY

To the extent that the North Vietnamese designed the Tet Offensive to influence the United States, they succeeded, for it sent instant shock waves across the nation. Early wire service reports exaggerated the success of the raid on the embassy, some even indicating that the guerrillas had occupied several floors of the building. Although these initial reports were in time corrected, the reaction was still one of disbelief. "What the hell is going on?" the venerable newscaster Walter Cronkite is said to have snapped. "I thought we were winning the war!"[6] Televised accounts of the bloody fighting in Saigon and Hue made a mockery of Johnson's and Westmoreland's optimistic year-

[6]Quoted in Oberdorfer, *Tet!* p. 158.

end reports, widening the credibility gap; cynical journalists openly ridiculed Westmoreland's claims of victory. The humorist Art Buchwald parodied the general's statements in terms of Custer at the Little Bighorn. "We have the Sioux on the run," Buchwald had Custer saying. "Of course we still have some cleaning up to do, but the Redskins are hurting badly and it will only be a matter of time before they give in."[7] The battles of Tet raised to a new level of public consciousness basic questions about the war that had long lurked just beneath the surface. The offhand remark of a U.S. Army officer who had participated in the liberation of the Mekong delta village of Ben Tre—"We had to destroy the town to save it"—seemed to epitomize the purposeless destruction of the war. Candid photographs and television footage of the police chief of Saigon holding a pistol to the head of an NLF captive—and then firing—starkly symbolized the way in which violence had triumphed over law.

The Tet Offensive left Washington in a state of "troubled confusion and uncertainty."[8] Westmoreland insisted that the attacks had been repulsed and that there was no need to fear a major setback, and administration officials publicly echoed his statements. Johnson and his advisers were shocked by the suddenness and magnitude of the offensive, however, and intelligence estimates were much more pessimistic than Westmoreland was. Many officials feared that Tet was only the opening phase of a larger Communist offensive. Some felt that Khe Sanh was still the primary objective, a fear that seemed borne out when the besieging forces renewed their attack in early February. Others feared a major offensive in the northern provinces or a second wave of attacks on the cities. An "air of gloom" hung over White House discussions, Taylor later observed, and General Wheeler likened the mood to that following the first Battle of Bull Run.[9]

The president responded with a stubborn determination to hold the line at any cost. He insisted that Khe Sanh be held and advised Westmoreland that he would send whatever reinforcements were needed to defend the fortress or meet any other threat. "The United States is not prepared to accept a defeat in South Vietnam," Wheeler advised Saigon, " . . . if you need more troops, ask for

---

[7]*Washington Post,* February 6, 1968.
[8]Townsend Hoopes, *The Limits of Intervention* (New York, 1970), p. 145.
[9]Earle Wheeler oral history interview, Johnson Papers, Lyndon Baines Johnson Library, Austin, Texas.

them." When Westmoreland indicated that he would appreciate any help he could get, Johnson immediately ordered an additional 10,500 men to Vietnam. In the first few weeks after Tet, the president's main concern seemed to be to "get on with the war as quickly as possible," not only by sending reinforcements but also by stepping up air attacks against North Vietnam.[10]

PROPOSALS FOR ESCALATION

From the standpoint of the military, the new mood of urgency in Washington provided a timely opportunity to force decisions that had been deferred for too long. Wheeler and the Joint Chiefs had been pressing for mobilization of the reserves since 1965, and by February 1968 they were certain this step must be taken at once. The Tet Offensive raised the distinct possibility that significant reinforcements would have to be sent to Vietnam. North Korea's seizure of the American warship *Pueblo* in January and a new flare-up in Berlin aroused fears that additional troops might have to be dispatched to these perennial Cold War trouble spots. Available forces were nearly exhausted, and Wheeler worried that unless the United States mobilized the reserves, it could not meet its global commitments.

Confident that he could exploit the enemy's defeat at Tet and buoyed by the president's apparent willingness to send substantial reinforcements, Westmoreland revived his 1967 proposals to expand the war. The enemy's decision to throw in "all his military chips and go for broke," the general advised Washington, provided the United States with a "great opportunity." The North Vietnamese and NLF could not afford the heavy losses sustained in the Tet Offensive, and with large numbers of additional troops, Westmoreland was certain he could gain the upper hand. His "two-fisted" strategy envisioned an "amphibious hook" against North Vietnamese bases and staging areas across the demilitarized zone, attacks on the sanctuaries in Laos and Cambodia, and an intensified bombing campaign against North Vietnam. By taking the offensive at a time when the enemy was overextended, the general was confident he could shorten the war.[11]

[10]Herbert Schandler, *The Unmaking of a President: Lyndon Johnson and Vietnam* (Princeton, N.J., 1977), p. 91; "March 31 Speech," Johnson Papers, National Security File, National Security Council Histories: March 31, 1968, Speech, Box 47.
[11]John B. Henry, "February 1968," *Foreign Policy* 4 (Fall 1971); 17.

Wheeler and Westmoreland conferred in Saigon in late February and devised an approach to force the president's hand. Wheeler appears to have been considerably less optimistic about the immediate prospects in Vietnam than Westmoreland was, but he agreed that whether Tet provided new opportunities or posed increased dangers, it justified a call for major reinforcements. The two men settled on the figure of 206,000 soldiers, a number large enough to meet any contingency in Vietnam and force mobilization of the reserves. Roughly half of the troops would be deployed in Vietnam by the end of the year; the rest would constitute a strategic reserve. Wheeler raised no objections to Westmoreland's proposed changes in strategy, but he persuaded the field commander that it would be best to defer such recommendations until the president had approved the new troop level. He was keenly aware of Johnson's opposition to widening the war, and he apparently feared that if he presented the case for additional troops on the basis of an optimistic assessment and an offensive strategy, he would be turned down again. Troops, not strategy, offered the "stronger talking point."[12]

Wheeler's report to Washington was deeply pessimistic. Describing the Tet Offensive as a "very near thing," he warned that the initial enemy attacks had almost succeeded in numerous places and had been turned back only by the "timely reaction" of U.S. forces. The North Vietnamese and NLF had suffered heavily, but they had repeatedly demonstrated a capacity for quick recovery, and they would probably attempt to sustain the offensive with renewed attacks. Without additional troops, he concluded, the United States must be "prepared to accept some reverses," a line calculated to sway a president who had already made clear he was not willing to accept defeat. Wheeler insisted that large-scale reinforcements were necessary to protect the cities, drive the enemy from the northern provinces, and pacify the countryside. His pessimism may have been sincere; he had never been as confident as Westmoreland was. It seems clear, however, that by presenting a gloomy assessment he hoped to stampede the administration into providing the troops to rebuild a depleted strategic reserve and meet any contingency in Vietnam. His proposal reopened in even more vigorous fashion the debate that had raged in Washington throughout 1967.[13]

[12]Ibid., 21.

[13]Wheeler Report, February 27, 1968, excerpted in Neil Sheehan et al., *The Pentagon Papers as Published by the New York Times* (New York, 1971), pp. 615–621.

Wheeler's report shocked a government already in a state of deep alarm. In terms of policy choices, it posed a hard dilemma. The general suggested that denial of the request for 206,000 troops could result in a military defeat, or at least in an indefinite continuation of the war. Acceptance of his recommendations, on the other hand, would force a major escalation of the war and impose heavy new demands on the American people in an election year and at a time when public anxiety about Vietnam was already pronounced. Not inclined to make a hasty decision on a matter fraught with such grave implications, Johnson turned the problem over to his new secretary of defense, Clark Clifford, with this grim instruction: "Give me the lesser of evils."[14]

THE CLIFFORD TASK FORCE

Clifford seized the opportunity to initiate a full reevaluation of Vietnam policy. The magnitude of the request was such that it demanded careful study. Clifford had consistently defended the president's policies in Vietnam, but his newness to the job and his need to clarify many fundamental issues also led him toward a full reassessment. He was encouraged in this regard by the senior civilians in the Pentagon, men such as Paul Warnke, Townsend Hoopes, and Paul Nitze, who had long been disenchanted with American strategy and had been partially responsible for McNamara's conversion. Thus, Clifford immediately began raising at the highest levels questions that had been avoided for years. He demanded of Wheeler and Westmoreland precise information on how the additional troops might be deployed and what results could be expected. He instructed his civilian advisers to study all the implications of the request and to review possible alternatives.

The Pentagon civilians responded with a sharp indictment of prevailing policy. Alain Enthoven of Systems Analysis attacked the request for more troops as another "payment on an open-ended commitment" and questioned whether it would shorten the war.[15] North Vietnam had already demonstrated that it could match

---

[14]Lyndon B. Johnson, *The Vantage Point* (New York, 1971), pp. 392–393.
[15]Quoted in U.S. Congress, Senate Subcommittee on Public Buildings and Grounds, *The Pentagon Papers (The Senator Gravel Edition)* (4 vols.; Boston, 1971), 4: 558. Hereafter cited as *Pentagon Papers (Gravel)*.

American increases and that it could limit its losses if it chose. Even with 206,000 additional troops, Enthoven and others concluded, the current strategy could "promise no early end to the conflict, nor any success in attriting the enemy or eroding Hanoi's will to fight." The costs would be heavy, moreover. The provision of substantial additional troops could lead to "total Americanization of the war," encouraging the ARVN's tendency to do nothing and reinforcing the belief of South Vietnam's "ruling elite that the U.S. will continue to fight while it engages in backroom politics and permits widespread corruption." Expansion of the war would bring increased American casualties and require new taxes, risking a "domestic crisis of unprecedented proportions." Clifford's advisers thus agreed that the administration should maintain existing limits on the war and give Westmoreland no more than a token increase in troops.[16]

The Pentagon civilians went further, however. In their final report, they urged a shift from search and destroy, with its goal of "attriting" the enemy, to a strategy of "population security." The bulk of American forces would be deployed along the "demographic frontier," an imaginary line just north of the major population centers, where they could defend against a major North Vietnamese thrust and, by engaging in limited offensive operations, keep the enemy's main forces off balance. At the same time, the United States would force the ARVN to assume greater responsibility for the war and compel the Saigon government to "end its internal bickering, purge corrupt officers and officials and move to develop efficient and effective forces." The goal of the new approach would be a negotiated settlement rather than military victory, and in this regard the civilians urged the scaling down of American objectives to a "peace which will leave the people of SVN [South Vietnam] free to fashion their own political institutions." The plan closely resembled McNamara's proposals of 1967, but it was stated more emphatically and went further in outlining specific alternatives.[17]

The military bitterly opposed the Defense Department recommendations. Recognizing the threat to his request for additional troops—indeed, to his entire strategy—Westmoreland, with the support of Wheeler, warned that rejection of his proposals would deny the United States a splendid opportunity to take advantage of

[16]Ibid., 563–564.
[17]Ibid., 564–568.

an altered strategic situation. Wheeler found "fatal flaws" in the population security strategy, admonishing that it would lead to increased fighting near the population centers, and hence to more civilian casualties, and that it would leave the initiative with the enemy.[18] The United States was at a "cross-road," warned Admiral U.S. Grant Sharp, commander in chief of the Pacific forces. It must choose between using its power without restriction to achieve victory, accepting a "campaign of gradualism" and a "long drawn-out contest," or retreating "in defeat from Southeast Asia," leaving its "allies to face the Communists alone." Along with Westmoreland, the Joint Chiefs continued to urge that the military be permitted to pursue enemy forces into Laos and Cambodia, "beat up" North Vietnam from the sea and air, and after an Inchon-type landing, take and occupy parts of North Vietnam as far as thirty miles north of the demilitarized zone.[19]

As had happened so often before, Clifford recommended against the military's proposals without resolving the debate on strategy. The secretary seems to have leaned toward the population security strategy and a scaling down of American objectives. "I see more and more fighting with more and more casualties on the U.S. side and no end in sight to the action," he complained on March 4.[20] He seems to have felt, however, that the proposed change, with its implicit assumption that U.S. policy had failed, would be more than the president could accept, and he may have wished to prepare Johnson gradually for change rather than confront him immediately. Clifford's formal report kept the strategic issue alive by calling for continued study of possible alternatives, but it did not address the issues raised by the civilians in the Pentagon. The secretary of defense merely recommended the immediate deployment to Vietnam of 22,000 troops, a reserve call-up of unspecified magnitude, and a "highly forceful approach" to Thieu and Ky to get the South Vietnamese to assume greater responsibility for the war.[21]

---

[18]Ibid., 568.

[19]Sharp is quoted in Schandler, *Johnson and Vietnam,* pp. 166–167. For the views of the Joint Chiefs, see Clifford notes on meeting, March 18, 1968, Clark Clifford Papers, Lyndon Baines Johnson Library, Austin, Tex.

[20]Notes on meeting, March 4, 1968, Johnson Papers, Tom Johnson Notes on Meetings, Box 1.

[21]Draft presidential memorandum, March 4, 1968, in *Pentagon Papers (Gravel),* 4:575–576.

THE PRESIDENT'S DECISIONS

The administration accepted Clifford's recommendations without serious debate. The president and his top civilian advisers had long opposed expansion of the war, and they seem to have agreed as early as November 1967 that American forces should not be enlarged above prevailing levels. In the immediate aftermath of the Tet attacks, Johnson had been ready to send additional troops if necessary to hold the line, but by the time he received Clifford's report, the military situation in South Vietnam seemed well in hand. Westmoreland and Ambassador Ellsworth Bunker reported that U.S. and South Vietnamese forces had fully recovered from the initial shock of the enemy offensive and were ready to mount a major counteroffensive. Under these circumstances, there seemed no need for immediate large-scale reinforcements, and although Johnson did not formally approve Clifford's recommendations at this time, he agreed with them and was prepared to act on them.

The administration also accepted the principle that South Vietnam should do more to defend itself. Johnson's advisers agreed that from a long-range standpoint the key to achieving American objectives was South Vietnam's ability to stand on its own, and they had concluded in late 1967 that more should be done to promote self-sufficiency. The ARVN's quick recovery from the initial panic of Tet and its surprising effectiveness in the subsequent battles reinforced this notion by suggesting that "Vietnamization" might work. Indeed, in the discussions of late February and early March 1968, some of the strongest arguments against sending massive reinforcements were that it would encourage the South Vietnamese to do less at a time when they should be doing more and that it would take equipment that might better be used by the ARVN. The administration thus agreed in early March that Thieu and Ky should be bluntly informed that the United States was willing to send limited reinforcements and substantial quantities of equipment but that continued American assistance would depend on South Vietnam's ability to put its house in order and assume a greater burden of the fighting.[22] The decision represented a significant shift in American policy—a return, at least in part, to

[22]Schandler, *Johnson and Vietnam*, p. 179.

the principle that had governed U.S. involvement before 1965 and adoption, at least in a rudimentary fashion, of the concept of Vietnamization, which would be introduced with much fanfare by the Nixon administration a year later.

While agreeing in principle to Clifford's recommendations, the administration also began serious consideration of a cutback in the bombing and a new peace initiative. The secretary of defense had recommended against further peace moves in his report and, perhaps as a sop to the military, had even urged intensification of the bombing. The initiative came from Secretary of State Rusk. Rusk had felt for some time that the bombing had produced only marginal gains at a heavy cost, and he proposed that the administration restrict it, without condition, to those areas "integrally related to the battlefield," namely, the supply routes and staging areas just north of the demilitarized zone. Such a move would cost the United States nothing, he argued, since inclement weather in the next few months would severely restrict raids over the northern part of North Vietnam. Bunker had speculated that Hanoi's purpose in launching the Tet Offensive may have been to establish a favorable position for negotiations, and in late February neutral intermediaries had brought several peace feelers to the State Department. Rusk believed that the chances for productive negotiations remained "bleak," but relaxation of the ambiguous San Antonio formula might entice Hanoi to the conference table and at least would test its intentions. Even if North Vietnam did not respond positively, domestic critics would be persuaded that the administration was trying to get negotiations under way. The United States could resume air attacks on Hanoi and Haiphong later, if necessary, the secretary pointed out, probably with increased public support.[23]

Johnson had steadfastly opposed any reduction of the bombing, but he was attracted to Rusk's proposal. The president was certain that North Vietnam had suffered heavily in the Tet Offensive, and he appears to have concluded that the United States could undertake negotiations from a vastly strengthened position. He recognized the need to do something to still the growing outcry against the war at home. And he was responsive to the idea because it came from Rusk, a man whose loyalty, caution, and measured

[23]Ibid., pp. 181–193.

judgment he had come to cherish.[24] Johnson later claimed to have accepted the idea of a reduction of the bombing and a new peace initiative as early as March 7, but he was not inclined to move hastily, and he remained outwardly noncommittal for several weeks. He urged his advisers to study the matter carefully and develop specific proposals for inclusion in a major speech he was to deliver at the end of the month.

PUBLIC OPINION AND POLITICS

The administration's inclination to move in new directions was strengthened by mounting evidence of public dissatisfaction with the war. Discussion of Vietnam during February and March 1968 took place in an atmosphere of gloom and futility. The media continued to depict events in highly unfavorable and sometimes distorted terms. Early reports of a smashing enemy victory went largely uncorrected. The fact that the United States and South Vietnam had hurled back the attacks and quickly stabilized their position was lost in the image of chaos and defeat.[25] For those television and newspaper commentators who had long opposed the conflict, Tet provided compelling evidence of its folly. "The war in Vietnam is unwinnable," the columnist Joseph Kraft reported, "and the longer it goes on the more the Americans will be subjected to losses and humiliation." Many opinion makers who had supported the president or had been only mildly critical now came out forcefully against the war. Tet made clear, *Newsweek* commented, that "a strategy of more of the same is intolerable." In a much-publicized broadcast on February 27, Cronkite eloquently summed up the prevailing mood: "To say that we are closer to victory today is to believe, in the face of the evidence, the optimists who have been wrong in the past. To suggest that we are on the edge of defeat is to yield to unreasonable pessimism. To say that

---

[24]Of Rusk, Johnson once said: "He has the compassion of a preacher and the courage of a Georgia cracker. When you're going in with the marines, he's the kind you want at your side." Max Frankel notes of conversation with Johnson, July 8, 1965, Arthur Krock Papers, Seeley G. Mudd Manuscript Library, Princeton, N.J., Box 1.

[25]For a critical analysis of press and television coverage of Tet, see Peter Braestrup, *Big Story* (New York, 1978).

we are mired in stalemate seems the only reasonable, yet unsatisfactory conclusion."[26]

A *New York Times* story of March 10, reporting that the administration was considering sending another 206,000 soldiers to Vietnam, added to the furor. By this time, Johnson had decided to turn down Westmoreland's request, but he had not revealed his intentions publicly, and the story set off a barrage of protest.[27] Critics asked why so many troops were needed and whether more would follow. Skeptics questioned the results of further escalation, warning that the North Vietnamese would be able to match any American increase. The only thing that would change, NBC's Frank McGee observed, would be the "capacity for destruction." The time had come, he concluded, "when we must decide whether it is futile to destroy Vietnam in the effort to save it."[28]

The possibility of another major troop increase provoked a stormy reaction in Congress. Democrats and Republicans, hawks and doves, demanded an explanation and insisted that Congress share in any decision to expand the war. On March 11 and 12, the Senate Foreign Relations Committee grilled Rusk for eleven hours, dramatically revealing a growing discontent with the administration's policies and a determination to exercise some voice in future decisions. A week later, 139 members of the House of Representatives sponsored a resolution calling for a full review of American policy in Vietnam. The congressional outcry reinforced the administration's conviction that it could not escalate the war without setting off a long and bitter debate, and persuaded some officials, Clifford included, that major steps must be taken to scale down American involvement.[29]

Indexes of public opinion also revealed a sharp rise in disillusionment. Support for the war itself remained remarkably steady between November 1967 and March 1968, hovering around 45 percent.[30] But approval of Johnson's conduct of it, which had risen to 40 percent as a result of the 1967 public relations campaign, plum-

[26]Oberdorfer, *Tet!* pp. 251, 275; Braestrup, *Big Story,* p. 137.
[27]Schandler, *Johnson and Vietnam,* pp. 200–205.
[28]Oberdorfer, *Tet!* p. 273.
[29]Schandler, *Johnson and Vietnam,* pp. 207–217.
[30]Approval and disapproval of the war were measured by the question "Do you think the United States made a mistake sending troops to Vietnam?"—at best an imperfect way of judging a complex issue.

meted to an all-time low of 26 percent during Tet. By March, more-over, an overwhelming majority of Americans (78 percent) were certain that the United States was not making any progress in Vietnam. The polls indicated no consensus for either escalation or withdrawal, only a firm conviction that the United States was hopelessly bogged down and a growing doubt that Johnson could break the stalemate.[31]

By mid-March, public discontent had assumed ominous political overtones. Senator Eugene McCarthy of Minnesota, an outspoken dove, had audaciously challenged Johnson's renomination, and his surprisingly strong showing in the New Hampshire primary on March 12 suddenly transformed what had seemed a quixotic crusade into a major political challenge. Johnson's name had not been on the ballot, but the party organization had mounted a vigorous write-in campaign for him, and when McCarthy won 42 percent of the vote, it was widely interpreted as a defeat for the president. Subsequent analysis revealed that hawks outnumbered doves by a wide majority among McCarthy supporters in New Hampshire. Early appraisals, however, emphasized that the vote reflected a growing sentiment for peace, and within several days a more formidable peace candidate had entered the field. After weeks of hesitation and soul-searching, Senator Robert F. Kennedy of New York announced that he, too, would run against the president on a platform of opposition to the war. With his name, his glamour, and his connections in the party, Kennedy appeared to be a serious threat to Johnson's renomination. Worried party regulars urged the president to do "something exciting and dramatic to recapture the peace issue" and to shift the emphasis of his rhetoric from winning the war to securing "peace with honor."[32]

The impact of public opinion on the decision-making process in March 1968 is difficult to measure. Westmoreland and others have charged that hostile and all-too-powerful members of the media, especially the television networks, seized defeat from the jaws of victory by turning the public against the war and limiting the government's freedom of action just when the United States had a battered enemy on the ropes.[33] Vietnam was the first television war, to

[31]Louis Harris, *The Anguish of Change* (New York, 1973), pp. 63–64, and Burns W. Roper, "What Public Opinion Polls Said," in Braestrup, *Big Story*, 1: 674–704.

[32]James Rowe to Johnson, March 19, 1968, Johnson Papers, Marvin Watson File, Box 32.

[33]Westmoreland, *A Soldier Reports*, p. 410; also Robert Elegant, "How to Lose a War," *Encounter* 57 (August 1981): 73–90.

be sure, and it is possible, over a long period of time, that nightly exposure to violence did contribute to public war-weariness. Up until the Tet Offensive, however, television coverage of the war had been overwhelmingly neutral or favorable to the government and, because of the isolated and remote nature of combat in Vietnam, had shown little of the actual horrors of war.[34] The intense and up-close action in the cities at Tet did expose the public more directly to the war, and the coverage was more critical. After the distorted accounts of the embassy battle, coverage was also for the most part more accurate and thus could not help but show the enemy's toughness and tenacity, increase already strong doubts about the South Vietnamese government and army, raise questions about the administration's claims of progress, and widen the president's already yawning credibility gap. It is difficult to measure the impact of television coverage on public attitudes, but it seems probable, as historian Chester Pach has concluded, that coverage of the battles at Tet intensified the "sense of shock, anguish, and uncertainty" felt by Americans and by top government officials.[35]

The Johnson administration itself was at least partially responsible for media and public disillusionment during Tet. Its unduly optimistic pronouncements of 1967 made the shock of Tet greater than it might otherwise have been and widened an already large credibility gap. The president and his advisers might have challenged the reporting of the media, but their public response to Tet was itself halting and confused, in part because they were uncertain what was happening and how to respond.

The idea that a hypercritical media undercut the media just at that point when the war could have been won is suspect on more basic grounds. That victory was within grasp, even had Westmoreland been given all the troops he requested, remains highly doubtful, and despite their later claims many top military officials knew this at the time. They perceived quite clearly the enormous damage

---

[34]Excellent analyses that challenge the view of the media as critic and minimize the media's impact on public opinion are Daniel Hallin, The "Uncensored War": The Media and Vietnam (Berkeley, 1986); William M. Hammond, Public Affairs: The Military and the Media, 1962–1968 (Washington, D.C., 1988); and Clarence R. Wyatt, Paper Soldiers: The American Press and the Vietnam War (New York, 1993).

[35]Chester J. Pach, Jr. "Tet on TV," in Carole Fink et al., eds., 1968: The World Transformed (Washington, D.C., 1998), pp. 55–81; Michael J. Arlen, The Living Room War (New York, 1969).

the enemy offensive had done to the war effort, and they recognized that success was not forthcoming. By making requests they knew would not be approved, in fact, some military leaders may have been trying to put the onus for failure on the backs of the civilians.[36] The influence of public opinion does not appear to have been as great as Westmoreland alleges. None of Johnson's civilian advisers favored expansion of the war and another large troop increase, and the president had rejected Westmoreland's proposals even before the public protest reached significant proportions. Evidence of growing popular discontent merely confirmed that it would be disastrous to escalate the war. Public anxiety persuaded some officials that the United States must move toward withdrawal from Vietnam, but the president did not go this far. He eventually concluded that he must make additional conciliatory gestures, but he did not alter his policy in any fundamental way or abandon his goals.

THE GOLD CRISIS

An economic crisis in mid-March, itself in part provoked by the war, also significantly affected post-Tet policy deliberations. Johnson had attempted to finance the war as he had dealt with public opinion—by deceit and trickery—and for the same reason. From the outset, he had a reasonably clear idea what the war would cost, but in dealing with the public and Congress he repeatedly minimized the price tag and he refused to ask for new taxes for fear such a request would force cuts in Great Society programs. Until 1967, he financed the war through budgetary sleight of hand. His tax request of that year was too little and came too late, and in any event, as he had feared, an increasingly restive Congress refused to pass it without domestic spending cuts he refused to make.

Thus by March 1968, the United States faced an economic crisis some harried officials compared to the Great Crash of 1929. The war imposed a burden of as much as $3.6 billion a year on a U.S. economy already strained by Great Society spending. Military expenditures stoked inflation and contributed to a spiraling balance-of-payments deficit that weakened the dollar in international money

---

[36]Robert Buzzanco, *Masters of War: Military Dissent and Politics in the Vietnam Era* (Cambridge, U.K., 1996), 316–328.

markets and threatened the world monetary structure. A late-1967 financial crisis in Britain, leading to devaluation of the pound, caused further problems, including huge losses from the gold pool. In March 1968, pressure on the dollar mounted again, and gold purchases reached new highs. On March 14, the United States lost $372 million in gold trading. At Washington's urging, the London gold market was closed. The economic crisis in the spring of 1968 marked the beginning of the end of the post–World War II economic boom. It shattered the postwar myth of American invincibility and raised severe doubts among business and government leaders that the nation could do it all and have it all in terms of domestic reform and national defense.[37]

As a result of the gold crisis of March 1968, Westmoreland's request for additional troops was increasingly linked to the nation's mounting economic woes. Secretary of the Treasury Henry Fowler warned that adoption of Westmoreland's proposals would cost $2.5 billion in 1968 and $10 billion in 1969, adding $500 million to the balance-of-payments deficit and requiring a major tax increase and cuts in domestic programs. Leading organs of business opinion began to question the nation's ability to finance the war at higher or even existing levels. "The gold crisis has dampened expansionist ideas," former Secretary of State Dean Acheson wrote a friend. "The town is in an atmosphere of crisis."[38]

In this context, some leading "establishment" figures, including the architects of America's major Cold War policies, concluded that the war was doing irreparable damage to the nation's overall national security position and began to press for disengagement. Acheson, W. Averell Harriman, and Paul Nitze, all of whom had served in the Truman administration and had helped formulate the original containment policy, agreed, as Acheson put it, that Vietnam was a dangerous diversion from Europe and that "our leader ought to be concerned with areas that count."[39] Fearing that the nation was hopelessly overextended and that Vietnam was eroding

[37]Robert M. Collins, "The Economic Crisis of 1968 and the Waning of the 'American Century,'" *American Historical Review* 101 (April 1996): 396–422.

[38]Acheson to John Cowles, March 14, 1968, Dean G. Acheson Papers, Yale University Library, New Haven, Conn., Box 7. The gold crisis is discussed at length in Paul Joseph, *Cracks in the Empire: State Politics in the Vietnam War* (Boston, 1981), pp. 262–266; Gabriel Kolko, *Anatomy of a War* (New York, 1986), pp. 313–320; and Diane B. Kunz, "The American Economic Consequence of 1968," in Fink, *1968*, pp. 83–110.

popular support for an internationalist foreign policy, they pressed for a review of Vietnam policy in the larger context of America's global national security concerns. In a long letter on March 26, Acheson warned the president that the gold crisis and concern with America's "broader interests in Europe" required a "decision now to disengage within a limited time."[40] The old Cold Warriors labored tirelessly behind the scenes to influence the president's decision, and they converted Clifford to their position.

On March 22, Johnson formally rejected Westmoreland's proposals to seek victory through an expanded war. He was undoubtedly influenced by public opinion and the economic crisis, and the steadily improving situation in South Vietnam seems to have been decisive. The Saigon government was responding to American pressures. Stability and order had been restored to the cities, and in late March, Thieu announced a massive increase in draft calls that would raise the ARVN'S strength by 135,000. The intensity of enemy rocket attacks was steadily diminishing. Enemy forces were withdrawing from the positions established before Tet and splitting into small groups to avoid destruction or capture. In mid-March, Westmoreland informed Johnson of plans for a major offensive in the northern provinces, the central objective of which was to relieve the siege of Khe Sanh.

Under these circumstances, Johnson saw no need for a major increase in American forces. Indeed, he did not even authorize the 22,000 soldiers recommended by Clifford, agreeing merely to deploy 13,500 support troops to augment the emergency reinforcements sent in February. At the same time, he decided to bring Westmoreland back to Washington to be chief of staff of the army. The general had come under heavy fire for his prophecies of victory and his failure to anticipate the Tet Offensive, and Johnson wanted to spare him becoming a scapegoat. The president may also have wished to remove him from the untenable position of fighting a war under conditions he did not approve. Whatever the precise purpose, the recall of Westmoreland signified the administration's determination to maintain the limits it had placed on the war and, tacitly at least, to check its further escalation.

---

[39]Quoted in Walter Isaacson and Evan Thomas, *The Wise Men: Six Friends and the World They Made* (New York, 1986), pp. 684, 689.
[40]Acheson to Johnson, March 26, 1968, Acheson Papers.

THE MARCH 31 SPEECH

During the last week of March, the internal debate reached a decisive stage and became increasingly sharp and emotional. Some of the president's advisers still insisted that the United States must "hang in there." At one time during the Tet crisis, Rostow had proposed sending to Congress a new Southeast Asia Resolution to rally the nation behind the war, and he continued to urge the president to stand firm at what could be a critical turning point. Rusk persisted in working for the partial bombing halt he had outlined in early March. He was concerned by the domestic protest, but he had not despaired of success in Vietnam, nor was he disposed to capitulate to the administration's critics. He seems to have been certain that the North Vietnamese would reject his proposal, but a conciliatory gesture would show the American people that the administration was doing everything possible to bring about negotiations, thus buying time to stabilize the home front and shore up South Vietnam.

By this time, Clifford had moved significantly beyond his position of late February. He was concerned by the apparent damage Vietnam was doing to the nation's international financial position. He was alarmed by the growing domestic unrest, particularly the "tremendous erosion of support" among the nation's business and legal elite. These executives felt the United States was in a "hopeless bog," he reported, and the idea of "going deeper into the bog" struck them as "mad." Although unclear about precisely how to proceed, he had set his mind on a "winching down" strategy that would put the United States irreversibly on a course of step-by-step de-escalation. U.S. forces should not be expanded above existing levels and should be used primarily to protect the South Vietnamese population from another enemy offensive. Thieu should be pressed to clean up and broaden his government. Clifford seems also to have been prepared to make major concessions to secure a negotiated settlement. He frankly conceded that the United States might have to settle for the best it could obtain. "Nothing required us to remain until the North had been ejected from the South and the Saigon government had established complete control of all South Vietnam," he later wrote. At a meeting on March 28, he delivered an impassioned plea to initiate the process of de-escalation. Working behind the scenes with Acheson and White House aide

Harry McPherson, he waged an unrelenting battle for the president's mind.[41]

While the debate raged about him, Johnson remained noncommittal. Instinctively, he leaned toward the Rusk position. He was infuriated by the desertion of Clifford, on whose support he had counted, and he was deeply opposed to abandoning a policy in which he had invested so much, particularly in view of the improved situation in South Vietnam. Publicly, he continued to take a hard line, proclaiming that "we must meet our commitments in Vietnam and the world. We shall and we are going to win!"[42]

On the other hand, he could not ignore the protest that was building around him, inside and outside the government, and he concluded, gradually and with great reluctance, that some additional conciliatory steps must be taken. In a highly emotional March 26 meeting with Generals Wheeler and Creighton Abrams, Westmoreland's successor, an obviously embattled commander in chief sought to head off military criticism of his peace moves. In tones that verged on despondency, he lamented an "abominable" fiscal situation, panic and demoralization in the country, near universal opposition in the press, and his own "overwhelming disapproval" in the polls. "I will go down the drain," he gloomily concluded.

Trusted advisers from outside the government seem to have clinched it for Johnson. To move the president from his indecision, Acheson suggested that he call his senior advisory group, the Wise Men, back to Washington for another session on Vietnam. After a series of briefings by diplomatic and military officials on March 26, the group, in a mood of obvious gloom, reported its findings. A minority advocated holding the line militarily and even escalating if necessary, but the majority favored immediate steps toward de-escalation. After its last meeting in November, McGeorge Bundy reported, the group had expected slow and steady progress. This had not happened, however, and the majority view, as summed up by Acheson, was that the United States could "no longer do the job we set out to do in the time we have left and we must begin to take

---

[41]Clark Clifford, "A Viet Nam Reappraisal," *Foreign Affairs* 47 (July 1969): 613; memorandum of conversation with Clifford, March 20, 1968, Krock Papers; Harry McPherson oral history interview, Johnson Papers.

[42]Schandler, *Johnson and Vietnam*, p. 248. Tom Johnson notes on meeting, March 26, 1968, Johnson Papers, Tom Johnson Notes on Meetings, Box 2.

steps to disengage." The Wise Men disagreed among themselves on what to do, some proposing a total and unconditional bombing halt, others a shift in the ground strategy. Most agreed, however, that the goal of an independent, non-Communist South Vietnam was probably unattainable and that moves should be made toward eventual disengagement. "Unless we do something quick, the mood in this country may lead us to withdrawal," Cyrus Vance warned.[43] "The establishment bastards have bailed out," an angry and dispirited Johnson is said to have remarked after the meeting.[44]

Keeping his intentions under wraps until the very end, the president in a televised address on March 31 dramatically revealed a series of major decisions. Accepting Rusk's proposal, he announced that the bombing of North Vietnam would henceforth be limited to the area just north of the demilitarized zone. Responding to the entreaties of Clifford and the Wise Men, however, he went further. "Even this limited bombing of the North could come to an early end," he stressed, "if our restraint is matched by restraint in Hanoi." He named the veteran diplomat W. Averell Harriman his personal representative should peace talks materialize, and he made clear that the United States was ready to discuss peace, any time, any place. In a bombshell announcement that caught the nation by surprise, Johnson concluded by stating firmly: "I shall not seek, and I will not accept, the nomination of my party for another term as your president." He later revealed that for some time he had considered not running for reelection. He was exhausted physically and emotionally from the strains of office. He realized that he had spent most of his political capital and that another term would be conflict-ridden and barren of accomplishment. By removing himself from candidacy, he could emphasize the sincerity of his de-

[43]Summary of notes, March 26, 1968, Johnson Papers, Meeting Notes File, Box 2. The Wise Men were Dean Acheson, George Ball, McGeorge Bundy, Douglas Dillon, Cyrus Vance, Arthur Dean, John McCloy, Omar Bradley, Matthew Ridgway, Maxwell Taylor, Robert Murphy, Henry Cabot Lodge, Abe Fortas, and Arthur Goldberg.
[44]Quoted in Roger Morris, *An Uncertain Greatness: Henry Kissinger and American Foreign Policy* (New York, 1977), p. 44. Johnson was furious with the negative tone of the March 26 briefings. The "first thing I do when you all leave is to get those briefers," he told one of the Wise Men. Notes, March 26, 1968, Johnson Papers, Diary Backup File, Box 95. See also Depuy oral history interview, William Depuy Papers, U.S. Army Military History Institute, Carlisle Barracks, Pa.

sire for negotiations and contribute to the restoration of national unity and domestic harmony.[45]

Johnson's speech is usually cited as a major turning point in American involvement in Vietnam, and in some ways it was. No ceiling was placed on American ground forces, and the president did not obligate himself to maintain the restrictions on the bombing. Indeed, in explaining the partial bombing halt to the embassy in Saigon, the State Department indicated that Hanoi would probably "denounce" it and "thus free our hand after a short period."[46] Nevertheless, the circumstances in which the March decisions were made and the conciliatory tone of Johnson's speech made it difficult, if not impossible, for him to change course. March 31, 1968, brought an inglorious end to the policy of gradual escalation.

The president did not change his goals, however. The apparent American success in the battles of Tet reinforced the conviction of Johnson, Rusk, and Rostow that they could yet secure an independent, non-Communist South Vietnam. "My biggest worry was not Vietnam itself," the president later conceded, "it was the divisiveness and pessimism at home. . . . I looked on my approaching speech as an opportunity to help right the balance and provide better perspective. For the collapse of the home front, I knew well, was just what Hanoi was counting on."[47] By rejecting major troop reinforcements, reducing the bombing, shifting some military responsibility to the Vietnamese, and withdrawing from the presidential race, Johnson hoped to salvage his policy at least to the end of his term, and he felt certain that history would vindicate him for standing firm. The March 31 speech did not represent a change of policy, therefore, but a shift of tactics to salvage a policy that had come under bitter attack.

The new tactics were even more vaguely defined and contradictory than the old, however. Johnson's decisions marked a shift from the idea of graduated pressure to the pre-1965 concept of saving South Vietnam by denying the enemy victory. Precisely how this goal was to be achieved was not spelled out. The debate over

[45]*Public Papers of Lyndon B. Johnson, 1968–1969* (2 vols.; Washington, D.C., 1970), 1:469–476. On Johnson's decision not to run, see also George Christian memorandum, March 31, 1968, Johnson Papers, Diary Backup File, Box 96.

[46]"March 31 Speech," Johnson Papers, National Security File, National Security Council Histories: March 31, 1968, Speech, Box 47.

[47]Johnson, *Vantage Point*, p. 422.

ground strategy was not resolved, and General Abrams was given no strategic guidance. Administration officials generally agreed that ground operations should be scaled down to reduce casualties, but it was not clear how they would contribute to the achievement of American goals. The bombing was to be concentrated against North Vietnamese staging areas and supply lines, but that tactic had not reduced infiltration significantly in the past, and there was no reason to assume it would be more effective in the future. The exigencies of domestic politics required acceptance of the concept of Vietnamization, and the surprising response of the ARVN during Tet raised hopes that it would work. There was little in the past record of various South Vietnamese governments to suggest, however, that Thieu and his cohorts could conciliate their non-Communist opponents and pacify the countryside while effectively waging war against a weakened but still formidable enemy. Negotiations were also desirable from a domestic political standpoint, but in the absence of concessions the administration was not prepared to make, diplomacy could accomplish nothing, and its failure might intensify the pressures the talks were designed to ease. In short, the tactics of 1968 perpetuated the ambiguities and inconsistencies that had marked American policy from the start.

FIGHTING WHILE NEGOTIATING

U.S. policy in the months after Tet makes clear that although the Johnson administration spoke a more conciliatory language and altered its tactics, it did not retreat from its original goals. The president made good on his pledge to negotiate, accepting, after numerous delays, Hanoi's proposal for direct talks. From the outset, however, he refused to compromise on the fundamental issues. In the meantime, the United States kept maximum pressure on enemy forces in South Vietnam, assisted the South Vietnamese in a frantic drive to gain control of the countryside, and made plans for a gradual shift of the military burden to the ARVN. The result was to harden the stalemate, leaving resolution of the problem to the next administration.

Divisions within the U.S. government became even more pronounced during this new phase of the war. Certain, as Westmoreland put it, that the enemy had suffered a "colossal" defeat and that in any negotiations the United States would "hold four aces," North Vietnam "two deuces," Rusk, Rostow, Ambassador Bunker, and the military staunchly opposed concessions and sought to apply intensive military pressure. They feared that the North Vietnamese would use negotiations to divide the United States from its South Vietnamese ally. They insisted that if the administration could shore up the home front and improve its military position in Vietnam, Hanoi could be forced to make major concessions. "We can afford . . . to be tough, patient and not too anxious in our negotiating stance," Bunker affirmed.[48]

Clifford and Harriman, on the other hand, sought to extricate the United States from what they viewed as a hopeless tangle. Certain that the war was crippling America's ability to deal with more important problems and undermining its position as the "standard-bearer of moral principle in the world," they sought through Clifford's "winching down process" mutual de-escalation and disengagement, even at the expense of South Vietnam.[49] A skillful bureaucratic infighter, Clifford attempted to move the president to positions he had not reached. At an April 11 press conference, for example, Clifford stated that a ceiling had been imposed on U.S. ground troops, a policy that the president had not yet approved but could not challenge and that therefore became established.

The battle raged throughout 1968. The two factions fought bitterly over such issues as the U.S. negotiating stance, the scale and purpose of ground operations, and resumption or full curtailment of the bombing. The stakes were high, the participants exhausted, their nerves frayed. Clifford remembered 1968 as a year that lasted five years; Rusk recalled it as a "blur." Personal attacks descended to unprecedented levels. The president himself was worn out, increasingly angry and frustrated, more indecisive than usual, at times petulant and petty. Rusk and Rostow's hard line appealed to his "nail that coonskin to the wall" mentality. On occasion, he regretted having made the March 31 speech, and he yearned to bomb Hanoi and Haiphong off the map. A man who thrived on consen-

[48]Bunker memorandum, "Viet-Nam Negotiations: Dangers and Opportunities," April 8, 1968, W. Averell Harriman Papers, Manuscript Division, Library of Congress, Washington, D.C., Box 521.
[49]Harriman memorandum, "General Review of the Last Six Months," December 10, 1968, Harriman Papers; Clark Clifford, *Counsel to the President: A Memoir* (New York, 1991), pp. 534–536.

sus, he could not deal with the bitter divisions among his advisers, and his administration in its last months never addressed, much less resolved, the fundamental issues of the war or developed a thought-out negotiating position. "The pressure grew so intense that at times I felt that the government itself might come apart at the seams," Clifford later recalled. "There was, for a brief time, something approaching paralysis, and a sense of events spiralling out of control.[50]

Despite the accommodating tone of his March 31 speech, the president approached the reality of negotiations with extreme caution. Some administration officials had expected the North Vietnamese to rebuff the U.S. proposal. In fact, Tet also produced pressures for negotiations in North Vietnam. Some officials there urged a scaling back of the war in the disastrous aftermath of Tet, and the North Vietnamese had long sought a respite from the bombing. Hanoi appears always to have intended, moreover, that negotiations would be an integral part of this new phase of the war. Its strategy of *danh va dam*, or "fighting while negotiating"—an integrated approach to warfare that blended military and diplomatic activities—sought to stimulate "internal contradictions" in the enemy camp. Specifically, the North Vietnamese hoped through a change of strategy to increase antiwar pressures in the United States and sow seeds of division between Washington and Saigon. Thus three days after Johnson's speech, they agreed to meet with the United States to discuss an unconditional end to the bombing.

Hanoi's positive response caught Washington by surprise, and some U.S. officials suspected a clever ploy to exploit antiwar sentiment in the United States. The administration had no choice but to accept the enemy's proposal for direct talks, but it was determined not to rush into negotiations. Although Johnson had vowed to send representatives "to any forum, at any time," he rejected Hanoi's proposed sites of Phnom Penh, Cambodia, and Warsaw, where, he said, the "deck would be stacked against us."[51]

---

[50]Clifford, *Counsel to the President,* p. 461; Dean Rusk as told to Richard Rusk, *As I Saw It* (New York, 1990), p. 417. See also George Elsey notes on Clifford staff conferences, May 4, May 18, June 12, George M. Elsey Papers, Lyndon Baines Johnson Library, Austin, Tex. My thanks to Professor Robert Buzzanco for helping me to get these valuable documents.

[51]Johnson, *Vantage Point,* pp. 505–506.

The two nations finally agreed to meet in Paris, and the administration took a hard line from the outset. Harriman and Clifford advocated a generous initial offer to get negotiations moving and extricate the United States from Vietnam as quickly as possible, but Johnson's other advisers were not persuaded. Westmoreland and Bunker insisted that the U.S. position in South Vietnam had improved significantly and that the administration would be negotiating from strength. Johnson and his more hawkish advisers expressed grave doubts that the talks would lead to anything. They sincerely desired peace, but the terms they were prepared to hold out for virtually ensured that nothing would be accomplished. The president assured a nervous delegation of Thais that "he was not about to run out on his commitments, his principles, or his friends." We "will never—we will never—compromise the future of Asia at the negotiating table," he vowed. Rusk insisted that the United States should get North Vietnam "to make concessions" or "take responsibility for breaking off the talks." In return for a complete bombing halt, administration officials seemed disposed to retreat from the San Antonio formula. The secretary of state even talked about holding out for North Vietnamese observance of the 1962 Geneva Accords on Laos and reestablishment of the demilitarized zone. The United States opposed a cease-fire that would tie its hands militarily in the south, and in terms of a political settlement, Rusk spoke hopefully of restoration of the status quo antebellum.[52]

Formal talks opened in Paris on May 13 and immediately deadlocked. North Vietnam had agreed to the meetings as part of its broader strategy of fighting while negotiating. It had little interest in substantive negotiations while the military balance of forces was unfavorable, and it viewed the Paris talks as a means of getting the bombing stopped, exacerbating differences between the United States and South Vietnam, and intensifying antiwar pressures in the United States. The North Vietnamese made clear that they were establishing contact with the United States to secure the "unconditional cessation of U.S. bombing raids and all other acts of war so that talks

[52]Robert J. Flynn, "Preserving the Hub: U.S.–Thai Relations during the Vietnam War" (Ph.D. diss. University of Kentucky), pp. 145–147; Notes on meeting, May 6, 1968, Johnson Papers, Meeting Notes File, Box 3; Harold Johnson notes on meetings, May 6, 8, 1968, Harold Johnson Papers, U.S. Army Military History Institute, Carlisle Barracks, Pa., Box 127; Andrew Goodpaster oral history interview, U.S. Army Military History Institute, Carlisle Barracks, Pa.

may start." The Johnson administration was willing to stop the bombing, but as in the past, it insisted on reciprocal de-escalation. Hanoi continued to reject the American demand for reciprocity and refused any terms that limited its ability to support the war in the south while leaving the United States a free hand there.

To break the impasse, chief American negotiator Harriman subsequently introduced a new proposal, actually a variant of the old two-track plan. The United States would stop the bombing "on the assumption that" North Vietnam would respect the demilitarized zone and refrain from further rocket attacks on Saigon and other cities and that "prompt and serious talks" would follow. The offer brought no formal response or any indication that one might be forthcoming. American officials complained that the North Vietnamese seemed prepared to sit in Paris "and even read the telephone directory if necessary to keep non-productive talks going," and the Joint Chiefs pressed relentlessly for reescalation, including B-52 strikes against North Vietnamese sanctuaries in Cambodia.[53]

Fearful that the talks might drag on inconclusively, perpetuating the war and exacerbating domestic divisions, Harriman urged the president to compromise. Although North Vietnam had not responded formally to the American proposal, NLF rocket attacks had subsided, and there were indications that significant numbers of North Vietnamese troops had been withdrawn from the south. Harriman argued that the military lull could be interpreted as a sign of de-escalation, and he pressed Johnson to stop the bombing and reduce the level of American military activity while making clear the next move he expected from Hanoi. Clifford supported Harriman's proposal, but the military argued that the lull was simply a regrouping for the next offensive and warned that stopping the bombing would endanger American troops. An enraged Johnson flatly rejected Harriman's proposal, privately dismissing it as "mush" and claiming that the enemy was using his "own people as dupes." Meeting with his advisers on July 30, he expressed a wish to "knock the hell" out of the North Vietnamese. At a press conference the following day he threatened that if there were no breakthrough in Paris, he might be compelled to undertake additional military mea-

[53]Notes on National Security Council meeting, May 22, 1968, Johnson Papers, National Security File, NSC Meetings, Box 3; notes on meetings, May 25, 28, Johnson Papers, Meeting Notes File, Box 3.

sures. "Our most difficult negotiations were with Washington and not Hanoi . . . ," one U.S. diplomat later lamented. "We just couldn't convince the President that summer."[54]

While standing firm in Paris, the administration used every available means to strengthen its position in South Vietnam. The United States stepped up the pace of military operations in the spring of 1968. The air war in South Vietnam reached a new level of intensity, as B-52s and fighter-bombers relentlessly attacked infiltration routes, lines of communication, and suspected enemy base camps. The number of B-52 missions tripled in 1968, and the bombs dropped on South Vietnam exceeded one million tons. In March and April, the United States and South Vietnam conducted the largest search-and-destroy mission of the war, sending more than 100,000 troops against enemy forces in the provinces around Saigon. "Charlie [the Vietcong] is being relentlessly pursued night and day and pounded to shreds whenever and wherever we catch him," one U.S. officer exclaimed.[55] The scale of American military operations diminished somewhat in the summer and fall as Abrams shifted to small-unit patrols and mobile spoiling attacks, but throughout the rest of the year the United States kept intense pressure on enemy forces in South Vietnam.

The United States and South Vietnam also launched an Accelerated Pacification campaign to secure as much of the countryside as possible in the event serious negotiations should begin. Abrams committed a major proportion of American and ARVN personnel to the program, and local defense forces were enlarged and given modern military equipment. To use their resources more effectively, the United States and South Vietnam focused on key areas and applied both carrot and stick to cripple an already weakened NLF. The Chieu Hoi Program, which offered amnesty and "rehabilitation" to defectors, was intensified, as was the Phoenix Program, a direct attack on the NLF infrastructure through mass arrests. By late 1968, for the first time, the United States and South Vietnam were firmly committed to controlling the countryside.[56]

[54]Quoted in Allan E. Goodman, *The Lost Peace: America's Search for a Negotiated Settlement of the Vietnam War* (Stanford, Calif., 1978), p. 69.

[55]Frank Clay to Mr. and Mrs. Lucius Clay, May 15, 1968, Frank Clay Papers, U.S. Army Military History Institute, Carlisle Barracks, Pa.

[56]Douglas S. Blaufarb, *The Counterinsurgency Era: U.S. Doctrines and Performance* (New York, 1977), pp. 264–265; James H. Embrey, "Reorienting Pacification: The Accelerated Pacification Campaign of 1968," (Ph.D. diss., University of Kentucky, 1997).

The United States also pressed forward with Vietnamization. American officials candidly admitted that the South Vietnamese were nowhere near ready to assume the burden of their own defense. "If you took out all the United States . . . forces now," Abrams conceded, "the Government would have to settle for a piece of Vietnam."[57] New plans were nevertheless drawn up to expand and upgrade the South Vietnamese armed forces and gradually shift to them primary responsibility for military operations. The force level was increased from 685,000 to 801,000, training programs were drastically expanded, and ARVN units were given the newest equipment. To improve the combat-readiness of Vietnamese troops and smooth the transition, Abrams employed ARVN and American units in combined operations.[58]

Pacification and Vietnamization were both long-range undertakings, however, and the frenzied efforts of 1968 could not make up for years of neglect. It was the end of the year before the pacification program got back to where it had been before Tet. The establishment of a presence in the villages was not tantamount to gaining the active support of the people, something that could not be accomplished overnight. The ARVN was larger and better equipped, but its basic problems remained uncorrected. Desertions reached an all-time high in 1968; an acute shortage of qualified officers persisted. At the end of the year, American advisers rated two ARVN divisions "outright poor," eight no better than "improving," and only one "excellent."[59] Americans detected among the Vietnamese a stubborn, if quiet, resistance to the whole notion of Vietnamization. Clifford returned from a visit to Saigon "oppressed" by the "pervasive Americanization" of the war. The United States was still doing most of the fighting and paying the cost. "Worst of all," he concluded, "the South Vietnamese leaders seemed content to have it that way."[60]

The crash programs of 1968 did not decisively alter the military or political balance in South Vietnam. The NLF hold on the country-

[57]A. J. Langguth, "General Abrams Listens to a Different Drummer," *New York Times Magazine*, May 5, 1968, 28.
[58]Jeffrey J. Clarke, *Advice and Support: The Final Years, 1965–1973* (Washington, D.C., 1988), pp. 293–296.
[59]Robert Shaplen, *The Road from War: Vietnam, 1965–1970* (New York, 1970), p. 250.
[60]Clifford, "Viet Nam Reappraisal," pp. 614–615; also Clifford to Johnson, July 16, 18, 1968, Clifford Papers, Box 5.

side was weaker than ever before, and defections increased significantly. The harsh methods used to rebuild the insurgents' depleted ranks alienated many villagers. The government was therefore able to regain much of what had been lost in the early days of Tet and even extend its influence into new areas. The United States held the military initiative throughout much of South Vietnam during 1968, and its spoiling attacks on base areas and supply lines kept the enemy off balance. Americans detected a marked deterioration in the quality of North Vietnamese Army (NVA) soldiers after Tet. The NLF clandestine organization and North Vietnamese main units remained intact, however, and the launching of major operations in May and August, as well as sporadic rocket attacks on the cities, made clear that they retained significant strength and the will to fight on.

Although it improved markedly in the aftermath of Tet, the performance of the government of South Vietnam remained at best uneven, its stability uncertain. Government and people worked together effectively in implementing Operation Recovery, a massive crash program to repair the damage done to the cities by the battles of Tet. At American urging, Thieu adopted a new economic program to combat inflation and instituted anticorruption measures to deal with one of South Vietnam's oldest and most pervasive problems. Some optimistic observers concluded late in the year that the government was functioning more effectively than at any other time since the mid-1950s. For every problem attacked, however, others remained unchallenged and new ones surfaced. Land reform moved forward at a snail's pace. Tet created thousands of new refugees, and American officials expressed grave concern at the government's apparent indifference to their plight. The prospect of negotiations made Thieu more reluctant than ever to broaden the base of his government. He made some cosmetic changes, appointing a civilian, Tran Van Huong, as prime minister and promising to expand civilian influence in the government. Increasingly, however, he withdrew into himself, trusting no one and making most decisions on his own. "He is his own Nhu," one American complained with more than a touch of resignation.[61]

The possibility of an American withdrawal exacerbated the fragmented political system of South Vietnam. "Divisiveness is still

---

[61]Quoted in Shaplen, *Road from War*, p. 248. See also William Colby oral history interview, Johnson Papers, and James P. Grant to Ernest Lindley, September 21, 1968, Johnson Papers, National Security File, Country File: Vietnam, Box 101.

endemic," Robert Shaplen observed in late 1968, "and rivalries exist across the board, in politics, in the Army, among religious groups, and so on." The rivalry between Ky and Thieu intensified, factionalizing much of the government. The Buddhists remained more alienated than ever, issuing open demands for the foundation of a "peace cabinet" and urging the soldiers to lay down their arms. Both the Buddhists and the sects appeared to look forward to the collapse of the government so that they could pick up the pieces. New political groups proliferated after the peace negotiations began, but they were dissension-ridden and could not work together. Much of the urban population persisted in its demeanor of watchful waiting. The South Vietnamese, Shaplen concluded, seemed "more and more like men who know they are suffering from an incurable malady."[62]

Vietnamese-American tensions increased significantly in the period after Tet. The government and its supporters angrily protested that they had been railroaded into negotiations before they were ready. Those Vietnamese who had come to depend on the United States expressed bitter fears that they would be left at the mercy of the Vietcong. American service personnel manifested more openly the accumulated frustrations of fighting in a hostile environment a war they could not "win," and the savagery of the battles of Tet and the heavy losses inflamed anti-Vietnamese feelings. A gallows humor solution to the Vietnam dilemma that went the round of firebases and GI bars typified the attitude. "What you do is, you load all the Friendlies onto ships and take them out to the South China Sea. Then you bomb the country flat. Then you sink the ship."[63] The murder of more than 500 civilians, including women and children, in the village of My Lai by an American company under the command of Lieutenant William Calley in March 1968 starkly revealed the hostility some Americans had come to feel for all Vietnamese.

YEAR OF ANGUISH

Divisions inside the United States also increased sharply and dramatically in that incredible year of tumult and torment, 1968, and although the war in Vietnam was only one of numerous causes, it was often the focal point. Campus unrest mounted significantly,

---

[62]Shaplen, *Road from War*, p. 208.
[63]Michael Herr, *Dispatches* (New York, 1978), p. 59.

some 200 demonstrations erupting at more than 100 colleges during the spring semester alone. The most publicized and violent demonstrations took place at Columbia University in New York City, where radicals took over several buildings and occupied the president's office. After eight days, 1,000 police wielding nightsticks forcibly drove out the protesters. The assassination of civil rights leader and antiwar activist Martin Luther King, Jr., in April brought latent racial unrest to the surface, provoking rioting, looting, and the burning of buildings in urban areas across the nation. The most visible and destructive rioting was in Washington, D.C., where members of Congress could see the flames of burning neighborhoods from their office windows and soldiers wielded guns on the steps of the Capitol building. Twelve people were killed, an estimated $25 million of damage was done, and the races were further polarized. The assassination of presidential candidate Robert Kennedy in June brought more grief to an already emotionally exhausted nation and seemed a graphic demonstration of the extent to which violence had triumphed.

More than anything else, the Democratic convention in Chicago in August dramatized the reality of a nation divided against itself. Within the movement, the radicals were in the ascendancy, and yippies circulated rumors that the Chicago water supply would be laced with drugs and 1,000 protesters would float nude in Lake Michigan. Chicago's hard-core mayor, William Daley, in turn mobilized more than 25,000 police, national guard, and army troops to maintain law and order. While delegates inside the stormy convention hall bitterly debated the war and other issues, antiwar protesters engaged Daley's police in bloody battles in the streets. The convention nominated Johnson's preferred candidate, Vice President Hubert H. Humphrey, and in general endorsed the president's policies, proving to some critics that the war could not be ended by working within the system. More important, the bloodshed in the streets of "nightstick city" was brought into the homes of Americans each night on television, and the nation "could no longer turn away from the fact that the war in Southeast Asia . . . was causing a kind of civil war in the United States."[64]

[64]Nancy Zaroulis and Gerald Sullivan, *Who Spoke Up? American Protest against the War in Vietnam, 1963–1975* (New York, 1984), p. 200. See also Terry H. Anderson, *The Movement and the Sixties* (New York, 1995), pp. 183–238; and Maurice Isserman and Michael Kazin, *America Divided* (New York, 2000), pp. 221–240.

THE OCTOBER BOMBING HALT

Largely in response to domestic pressures, Johnson in late 1968 made one last effort to get the peace talks off dead center. The convention in Chicago badly discredited the Democrats, and in its aftermath some party leaders pleaded for a dramatic peace move to assist Humphrey, who lagged well behind Republican candidate Richard M. Nixon in the early polls. The president had repeatedly insisted that he would not be swayed by political considerations, and when Humphrey sought to distance himself from the administration's Vietnam policy, the president for a time seemed to prefer a Nixon victory. But Johnson was sympathetic to the concerns of leading Democrats, and he was eventually persuaded that he might be able to break the deadlock in Paris without undue risk. Harriman continued to argue that the military lull in South Vietnam was a clear sign of North Vietnamese interest in substantive negotiations, and Abrams assured Johnson that a bombing halt would not pose a military threat. The North Vietnamese had been badly hurt by the spring campaigns. In any case, the approach of the monsoon season would severely limit the effectiveness of the bombing for several months. To appease the military and keep pressure on North Vietnam, Johnson agreed, in the event of a bombing halt, to redeploy American airpower against North Vietnamese supply lines in Laos. The president, with apparent reluctance, finally committed himself to stop the bombing altogether if some concessions could be obtained from the North Vietnamese.[65]

Over the next few weeks, Harriman diligently negotiated an "understanding." To meet Hanoi's continuing objections to reciprocity, he indicated that the bombing would be stopped unilaterally, and North Vietnam eventually dropped its insistence on an unconditional bombing halt. The U.S. delegation made clear, however, that the enemy would be expected to stop rocket and mortar attacks on South Vietnamese cities and limit the infiltration of soldiers and supplies across the demilitarized zone. In addition, the North Vietnamese informally agreed that serious peace talks would begin within four days after the bombing had been stopped. The administration was especially pleased to secure Hanoi's consent to

[65]Johnson, *Vantage Point*, pp. 514–515; memorandum for the record, October 23, 1968, Johnson Papers, Diary Backup, November 11, 1968, Box 115.

the Saigon government's participation in the peace talks. To get around North Vietnam's repeated refusal to negotiate directly with the "puppet" Saigon government and Thieu's refusal to join negotiations in which the NLF participated, Harriman devised an ingenious "our side, your side" formula. The negotiations would be two-sided, but each side was free to work out its own composition and to interpret the makeup of the other as it chose. The NLF and the Saigon government could thus participate without recognizing each other as an independent entity. The North Vietnamese refused to commit themselves formally to these "understandings," but they gave private assurances that they would "know what to do" once the bombing had stopped. Hesitant to the end, Johnson finally agreed to "go the last mile" for peace, although administration officials agreed that if the North Vietnamese took advantage of the bombing halt or appeared not to be negotiating seriously, the United States might resume air operations.[66]

No sooner had these arrangements been completed than the South Vietnamese balked. Thieu may have been responding to right-wing politicians in his own country, Ky included, who issued dire warnings of an American sellout.

His intransigence was encouraged by Republicans who feared a Democratic preelection "peace gimmick" that would undercut Nixon's candidacy. In one of the more sordid episodes in recent political history, Harvard professor Henry A. Kissinger, eager for a top-level foreign policy position whoever won and adept at playing several ends against the middle, used his contacts in the Johnson administration to ingratiate himself with the Nixon camp by keeping it informed of what was happening in Washington and Paris. While candidate Nixon was issuing public statements putting the war above politics, his advisers used Madame Anna Chennault, widow of the legendary founder of China's World War II Flying Tigers and a devotee of Taiwan and other right-wing causes, as a go-between to urge Thieu to sabotage the administration's diplomacy, making clear that South Vietnam might fare better with a Nixon administration in January than with an incumbent desperate for a settlement in his last days in office. Johnson found out about the conspiracy through wiretaps and surveillance of some of the major participants, but he refused to expose it because to do so

---

[66]Johnson, *Vantage Point*, p. 518; notes on meetings, October 14, 31, 1968, Johnson Papers, Meeting Notes File, Box 3.

might require divulging the sources of his information and reveal his own unsavory practices.[67]

Only forty-four years old at this crucial juncture in his career, Nguyen Van Thieu had demonstrated above all else in his rapid rise to military and political power a keen instinct for survival. He had collaborated with the Vietminh, the French, and the Americans at various times, and he had shown rare cunning in mastering the Byzantine intricacies of South Vietnamese politics. Shrewd and suspicious, he was painfully aware of his dependence on the United States, but he also increasingly recognized that he could not trust his ally. A wily, calculating politician, desperately fearful for his country's future and his own, Thieu probably would have concluded without any prompting that he would do better with the Republicans than with the Democrats and that delay was essential. Proclaiming that his government was not a "car that can be hitched to a locomotive and taken anywhere the locomotive wants to go," he insisted that he would not meet with the Vietcong and that the American-arranged understanding was a "clear admission of defeat." Hanoi, he said, must issue formal assurances that it would de-escalate the war and must negotiate directly with Saigon.[68]

Intensive U.S. pressure failed to budge the embattled South Vietnamese. Johnson sternly warned Thieu on October 30 that if Americans held Thieu responsible for blocking peace, "God help South Vietnam, because no president could maintain the support of the American people." An emotional Thieu stubbornly retorted: "You are powerful. You can say to small nations what you want . . . but you cannot force us to do anything against our interests. This negotiation is not a life and death matter for the US, but it is for Vietnam."[69]

Thieu's obstinacy posed a dilemma for the United States. Johnson recognized that to concede to Saigon's demands would "blow the whole peace effort sky high," perhaps wrecking Humphrey's chances as well.[70] On the other hand, he feared that to negotiate

[67]The fullest accounts of this sorry story are Anthony Summers, *The Arrogance of Power: The Secret World of Richard Nixon* (New York, 2000), pp. 297–308; and Christopher Hitchens, "The Case against Henry Kissinger: Part One, The Making of a War Criminal," *Harper's Magazine,* February 2001, 37–42.

[68]Quoted in Shaplen, *Road from War,* p. 243.

[69]Secretary of State to Embassy Saigon, Embassy Saigon to Secretary of State, October 30, 1968, copies in Harriman Papers, Box 554.

[70]Johnson, *Vantage Point,* pp. 517–519.

without Saigon, as Harriman and even Rusk urged, offered little prospect of an acceptable settlement and risked Republican charges of a sellout. The president thus announced the bombing halt on October 31 without South Vietnamese approval, but he delayed the opening of formal talks. In the meantime, the United States combined renewed assurances that it would not recognize the NLF or impose a coalition government on South Vietnam with private pressures and eventually a public threat to begin talks without Saigon. After a two-week delay, during which Nixon won a precariously thin victory, Thieu agreed to send representatives to Paris.

Once in Paris, the South Vietnamese raised procedural objections that nullified any hope of a peace settlement. The United States had originally proposed that the delegations be seated at two long tables to emphasize the two-sided nature of the talks, but North Vietnam had demanded a square table with one delegate on each side to underscore its contention that the NLF was a separate party to the talks. To get around this impasse, Harriman had proposed a round table, and the North Vietnamese had acquiesced. But Saigon refused to go along. Thieu may have felt that the issue was of sufficient symbolic or even practical importance to merit resistance, or he may simply have seized on it to stall the talks until a presumably more sympathetic Nixon took office.

Americans railed at South Vietnamese intransigence, and the North Vietnamese mocked American weakness. Harry McPherson lamented that the "American Gulliver is tied down by the South Vietnamese Lilliputians." Outraged at what he later denounced as a "ridiculous performance" on the part of the South Vietnamese, Harriman again urged Johnson to negotiate without them. The South Vietnamese has been "coddled and cuddled beyond belief," an impatient and irate Clifford complained. "They're making all the decisions, but we pay, we die, we fight." He pressed Johnson to begin to withdraw U.S. troops irrespective of what Saigon and Hanoi did.[71] North Vietnamese negotiators snidely observed that "usually the man leads the horse. This time the horse is leading the man."[72] The president upheld Thieu's objections, however, and the

[71]McPherson to Clifford, August 13, 1968, Johnson Papers, McPherson File, Box 53; Clifford notes for meeting with Johnson, November 18, 1968, Clifford Papers, Box 6; Elsey Notes, December 18, 1968, January 4, 1969, Elsey Papers.
[72]Harriman memorandum of conversation with Robert Shaplen, November 30, 1968, Harriman Papers, Box 556.

so-called battle of the tables raged for weeks. Instead of drafting cables at night, the U.S. delegation sketched table designs, the two sides proposing at various times such inventive geometric creations as a broken parallelogram, four arcs of a circle, a flattened ellipse, and two semicircles that touched but did not form a circle. Finally, under pressure from the Soviet Union, Hanoi agreed to a compromise: a round table placed between two rectangular tables. By the time the infamous battle had been resolved, the Johnson administration was in its last days, and any chance of substantive negotiations had passed.[73]

It seems doubtful that South Vietnamese intransigence sabotaged an opportunity for a peace settlement. Hanoi's approach on procedural issues was more flexible in late 1968 than previously, probably because it wanted to get the bombing stopped, possibly because it hoped to extract an acceptable settlement from Johnson before he left office. Its flexibility most likely did not extend to substantive issues, however. There is nothing to indicate that Hanoi would have agreed to anything short of an American withdrawal and a coalition government. These terms would not have been acceptable to the United States. Although he had given in on the bombing halt and was deeply annoyed with Thieu, Johnson still clung to the goals he had pursued so doggedly since taking office. He made clear to Thieu that he would not recognize the NLF or accept a coalition government or some form of cosmetic settlement that would permit an American withdrawal. He seems to have felt that he could still achieve his original goals, and he remained convinced that he had the enemy on the ropes.[74] On the day he ordered the bombing halt, he instructed Abrams to "use his manpower and resources in a maximum effort" to "keep the enemy on the run." "Don't give them a moment's rest. Let the enemy feel the weight of everything you've got."[75] Thus, even if Thieu had gone along from the start, it appears

[73]Harriman to Rusk, December 21, 28, 1968, Harriman Papers, Box 553; Rudy Abramson, *The Life of W. Averell Harriman: Spanning the Century, 1891–1986* (New York, 1992), p. 671.
[74]The enemy could "still knock out a window light," Johnson remarked in November, but "they have been out of it since September." Henry Graff, *The Tuesday Cabinet* (Englewood Cliffs, N.J., 1970), p. 163. Also notes on meeting with Nixon, November 11, 1968, Johnson Papers, Tom Johnson Notes, Box 1.
[75]Johnson, *Vantage Point,* p. 523; Lewis Sorley, *Thunderbolt: General Creighton Abrams and the Army of His Times* (New York, 1992), p. 253.

Comparative Military Casualty Figures

Year	Killed in Action		Wounded	
	U.S.	South Vietnam	U.S.	South Vietnam
1960	0	2,223	0	2,788
1961	11	4,004	2	5,449
1962	31	4,457	41	7,195
1963	78	5,665	218	11,488
1964	147	7,457	522	17,017
1965	1,369	11,242	3,308	23,118
1966	5,008	11,953	16,526	20,975
1967	9,377	12,716	32,370	29,448
1968	14,589	27,915	46,797	70,696
1969	9,414	21,833	32,940	65,276
1970	4,221	23,346	15,211	71,582
1971	1,381	22,738	4,767	60,939
1972	300	39,587	587	109,960
1973	237	27,901	24	131,936
1974	207	31,219	0	155,735
Totals	46,370	254,256	153,313	783,602

Source: Jeffrey J. Clarke, *Advice and Support: The Final Years,* p. 275.

highly unlikely that any meaningful peace agreement could have been reached in 1968, particularly in view of the short timetable.

The year 1968 ended as it had begun, with deadlock on the battlefield and in diplomatic councils. Each side in the aftermath of Tet saw itself on the offensive seeking a knockout blow against a weakened enemy. In fact, each had suffered enormous losses. In the eight weeks after March 31 alone, 3,700 Americans were killed, an estimated 43,000 enemy. Despite claims of victory, moreover, each combatant was significantly weakened, and neither emerged with sufficient leverage to force a settlement. Tet merely hardened the deadlock, and it would take four more years of "fighting while negotiating" before it was finally broken.

In the long run, as historian Ronald Spector has observed, the battles of Tet were decisive "because they were so indecisive."[76]

[76]Ronald H. Spector, *After Tet: The Bloodiest Year in Vietnam* (New York, 1993), pp. 311–314.

Whatever its costs, Tet represented a major political victory for the enemy because it convinced most Americans that the war could not be won in an acceptable time and at an acceptable cost. Thus, although Johnson clung stubbornly to his goals and refused to make the concessions necessary to get a settlement, he initiated what turned out to be an irreversible process of de-escalation that would in time work in North Vietnam's favor. In a still larger sense, Tet represented the high-water mark of post–World War II American hegemony, that point at which the nation's establishment came to recognize that its international commitments had begun to exceed its ability to pay for them. From this point on, in Vietnam and elsewhere, the United States struggled with the dilemma of scaling back its commitments or finding alternative ways of maintaining its domestic and international well-being at a lower cost.

Nixon and Kissinger
Certain at the outset of success in Vietnam, Richard M. Nixon and Henry A.
Kissinger prolonged the war for four bloody years, with huge costs for
Americans, Vietnamese, and ultimately themselves.
AP/Wide World Photos

CHAPTER 7

A War for Peace

Nixon, Kissinger, and Vietnam, 1969–1973

"We will not make the same old mistakes," Henry A. Kissinger proclaimed of Vietnam in 1969. "We will make our own."[1] Kissinger's remark underscored the Nixon administration's determination to find new solutions to an old problem, and the self-effacing humor, a Kissinger trademark, suggested a certainty of success. But the prediction turned out to be only partially correct. Kissinger and Nixon did try new approaches, some of which in time produced their own mistakes, but their policy suffered from the same flaws as those of their predecessors. Although disguising it in the rhetoric of "peace with honor," the Nixon administration persisted in the quixotic search for an independent, non-Communist Vietnam. This goal was to be achieved primarily by a massive buildup of South Vietnamese military strength and by the application of military pressure against North Vietnam, methods that had been tried before in various forms and found wanting. The result was four more years of bloody warfare in Indochina, a marked increase in domestic strife, and a peace settlement that permitted American extrication but was neither honorable nor lasting.

PEACE WITH HONOR

U.S. foreign policy in the Nixon-Kissinger era bore the distinct personal imprint of its shapers. The middle-American professional

---

[1]Quoted in Roger Morris, *An Uncertain Greatness: Henry Kissinger and American Foreign Policy* (New York, 1977), p. 4.

271

politician and the German-born Harvard professor could hardly have been more different in background, but they shared a love of power and a burning ambition to mold a fluid world in a way that would establish their place in history. Loners and outsiders in their own professions, they were perhaps naturally drawn to each other. Insecure to the point of paranoia, they eventually became bitter rivals, but in the first years their mutual suspicion was kept in check by mutual dependence, Kissinger viewing Nixon as a means to prominence and power, Nixon relying on Kissinger to shape and implement his broad designs.

Although both men had reputations as rigid ideologues, they were pragmatic and flexible in their approach to foreign policy. They shared an obsession with secrecy, a zest for intrigue, and a flair for the unexpected move. They also shared a certain disdain for democracy, equating dissent with treason and carrying to extremes the Cold War dogma that national security was too important to be left to an ignorant public and a parochial and cumbersome Congress. Above all, they shared a contempt for bureaucracy. They took the foreign policy controls firmly and exclusively in their own hands and jealously guarded them, using, but rarely relying on or even keeping informed, the rest of the government and employing deception and backchannel communications to dominate their colleagues. Internecine warfare is a way of life in the American system of government, but Nixon and Kissinger created an atmosphere of oppressive secretiveness, paranoia, backbiting, and conspiracy that makes the word *Byzantine* seem tame by comparison. At one point, the Joint Chiefs of Staff felt compelled to engage a "spy" to find out what was going on in the White House!

The result was a foreign policy sometimes bold and imaginative in conception, sometimes crude and improvised; sometimes brilliant in execution, sometimes bungling; a policy dedicated to the noble goal of a "generation of peace" but frequently ruthless and cynical in its use of military power and callous in its obliviousness to the enormous human costs inflicted at home and especially abroad. The result also was a systematic abuse of power that ultimately forced Nixon's humiliating resignation from the office he had pursued relentlessly throughout his entire career.

Prior to taking office, Nixon and Kissinger had firmly defended the American commitment in Vietnam. At the height of the domestic debate in 1967, Nixon had insisted that the presence of U.S.

troops in Southeast Asia had helped contain an expansionist China and given the "free" Asian nations time to develop stable institutions. "Whatever one may think of the 'domino theory,' " he asserted, "it is beyond question that without the American commitment in Vietnam, Asia would be a far different place today."[2] Kissinger was more equivocal, conceding that the United States may have exaggerated the significance of Vietnam in the early stages of its involvement. "But the commitment of five hundred thousand Americans has settled the issue of the importance of Vietnam," he quickly added. "For what is involved now is confidence in American promises."[3]

By 1969, Nixon and Kissinger recognized that the war must be ended. It had become, in the words of one of Nixon's speechwriters, a "bone in the nation's throat," a divisive force that had torn the country apart and hindered any constructive approach to domestic and foreign policy problems.[4] Nixon clearly perceived, moreover, that his ability to extricate the nation from Vietnam would decisively affect his political future and his place in history. "I'm not going to end up like LBJ," he once remarked, "holed up in the White House afraid to show my face on the street. I'm going to stop that war. Fast."[5]

The two men nevertheless insisted that the war must be ended "honorably." Simply to pull out of Vietnam, they believed, would be a callous abandonment of those South Vietnamese who had depended on American protection and would be unworthy of the actions of a great nation. As a young Congressman, Nixon had led the right-wing Republican attack on Truman for "losing" China, and like Johnson before him, he feared the domestic upheaval that might accompany the fall of South Vietnam to communism. The reaction would be "terrible," he told a journalist in May 1969, ". . . we would destroy ourselves if we pulled out in a way that wasn't really honorable."[6]

Most important, Nixon and Kissinger feared the international consequences of a precipitous withdrawal. Even before taking office,

---

[2]Richard M. Nixon, "Asia after Vietnam," *Foreign Affairs* 46 (October 1967); 111.
[3]Henry A. Kissinger, "The Vietnam Negotiations," *Foreign Affairs* 47 (January 1969); 219.
[4]William Safire, *Before the Fall* (New York, 1975), p. 121.
[5]H. R. Haldeman, *The Ends of Power* (New York, 1978), p. 81.
[6]Quoted in C. L. Sulzberger, *Seven Continents and Forty Years* (New York, 1977), pp. 505–507.

they had begun sketching the outlines of a new world order based on American primacy. Their grand design included at least a limited accommodation with the Soviet Union and China, and they felt that they must extricate the United States from the war in a manner that would demonstrate to these old adversaries resoluteness of purpose and certainty of action, a manner that would uphold U.S. credibility with friends and foes alike. "However we got into Vietnam," Kissinger observed, "whatever the judgment of our actions, ending the war honorably is essential for the peace of the world. Any other solution may unloose forces that would complicate the prospects of international order."[7] Nixon agreed. "The true objective of this war is peace," he affirmed shortly after taking office—with no apparent sense of the paradox—"It is a war for peace."[8]

An "honorable" settlement had to meet several essential conditions. The American withdrawal from Vietnam must be conducted in a way that avoided even the slightest appearance of defeat. There must be no face-saving political settlement designed merely to permit a graceful American exit from Vietnam. Kissinger explicitly rejected the idea of a coalition government, which, he said, would "destroy the existing political structure and thus lead to a Communist takeover." Nixon and Kissinger set as their optimum goal a "fair negotiated settlement that would preserve the independence of South Vietnam." At a minimum, they insisted on a settlement that would give South Vietnam a reasonable chance to survive.[9]

Although this objective had eluded the United States for more than a decade, Nixon and Kissinger believed that they could succeed where others had failed. They perceived that the Saigon government could not survive an abrupt American withdrawal, but it appeared stronger than ever in early 1969, and with continued U.S. backing, Thieu might hold on indefinitely. The North Vietnamese must recognize, Kissinger reasoned, that they could not eject the United States from Vietnam by force. They might therefore be persuaded to exchange an American withdrawal for a political settlement that would leave Thieu firmly in control.

[7]Kissinger, "Vietnam Negotiations," 234.
[8]Sulzberger, *Seven Continents*, p. 507.
[9]Richard M. Nixon, *RN: The Memoirs of Richard Nixon* (New York, 1978), p. 349; Safire, *Before the Fall*, p. 134.

Nixon and Kissinger were confident, moreover, that they could compel Hanoi to accept the terms it had consistently rejected. The Soviet Union had made clear its keen interest in expanded trade with the United States and an agreement limiting strategic arms, and this leverage could be used to secure Russian assistance in getting North Vietnam to agree to a "fair" settlement. Great power diplomacy would be supplemented by the use of force. Nixon felt that military pressure had failed thus far because it had been employed in a limited, indecisive manner. A "fourth-rate power like North Vietnam" must have a "breaking point," Kissinger insisted, and he and Nixon were prepared to use maximum force, threatening the very survival of North Vietnam, to get what they wanted.[10] Nixon compared his situation to that faced by Eisenhower in Korea in 1953, and he was certain that the threat of "massive retaliation" would intimidate the North Vietnamese as he believed it had the North Koreans. He counted on his image as a hard-line anti-Communist to make the threat credible. "They'll believe any threat of force Nixon makes because it's Nixon," he told one of his advisers. "We'll just slip the word to them that, 'for God's sake, you know Nixon's obsessed about Communism . . . and he has his hand on the nuclear button.' "[11]

The Nixon-Kissinger strategy for ending the war was deeply flawed and based on a large dose of wishful thinking. Their concern for U.S. credibility was exaggerated and was based on dubious reasoning to begin with. In any event, as Walter Isaacson has concluded, in their stubborn and ultimately futile pursuit of a settlement that would uphold the credibility of the United States, they "squandered the true sources of its influence—and of its credibility—in the world: its moral authority, its sense of worthy purpose and its reputation as a reasonable and sensible player." It was naive to assume that they could accomplish what Johnson had failed to do at a time when they had less military power at their disposal and when the patience of the American public had already worn thin. Like their predecessors, they grossly underestimated their adversaries and they also overestimated the willingness and ability of the Kremlin to pressure North Vietnam to accept a settlement favorable to the United States. And the lessons

[10]Quoted in Morris, *Uncertain Greatness*, p. 164.
[11]Quoted in Haldeman, *Ends of Power*, p. 83.

Nixon drew from Eisenhower's ending of the Korean War represented yet another example of misuse of historical analogy by
American leaders.[12]

PEACE THROUGH COERCION

With that sublime self-confidence common among leaders new to
power, Nixon and Kissinger were certain they could end the war
within six months to a year. Through French intermediaries, the
president conveyed a personal message to the North Vietnamese
expressing his sincere desire for peace and proposing as a first step
the mutual withdrawal of American and North Vietnamese troops
from South Vietnam and the restoration of the demilitarized zone
as a boundary between north and south. Kissinger informed Soviet
ambassador Anatoly Dobrynin that the administration was eager to
negotiate on a variety of urgent topics but bluntly warned that
peace in Vietnam must come first.

As a signal to both Hanoi and Moscow that the United States
meant business, Nixon ordered intensive bombing attacks against
North Vietnamese sanctuaries in neutral Cambodia, a step repeatedly advocated by the Joint Chiefs of Staff but rejected by Johnson.
The military objective was to limit North Vietnam's capacity to
launch an offensive against the south, but Nixon's primary motive
was to indicate that he would take measures Johnson had avoided,
thus frightening Hanoi into negotiating on his terms. Over the next
fifteen months, 3,630 B-52 raids were flown, dropping more than
100,000 tons of bombs on Cambodia. The operation was dubbed
(with singular inappropriateness) MENU, its individual components
BREAKFAST, LUNCH, SNACK, DESSERT. At Nixon's insistence, it was kept secret from the public—and indeed from much of the government—
and elaborate methods of bookkeeping were devised to conceal its
existence. The number of civilian deaths among Cambodians will
never be known, and to avoid the American bombs, the North Vietnamese moved deeper into Cambodian territory. When a story on
the bombing appeared in the *New York Times* shortly after it was initi-

---

[12]Walter Isaacson, *Kissinger: A Biography* (New York, 1992), p. 161. Edward C. Keefer,
"President Dwight D. Eisenhower and the end of the Korean War," *Diplomatic History* 10 (Summer 1986): 267–289.

ated, an enraged Nixon, with Kissinger's ardent support, ordered wiretaps on the phones of seventeen government employees and journalists, including some members of Kissinger's staff.[13]

Recognizing that the success of his Vietnam policy hinged on his ability to maintain at least the appearance of unity at home, Nixon mounted a public relations strategy to parallel his secret diplomacy. His aides used extensive polling both to measure and influence public opinion, often framing questions to get the sort of responses they wanted and then publicizing the answers to prove that their policies had popular backing.[14] In May 1969, Nixon unveiled what he described as a "comprehensive peace plan," publicly revealing the proposals he had privately made to North Vietnam and adding his hope that all "foreign" troops might be removed from South Vietnam within a year after the signing of a peace agreement. To make plain his intention of terminating U.S. involvement in the war, he initiated planning for the phased withdrawal of American combat troops, and after conferring with Thieu on Midway Island in June, he announced the immediate withdrawal of 25,000 American combat forces. To emphasize to the Russians, the North Vietnamese, and the right wing at home that he had not gone soft, Nixon delivered several tough speeches, attacking as "new isolationists" those doves who argued that the war was diverting the nation from more pressing problems at home and stressing his determination to uphold America's international responsibilities.

Nixon's secret diplomacy and implied military threats failed to wrench concessions from Hanoi. From the North Vietnamese standpoint, the president's proposals were no improvement over those of Johnson, and to have accepted them would have represented abandonment of goals for which they had been fighting for nearly a quarter of a century. Painfully aware of their weakness in the south, the North Vietnamese recognized that they must take time to rebuild the National Liberation Front (NLF) and that in this "tough period" acceptance even of a coalition government would pose serious problems for them. They saw the need to wait for a

---

[13]William Shawcross, *Sideshow: Kissinger, Nixon, and the Destruction of Cambodia* (New York, 1979), pp. 26–35.

[14]Andrew Z. Katz, "Public Opinion and Foreign Policy: The Nixon Administration and the Pursuit of Peace with Honor in Vietnam," *Presidential Studies Quarterly* 27 (Summer 1997): 499–501.

"more propitious opportunity." The delegation to the Paris peace talks thus publicly dismissed Nixon's offer as a "farce" and vowed that if necessary they would sit in Paris "until the chairs rot."[15] They continued to demand the total and unconditional withdrawal of all U.S. forces from Vietnam and called for the establishment of a government from which Thieu would be excluded. In 1969, Hanoi shifted to a defensive, protracted war strategy, sharply curtailing the level of military activity in the south and withdrawing some troops back across the demilitarized zone. Certain that public opinion would eventually force Nixon to withdraw from Vietnam, they prepared to wait him out, no matter what the cost might be.

Nixon's peace moves also failed to contain the opposition at home. When it was clear that there would be no breakthrough in Paris, public approval of the president's handling of the war dropped sharply. Expressing the growing frustration of the hawks, Senator Richard Russell of Georgia insisted that if the Paris talks did not soon produce results, the United States must make a "meaningful move" against North Vietnam.[16] The organized peace movement, dormant since the Democratic convention of 1968, began to stir again, announcing plans for massive demonstrations in the fall. Congressional doves had remained silent during the administration's first hundred days, giving the president an opportunity to end the war, but by June they began to speak out anew. Republican Senator Jacob Javits of New York charged Nixon with pursuing the same "sterile and unsuccessful approach" followed by Johnson, and Arkansas Senator J. William Fulbright denounced the "new isolationism" speech as "demagogy and personally offensive." Senate doves were not satisfied with Nixon's peace offer and troop withdrawal, and many Democrats rallied behind Clark Clifford's call for the withdrawal of all American forces by the end of 1970. By mid-summer, Nixon's brief honeymoon with the Democratic-controlled Congress had ended.

Never one to avoid a fight, the pugnacious Nixon struck back at his foes. White House spokespeople sought to link Democrats and liberals to the radical left, thereby portraying them as danger-

---

[15]Robert Shaplen, *The Road from War: Vietnam, 1965–1970* (New York, 1970), pp. 300–301; the North Vietnamese perspective is well covered in Luu Van Loi and Nguyen Anh Vu, *Le Duc Tho–Kissinger Negotiations in Paris* (Hanoi, 1996), pp. 75, 85, 104.

[16]Russell to L. M. Thacker, July 26, 1969, Richard M. Russell Papers, University of Georgia Library, Athens, Georgia, Dictation File, Box IJ7.

ous fringe groups. The government prosecuted the ringleaders of the 1968 Chicago protest, the so-called Chicago Seven, initiating a show trial that at times would take on all the solemnity of a circus and would eventually be thrown out of court. The administration used all its public relations skills to draw attention to those who supported the president's policies and discredit those who opposed him. Nixon unleashed his equally combative vice president, Spiro Agnew, for a series of vitriolic attacks against antiwar protesters and the liberal media that allegedly supported them. Believing that student protest derived mainly from narrow self-interest, the administration modified the draft laws, making fewer young men susceptible to being inducted and gradually reducing draft calls.

Nixon's early curiosity about what drove the antiwar protesters evolved into an obsession. He and his top aides developed a voyeurlike and nearly insatiable appetite for information about the movement. They spent hours agonizing over how to deal with it and concocted schemes ranging from the bizarre to the sinister, discussing such options as using helicopters to blow out candles held by protesters and hiring thugs to beat up protesters. Above all, the White House viewed the movement as an enemy that must be crushed and launched a systematic campaign to destroy it. The administration increased government surveillance of antiwar organizations and their leaders. The FBI, CIA (through the illegal CHAOS operation initiated by Johnson), and military expanded their surveillance activities, tapping phones and ransacking files of antiwar groups. Like Johnson, Nixon was certain that the Communists were masterminding the movement, and when extensive analysis again failed to establish a direct connection he disparaged the intelligence rather than reexamine his assumptions. The administration went well beyond intelligence to infiltration and sabotage. Government agencies spread disinformation to discredit antiwar groups. The Internal Revenue Service and FBI harrassed major organizations and their leaders. Agents working inside these organizations helped disrupt their lawful activity, incited them to violent acts against each other, and engaged in actions to make them look bad.[17]

---

[17]Terry H. Anderson, *The Movement and the Sixties* (New York, 1995), pp. 323–325; Tom Wells, *The War Within: America's Battle over Vietnam* (Berkeley, Calif., 1994), pp. 306–377.

DUCK HOOK

Fearful that the rising domestic protest might doom his efforts to pressure the North Vietnamese into a settlement, Nixon also improvised in July a "go-for-broke" strategy, an all-out attempt to "end the war one way or the other—either by negotiated agreement or by force." Again through French intermediaries, he sent a personal message to Ho Chi Minh, reiterating his desire for a "just peace" but adding an ultimatum: unless some progress toward a settlement were made by November 1, he would have no choice but to resort to "measures of great consequence and force." Kissinger again spoke with Dobrynin, warning that "as far as Vietnam is concerned, the train has just left the station and is now headed down the track."[18] On Nixon's orders, Kissinger convened a special, top-secret National Security Council study group to draw up plans (code-named DUCK HOOK) for what he described as "savage, punishing blows" against North Vietnam, including massive bombing attacks on the major cities, a blockade of the ports, and even, possibly, the use of tactical nuclear weapons in certain "controlled" situations. To give force to his warnings, Nixon leaked word to journalists that he was considering such options, and he emphatically told some members of Congress that he would not be the first American president to lose a war.[19]

Nixon's ultimatum had no effect. Hanoi did agree to secret peace talks outside the Paris framework, and on August 4, in the first of a long series of secret meetings, Kissinger met privately with North Vietnamese diplomat Xuan Thuy. Kissinger reiterated Nixon's peace proposals and ultimatum, but Thuy responded with the standard line that the United States must withdraw all its troops and abandon Thieu to secure an agreement. Ho Chi Minh's formal response, written shortly before his death on September 2, 1969, conveyed the same message and was, in Nixon's words, a "cold rebuff." From Nixon's standpoint, the North Vietnamese were not only intransigent but also deliberately provocative. Hanoi Radio tossed back at the president statements made by Senate doves that Nixon's policies were prolonging the war and expressed

---

[18]Nixon, *RN*, pp. 393–394, 399.
[19]The most complete discussion of the DUCK HOOK planning is in Jeffrey Kimball, *Nixon's Vietnam War* (Lawrence, Kansas 1998), pp. 158–170.

to the "American people" hope that their "fall [peace] offensive" would "succeed splendidly."[20]

Unable to intimidate Hanoi into making even the slightest concession, Nixon had to choose between a major escalation of the war and an embarrassing retreat. He was infuriated by North Vietnam's defiance and by the domestic criticism, which he felt encouraged it. His natural inclination was to strike back. But Secretary of Defense Melvin Laird and Secretary of State William Rogers implored him not to take any action that would inflame the opposition at home. And after weeks of careful analysis, Kissinger's study group concluded that air strikes and a blockade might not force concessions from Hanoi or even significantly limit its capacity to continue the war in the south. Haunted throughout his political career by a near-obsessive fear of defeat and humiliation, Nixon abandoned the plan for "savage, punishing blows" with the greatest reluctance and only after being persuaded that it would not work. Having relied on military pressure to bring a quick and decisive end to the war, he suddenly found himself without a policy.

VIETNAMIZATION

Unwilling to make concessions and unable to end the war by force, Nixon again improvised, this time falling back on the Vietnamization policy he had inherited from Johnson. While he was still pondering escalation in October, the British counterinsurgency expert Sir Robert Thompson informed him that South Vietnam was daily growing stronger and that if the United States continued to furnish large-scale military and economic assistance, the Saigon government might be strong enough within two years to resist a Communist takeover without external help. With no place else to go, Nixon eagerly and uncritically embraced Thompson's conclusions as the foundation for a new approach to extricate the United States from the war. He seems to have reasoned that if he could mobilize American opinion behind him, persuade Hanoi that he would not abandon Thieu, and intensify the buildup of South Vietnamese military strength, the North Vietnamese might conclude that it would be better to negotiate with the United States now than with South

---

[20]Nixon, *RN*, pp. 397–399.

Vietnam later, and he could extract from them the concessions necessary to secure peace with honor.

In a major speech on November 3, Nixon set out to isolate his critics and mobilize popular backing for his policy. He firmly defended the commitment in Vietnam, warning that a pullout would produce a bloodbath in South Vietnam and a crisis of confidence in American leadership at home and abroad. Spelling out his Vietnamization policy in some detail, he offered the alluring prospect that it not only would reduce American casualties but also might terminate American involvement in an honorable fashion regardless of what North Vietnam did. Although some members of his staff cautioned against a confrontation with the peace movement, Nixon rejected their advice. He dismissed the protesters as an irrational and irresponsible element and accused them of sabotaging his diplomacy. He openly appealed for the support of those he labeled the "great silent majority," and he concluded with a dramatic warning: "North Vietnam cannot humiliate the United States. Only Americans can do that."[21]

Nixon's "silent majority" speech was a shrewd and, for the most part, successful political maneuver. He placed his opponents squarely on the defensive. By offering a policy that could achieve an honorable peace with minimal American sacrifice, he appeared to have reconciled the contradictory elements of popular attitudes toward the war. He cleverly appealed to the patriotism of his listeners and to their reluctance to accept anything resembling defeat. By specifically identifying a "silent majority," he helped mobilize a bloc of support where none had existed.

The moratoriums of October 15 and November 15 were spectacularly successful and signaled a new turn in the evolution of the antiwar movement. Organized by liberals, the demonstrations attracted millions of sober, middle-class citizens, constituting "the greatest outpouring of mass protest that the country had ever known" and making clear that the peace movement was becoming "respectable."[22] In contrast to the bedlam and violence of Chicago, the fall moratoriums were peaceful and dignified affairs with religious overtones. Across the nation, church bells tolled, the names of

[21]*Public Papers, Richard M. Nixon, 1969* (Washington, D.C., 1971), pp. 901–909.
[22]Charles DeBenedetti, *The Peace Reform in American History* (Bloomington, Ind., 1984), pp. 184–185.

American war dead were called out at candlelight services, and participants solemnly intoned songwriter John Lennon's haunting antiwar chant, "Give Peace a Chance." In Washington's March of Death, thousands of protesters carrying candles walked through high winds and rain from Arlington Cemetery to the Capitol, where they placed into wooden coffins signs bearing the names of GIs killed in Vietnam.

The fall demonstrations did not produce a change in policy. Although alarmed and deeply angered by the protest, Nixon publicly feigned indifference, and his silent majority speech temporarily neutralized the effects of the demonstrations. Low on funds, its leadership increasingly splintered, and demoralized by a crippling sense of helplessness, the organized peace movement in the immediate aftermath of the moratoriums grew quiescent again. The polls indicated solid support for the administration, and in late November pro-Nixon rallies were held in a number of cities. "We've got those liberal bastards on the run now," the president exulted, "and we're going to keep them on the run."[23]

VIETNAMIZATION IN PRACTICE

Making Vietnamization work proved an even more formidable task than did manipulating American public opinion. Whatever they said publicly, U.S. officials undertook the program with grave doubts. Most military experts agreed that without full American assistance, the South Vietnamese could not stand up against the combined threat of the North Vietnamese Army (NVA) and NLF forces. General Creighton Abrams criticized Vietnamization as "slow surrender" and repeatedly protested the size and pace of U.S. troop withdrawals.[24]

The South Vietnamese also objected to the Nixon policy. Typically, they were not consulted in decisions on and planning for Vietnamization. Although Nixon publicly proclaimed that Thieu had recommended U.S. troop withdrawals, in fact he bitterly opposed them. The South Vietnamese grudgingly acquiesced in what they saw as a political expedient for the United States. But they

[23]Quoted in Tad Szulc, *The Illusion of Peace* (New York, 1973), p. 158.
[24]Quoted in Isaacson, *Kissinger,* pp. 235–236.

found the term *Vietnamization* demeaning, protesting that they had been fighting for years before the Americans became involved and even after 1965 had "sacrificed and suffered the most." Some Vietnamese cynically dismissed Vietnamization as a "U.S. Dollar and Vietnamese Blood Sharing Plan." Most saw it as a fig leaf to cover U.S. abandonment.[25]

By the time Nixon formally announced his "new" plan to end the war, Vietnamization had been in effect for more than a year and a half. A tank commander under the legendary General George S. Patton in World War II and the polar opposite of Westmoreland in appearance and leadership style, the rugged, profane, often unkempt Abrams made major adjustments in fighting the war. He scrapped Westmoreland's costly and ineffectual search-and-destroy approach for a strategy that integrated combat operations more closely with pacification, the main object of which was to protect the population of South Vietnam. He sought to curb the excessive and counterproductive use of firepower and the corrupting emphasis on body counts. He shifted from large-scale search-and-destroy operations against enemy main-force units to small-unit operations aimed at disrupting the enemy's logistic systems and thereby limiting its ability to conduct offensive operations.[26]

While U.S. combat forces sought to keep the North Vietnamese and NLF off balance by relentlessly attacking their supply lines and base areas, American advisers worked frantically to build up and modernize the South Vietnamese armed forces. The force level, about 850,000 when Nixon took office, was increased to more than one million, and the United States turned over to South Vietnam huge quantities of the newest weapons: more than a million M-16 rifles, 12,000 M-60 machine guns, 40,000 M-79 grenade launchers, and 2,000 heavy mortars and howitzers. The Vietnamese were also given ships, planes, helicopters, and so many vehicles that one congressmen wondered whether the object of Vietnamization was to "put every South Vietnamese soldier behind the wheel."[27] Military schools were expanded to a capacity of more than 100,000 students

---

[25]George C. Herring, " 'Peoples Quite Apart': Americans, South Vietnamese, and the War in Vietnam," *Diplomatic History* 14 (Winter, 1990): 17–18.

[26]Lewis Sorley, *A Better War* (New York, 1999), pp. 17–30.

[27]Thomas Buckley, "The ARVN Is Bigger and Better, But—," *New York Times Magazine*, October 12, 1969, 132.

a year. To improve morale and check the desertion rate, the promotion system was modernized, leaves improved, pay scales increased, veterans' benefits expanded, and systematic efforts made to improve conditions in military camps and dependent housing.

The Accelerated Pacification Campaign, originally designed as a crash program to extend government control over the countryside prior to negotiations, was institutionalized and expanded in 1969 and 1970. To improve security in the villages, which had been the major weakness of earlier programs, regular forces assigned to pacification were expanded to 500,000 soldiers armed with M-16 rifles and supplemented by a hastily created militia numbering in the thousands. Americans and South Vietnamese also attempted to infuse new life into old programs of village development. Village elections were held, restoring the autonomy that had been taken away in the Diem era. Elected officials were trained in civic responsibilities at the Rural Development Center in Vung Tau and upon graduation given black pajamas furnished by the CIA. The government turned over to individual villages control of the militia and funds to be used for local projects. Strenuous efforts were made to clear roads, repair bridges, establish schools and hospitals, and expand agricultural production. In March 1970, the government launched an ambitious land reform program through which nearly one million hectares were eventually redistributed.

Vietnamization was in full swing by early 1970, and most observers agreed that significant gains had been made. Almost overnight the South Vietnamese Army had become one of the largest and best-equipped in the world. When properly led, moreover, Army of the Republic of Vietnam (ARVN) units fought well, and some American advisers began to detect that perhaps out of necessity, their performance improved noticeably as U.S. support units were withdrawn. In some areas, improvement in the performance of the separate South Vietnamese militia was even greater than that of the ARVN. American "spoiling" tactics, along with North Vietnam's decision to go on the defensive, left the countryside more secure than at any other time since the war began. The ability of the NLF to tax and recruit had been sharply reduced, and NVA units in South Vietnam appeared to be suffering from serious personnel and material shortages. In former guerrilla strongholds, roads were passable at least by day, and the number of terrorist incidents declined markedly. On the surface, at least, the insurgency appeared to be under control. Even long-time skeptics like pacification expert John Vann concluded that "we are now on the right road."[28]

Real progress in Vietnamization remained uncertain, however. American officials claimed to have "neutralized" as many as 20,000 members of the NLF infrastructure through the Phoenix Program, and NLF operatives later conceded that in some areas Phoenix was "dangerously effective."[29] The figures were grossly inflated, however, and although the insurgents' clandestine apparatus was severely damaged, it remained intact. In addition, the abuses that accompanied the program sometimes generated support for the NLF. American officials also conceded that the gains in security had resulted primarily from U.S. military operations and the enemy stand-down, and they were unsure whether these factors could be sustained in the face of the withdrawal of U.S. forces and the renewal of enemy attacks.

The biggest question mark remained the government itself. Thieu had skillfully built a durable governing structure comprising Chinese merchants, loyal bureaucrats, and army officers and held together by the glue of corruption. It was, however, a narrowly based operation entirely dependent on the continued infusion of U.S. funds and, ironically, largely resistant to U.S. influence. Despite the frenetic activity in the villages, there was nothing to indicate that the pacification program had generated any real enthusiasm for the Thieu government. One senior U.S. officer observed, moreover, that although significant progress had been made in numerous areas, the government had not yet "succeeded in mobilizing the will and energies of the people against the enemy and in support of national programs."[30]

---

[28]Vann to General Frederick Weyand, January 22, 1970, John P. Vann Papers, U.S. Army Military History Institute, Carlisle Barracks, Pa.

[29]Truong Nhu Tang, *A Vietcong Memoir* (New York, 1985), pp. 201–202. The Phoenix Program was highly controversial during its own time and remains so today. For recent, conflicting assessments, see Dale Andradé, *Ashes to Ashes: The Phoenix Program and the Vietnam War* (Lexington, Mass., 1990); Douglas Valentine, *The Phoenix Program* (New York, 1990); and Mark Moyar, *Phoenix and the Birds of Prey* (Annapolis, Md., 1997).

[30]Memorandum by General Arthur S. Collins, fall 1970, A. S. Collins Papers, U.S. Army Military History Institute, Carlisle Barracks, Pa.; see also Report by Vietnam Special Studies Group, January 10, 1970, and Charles S. Whitehouse to William Colby, September 22, 1970, both in Vann Papers.

On paper, the ARVN appeared a formidable force, but many of its fundamental weaknesses remained uncorrected. Americans estimated that the practice of "ghosting"—keeping on rosters the names of dead and deserted soldiers so the officer in charge could pocket the pay—ran as high as 20 percent, and "flower soldiers" commonly paid off their superiors to avoid serving in combat. Desertion remained a chronic problem, and there was thus a huge gap between the authorized and actual strength of most units. Increases in pay were offset by inflation, and in an economy where prostitutes could earn as much in a week as senior military officers in a year, corruption was accepted as a means to redress economic inequities. There was a severe shortage of qualified, competent, and honest officers at all levels.

Americans continued to doubt that the ARVN could fill the vacuum left by U.S. troop withdrawals. Even the better units still manifested a reluctance to engage the enemy in sustained combat, provoking a senior U.S. officer to question whether the United States would ever "be able to create an army with the offensive and aggressive spirit that will be necessary to counter either the VC or the NVA."[31] Americans also began to realize belatedly the extent to which the South Vietnamese had come to depend on them. The "nagging question" was whether the ARVN could fend for itself after the United States withdrew, and many advisers conceded that, at best, much time would be required before the South Vietnamese would be able to stand on their own against Hanoi's seasoned and disciplined forces.[32] North Vietnamese negotiator Le Duc Tho openly posed to Kissinger the fundamental question. If the United States could not win with a half million of its own troops, "how can you succeed when you let your puppet troops do the fighting?" It was a question, Kissinger conceded, that "also torments me."[33]

By the spring of 1970, the contradictions in Nixon's Vietnamization strategy had become all too apparent. The silent majority speech had quieted the opposition temporarily, but Nixon realized that his success was only transient. In March he announced

[31]Collins memorandum, April 25, 1970, Collins Papers.
[32]Collins memorandum, fall 1970, Collins Papers; William Rosson oral history interview, U.S. Army Military History Institute, Carlisle Barracks, Pa. Jeffrey J. Clarke, *Advice and Support: The Final Years, 1965–1973* (Washington, D.C., 1988), pp. 341–359, provides a balanced and persuasive analysis of Vietnamization.
[33]Quoted in Isaacson, *Kissinger*, p. 253.

the phased withdrawal of 150,000 troops over the next year in order to "drop a bombshell on the gathering spring storm of anti-war protest."[34] Nixon recognized that this withdrawal, however necessary from the standpoint of domestic politics, would weaken his hand in other areas. Abrams had bitterly protested the new troop withdrawals, warning that they would leave South Vietnam vulnerable to enemy military pressure and could be devastating to the Vietnamization program. Nixon had rather naively hoped that his professed determination to remain in Vietnam indefinitely and the demonstrations of public support that had followed his November 3 speech would persuade the North Vietnamese to negotiate. But there had been no breakthrough in Paris, and he recognized that the announcement of additional troop withdrawals would probably encourage Hanoi to delay further. Increasingly impatient for results and still certain that he could end the war by a dramatic show of force, he once more began looking for "initiatives" to "show the enemy that we were still serious about our commitment in Vietnam."[35]

CAMBODIA

The overthrow of Cambodia's neutralist Prince Sihanouk in March by a pro-American clique headed by Prime Minister Lon Nol posed new dangers to the Vietnamization policy and presented enticing opportunities for the initiative Nixon sought. Kissinger has vigorously denied American complicity in the coup, and no evidence has ever been produced to prove that the United States was directly involved. The administration appears not to have been surprised by Lon Nol's move, however, and Washington's long-standing and obvious dislike for Sihanouk and its interest in attacking the North Vietnamese sanctuaries in Cambodia may have encouraged Lon Nol to believe that a successful coup would be rewarded with U.S. support.[36]

---

[34]Nixon, *RN*, p. 448.

[35]Ibid., p. 445.

[36]The controversy over Cambodia is one of the most bitter and emotional to come out of the war. The respective positions are spelled out in Shawcross, *Sideshow*, especially pp. 112–127, and in Henry A. Kissinger, *White House Years* (Boston, 1979), pp. 457–521.

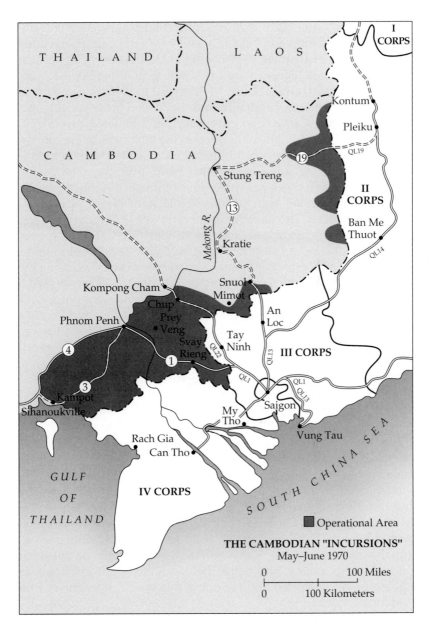

THAILAND

LAOS

I CORPS

Kontum

Pleiku

QL19

CAMBODIA

19

II CORPS

Stung Treng

13

Ban Me Thuot

Kratie

QL14

Kompong Cham

Snuol

Mimot

An Loc

Chup

Prey Veng

Phnom Penh

Svay Rieng

Tay Ninh

III CORPS

4

1

QL22

QL1

QL13

3

Kampot

QL1

QL13

Sihanoukville

My Tho

Saigon

Rach Gia

Vung Tau

Can Tho

SOUTH CHINA SEA

GULF

OF

THAILAND

IV CORPS

■ Operational Area

THE CAMBODIAN "INCURSIONS"
May–June 1970

0   100 Miles

0   100 Kilometers

Kissinger's later claim that the United States intervened in Cambodia only hesitantly and belatedly and only after being persuaded that the North Vietnamese were committed to the destruction of Lon Nol's government appears at best misleading. Shortly after the coup, with U.S. authorization, South Vietnamese units conducted raids across the border into Cambodia, and the United States quickly recognized the new Cambodian government and initiated covert military aid. That North Vietnam decided in the aftermath of the coup to take over Cambodia remains unproven today and was open to serious question at the time. On the other hand, from the outset, some U.S. officials were eager to exploit developments in Cambodia. The military for years had been anxious to attack the North Vietnamese sanctuaries there. The change of government in Phnom Penh removed the long-standing concern about violating Cambodian neutrality, and attacks on the sanctuaries could now be justified in terms of sustaining a friendly Cambodian government as well as easing the military threat to South Vietnam. Nixon therefore quickly endorsed a Defense Department proposal that South Vietnamese units with American air support attack an enemy sanctuary on the Parrot's Beak, a strip of Cambodian territory thirty-three miles from Saigon. Even before plans for this operation had been completed, the president approved a more dramatic—and much more risky—move. After nearly a week of careful and apparently agonizing study and over the vigorous opposition of Laird and Rogers, he approved Abrams's proposal that American forces attack Fishhook, a North Vietnamese base area fifty-five miles northwest of Saigon.

Nixon's decision to send American troops into Cambodia, one of the most important and controversial decisions of his tumultuous presidency, was motivated by a variety of considerations. He was swayed by the military's argument that the operation would buy time for Vietnamization and help sustain a friendly government in Cambodia. On the other hand, he realized that his decision would have a "shattering effect" at home.[37] Nixon's willingness to run this risk for uncertain gains reflected, in part, what he called his "big play philosophy," his belief that since the administration was "going to get unshirted hell for doing this at all," it might as well "go for all the marbles."[38]

---

[37]Kissinger, *White House Years,* p. 449.
[38]Safire, *Before the Fall,* pp. 102–103.

Rather than fearing the domestic backlash he was sure would come, he seems to have welcomed it. By the spring of 1970, he was embattled at home as well as abroad. The Democratic-controlled Senate had just rejected for the second time his nominee for a Supreme Court vacancy, and he was determined to show "those Senators . . . who's really tough."[39]

Most important, he was still confident that he could make peace by threatening Hanoi. Embarrassed by backing down from the November ultimatum, a move that conveyed precisely the wrong message, he seems to have reasoned that widening the war into previously off-limits Cambodia would make it clear that unlike his predecessor, he would not be bound by restraints. The North Vietnamese would then have to decide "whether they want to take us on all over again," he explained to his staff, and in terms of pressures on them to negotiate, "this was essential."[40]

Preoccupied throughout his career with the urgency of responding to crises, Nixon put himself through an emotional wringer in making the Cambodian decision. Kissinger described him as "overwrought," "irritable," and "defiant."[41] Exhausted from stress and lack of sleep, obviously agitated, at times frenetic, Nixon repeatedly viewed the epic World War II film *Patton,* apparently as a way of pumping himself up to make a tough decision. The Cambodian crisis represented yet another effort on the part of a profoundly insecure individual to prove his toughness to an ever-widening list of enemies, real and imagined, an opportunity he felt he must seize to demonstrate his courage under fire and show his adversaries that he would not be intimidated. Although he later depicted himself as a voice of reason and a calming influence, Kissinger too was strung out during this period. He seems to have had reservations about going into Cambodia, but he went along with the president, in part as a way of outflanking Laird and Rogers in the raging turf war that was Nixon's Washington.

The president explained his decision in a belligerent, provocative televised speech on April 30. He justified the Cambodian "incursion" as a response to North Vietnamese "aggression," although Hanoi's intentions remained unclear, and as a necessary action to

[39]Morris, *Uncertain Greatness,* pp. 174–175.
[40]Safire, *Before the Fall,* p. 190.
[41]Kimball, *Nixon's Vietnam War,* pp. 204–205.

protect American forces in Vietnam, although he did not explain why an old threat suddenly required such a vigorous response. The real target of the operation, he explained, was the Central Office for South Vietnam (COSVN), the "nerve center" of North Vietnamese military operations, although the Defense Department had made clear to him its uncertainty where COSVN was located or whether it even existed. Anticipating a furor at home, Nixon indicated that he would rather be a one-term president than preside over America's first defeat. He concluded with a bit of inflated rhetoric that appeared to make America's very survival hinge on his Cambodian venture. "If when the chips are down," he warned, "the world's most powerful nation acts like a pitiful helpless giant, the forces of totalitarianism and anarchy will threaten free nations and free institutions throughout the world."[42]

From a military standpoint, Nixon's Cambodian venture produced significant, if limited, results. The U.S. command claimed to have some 2,000 enemy troops, cleared over 1,600 acres of jungle, and destroyed 8,000 bunkers. It uncovered huge caches of supplies and "treasure troves" of intelligence. The incursion rendered the sanctuaries temporarily unusable and vastly complicated North Vietnam's supply problems, thus buying vital time for Vietnamization. The South Vietnamese army performed very well in most areas. Predictably, on the other hand, the invaders did not locate the elusive COSVN. Americans were also painfully aware that the gains made in Cambodia were no more than "ephemeral." As Abrams himself lamented about the resilience of the enemy, "you give them thirty-six hours and, goddamn it, you've got to start the war all over again."[43] Whatever advantages the operation gained for Vietnamization may have been more than offset by enlargement of the theater of war. At a time when the United States was seeking to scale down its role in Vietnam, it had to divert precious resources to support an even more fragile client state in Cambodia.

In Cambodia itself, U.S. actions contributed to one of the great tragedies of recent history. The United States was not exclusively responsible for Cambodia's misery. North Vietnam had violated Cambodia's precarious neutrality first, and Cambodians of all polit-

---

[42]*Public Papers, Richard M. Nixon, 1970* (Washington, D.C., 1971), pp. 405–410.
[43]Quoted in Sorley, *Better War*, p. 204. See also John M. Shaw, "The U.S. Army in the 1970 Cambodian Incursion" (Ph.D. diss. University of Kentucky, 1995).

ical factions inflicted their share of suffering on one another. The United States did, however, encourage the Lon Nol government to initiate a war it could not win. The American invasion forced the North Vietnamese to move out of their sanctuaries and into the heartland of Cambodia. Whether as a direct or indirect consequence of the American invasion, North Vietnam initiated large-scale support for the Khmer Rouge insurgents fighting Lon Nol. In the particularly brutal civil war that followed, the United States lavishly supported the Cambodian government and unleashed thousands of tons of bombs on Cambodia. The ultimate tragedy was that from beginning to end, the Nixon administration viewed its new ally as little more than a pawn to be used to help salvage the U.S. position in Vietnam, showing scant regard for the consequences for Cambodia and its people.

The domestic reaction exceeded Nixon's worst expectations— in tragic ways. The incursion into Cambodia "reignited an antiwar movement that had been smoldering that spring." The unexpected expansion of a war the president had promised to wind down enraged his critics, and his intemperate defense of his actions, including a statement indiscriminately branding protesters as "bums," added to the furor. Demonstrations erupted at campuses across the nation, and the protest took on new force when four students at Kent State University in Ohio and two at Jackson State College in Mississippi were killed in angry confrontations with the National Guard and police. More than 100,000 demonstrators gathered in Washington the first week of May to protest Cambodia and Kent State. Students at 350 colleges and universities went on strike, and as many as 500 schools were closed down to avert further violence. The Kent State killings provoked outbreaks even at normally conservative and placid institutions. At the University of Kentucky, a building was burned, and student demonstrations were broken up by armed National Guards troops using tear gas.[44]

The Cambodian incursion also provoked the most serious congressional challenge to presidential authority since the beginning of the war. The president had consulted with only a handful of members of Congress, all known to be sympathetic. Many legislators,

[44]Anderson, *Movement*, pp. 351–352; Mitchell K. Hall, " 'A Crack in Time': The Response of Students at the University of Kentucky to the Tragedy at Kent State," *Kentucky Historical Register* 83 (Winter 1985): 36–63.

Kent State, 1970
This classic photograph of a young woman kneeling near one of the students felled by National Guard bullets at Kent State University in Ohio captured the shock and anguish of a war now come home. The shooting at Kent State following the invasion of Cambodia sparked massive protests at colleges and universities across the country.
John Filo

including Senate Minority Leader Hugh Scott, were outraged at having been kept in the dark, and others were infuriated by Nixon's broadening of the war.[45] In a symbolic act of defiance, the Senate voted overwhelmingly in June to terminate the Tonkin Gulf Resolution of 1964. An amendment sponsored by Senators John Sherman Cooper (a Republican from Kentucky) and Frank Church (a Democrat from Idaho) proposed to cut off all funds for American military operations in Cambodia after June 30. An even more restrictive amendment sponsored by Senators George McGovern (a Democrat from South Dakota) and Mark Hatfield (a Republican

[45]Scott to Kissinger, May 21, 1970, Hugh Scott Papers, University of Virginia Library, Charlottesville, Va., Box 65.

from Oregon) would have required the administration to withdraw all U.S. forces from Vietnam by the end of 1971.

Thin-skinned and combative, Nixon throughout his career had shown a singular capacity to provoke virulent attacks, and he responded in kind. There would be no more "screwing around" with congressional foes, he instructed his staff. "Don't worry about divisiveness. Having drawn the sword, don't take it out—stick it in hard."[46] The president publicly blamed his domestic opponents for prolonging the war, and he bluntly warned congressional leaders that if "Congress undertakes to restrict me, Congress will have to assume the consequences."[47] He approved one of the most blatant attacks on individual freedom and privacy in American history, the so-called Huston Plan, which authorized the intelligence agencies to open mail, use electronic surveillance methods, and even burglarize to spy on Americans. The agencies subsequently refused to implement this specific plan, but they did use many of its methods in the futile effort to verify suspected links between radical groups in the United States and foreign governments.[48]

The administration eventually rode out the storm. Nixon removed American troops from Cambodia by the end of June, depriving his opponents of their most telling issue, and the protests gradually abated. Despite the flurry of activity, Congress was not yet ready to challenge the president directly or assume responsibility for ending the war. The more dovish Senate approved the Cooper-Church amendment, but the House rejected it, permitting the administration to continue air operations in Cambodia and send money and supplies to Lon Nol. The Hatfield-McGovern amendment could not even secure a majority of the Senate.

Although Nixon escaped with his power intact, the Cambodian venture tightened the trap he had set for himself. The domestic reaction reinforced his determination to achieve "peace with honor" while sharply limiting his options for attaining it. Cambodia may have bought some time for Vietnamization, but it also imposed clear-cut, if implicit, limits on the future use of American combat forces and increased the pressures for speeding the pace of

---

[46]Safire, *Before the Fall*, p. 190.

[47]Henry Brandon, *The Retreat of American Power* (New York, 1974), pp. 146–147.

[48]Athan Theoharis, *Spying on Americans: Political Surveillance from Hoover to the Huston Plan* (Philadelphia, 1978), pp. 13–39.

withdrawal. Divisiveness within the United States increased even beyond the level of 1968, with far-reaching, if still unforeseen, implications for Nixon's future. In the summer of 1970, an embittered president declared war on his enemies: the "madmen" on the Hill, the "liberal" press, the "trash" and "rabble" who marched in protest. "Within the iron gates of the White House, quite unknowingly, a siege mentality was setting in," one of Nixon's aides later stated. "It was now 'us' against 'them.' Gradually, as we drew the circle closer around us, the ranks of 'them' began to swell."[49]

Hoping to break the diplomatic deadlock by going into Cambodia, Nixon seems merely to have hardened it. North Vietnamese and NLF delegates boycotted the formal Paris talks until U.S. troops had been withdrawn from Cambodia, and the secret talks lapsed for months. Hanoi continued to bide its time, and the uproar in the United States certainly reinforced its conviction that domestic pressures would eventually force an American withdrawal.

DEADLOCK AND DISSENSION

To resolve his foreign and domestic problems, Nixon launched in October 1970 what he described as a "major new initiative for peace." The proposals he made in a televised speech, while cleverly phrased, offered no concessions on the fundamental issues, and Hanoi promptly rejected his call for a cease-fire in place, which, it perceived, would restrict the NLF to areas they presently controlled without assuring them any role in a political settlement. In any case, the speech appears to have been designed primarily for the upcoming congressional elections. Nixon followed it up by touring ten states, angrily denouncing the antiwar protesters and urging the voters to elect representatives who would "stand with the President." Even here, the results were disappointing. Several doves were defeated, but the Republicans gained only two seats in the Senate and lost nine in the House.

After two years of continued heavy fighting, intensive secret diplomacy, and political maneuvering, Nixon's position was worse than when he had taken office. The negotiations with North Vietnam remained deadlocked, and a National Security Council study

---

[49]Charles W. Colson, *Born Again* (Old Tappan, N.J., 1976), p. 41.

of late 1970 grimly concluded that the United States could neither persuade nor force Hanoi to remove its troops from the south. At home, Nixon kept "one step ahead of the sheriff," as he would put it, narrowly heading off restrictions on his war-making powers. But he still faced a hostile and even more determined opposition in Congress and a revived antiwar movement, which had seemed moribund just a year before. The situation in South Vietnam remained stable. By the end of the year, however, intelligence reported a sharp increase in the infiltration of troops and supplies into Laos, Cambodia, and South Vietnam, posing an ominous threat to the northern provinces and Hue, where sizable American forces had been withdrawn.

Instead of rethinking a policy that had brought no results, Nixon clung stubbornly throughout much of 1971 to the approach he had improvised the preceding year. To appease critics at home, he speeded up the timetable of American troop withdrawals. Over the protests of Abrams, he ordered the removal of 100,000 troops by the end of the year, leaving 175,000 troops in Vietnam, of whom only 75,000 were combat forces. To make clear, at the same time, his continued determination to secure a "just" peace and to counter the threat to Vietnamization posed by increased North Vietnamese infiltration and American troop reductions, he stepped up the military pressure against North Vietnam. U.S. aircraft mounted heavy attacks against supply lines and staging areas in Laos and Cambodia. Using as a pretext North Vietnamese firing upon American "reconnaissance" planes, the administration ordered "protective reaction" air strikes against bridges, base camps, and trails across the demilitarized zone and in the Hanoi-Haiphong area.

In February 1971, Nixon again expanded the war, approving a major ground operation into Laos. LAM SON 719 was conceived in the White House and approved over Abrams's vigorous opposition. The objective was the same as in Cambodia—to buy time for Vietnamization by disrupting enemy supply lines—but this time the ARVN assumed the burden of the fighting, with only U.S. air support.

The Laotian operation was at best a costly draw. U.S. intelligence had anticipated only light resistance, but North Vietnam apparently saw an opportunity to strike a body blow at Vietnamization and hurled some 36,000 troops, supported by the newest Russian-made tanks, against the two South Vietnamese divisions that crossed the border. ARVN performed well at first, inflicting huge losses on the enemy, and Abrams now urged that they sustain the attack until the end of the dry season. But Thieu was nervous about his army's losses and refused unless U.S. ground forces joined the battle. In time, the NVA gained the upper hand, and after six weeks of the bloodiest fighting of the war, the battered ARVN forces retreated back into South Vietnam. Official spokespeople claimed that the ARVN killed as many as 15,000 enemy troops and destroyed North Vietnam's supply network in Laos, thus delaying a major offensive for a year. Nixon and Kissinger continued to delude themselves into claiming a major victory while blaming Abrams for the failures. In fact, the ARVN took a beating, suffering a casualty rate as high as 50 percent and an estimated 2,000 dead. The losses would have been much higher without American air support, which flew one sortie every ten minutes around the clock during the entire operation and dumped 48,000 tons of bombs. Administration assertions that ARVN had conducted an "orderly retreat" appeared ludicrous amid the haste and confusion that accompanied the withdrawal from Laos, and the sight of South Vietnamese soldiers clinging desperately to the skids of departing helicopters raised serious questions about the progress of Vietnamization. In the aftermath of the operation, Abrams concluded that South Vietnam could not "sustain large-scale cross border operations . . . without external support."[50]

At home, the protests and demonstrations continued, drawing new faces and becoming more rancorous and unruly. In early 1971, at a Howard Johnson's Motor Lodge in Detroit, the newly formed Vietnam Veterans Against the War (VVAW) conducted its "Winter Soldier" investigation of U.S. war crimes; members testified to the atrocities they had seen in the war, such as prisoners being tossed out of helicopters and ears being cut off dead enemy soldiers. In April, in Operation Dewey Canyon III, a limited incursion into the country of Congress, Vietnam veterans clothed symbolically in faded uniforms adorned with combat ribbons and peace symbols gathered in front of the Capitol, told of their own war crimes, and ceremoniously tossed away their medals. Speaking before the Fulbright committee, former Navy lieutenant John Kerry raised a haunting question: "How do you ask a man to be the last man to die for a mistake?"

[50]Clarke, *Final Years*, p. 473; Sorley, *Better War*, pp. 237–263.

Several days later, 30,000 self-styled members of the Mayday Tribe descended on Washington with the avowed intention of shutting the government down and proceeded to conduct lie-ins on bridges and major thoroughfares and at the entrances of government buildings. Mobs roamed the streets, stopped traffic, and broke windows, leading to one of the worst riots in Washington's history.

Many Americans would undoubtedly have preferred that the war simply go away, but by the summer of 1971 the history of a conflict now more than a decade old had begun to come back to haunt the nation. After a long and much-publicized trial, a military court found Lieutenant William Calley guilty of at "least twenty-two murders" in the My Lai incident of 1968 and sentenced him to life imprisonment, once more bringing before public attention the horrors that had attended the war and setting off a brief but bitter debate on the question of responsibility for alleged war crimes. No sooner had the Calley furor abated than the *New York Times* began publication of the so-called Pentagon Papers, a history of decision making in Vietnam based on secret Defense Department documents and leaked by a former Pentagon official, Daniel Ellsberg. The documents confirmed what critics of the war had long been arguing, among other points that Kennedy and Johnson had consistently misled the public about their intentions in Vietnam.

An increasingly isolated and embattled Nixon responded fiercely to what he regarded as sinister threats to his authority to govern. The White House mounted a major campaign to smear the VVAW and especially Kerry. The Justice Department secured an injunction to prevent the veterans from sleeping on the Mall, and the government hauled off to jail some 12,000 Mayday protesters, often without bothering to charge them with any specific offense. Nixon personally intervened in the Calley case while it was still under appeal, ordering Calley released from prison and indicating that he would review the conviction.

Nixon also took a tough line on the Pentagon Papers. Some of his advisers shrewdly suggested that, since the documents seemed to deal entirely with the Kennedy and Johnson presidencies and would therefore embarrass the Democrats, the administration might best ignore them. But Kissinger flew into a rage, perhaps nervous about his own prior association with Ellsberg, and the president, already obsessed with leaks, determined to act. He took the unprecedented step of securing an injunction to stop publication of the Papers. Enraged when the Supreme Court over-turned the order, he approved the creation of a clandestine group of "plumbers," ostensibly to plug leaks within the government but in fact to do all kinds of dirty work. Labeling Ellsberg a "rat" (Kissinger called him "the most dangerous man in America today"), Nixon instructed the group to use any means necessary to discredit him. Nixon even discussed the possibility of fire-bombing and burglarizing the Brookings Institution, a Washington think tank, to determine whether additional classified documents might be held there. Nixon's certainty that he faced a vast and sinister conspiracy intent on destroying him, and his growing willingness to use any means to fight back led straight to the Watergate break-in and the demise of his presidency.[51]

Neither Nixon's withdrawal policy nor his vigorous counterat-tacks against the opposition could stem the war-weariness and general demoralization that enveloped the nation by the summer of 1971. Former Secretary of State Dean Acheson lamented the plight of "this floundering republic," and journalist Robert Shaplen labeled the United States "the sick man of the western hemisphere."[52] While the antiwar movement was splintering into hundreds of groups often in conflict with each other, an antiwar mood increasingly per-vaded the nation. Disillusionment with the war reached an all-time high, a whopping 71 percent agreeing that the United States had made a mistake by sending troops to Vietnam and 58 percent regarding the war as "immoral." Nixon's public approval rating on Vietnam had dropped to a low of 31 percent, and opposition to his policies had increased sharply. A near majority felt that the pace of troop withdrawals was too slow, and a substantial majority approved the removal of all troops by the end of the year, even if the result was a Communist takeover of South Vietnam.[53]

Congress reflected the growing public uneasiness, although it continued to stop short of decisive action. On two separate occa-

[51]See especially Stanley I. Kutler, ed., *Abuse of Power: The New Nixon Tapes* (New York, 1998), pp. 1–17.

[52]Acheson to Matthew B. Ridgway, July 5, 1971, and Shaplen to Robert Aspey, n.d., both in Matthew B. Ridgway Papers, U.S. Army Military History Institute, Carlisle Barracks, Pa., Box 34B.

[53]Louis Harris, *The Anguish of Change* (New York, 1973), pp. 72–73. See also Charles DeBenedetti with Charles Chatfield, *An American Ordeal: The Antiwar Movement of the Vietnam Era* (Syracuse, N.Y., 1990), p. 298.

sions, the Senate approved resolutions setting a specific deadline for the removal of all American troops pending Hanoi's release of the prisoners of war. Each time, the House removed the deadline and otherwise watered down the language.

The malaise that afflicted the nation spread to the U.S. armed forces in Vietnam. Until 1969, American GIs had fought superbly. But the failure to call up the reserves and the well-intentioned policy of requiring Americans to serve one-year tours in Vietnam deprived the army of experienced leaders, forced constant turnover in units, and transported to Vietnam problems already deeply entrenched in the United States. After the initiation of Nixon's troop-withdrawal policy, moreover, the purpose of the war became increasingly murky to those called on to fight it, and many GIs became much more reluctant to put their lives on the line. Discipline broke down in some units, with enlisted personnel simply refusing to obey their officers' orders. Attempts to assassinate officers in time of war were not unique to Vietnam, but fragging (so called because of the fragmentation grenades often used) reached unprecedented proportions in the Vietnamization period; more than 200 incidents were reported in 1970 alone. The availability and high quality of drugs in Southeast Asia meant that the drug culture that attracted growing numbers of young Americans at home was easily transported to Vietnam. The U.S. command estimated in 1970 that as many as 65,000 American service personnel were using drugs and that 40,000 were hooked on heroin. In addition, the armed services were not immune to the racial tensions that tore America apart in the Vietnam era, and numerous outbreaks of racial conflict in units in Vietnam and elsewhere drew growing attention to the breakdown of morale and discipline. "I need to get this Army home to save it," Abrams moaned to a friend.[54]

Although determined not to be stampeded, Nixon and Kissinger were sufficiently concerned by their predicament to try once again to break the stalemate in Paris. Kissinger expressed repeated fear that the administration might not be able to get through the year without Congress "giving the farm away."[55] Nixon recognized that he would probably need a peace settlement to win reelection, but he hoped to get it far enough in advance to avoid the

[54]Quoted in Sorley, *Better War*, 289.
[55]Quoted in Vernon A. Walters, *Silent Missions* (New York, 1978), p. 516.

appearance of desperation or a blatant political maneuver. As a consequence, in May 1971 Kissinger secretly presented to the North Vietnamese the most comprehensive peace offer yet advanced by the United States. In exchange for release of the American prisoners of war (POWs), he pledged to withdraw all troops within seven months after an agreement had been signed. The United States also abandoned the concept of mutual withdrawal, insisting only that North Vietnam stop further infiltration in return for the removal of American forces.

This offer initiated the most intensive peace discussions since the war had begun. The North Vietnamese quickly rejected Kissinger's proposal, perceiving that it would require them to give up the prisoners of war (their major bargaining weapon), to stop fighting, and to accept the Thieu regime in advance of any political settlement. Hanoi's delegate, Le Duc Tho, promptly made a counteroffer, however, agreeing to release the POWs simultaneously with the withdrawal of American forces, provided that the United States dropped its support for Thieu prior to a political settlement. Kissinger found the North Vietnamese offer unacceptable, but he was deeply impressed by Tho's serious and conciliatory demeanor and sensed "the shape of a deal" between the two offers. He could "almost taste peace," he remarked excitedly to friends.[56]

The discussions eventually broke down over the issue of the Thieu regime. From the start of the secret talks, the North Vietnamese had insisted on Thieu's removal as an essential precondition for any peace agreement and on several occasions had even hinted that the United States might assassinate him. Elections were scheduled to be held in South Vietnam in September, and Tho now proposed that if the United States would withdraw its support for Thieu, permitting an open election, it could take the first step toward a settlement without losing face. Uninformed of the substance of the secret talks but sensing just such a deal, Thieu vastly complicated matters by forcing the removal of the two opposition candidates, Nguyen Cao Ky and Duong Van Minh. Thieu's blatant interference in the political process so enraged the American embassy that Ambassador Ellsworth Bunker urged Nixon to publicly disassociate himself from Thieu and privately force him to accept a contested election. Nixon and Kissinger were unwilling to run the risk

[56]Quoted in Marvin and Bernard Kalb, *Kissinger* (Boston, 1974), p. 180.

of abandoning Thieu at this critical juncture, however, and rejected both the North Vietnamese proposal and Bunker's advice. The administration would only declare its "neutrality," a position that was meaningless while Thieu was running unopposed.

After Thieu had been safely reelected, Kissinger attempted to keep the secret talks alive, proposing elections within sixty days after a cease-fire and Thieu's withdrawal one month in advance. From Hanoi's standpoint, this offer was undoubtedly an improvement over earlier ones, but it did not guarantee that Thieu would not be a candidate or that he would be prevented from using the machinery of the government to rig the election. The North Vietnamese thus concluded that it was "necessary not to appear impatient." They promptly rejected the American proposal. The secret talks once again broke off in late November, leaving a frustrated Kissinger to fantasize about building a dam across the Mekong River and flooding all of Vietnam.[57]

Although the negotiations of late 1971 were the most serious yet undertaken, they eventually broke down for the same reasons earlier efforts had failed. Having invested so much blood, treasure, and prestige in a struggle of more than ten years' duration, neither side was yet willing to make the sort of concessions necessary for peace. Perhaps more important, each side still felt that it could get what it wanted by means other than compromise. Since 1969, North Vietnam had remained on the defensive, carefully husbanding its resources and personnel for a final military offensive it hoped would topple the Thieu regime and force the United States out of Vietnam. While attempting, without much success, to keep Vietnam on the back burner in 1971, Nixon and Kissinger had focused on achieving a dramatic reversal in relations with the Soviet Union and China, thus making good their promises of a "generation of peace." By the end of 1971, summit meetings had been scheduled for both Beijing and Moscow, giving Nixon and Kissinger renewed hope that they could salvage the administration, ensure the president's reelection, and force an isolated North Vietnam to come to terms. Neither side would achieve what it hoped with the dramatic military and diplomatic moves of 1972, and each would pay a high price trying, but they did bring the war into a final, convulsive phase that would ultimately produce a compromise peace.

[57]Ibid., p. 185.

THE EASTER OFFENSIVE

On March 30, 1972, North Vietnam launched a massive, conventional invasion of the south. At the time, only 95,000 U.S. forces remained there, only 6,000 of them combat troops, and Hanoi correctly reasoned that domestic pressures would prevent Nixon from putting new forces into Vietnam. The North Vietnamese were increasingly uneasy about U.S. negotiations with their major allies, the Soviet Union and China. They timed the invasion to coincide with the beginning of the American presidential campaign in hopes that, as in 1968, by striking a decisive blow they could cripple Nixon as they had Johnson, thus giving them the upper hand in negotiating a settlement. They aimed the offensive directly at ARVN main-force units, hoping to discredit the Vietnamization policy and tie down as many enemy regular forces as possible, enabling the NLF to resume the offensive in the countryside, disrupt pacification, and strengthen its position prior to the final peace negotiations.

In its first stages, the offensive was an unqualified success. Spearheaded by Soviet tanks, 120,000 North Vietnamese troops struck on three fronts: across the demilitarized zone; in the Central Highlands; and across the Cambodian border northwest of Saigon. Expecting a series of smaller attacks during the Tet holidays, American intelligence completely misjudged the timing, magnitude, and location of the invasion. Achieving near complete surprise, the North Vietnamese routed the thin lines of defending forces and quickly advanced toward the towns of Quang Tri in the north, Kontum in the highlands, and An Loc just sixty miles north of Saigon. Thieu was forced to commit most of his reserves to defend the threatened towns, thus freeing the NLF to take the offensive in the Mekong delta and in the heavily populated regions around Saigon.

Although stunned by the swiftness and magnitude of the invasion, Washington responded forcefully. Nixon refused to allow South Vietnam to fall. He was unwilling to send U.S. ground troops back to Vietnam, but he was determined to give North Vietnam a "bloody nose," and he saw in the enemy invasion an opportunity to revive the end-the-war strategy he had been forced to discard in 1969.[58] He quickly approved B-52 strikes across the demilitarized zone and followed with massive air attacks on fuel depots in the

[58]Elmo R. Zumwalt, Jr., *On Watch* (New York, 1976), p. 379.

Kim Phuc, 1972
This photograph of Kim Phuc, taken on June 8, 1972, during the furious battles of the Easter Offensive, became one of the defining images of the war. A nine-year-old peasant girl, Kim Phuc was running in terror in a futile effort to escape the napalm clinging to her body after an inadvertant South Vietnamese attack on her village. Used by Hanoi for a time as a poster child for the evils of capitalism, Kim Phuc later defected to Canada. In a moving ceremony on Veteran's Day, 1996, she joined with a former American POW in laying a wreath at the base of the Vietnam Mermorial in Washington.
AP/Wide World Photos

Hanoi-Haiphong area. In the meantime, Kissinger met secretly with Soviet Premier Leonid Brezhnev. For the first time, Kissinger made explicit an American willingness to permit North Vietnamese forces to remain in South Vietnam after a cease-fire. He also stated emphatically that the United States held the Soviet Union responsible for the invasion, and he warned that a continuation of the war could severely damage Soviet-American relations and have grave

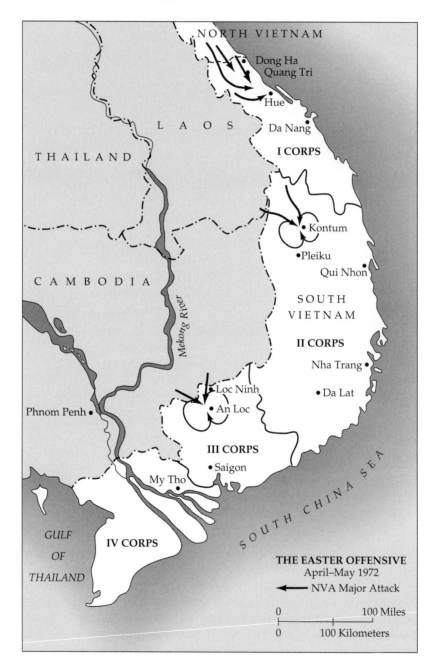

NORTH VIETNAM

Dong Ha
Quang Tri

Hue

L A O S

Da Nang

I CORPS

THAILAND

Kontum

•Pleiku

Qui Nhon

SOUTH
VIETNAM

C A M B O D I A

II CORPS

Nha Trang •

Mekong River

• Da Lat

•Loc Ninh

Phnom Penh •

• An Loc

III CORPS

• Saigon

My Tho

SOUTH CHINA SEA

GULF
OF
THAILAND

IV CORPS

THE EASTER OFFENSIVE
April–May 1972
◄─── NVA Major Attack

0   100 Miles

0   100 Kilometers

consequences for North Vietnam. The offer and the threats were repeated to Le Duc Tho on May 1.

Still confident of victory, the North Vietnamese flatly rejected Kissinger's offer, leaving Nixon a set of difficult choices. Warning that Hue and Kontum might soon fall and that the "whole thing may be lost," Abrams on May 8 pressed for intensification of the bombing of North Vietnam and for the mining of Haiphong harbor.[59] On the other hand, Secretaries Laird and Rogers warned that drastic countermeasures could have disastrous domestic consequences, and Kissinger expressed concern that the Soviets might cancel Nixon's impending visit to Moscow, undoing months of tedious negotiations on strategic arms limitation and other major issues.

Enraged by the North Vietnamese challenge and unwilling to accept defeat, Nixon struck back furiously. Still intent on persuading the enemy of his resolve and his unpredictability, he set out to make clear that he was "absolutely determined to end the war" and would take *"whatever steps* are necessary to accomplish this goal." Johnson lacked the will, he boasted. "I have the *will* in spades." A number of Washington officials reassured him that the Russians had too much at stake in their negotiations with the United States to cancel the summit. Even should they do so, he was willing to take the risk, as always for the sake of his credibility. "If we were to lose in Vietnam," he insisted, "there would have been no respect for the American President . . . because we had the power and didn't use it. . . . We must be credible." The president thus decided to "go for broke." He would seize the opportunity presented by the Easter Offensive to destroy the enemy's capacity to make war. The United States pulled together from bases across the world the greatest armada of naval and air power assembled during the war. On May 8, Nixon announced to a startled nation the most drastic escalation since 1965: the mining of Haiphong harbor, a naval blockade and massive, sustained bombing of North Vietnam. "The bastards have never been bombed like they're going to be bombed this time," he vowed.[60]

Nixon's gamble succeeded, at least to a point. Caught up in an extremely delicate diplomatic game, the two major Communist

---

[59]Nixon, *RN*, p. 594.
[60]Kimball, *Nixon's Vietnam War*, pp. 312–315; *New York Times*, June 30, 1974, April 30, 2000; Raymond Price, *With Nixon* (New York, 1977), p. 112.

powers responded to the events of 1972 with the greatest care. Because of their continuing rivalry, neither was prepared to sacrifice North Vietnam on the altar of political expediency. At the same time, each had increasingly come to regard the war as a sideshow that must not be allowed to jeopardize the major diplomatic realignment then taking place in the world. The Soviet Union continued to provide North Vietnam with massive military and economic assistance. But the summit went ahead as scheduled. During Nixon's visit to Moscow in late May, Brezhnev and his colleagues went through the motions of protesting, charging the United States with "sheer aggression" in Vietnam and even comparing it to Nazi Germany. The negotiations then proceeded in a cordial and businesslike manner, however, and major agreements were concluded. The Soviet Union also sent a top-level diplomat to urge Hanoi to make peace. The Chinese protested Nixon's escalation of the war and provided North Vietnam crucial assistance, especially with minesweeping Haiphong Harbor. But they too urged Hanoi to reach an agreement with the United States.[61]

The domestic reaction was also manageable. A new round of protests and demonstrations erupted. Senate doves were "shocked," "mad," and "depressed," according to George Aiken (a Republican from Vermont), and another flurry of end-the-war resolutions went into the congressional hopper.[62] The American public had always considered bombing more acceptable than the use of ground forces, however, and many Americans felt that the North Vietnamese invasion justified Nixon's response. As on earlier occasions, the public and Congress rallied around decisive presidential initiatives, and the success of the summit cut the ground from beneath those who argued that Nixon's rash action would undermine détente. Unwilling to leave anything to chance, zealous operatives on the Committee for the Reelection of the President forged thousands of letters and telegrams to the White House expressing approval of Nixon's policies, but even without such antics the president enjoyed broad support. His public approval rating shot up dramatically, Congress did nothing, and he emerged in a much stronger position than before the North Vietnamese invasion.[63]

---

[61]Kissinger, *White House Years*, pp. 1226–1227; Qiang Zhai, *China and the Vietnam Wars, 1950–1975* (Chapel Hill, N.C., 2000), pp. 202–206.
[62]George Aiken, *Senate Diary* (Brattleboro, Vt., 1976), pp. 55–57.
[63]Harris, *Anguish of Change*, p. 74.

Nixon's decisive response appears also to have averted defeat in South Vietnam. Code-named LINEBACKER (because of the president's well-known love for football), the bombing operations ordered in May vastly exceeded all previous attacks on North Vietnam. In June alone, U.S. planes dropped 112,000 tons of bombs, including new so-called smart bombs precisely guided to their targets by computers receiving signals from television cameras and laser beams. The attacks devastated the North Vietnamese economy, paralyzed the transportation system, and exhausted air defenses. The conventional military tactics employed by the NVA in the summer of 1972 required vast quantities of fuel and ammunition, and the bombing and blockade made resupply extremely difficult. Even more critical was U.S. tactical air support in South Vietnam. American bombers flew round-the-clock missions—B-52 sortie rates reached an unprecedented three per hour each twenty-four hours—pummeling enemy supply lines and encampments. With the crucial assistance of U.S. airpower, the ARVN eventually stabilized the lines in front of Saigon and Hue and even mounted a small counteroffensive.

In the final analysis, the ferocious campaigns of the summer of 1972 merely raised the stalemate to a new level of violence. Both sides endured huge losses—the North Vietnamese suffered an estimated 100,000 casualties, the South Vietnamese lost as many as 30,000 killed, 78,000 wounded, and 14,000 missing in action—but neither emerged appreciably stronger. Although it fought determinedly at times, ARVN continued to be afflicted by severe leadership problems, especially in top positions, and its ability to prevail without the support of U.S. airpower was highly suspect. The Easter Offensive again demonstrated, one scholar has concluded, that the " 'strategy' of Vietnamization could never compensate for a lack of national will."[64] North Vietnam had exposed ARVN's continued vulnerability, gained a sizable slice of territory along the Laotian and Cambodian borders that would be important in its final offensive, and retained sizable troops in the South. The NLF scored some major gains in the Mekong delta. But Hanoi had again badly miscalculated the U.S. response, and by spreading its forces over three fronts rather than concentrating on one, it succeeded nowhere. The North Vietnamese again paid a huge price for their mistakes: their offensive capabilities were set back for

---

[64]Dale Andradé, *Trial by Fire: The 1972 Easter Offensive, America's Last Vietnam Battle* (New York, 1995), p. 533. See also Sorley, *Better War*, pp. 339–342; and Kimball, *Nixon's Vietnam War*, pp. 324–327.

three years. Thieu clung stubbornly to power, and the United States remained in South Vietnam.

Frustrated in their hopes of breaking the diplomatic stalemate by military means, each side, by the fall of 1972, found compelling reasons to attempt to break the military deadlock by diplomacy. The Nixon administration was by no means desperate to get a settlement. The Democrats had nominated George McGovern, an outspoken dove whose extreme views appeared to make him the easiest of the Democratic contenders to defeat and left Nixon a great deal of room to maneuver. Nonetheless, Nixon and especially Kissinger recognized that an indefinite continuation of the air war could cause problems at home. They were increasingly frustrated, moreover, by the persistence of a war they had come to regard as a major obstruction to their grand design for a generation of peace, and they were eager to uphold their earlier promises to end it.

For North Vietnam, the pressures were equally compelling. Its allies could no longer be relied on for crucial diplomatic support. The nation had survived "the second US war of destruction," but it had suffered heavily. Although the leadership was prepared to continue the war if necessary, it was anxious for a peace that could be accomplished without sacrificing long-term goals. It was eager to see the removal of all U.S. troops from South Vietnam, because it recognized that dealing with the Saigon forces alone would be much easier. It was confident that the autumn "race to the White House" would put pressure on Nixon to settle. Thus the North Vietnamese in late summer shifted to a "strategy of peace," hoping to ease the United States toward "real negotiations" while preparing for a possible continuation of the war. Even if the North Vietnamese could not secure the ouster of Thieu, they were prepared to settle, recognizing that it was vital to exploit the opportunity provided by the American election. By September, when it became obvious that Nixon would win by a landslide, they were even more certain that they must try to settle as soon as possible.[65]

PEACE IS AT HAND

From late summer on, the two nations began inching toward a compromise. Having already indicated its willingness to allow

---

[65]Loi and Vu, *Le Duc Tho–Kissinger Negotiations*, pp. 239–272.

North Vietnamese troops to remain in the south after a cease-fire, the United States took a major step away from its absolute commitment to Thieu by agreeing to accept a tripartite electoral commission. Composed of the Saigon regime, the Provisional Revolutionary Government [(PRG), the functioning government created in 1969 by the NLF as a rival to the Government of Vietnam (GVN)], and the neutralists, this body would in theory be responsible for arranging a settlement after the cease-fire went into effect. In the meantime, the North Vietnamese dropped their insistence on the ouster of Thieu, accepting the principle of a cease-fire that would leave him in control temporarily but would also grant the PRG status as a political entity in the south.

Serious discussions of a settlement along these lines began in late September, and during three weeks of intensive, sometimes frantic negotiations, Kissinger and Tho hammered out the fundamentals of an agreement. Within sixty days after a cease-fire, the United States would withdraw its remaining troops, and North Vietnam would return American POWs. A political settlement would then be arranged by the tripartite National Council of Reconciliation and Concord, which would administer elections and assume responsibility for implementing the agreement. By October 11, all but several issues had been resolved. Eager to wrap up the matter as quickly as possible, Kissinger and Tho agreed that these items could be left until later. After consulting with Nixon and Thieu, Kissinger would proceed on to Hanoi to initial the treaty on October 22.

In his haste to work out an agreement, Kissinger made several critical mistakes. He had routinely deceived both Vietnams, on important issues taking one position with Hanoi and quite another with Saigon. He also badly overestimated Thieu's willingness to do what the United States told him and underestimated Nixon's willingness to go along with Thieu.

The imperious and impatient American spent five tension-filled days in Saigon employing what he called "shock tactics," going over the treaty item by item, embellishing its advantages for South Vietnam and issuing only slightly veiled warnings that a refusal to go along would compel the end of American support. Increasingly frustrated that the leader of a mere client state could threaten his grand design, Kissinger complained that Thieu's objections "verge on insanity." While trying to sway the South Vietnamese, he continued to practice masterful self-deception. "We face the paradoxical situation," he wrote Nixon, "that the North, which has effectively lost, is acting as if it had won, while the South, which effectively won, is acting as if it has lost."[66]

Thieu was not appeased. He deeply resented his dependence on the United States, and he was frightened at the prospect of abandonment. He was furious that he had not been consulted during the negotiations and especially that he had first learned of the terms through captured NLF documents. He was incensed that the draft Kissinger presented to him was in English. Kissinger's heavy-handed and arrogant efforts to present him with a fait accompli reinforced his already deep-seated suspicion of the United States. Of all the parties concerned, Thieu had the least interest in an agreement providing for an American withdrawal, and he found the terms completely unacceptable. He could not go along with an agreement that permitted North Vietnamese troops to remain in the south and that accorded the PRG sovereignty. He brought to Kissinger's attention some notably careless phraseology in the text that accorded the tripartite commission the status of a coalition government. He had been faithful to his ally, he claimed, but now he was being sacrificed. "If we accept the document as it stands, we will commit suicide—and I will be commmitting suicide." He demanded wholesale changes, including establishment of the demilitarized zone as a boundary between two sovereign states and removal of North Vietnamese troops from the south. Perhaps attempting to repeat his maneuver of 1968 (although McGovern was of no help to him), he sought to drive a wedge between the United States and North Vietnam by blocking the treaty and allowing the war to continue.[67]

Thieu succeeded for the short term. Outraged at this unexpected threat to his handiwork, Kissinger denounced Thieu's demands as "preposterous" and urged Nixon to go ahead without Thieu's cooperation. Concerned primarily with getting the United States out of Vietnam, Kissinger seems to have sought nothing more than a "decent interval" between an American withdrawal and the inevitable North Vietnamese conquest of South Vietnam. Nixon, on the other hand, was at best ambivalent. Increasingly jeal-

[66]Quoted in *New York Times,* April 30, 2000.
[67]Ibid.; Kimball, *Nixon's Vietnam War,* pp. 328–332. For the South Vietnamese perspective, see Nguyen Tien Hung and Jerrold L. Schecter, *The Palace File* (New York, 1986), pp. 98–106.

ous of Kissinger's accomplishments and suspicious of his ambitions, the president suspected that his aide was rushing a peace agreement in order to claim credit for his reelection, and he feared that a peace settlement on the eve of the election might be dismissed as a political ploy. Unlike Kissinger, Nixon never abandoned his quest for "peace with honor." He shared some of Thieu's reservations about the October draft, and although he had approved it on condition of Thieu's acquiescence, he seems to have sensed in Saigon's rejection an opportunity to achieve what he had sought from the start. Certain of an "enormous mandate" in the upcoming election, he was inclined to wait until after he had been reelected, at which point he could demand that North Vietnam settle or "face the consequences of what we could do to them."[68] He was not willing to let Thieu block an agreement indefinitely, but a brief delay would permit the United States to provide South Vietnam with additional assistance, patch up fundamental shortcomings in the treaty, and weaken North Vietnam's ability to threaten the peace. He seems already to have committed himself to using airpower or the threat of airpower to uphold the peace agreement and keep South Vietnam afloat until the end of his second term. Kissinger attempted to keep alive hopes of an early settlement by stating publicly on October 31 that "peace is at hand," but Nixon's support of Thieu ensured the breakdown of the October agreement.

When the secret discussions resumed in early November, the United States brought up for reconsideration sixty-nine points, many of them minor but others central to the compromise. Kissinger asked for at least a token withdrawal of North Vietnamese troops from the south and requested changes in the text that would have weakened the political status of the NLF, restricted the powers of the tripartite commission, and established the demilitarized zone as a virtual boundary. He added stern warnings that Nixon, having secured a landslide victory over McGovern, would not hesitate to "take whatever action he considers necessary to protect United States interests."[69] Certain that they had been betrayed, refusing to give way in the face of threats, and determined not to be steamrolled into a disadvantageous agreement,

[68]Nixon, *RN*, p. 701. See also Larry Berman, *No Peace, No Honor* (New York, 2001), p. 140.
[69]Ibid., p. 721.

the North Vietnamese angrily rejected Kissinger's proposals. The NLF, no happier with the agreement than the Saigon regime was, bitterly protested that it gave Thieu a veto over negotiations and did not adequately provide for the release of political prisoners held by the GVN. Under extreme pressure from their southern compatriots, Hanoi's negotiators raised numerous demands of their own, even reviving their old insistence on the ouster of Thieu.[70]

For days, Kissinger and Tho sparred back and forth across the negotiating table in an atmosphere ridden with tension and marked by frequent outbursts of anger. Fearful that the peace that had seemed so close might yet slip away, each side made concessions, and by mid-December they had returned to the essence of the original compromise with only the status of the demilitarized zone unresolved.

Strangely, just when peace once again seemed at hand, Nixon and Kissinger broke off the talks. Thieu had still not given in, and a peace settlement at this point would have required an embarassing break with a long-standing ally. Kissinger was increasingly frustrated with North and South Vietnam, neither of whom would bend to his will. Decision making was complicated by the growing suspicion and mutual antagonism between Nixon and Kissinger themselves. Although dependent on his adviser to implement his diplomacy, Nixon seethed with resentment that Kissinger was gaining recognition that should rightfully be his. Communication between them was poor during this critical period. Kissinger may have proposed a tougher line to reestablish his credibility and influence with an increasingly angry and suspicious boss. Rather than being charitable in his hour of triumph, Nixon was more tormented and vengeful than ever, reluctant to compromise with anyone and even more determined to settle old scores and stick it to his enemies. Conveniently ignoring America's role in the impasse, Kissinger denounced the North Vietnamese as "insolent" and "tawdry" and complained that they had "goaded us beyond endurance."[71] Frustrated and impatient for results, the two men decided to terminate the talks and resolve the dual impasse by diplomatic pressure and military force.

---

[70]Robert K. Brigham, *Guerrilla Diplomacy: The NLF's Foreign Relations and the Vietnam War* (Ithaca, N.Y., 1999), pp. 104–109.

[71]Sulzberger, *Seven Continents*, p. 593; Nixon, *RN*, pp. 725–726. The best discussion of these events is Kimball, *Nixon's Vietnam War*, pp. 348–362.

Over the next few weeks, Nixon stepped up the pressure on South Vietnam. He ordered the immediate delivery of more than $1 billion of military hardware, leaving Thieu with, among other assets, the fourth largest air force in the world. Nixon gave "absolute assurances" that if the North Vietnamese violated the peace agreement, he would order "swift and severe retaliatory action," and he instructed the Joint Chiefs of Staff to begin immediate planning for such a contingency.[72] At the same time, in Kissinger's words, Nixon sought to "brutalize" Thieu, warning in what he termed his "absolutely final offer" that if South Vietnam rejected the best treaty that could be obtained the United States would "seek a settlement with the enemy which serves U.S. interests alone."[73] Thieu continued to defy his more powerful patron, refusing to give Nixon carte blanche to negotiate for him and brazenly informing the press that he had rejected a U.S. ultimatum. Although enraged at the intransigence of an ally he now labeled a "complete SOB," Nixon was not entirely displeased, perceiving that Thieu's defiance gave him ample pretext for a break should it come to that later.[74]

While attempting to bludgeon Thieu into submission, Nixon employed what Kissinger called "jugular diplomacy" against North Vietnam, ordering over the Christmas season a massive dose of bombing against Hanoi and Haiphong. The ostensible motive was to force the North Vietnamese to conclude an agreement. But the decision reflected the accumulated anger and frustration of four years. It may have been designed to reassure Thieu and to reduce North Vietnam's capacity to threaten South Vietnam after a settlement had been concluded. Nixon knew that he must end the war quickly or Congress might take control out his hands. He was egged on by hard-liners such as Secretary of the Treasury John Connally and Kissinger's aide and rival General Alexander Haig. An intensive bombing attack could end the war with a dramatic flourish—a bang rather than a whimper—as Nixon had predicted at the outset of his presidency. It would enable him to portray this

---

[72]Nixon, *RN*, p. 718; Zumwalt, *On Watch*, pp. 413–414.

[73]H. R. Haldeman, *The Haldeman Diaries: Inside the Nixon White House* (New York, 1994), p. 543; Nixon to Thieu, December 17, 1972, Richard Cheney Files, Gerald R. Ford Library, Ann Arbor, Mich., Box 13.

[74]Haldeman, *Haldeman Diaries*, p. 558.

peace that in fact had resulted from compromise as a victory for U.S. military power and his own courage and diplomatic skill.[75] It would demonstrate to the North Vietnamese that he was prepared to uphold the peace that was negotiated.

Nixon thus again determined to go for broke. He made absolutely clear to the military his determination to inflict maximum damage on North Vietnam. "I don't want any more of this crap about the fact that we couldn't hit this target or that one," he lectured Admiral Thomas Moorer, chairman of the Joint Chiefs of Staff. "This is your chance to use military power to win this war, and if you don't, I'll consider you responsible."[76] Over the next twelve days, the United States unleashed the most intensive and devastating air attacks of the war, dropping more than 36,000 tons of bombs, exceeding the tonnage for the entire period between 1969 and 1971.

Nixon's and Kissinger's later claims that the so-called Christmas bombing forced the North Vietnamese to accept a settlement satisfactory to the United States do not hold up under close scrutiny. Despite its ferocity, the bombing did not severely set back North Vietnam's war-making capacity. It did not compare in terms of destructiveness to the bombing of Tokyo, Hiroshima, or Dresden during World War II, as critics charged. American pilots went to extraordinary lengths to avoid civilian casualties, and large numbers of civilians had already been evacuated from the major cities. Still, the destruction in parts of Hanoi and Haiphong was heavy, and more than 1,600 civilians were killed. The bombing certainly gave the North Vietnamese reason to resume negotiations, especially since they had exhausted their stock of surface-to-air missiles by December 30.[77]

The bombing also gave Nixon compelling reasons to return to the negotiating table. In part because of U.S. tactics designed to avoid civilian casualties, North Vietnamese air defenses exacted a heavy toll, bringing down fifteen B-52s (nine the first three days) and eleven other aircraft, leaving ninety-three crew members missing and thirty-one new POWs. The Christmas bombing provoked

[75]Kimball, *Nixon's Vietnam War*, pp. 362–364.
[76]Sulzberger, *Seven Continents*, p. 593; Nixon, *RN*, pp. 725–726.
[77]For a balanced discussion of the effects of the Christmas bombing, see James R. Powell, "Going for Broke: Richard Nixon's Search for 'Peace with Honor,' October 1972–January 1973" (Ph.D. diss., University of Kentucky, 1998), pp. 169–200.

cries of outrage across the world. The Soviets and Chinese, in marked contrast to their restraint in May, heatedly protested, and in a remark that especially stung Nixon, Swedish prime minister Olof Palme compared it as an act of cruelty to those perpetrated by the Nazis. The reaction at home was one of shock and anger. Critics condemned Nixon as a "madman" and accused him of waging "war by tantrum." Columnist Joseph Kraft denounced the bombing as an act of "senseless terror which stains the good name of America."[78] Many Americans who had accepted the May bombings questioned both the necessity and unusual brutality of the December attacks, a "sorry Christmas present" for the American people, in the words of Senator Aiken.[79] Nixon's popular approval rating plummeted to 39 percent overnight, and congressional doves made it clear that when they returned to Washington after the Christmas recess, they would be ready to do battle with the president. "We took the threats from Congress seriously," one of Nixon's aides later observed; "we knew we were racing the clock," and if North Vietnam refused to negotiate, "we faced stern action."[80] To keep his options open, Nixon had indicated to the North Vietnamese that he would stop the bombing if they agreed to resume the peace talks. Hanoi consented, and Nixon got himself off the hook.

Most important, the bombing did not produce a settlement markedly different from the one the United States had earlier rejected. The negotiations resumed in Paris on January 8. The atmosphere was grim and icy, but this time both parties were committed to a settlement, and after six days of marathon sessions, marked by compromise on both sides, Kissinger and Tho resolved their differences. The changes from the October agreement were largely cosmetic, enabling each side to claim that nothing had been given up. On the demilitarized zone, which had been the major sticking point of the December negotiations, the North Vietnamese agreed to make explicit reference to it in the treaty, but the United States accepted its description as a "provisional and not a political and territorial boundary," preserving the substance of Hanoi's position. The question of civilian movement across the demilitarized zone was left to be resolved later in negotiations between North and South Vietnam,

[78]Quoted in ibid., 205.
[79]Aiken, *Senate Diary*, p. 136.
[80]Colson, *Born Again*, pp. 77–79.

and North Vietnamese Troops remained in the south. "We bombed the North Vietnamese into accepting our concessions," Kissinger aide John Negroponte observed with obvious irony.[81]

This time, the United States imposed the agreement on Thieu. To sweeten the pill, Nixon reaffirmed that if Thieu accepted the treaty, he would provide South Vietnam with continued support and would "respond with full force" if North Vietnam violated the agreement. At the same time, he made clear that if Thieu continued to resist, he would cut off further assistance and that he was prepared to sign the treaty alone, if necessary. In one especially heavy-handed letter, he reminded Thieu of the fate of Ngo Diuh Dien in 1963.[82] Thieu stalled for several days, but when it was apparent that he could do no better, he gave in, remarking with resignation, "I have done all that I can for my country." The Saigon government never formally endorsed the treaty, but Thieu let it be known in a cryptic way that he would not oppose it.

Nixon and Kissinger later claimed to have achieved the peace with honor to which they had committed themselves in 1969.[83] Despite the perfidy of North Vietnam, the intractability of South Vietnam, and the vicious, unrelenting attacks from their domestic critics, the two men saw themselves as having courageously persisted and put together a peace agreement that extricated the United States from the war, secured the return of American prisoners of war, and kept South Vietnam intact. That peace with honor could have been upheld, they insisted, had not North Vietnam repeatedly violated the Paris agreements and had not a vengeful and feckless Congress, bolstered by the Watergate scandals, prevented the administration from using American power to defend a peace for which so much had been paid in blood and treasure.

In fact, there was no peace. The Paris agreements permitted American extrication from the war and secured the return of most of the POWs while leaving the Thieu government in place, at least for the moment. But the major question over which the war had been fought—the political future of South Vietnam—was left unresolved. The political mechanism established to resolve it was inherently unworkable. At the time Kissinger and Tho emerged from the

---

[81]Quoted in Powell, "Going for Broke," p. 286.
[82]Hung and Schecter, *The Palace File*, pp. 73–74.
[83]Richard M. Nixon, *No More Vietnams* (New York, 1985).

Hotel Majestic in Paris smiling broadly at their achievement, the combatants in South Vietnam were busily preparing for the final round. As all sides recognized at the time, the 1973 agreements marked the beginning of yet another phase in the thirty-year struggle for the control of Vietnam.

Nor was there honor. Although South Vietnam was indeed intact when the peace agreement was signed, the presence of 150,000 North Vietnamese troops below the demilitarized zone, along with the U.S. withdrawal and recognition of the PRG, represented huge concessions on the part of the United States, concessions that Thieu saw so clearly as imperiling the existence of his already rickety government. With the use of or the threat of using American airpower, Nixon might have been able to delay the outcome. But U.S. forces would not be deployed in Vietnam again, and even the threat increasingly lacked credibility. This inability to act was in fact a result of the Watergate scandal, as Nixon and Kissinger later claimed. What they conveniently omit is that Watergate was the result of illegal actions taken by a paranoid administration and a vindictive president determined to destroy his political enemies. Even without Watergate, Nixon's threats to use American airpower and his promises to Thieu would probably have turned out to be empty. They were of dubious legality, in part because Nixon had not consulted with Congress. In any event, once U.S. forces had been removed from Vietnam, a war-weary nation and a rebellious Congress were not inclined to permit them to return. Nixon may have seen this outcome and sought to shift blame for the inevitable fall of South Vietnam to Congress. Or, as Larry Berman has persuasively argued, he may have planned through American airpower to maintain a perpetual stalemate.[84] Whatever the case, Nixon failed. Although he had succeeded in buying some time for Vietnamization, he had never built a base of public support to uphold the standards he had set for peace with honor. In the end, his standards had to give way to public unwillingness to invest more resources in a losing cause.[85]

For all concerned, "peace with honor" came at an enormous price. Official U.S. estimates place the number of South Vietnamese battle deaths for the years 1969 to 1973 at 107,504 and North Vietnamese and NLF at more than a half million. There will probably

[84]Berman, *No Peace, No Honor,* pp. 9, 204.
[85]Katz, "Public Opinion and Foreign Policy," 507.

never be an accurate accounting of civilians deaths and casualties. The tonnage of bombs dropped on Indochina during these years far exceeded that of the Johnson years, wreaking untold devastation, causing permanent ecological damage to the countryside, and leaving millions of civilians homeless.

The United States suffered much less than Vietnam did, but the cost was still substantial. An additional 20,553 Americans were killed in the last four years of the war, bringing the total to more than 58,000. Continuation of the war fueled an inflation that neither Nixon nor his successors could control. The war polarized the American people and poisoned the political atmosphere as no other issue since slavery a century before. Although Nixon had prolonged the fighting four years mainly to uphold America's position and credibility in the world, the United States emerged from the conflict with its international image substantially tarnished and its people weary of international commitment.

For Nixon, too, the price was steep. In January 1973, at the very moment when he should have been savoring his electoral triumph and his diplomatic successes, he was exhausted, embittered, and isolated, his administration reduced to a "small band of tired, dispirited, sometimes mean and petty men, bickering among themselves, wary and jealous of one another."[86] Ironically, at the very height of their political and diplomatic triumphs, Nixon and Kissinger gave vent to jealousy and backbiting over who deserved the credit. Nixon, enraged when Kissinger leaked to the press that he had opposed the Christmas bombing, characteristically ordered the monitoring of his key adviser's telephone. He was furious that Kissinger shared the Nobel Peace Prize with Le Duc Tho. At the beginning of the second term, the president and his staff were preparing to remove Kissinger from his position.

More than any other single issue, the Vietnam War brought a premature end to the Nixon presidency. The extreme measures he took to defend his Vietnam policies led directly to Watergate, which would eventually force his resignation. Thus, when the final crisis came in 1975, the person who claimed to have achieved peace with honor was no longer in the White House, and the nation was in no mood to defend the agreement he had constructed at such great cost.

[86]Colson, *Born Again,* p. 80.

"Night Patrol"
The Vietnam War touched the soul of Americans as few
other events in their history. The Vietnam Veterans
Memorial in Washington—the Wall—came to symbolize
the nation's grief and served as a place of healing and
reconciliation.
Larry Powell Photo

CHAPTER 8

The Postwar War
and the Legacies of Vietnam

The "peace" agreements of January 1973 established a framework for continuing the war without direct American participation. North Vietnam still sought unification of the country on its terms; South Vietnam still struggled to survive as an independent nation; and President Nixon still supported its aspirations and was prepared to keep the war going. The cease-fire thus existed only on paper.

This last phase of the war was of remarkably short duration. Dependent on the United States from its birth, the Saigon government had great difficulty functioning on its own. Because of the Watergate scandals and American war-weariness, moreover, Nixon was not able to live up to his secret commitments to Thieu, and indeed in August 1974 he was forced to resign. Congress drastically cut back aid to South Vietnam, further eroding the Saigon government's faltering will to resist. When North Vietnam and the National Liberation Front (NLF) mounted a major offensive in the spring of 1975, South Vietnam collapsed with stunning rapidity, dramatically ending the thirty-year war and leaving the United States, on the eve of its third century, frustrated, angry, and bewildered.

THE POSTWAR WAR

The "postwar war" began the instant peace was proclaimed. The United States had some difficulty arranging with the North Vietnamese for the return of the 591 prisoners of war, at one point threatening to delay troop withdrawals in the absence of cooperation. By the end of March, the details had been worked out and the POWs were released. Some had been held more than eight years. All had suffered through horrible living conditions, cruel captors, isolation, beatings, and other forms of torture. Some broke under the stress and made statements demanded by their captors. As a group, however, the POWs bore their captivity with courage, dignity, and remarkable inner strength. They developed ingenious methods to communicate with each other—and to survive. They returned in March 1973 to a heroes' welcome, and Jeremiah Denton's understated response—"We are honored to have had the opportunity to serve our country under difficult circumstances"—added to their appeal. That the POWs were singled out as the only true heroes of an unpopular war did a disservice to the thousands of Americans who performed heroic feats, but their dramatic return helped a divided and war-weary nation salvage some pride and redemption.[1]

The return of the POWs and the withdrawal of U.S. troops, however, were the only tangible accomplishments of the teams assigned to implement the peace accords. From the start, efforts to effect a cease-fire proved unavailing. The Vietnamese combatants had not abandoned their goals, and they were willing to observe the agreements only to the extent that it suited their interests. For Saigon, the agreement permitted, with U.S. assistance, continuation of the war and possible improvement of its position. For North Vietnam and the NLF, it provided a political mechanism to win the war.

Buoyed by Nixon's promises, Thieu defied the peace agreement from the outset. The NLF had launched a series of land-grabbing operations immediately before the cease-fire, and Thieu wanted to retrieve as much of the lost territory as possible. Although he controlled an estimated 75 percent of the land and 85 percent of the people when the agreements were signed, he sought to solidify his position while U.S. support remained firm. To secure as much additional territory as possible, he resettled refugees and built forts in contested areas. Army of the Republic of Vietnam (ARVN)

[1]Vernon E. Davis, *The Long Road Home: U.S. Prisoner of War Policy and Planning in Southeast Asia* (Washington, D.C., 2000), pp. 527–528. For a companion official history of the POWs' captivity, see Stuart I. Rochester and Frederick Kiley, *Honor Bound: The History of American Prisoners of War in Southeast Asia, 1961–1973* (Washington, D.C., 1998). A recent, personal account is John McCain with Mark Salter, *Faith of My Fathers* (New York, 1999).

units attacked North Vietnamese bases and supply lines, and artillery and aircraft indiscriminately shelled and bombed villages under Provisional Revolutionary Government (PRG) control. During the first three months of "peace," the ARVN lost more than 6,000 soldiers, among its highest casualties during the entire war.[2]

The North Vietnamese and NLF were more cautious but no less purposeful. Battered and exhausted from the bloody campaigns of 1972 and short of food, personnel, and ammunition, they desperately needed time to regroup. They were also eager to secure a complete U.S. withdrawal from Vietnam and to avoid blatant moves that might provoke a resumption of the bombing or threaten American promises of aid. During the first six months after the cease-fire, the PRG sought primarily to consolidate the territory under its control and to undermine Thieu's position through political agitation. By appearing to support the peace accords, it attempted to win sympathy from war-weary peoples in South Vietnam and the United States and to portray Thieu as an enemy of peace. Meanwhile, the North Vietnamese quietly infiltrated troops and equipment into the south, built a system of modern highways linking staging areas to strategic zones in South Vietnam, and even constructed a 1,000-mile pipeline to ensure adequate supplies of petroleum for forces in the field.

Although the Paris agreements provided that the future of South Vietnam would be settled by the Vietnamese, the United States persisted in its commitment to Thieu. Deeply frustrated by the months of tortuous negotiations and anxious to move on to other issues, Kissinger appears to have sought nothing more than a "decent interval" between the signing of the agreements and a North Vietnamese victory. Nixon, on the other hand, was no more willing in 1973 than in 1969 to be the first American president to lose a war. The January accords gave the PRG political status in the south, but the president made clear that the United States would

---

[2]The best account of the postwar war is Arnold R. Isaacs, *Without Honor: Defeat in Vietnam and Cambodia* (New York, 1984). See also Maynard Parker, "Vietnam: The War That Won't End," *Foreign Affairs* 53 (January 1975), especially 365–366; and Gareth Porter, *A Peace Denied: The United States, Vietnam, and the Paris Agreements* (Bloomington, Ind., 1975), pp. 174–184, 188–196. For the South Vietnamese perspective, see Nguyen Tien Hung and Jerrold L. Schecter, *The Palace File* (New York, 1986), pp. 159–349.

"continue to recognize the government of the Republic of Viet-Nam as the sole legitimate government of South Viet-Nam."[3]

Fully aware of the fragility of the agreements, Nixon deluded himself into believing that he could sustain the Thieu government. To secure Saigon's acquiescence, he had secretly promised to continue "full economic and military aid" and to "respond with full force" should North Vietnam violate the agreements.[4] In a meeting at San Clemente, California, in March, he reassured Thieu that "you can count on us."[5] Throughout the rest of 1973, the administration employed various subterfuges to maintain a high level of military aid without overtly violating the Paris accords. Instead of dismantling its bases, the United States transferred title to the South Vietnamese before the cease-fire went into effect. Supplies were designated "nonmilitary" and thus rendered eligible for transfer. The military advisory group was replaced by a "civilian" team of some 9,000 people, many of them hastily discharged from military service and placed in the employ of the government of Vietnam.[6]

The administration believed that it had the leverage to prevent North Vietnam from upsetting the delicate equilibrium in the south. As part of the Paris package, Nixon had secretly promised to provide Hanoi with $3.25 billion in aid for reconstruction and another $1.5 billion in commodities. On several occasions in the spring of 1973, he threatened to withhold the funds unless North Vietnam adhered to the letter of the agreements, and he eventually suspended talks on postwar aid to protest continued infiltration into South Vietnam and intensification of the fighting in Cambodia. The president and Kissinger also sought to keep alive the threat of American military intervention. "The only way we will keep North Vietnam under control is not to say we are out forever," Kissinger observed. "We don't want to dissipate with them the reputation for fierceness that the President has earned."[7] The last American troops were withdrawn from Vietnam by the end of March, but the United States kept a formidable armada of naval and air power in the Gulf

---

[3]Quoted in Porter, *Peace Denied,* p. 186.

[4]Richard M. Nixon, *RN: The Memoirs of Richard Nixon* (New York, 1978), pp. 749–750; *New York Times,* May 1, 1975.

[5]Stephen T. Hosmer et al., *The Fall of South Vietnam* (Santa Monica, Calif., 1978), p. 11.

[6]Tad Szulc, *The Illusion of Peace: Foreign Policy in the Nixon Years* (New York, 1978), pp. 672–676.

[7]Quoted in William Safire, *Before the Fall* (New York, 1975), p. 673.

of Tonkin and in Thailand and Guam. The bombing of Cambodia was continued, in part to support Lon Nol against a determined Khmer Rouge offensive, in part to maintain Nixon's "reputation for fierceness." Several times, the president seriously considered resuming the bombing of North Vietnam, and in April he reinstituted reconnaissance flights north of the seventeenth parallel.

VIETNAM, WATERGATE, AND CONGRESS

By the early summer of 1973, Nixon's ability to dangle carrots or brandish sticks had been sharply curtailed by an increasingly rebellious Congress. The congressional challenge reflected a pervasive war-weariness and a widespread feeling among Americans that once their troops had been safely removed, the nation should extricate itself entirely from the conflict. Mounting evidence of White House involvement in the Watergate scandal increased Nixon's vulnerability. Republicans joined Democrats in condemning the bombing of Cambodia as illegal, and on May 10 the House voted to cut off funds for further air operations. Congress displayed no enthusiasm for aid to North Vietnam, doves protesting that it would not ensure peace, hawks denouncing it as "reparations." In the fall of 1973 it voted that no funds would be provided until Hanoi gave a full accounting of U.S. personnel missing in action (MIAs), something it refused to do.

Perceiving the steady erosion of administration control over events in Indochina, Kissinger journeyed to Paris in May in a last-ditch and ultimately futile effort to persuade Le Duc Tho to observe the cease-fire. The North Vietnamese responded angrily to American charges of violations with countercharges that South Vietnam and the United States were not upholding their commitments. More annoying to Kissinger, they dismissed his accusations as attempts to deceive public opinion, "as you have done with Watergate." The diplomats could agree on nothing more than an innocuous communiqué reaffirming the January accords. Upon returning to Washington, a weary Kissinger informed newsmen that he was going to reduce his involvement in Indochina affairs "in order to preserve my emotional stability."[8]

---

[8]Quoted in Marvin and Bernard Kalb, *Kissinger* (Boston, 1974), p. 432.

Kissinger's remark was more prophetic than he realized, for in June Congress deprived the administration of what little leverage it retained. By this time, the Watergate investigations had turned up sensational revelations of abuses of presidential power. Long-embittered Democrats were encouraged to take on the president, and Republicans were increasingly reluctant to support him. Nixon and Kissinger vigorously defended the bombing of Cambodia as necessary to sustain Lon Nol and uphold the cease-fire. But an overwhelming majority of congressal representatives agreed with Senator George Aiken that the bombing was "ill-advised and un-warranted," and many accepted the outspoken affirmation of Representative Norris Cotton (a Republican from New Hampshire): "As far as I'm concerned, I want to get the hell out."[9] In late June, Congress approved an amendment requiring the immediate cessation of all military operations in and over Indochina. The House upheld Nixon's angry veto, but the president was eventually forced to accept a compromise extending the deadline to August 15. For the first time, Congress had taken decisive steps to curtail American involvement in the war. "It would be idle to say that the authority of the executive has not been impaired," Kissinger remarked with obvious understatement and disappointment.[10]

By the end of 1973, Nixon was virtually powerless. Watergate had reduced his popular approval ratings to an all-time low and left him fighting a desperate rearguard action to save his political life. His complete absorption with his survival rendered him increasingly incapable of dealing with other issues. In November, Congress passed, over another veto, the so-called War Powers Act, a direct response to the abuse of presidential authority in Vietnam. The legislation required the president to inform Congress within forty-eight hours of the deployment of American military forces abroad and to withdraw them in sixty days in the absence of explicit congressional endorsement. Some members of Congress protested that the act conferred on the president a more direct power to commit American troops to war than was provided by the Constitution, but the circumstances under which the debate took place, combined with Watergate and the vote terminating opera-

---

[9]George Aiken, *Senate Diary* (Brattleboro, Vt., 1976), p. 198; Kalb and Kalb, *Kissinger*, p. 432.
[10]Kalb and Kalb, *Kissinger*, p. 434.

tions in Indochina, made virtually certain the end of direct American involvement in Vietnam.

A CRUMBLING BASTION

In the meantime, the Paris agreements had become a dead letter. Discussions of a political settlement had begun in early 1973 and continued sporadically throughout the year, but the basic issue— the future of South Vietnam—was nonnegotiable. From the outset, Thieu took a position he labeled the "Four Nos": no recognition of the enemy; no coalition government; no neutralization for South Vietnam; no concession of territory. Still confident of U.S. support despite the darkening cloud of Watergate, he formally proclaimed in late 1973 the start of the "Third Indochina War," stepping up ground and air attacks on enemy bases and launching a series of land-grabbing operations in PRG-held territories along the eastern seaboard, in the Iron Triangle, and in the Mekong delta.

This time, the North Vietnamese and PRG counterattacked. Fearing a repetition of events in 1955 to 1959, when Vietminh stay-behinds had nearly been exterminated by the Diem regime, southerners pressed for action, and in October 1973 the Politburo authorized the use of "revolutionary violence." Still eager to avoid provoking a U.S. return, it stopped short of a large-scale offensive, but NLF forces were authorized to engage in armed conflict. Over the next few months they scored success after success, mauling ARVN units in the Iron Triangle, retaking much of the territory that had been lost, and seizing additional territory formerly under Saigon's control.

By the fall of 1974, the military balance had shifted in favor of North Vietnam and the NLF. In seeking to control more territory, Saigon had unwisely overextended itself; the more hamlets it acquired, the more vulnerable it became. More than half of its million-soldier army was tied down in static defense positions and scattered throughout the northern provinces. Modeled after the U.S. Army, the ARVN had a huge logistics tail. Only about 150,000 of its regular forces were actual combat troops, and as many as 20,000 of these were "flower soldiers" who had purchased their freedom from fighting. The crippling sense of dependency persisted as South Vietnamese still insisted on "checking with the Americans," even though it was unclear what Americans should be checked with. By this time, the North Vietnamese had an estimated 285,000 troops in the south. They had stockpiled vast quantities of supplies and built a highly sophisticated logistics system that permitted them to move regulars, along with tanks and artillery, to any battlefront within hours. The once primitive Ho Chi Minh Trail was now a gravel-paved, two-lane highway with way stations every 100 kilometers. In the crucial Mekong delta, the PRG had regained most of the territory lost the preceding year.[11]

At the same time, South Vietnam's perennial economic and political problems had been sharply aggravated by the American withdrawal. Loss of the $400 million the United States spent annually in South Vietnam, reduction of military aid from $2.3 billion in 1973 to about $1 billion in 1974, and a sharp rise in worldwide inflation combined to produce an annual inflation rate of 90 percent, massive unemployment, a drastic decline in morale in the armed forces and among the urban population, and an increase in the ever present corruption. Scavengers stripped the American-built port at Cam Ranh Bay to a bare skeleton. Pilots demanded bribes to fly missions in support of ground troops.

Thieu's policies compounded the problems. In the spring of 1974, he attempted to starve out the enemy by blockading PRG areas, enacting various measures to deny them rice. The so-called Rice War backfired, causing enormous suffering throughout all of South Vietnam, even in Saigon. By 1974, there were three to four million unemployed people in areas controlled by the Government of Vietnam (GVN), and the increase in hunger and joblessness stimulated a rise in crime and corruption. The economic crisis of 1974 compounded Thieu's political woes. The Buddhists became more active than at any other time since 1966, agitating for peace and reconciliation with the Communists. The Catholics, the government's most important base of support, organized an anticorruption campaign, the major target of which was Thieu himself. A spirit of defeatism grew among those fence-sitters who had not supported the government but had not actively opposed it either. Growing political unrest spurred demonstrations. The government responded as it always had with jailings and beatings.[12]

---

[11]Parker, "Vietnam," 366–367.
[12]Ngo Vinh Long, "Post-Paris Struggles and the Fall of Saigon," in Jayne S. Werner and Luu Doan Huynh (eds.), *The Vietnam War: Vietnamese and American Perspectives* (New York, 1993), pp. 206–212.

The American abandonment of South Vietnam was manifest by the end of 1974. Nixon was forced to resign in August, removing from power the individual who had promised continued support and leaving a despondent Thieu to contemplate abandoning the northern part of South Vietnam and building a new nation around the former Cochin China. Throughout the year, Kissinger pleaded with an increasingly defiant Congress to expand military aid to $1.5 billion, insisting that the United States had a moral obligation to South Vietnam and warning that failure to uphold it would have a "corrosive effect on our interests beyond Indochina."

The arguments that had been accepted without challenge for nearly a quarter of a century now fell flat. Runaway inflation in the United States evoked insistent demands for reducing expenditures, and many members of Congress agreed with Senator William Proxmire (a Democrat from Wisconsin) that there was less need for continued military aid to South Vietnam than for "any other single item" in the budget. Critics pointed out that the Thieu government was in no immediate peril and warned that much of the money would line the pockets of Saigon's corrupt bureaucrats. A continuation of massive American military aid would encourage Thieu to prolong the war, while a reduction might impress on him the need to seek a political settlement. It was time to terminate America's "endless support for an endless war," Senator Edward Kennedy insisted. In September 1974, Congress approved an aid program of $700 million, half of which comprised shipping costs.[13]

The aid cuts of 1974 had a tremendous impact in South Vietnam. Without the continued large infusion of American funds and equipment, the armed forces could not fight the way the Americans had trained them. Air force operations had to be curtailed by as much as 50 percent because of shortages of gasoline and spare parts. Ammunition and other supplies had to be severely rationed. The inescapable signs of waning American support had a devastating effect on morale in an army already reeling under North Vietnamese blows, and desertions reached an all-time high of 240,000 in 1974. The aid cutbacks heightened Thieu's economic and political difficulties, spurring among many Vietnamese a "growing psychology of accommodation and retreat that sometimes approached despair."[14]

---

[13]*Congressional Record*, 93d Cong., 2d Sess., 29176–29180.
[14]Guenter Lewy, *America in Vietnam* (New York, 1978), p. 208.

THE END OF THE TUNNEL

From the time of the First Indochina War, overly optimistic French and U.S. officials had promised a light at the end of the tunnel. When that light finally appeared in 1975 it came with a stunning rapidity and brought an outcome that turned a cliche into a cruel irony. Since the beginning of the postwar war, North Vietnamese and NLF leaders had watched events in South Vietnam and especially in the United States with "an almost obsessive curiosity," and in early 1975 they concluded that the opportune moment was at hand.[15] In December 1974, North Vietnamese main units and PRG regional forces had attacked Phuoc Long, northeast of Saigon, and within three weeks had killed or captured 3,000 ARVN troops, seized huge quantities of supplies, and "liberated" the entire province. The ease of the victory underscored the relative weakening of the ARVN during the past year and made clear, as the North Vietnamese chief of staff, General Van Tien Dung, later put it, that Thieu was now forced to fight a "poor-man's war." Aware from intelligence that Saigon was not expecting a major offensive in 1975, the North Vietnamese in January adopted a two-year plan, a series of large-scale offensives in 1975 to create the conditions for a "general offensive, general uprising" in 1976. Washington's failure to respond to the fall of Phuoc Long confirmed what many North Vietnamese strategists had long suspected, that having pulled out of South Vietnam, the Americans would not "jump back in." After days of sometimes heated debate, the leadership concluded that even if the United States responded with naval and air power, it could not "rescue the Saigon administration from its disastrous collapse."[16]

The collapse came with a suddenness that surprised even the North Vietnamese. Massing vastly superior forces against the stretched-out ARVN defenders, Dung attacked Ban Me Thuot in the Central Highlands on March 10 and took it within two days. To secure control of the highlands before the end of the dry season, he quickly moved north against Pleiku and Kontum. A panicky Thieu foolishly ordered a withdrawal from the highlands, but no plans

[15]Truong Nhu Tang with David Chanoff and Doan Van Toai, *A Vietcong Memoir* (New York, 1985), p. 225.
[16]Van Tien Dung, *Our Great Spring Victory* (New York, 1977), pp. 17, 19–20.

had been drawn up for retreat, and the North Vietnamese had cut the major roads. The withdrawal turned into a rout. Hundreds of thousands of refugees fled with the departing soldiers, clogging the avenues of escape. Much of the army was captured or destroyed, and thousands of civilians died from enemy or ARVN gunfire and from starvation in what journalists called the "Convoy of Tears." Pleiku and Kontum fell within a week. The disastrous abandonment of the highlands cost Thieu six provinces, at least two divisions of soldiers, and the confidence of his army and people. It opened the way for even greater catastrophe in the coastal cities of South Vietnam.

Hanoi now sensed that total victory was within reach and immediately put into effect contingency plans for the conquest of all of South Vietnam. When North Vietnamese forces advanced on Hue and Da Nang, the defending army, along with hundreds of thousands of civilians, fled for Saigon, duplicating on an even larger and more tragic scale the debacle in the highlands. Soldiers looted, and money-hungry citizens charged refugees up to $2 for a glass of water. Ten days after the attack had begun and almost ten years to the day after the U.S. Marines had splashed ashore at Da Nang, the two coastal cities were in North Vietnamese hands. South Vietnam had been cut in two, half its army lost without putting up any resistance. Nha Trang and Cam Ranh Bay were abandoned before they were even threatened by enemy troops. Dung now threw all his forces into the "Ho Chi Minh Campaign" to liberate Saigon.

The United States was stunned by the collapse of South Vietnam but resigned to the outcome. American intelligence had correctly predicted that the major North Vietnamese thrust was not planned until 1976, but the capacity of the South Vietnamese to resist was again overestimated, and Washington was shocked by the sudden fall of the highlands. America's disinclination for further involvement was obvious; on the day Ban Me Thuot fell, Congress rejected President Gerald Ford's request for an additional $300 million in military aid for South Vietnam.

The legislators' vote seems to have reflected the wishes of the American people. A few diehards issued one last appeal to honor the nation's commitments and defend the cause of freedom, and some Americans raised the specter of a bloodbath in which hundreds of thousands of South Vietnamese would be slaughtered by the Communist conquerors. For the most part, however, such appeals fell on deaf ears. Weary of the seemingly endless involvement in Vietnam and pinched by an economic recession at home, Americans were not in a generous mood. Why throw good money after bad, they asked. At a time when they themselves were in "desperate financial straits," they saw no reason to sacrifice for a government that was "not only corrupt but grossly wasteful and inefficient." It was about time that the South Vietnamese were made to stand on their own feet, one "fed-up taxpayer" exclaimed. "My God, we're all tired of it, we're sick to death of it," an Oregonian wrote. "55,000 dead and $100 billion spent and for what?"[17]

The fall of Da Nang and Hue and the imminent threat to Saigon did nothing to change Americans' views. Ford gave no thought to employing U.S. air and naval power. To stiffen South Vietnamese morale and to shift to the legislative branch blame for a debacle that seemed likely if not inevitable, he asked Congress for $722 million in emergency military assistance, setting off a final, bitterly emotional debate on the war. Persisting in the self-delusion that had marked U.S. involvement from the outset, administration spokespeople held out the chimera that additional aid might yet bring about a stalemate and a negotiated settlement within the framework of the Paris accords. Now insisting for the sake of expediency that the domino theory was not valid, Secretary of State Kissinger reiterated the shopworn warning that if America let South Vietnam down, the "impact on the United States in the world would be very serious indeed." The nation must not have on its conscience "pulling the plug" on the South Vietnamese. It must give them some chance to succeed rather than "doom them to lingering deaths."[18]

Such arguments evoked little support. Legislators responded heatedly that the South Vietnamese had abandoned more equipment in the northern provinces than could be purchased with the additional funds, and they argued that no amount of money could save an army that refused to fight. It was time for the United States

---

[17]Mrs. J. S. Mozzanini to James J. Kilpatrick, February 6, 1975, and numerous other letters in James J. Kilpatrick Papers, University of Virginia Library, Charlottesville, Va., Box 5.

[18]Notes on cabinet meeting, April 16, 1975, Ron Nessen Papers, Gerald Ford Library, Ann Arbor, Mich., Box 294; memorandum of conversation, Kissinger, Ford, and congressional leaders, March 5, 1975, Kissinger/Scowcroft File, Box A1, Ford Library.

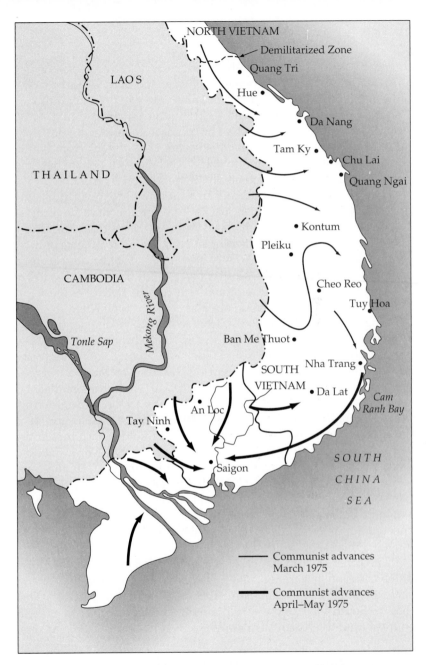

The Ho Chi Minh Campaign: North Vietnam's Final Offensive, 1975
Stanley Karnow, *Vietnam—A History*, p. 662.

to end its involvement in "this horrid war."[19] The specter of the Gulf of Tonkin and Watergate hung over the debate, and revelations of Nixon's secret promises to Thieu provoked cries of outrage. Congress eventually approved $300 million for the evacuation of Americans and for humanitarian purposes and endorsed Ford's request to use American troops to evacuate U.S. citizens from South Vietnam. But it would go no further. "The Vietnam debate has run its course," Kissinger commented with finality on April 17.[20]

The certainty that the United States would not intervene doomed what glimmer of hope South Vietnam may have had. North Vietnamese forces advanced from Da Nang to the outskirts of the capital in less than a month, meeting strong resistance only at Xuan Loc, where a small ARVN contingent fought desperately against superior numbers and firepower. With the fall of that town on April 21 and the congressional rejection of Ford's request for aid, the intransigent Thieu finally and reluctantly resigned, bitterly blaming the debacle on his ally. "It is so easy to be an enemy of the United States," he moaned, "but so difficult to be a friend." He was replaced by the aged and infirm Tran Van Huong, who vainly attempted to negotiate a settlement on the basis of the 1973 agreements, and then by the pathetic Duong Van Minh, the architect of the 1963 coup, to whom was left the odious task of surrendering unconditionally. On April 30, 1975, enemy tanks crashed through the gates of the presidential palace, and NLF soldiers triumphantly ran up their flag over a quickly renamed Ho Chi Minh City. A week earlier, Gerald Ford had formally pronounced at Tulane University in New Orleans what had already become obvious: the Vietnam War was "finished as far as the United States was concerned." When he uttered the word "finished," the crowd of mostly students cheered robustly, many jumped to their feet, and there was prolonged applause.[21]

The American evacuation of Saigon revealed in microcosm much of the delusion, frustration, and tragedy that had marked the American experience in Vietnam. Some U.S. officials persisted in the belief that the South Vietnamese would mount an effective defense of their country until the North Vietnamese were at the gates of Saigon, and

[19]*Congressional Record*, 94th Cong., 1st Sess., 10101–10108.
[20]*New York Times*, April 18, 1975.
[21]New Orleans *Times-Picayune*, April 23, 2000.

they clung stubbornly to hopes of a negotiated settlement long after any such hope had vanished. Ambassador Graham Martin had pronounced upon his appointment in 1973 that he was "not going to Vietnam to give it away to the Communists," and he stubbornly supported Thieu long after it was evident that the president had no backing within his own country. Martin thwarted several coup attempts and encouraged Thieu's refusal to resign, resignation being perhaps the only chance of avoiding unconditional surrender.

Fearful of spreading panic in Saigon and hoping to arrange the American exit in a way that "would not add a further disgrace to the sad history of our involvement," Martin delayed implementation of evacuation plans until the last minute.[22] Through Operation Frequent Wind, the United States managed to get its own people out. Many Washington officials were intent only on extricating Americans, but Ford insisted that the United States had a moral obligation to do what it could to get out as many as possible of those South Vietnamese who had worked closely with their ally. As many as 130,000 were rescued, but the operation was chaotic and fraught with great human agony, a "vision out of a nightmare," one participant later recalled. Corruption ran rampant, escape frequently going to the highest bidder, and the U.S. embassy paid exorbitant fees to get exit visas for some of those seeking to flee. Because of the delays in implementing the evacuation plan and the unavailability of adequate transport, many who wished to leave could not. The spectacle of U.S. Marines using rifle butts to keep desperate Vietnamese from blocking escape routes and of angry ARVN soldiers firing on the departing Americans provided a tragic epitaph for twenty-five years of U.S. involvement in Vietnam. The indelible image of the last helicopter departing the rooftop of the embassy in Saigon starkly symbolized America's failure. Ford recalled April 30, 1975, as "one of the saddest days in my life"; journalist Evan Thomas labeled it a "low moment in the American century."[23]

The United States shared with the South Vietnamese leadership responsibility for the debacle of April 1975. In the two years after the signing of the Paris agreements, the Nixon administration gave Thieu enough support to encourage his defiance but not enough to ensure his survival. Nixon's ill-advised promises tempted Thieu to

[22]Martin to Kissinger, April 18, 1975, Kissinger/Scowcroft File, Box A1, Ford Library.
[23]Evan Thomas, "The Last Days of Saigon," *Newsweek,* May 1, 2000, 37–42.

The End of the Tunnel
Such images of the frantic efforts to evacuate Americans and South
Vietnamese and of the last helicopter departing the rooftop of the U.S.
Embassy in Saigon, April 30, 1975, brought home to Americans the harsh
reality of the outcome of the Vietnam War and served as an enduring
reminder of the nation's failure.
Bettmann/Corbis

reject the admittedly risky choice of negotiations and to launch a
war he could not win. The reduction of American involvement in
the war and the cutbacks of American aid weakened South Vietnam's capacity and will to resist, and the refusal of the United
States to intervene in the final crisis sealed its downfall. On the
other hand, Thieu's intransigence, his gross tactical errors, and his
desperate attempts to save himself while his nation was dying suggest that the outcome would probably have been the same regardless of what the United States had done. Without leadership from
Thieu and the army's high command, the South Vietnamese people
gave way to hysteria, each person seeking merely to save his or her
own skin. The nation simply collapsed.

The fall of South Vietnam just fifty-five days after the onset of
the North Vietnamese offensive was symptomatic of the malaise
that had afflicted that ill-fated nation since its birth. Originally created by the French, the Saigon regime could never overcome its ori-

gins as a puppet government. Political fragmentation, the lack of able and far-sighted leaders, and a tired and corrupt elite that could not adjust to the revolution that swept Vietnam after 1945 afforded a perilously weak basis for nationhood. Given these harsh realities, the American effort to create a bastion of anticommunism south of the seventeenth parallel was probably doomed from the start. The United States could not effect the needed changes in South Vietnamese society without jeopardizing the order it sought, and there was no long-range hope of stability without revolutionary change. The Americans could provide money and weapons, but they could not furnish the ingredients necessary for political stability and military success. Despairing of the capacity of the South Vietnamese to save themselves, the United States had assumed the burden in 1965, only to toss it back in the laps of its clients when the American people tired of the war. The dependency of the early years persisted long after the United States had shifted to Vietnamization, however. To the very end and despite overwhelming evidence to the contrary, Thieu and his cohorts clung desperately to the belief that the United States would return and rescue them.[24]

As comforting as it has been for Americans to find the causes of failure primarily in South Vietnam's weakness and Washington's errors, these alone do not explain the outcome of the war. The North Vietnamese and NLF were not superpeople, as they were often portrayed in antiwar propaganda. They made colossal blunders by repeatedly miscalculating U.S. responses to their actions. They paid an enormous price for their success. Still, in waging this war they had distinct advantages. From the outset of the revolution, the Communists drew into the fold the best of the traditional Vietnamese ruling class and the most able and dedicated political activists, and they were thus blessed with superior leadership, from Ho Chi Minh at the top down to the village level. Skillful organizers, they tapped the wellsprings of Vietnamese nationalism and the urge for social reform to effectively mobilize the people and resources of Vietnam "in a total and concentrated effort to seize power." Sold out by their allies at Geneva in 1954, they exploited the Sino-Soviet split in the Second Indochina War to secure maximum aid and retain maximum freedom of action. Drawing on Chinese models of revolutionary war, they improvised through trial and error a comprehensive, integrated

[24]Hosmer et al., *Fall of South Vietnam*, pp. 118–120.

strategy that blended military, diplomatic, and political methods to achieve the goal of liberating and unifying their country. They skillfully employed the concept of protracted war, perceiving that the Americans, like the French, could become impatient and that if they bled long enough might tire of the war. Above all, as William Duiker has written, they "mobilized the inchoate frustration and anger of the mass of the population and fashioned it into a fierce and relentless weapon of revolutionary war."[25]

CONSEQUENCES AND IMPACT

With the North Vietnamese/NLF victory, the "dominoes" in Indochina quickly toppled. Cambodia, in fact, fell before South Vietnam, ending a peculiarly brutal war and initiating a period of enormous cruelty. Between 1970 and 1972, the United States had spent over $400 million in support of Lon Nol's government and army, and heavy bombing continued until Congress legislated its end in August 1973. In six months of 1973, the bombing exceeded 250,000 tons, more than was dropped on Japan in all of World War II. Lon Nol's government and army were ineffectual even by South Vietnamese standards, however, and with extensive support from North Vietnam and China, the Khmer Rouge pressed on toward Phnom Penh, using human-wave assaults in some areas. The government collapsed in mid-April, and the Khmer Rouge took over the capital on April 17. Thousands of lives were lost in the war, and over two million people were left refugees. The country as a whole faced starvation for the first time in its history. Upon taking over, the Khmer Rouge imposed a gruesome totalitarianism and began the forced relocation of much of the population.

The end in Laos was only slightly less convulsive. The Laotian settlement of 1962 had been a dead letter from the start. A flimsy coalition government nominally upheld a precarious neutrality, while outsiders waged war up and down the land. The North Vietnamese used Laotian territory for their infiltration route into South Vietnam and supported the insurgent Pathet Lao with supplies and as many as 20,000 "volunteers." While backing the neutralist gov-

---

[25]William Duiker, *The Communist Road to Power in Vietnam* (Boulder, Colo., 1981), pp. 320–329.

ernment, the United States from 1962 to 1972 waged a secret war against North Vietnamese positions in Laos. When the bombing of North Vietnam was stopped at the end of 1968, Laos became the primary target. By 1973 the United States had dropped more than two million tons of bombs there, leaving many areas resembling a desert. At the same time, the CIA sponsored an army of Hmong tribespeople, led by General Vang Pao, that waged guerrilla warfare against the Ho Chi Minh Trail in Laos at a huge cost: more than 17,000 soldiers and 50,000 civilians had been killed by 1975. The U.S. withdrawal from South Vietnam left the government without any chance of survival. An agreement of February 1973 created a coalition government in which the Pathet Lao held the upper hand. With the fall of Cambodia and South Vietnam, the Pathet Lao took over, making no effort to hide its subservience to Vietnam. In one of the great human tragedies of the Indochina wars, America's loyal allies, the Hmong, were the victims of Pathet Lao genocide. Roughly 100,000, including the legendary Vang Pao, escaped. Another 100,000 were killed in a systematic campaign of extermination that employed bombing, artillery, and possibly chemical-biological weapons. Thousands more suffered in what the Pathet Lao euphemistically called "seminar camps."[26]

The impact on world politics of America's failure in Vietnam was considerably less than U.S. policy makers had predicted. From Thailand to the Philippines, there was obvious nervousness, even demands for the removal of U.S. bases. Outside Indochina, however, the dominoes did not fall. On the contrary, in the years after the end of the war, the non-Communist nations of Southeast Asia prospered and attained an unprecedented level of stability. The Soviet Union continued to build up its military arsenal in the 1970s, and spurred by a hubris deriving from American failure, it intervened in civil wars in Angola, Zaire, and Ethiopia. As with the United States, however, the Soviets' reach soon exceeded their grasp, luring them into their own quagmire in Afghanistan, a "bleeding wound" that reformist Soviet premier Mikhail Gorbachev bound up in the late 1980s only at great cost.

One of the most significant and ironic effects of the end of the Vietnam War was to heighten tensions among the various Communist

[26]Jane Hamilton-Merritt, *Tragic Mountains: The Hmong, the Americans, and the Secret Wars for Laos, 1942–1962* (Bloomington, Ind., 1993), pp. 337–410.

nations of East Asia. The brutal Pol Pot regime launched a grisly effort to rebuild Cambodia from the "Year Zero," killing millions of its own people in the process. More important from the Vietnamese standpoint, Cambodia established close ties with China. In response to Khmer Rouge cross-border raids and to preserve a "friendly" government next door, Vietnam invaded Cambodia in 1978, drove out Pol Pot, and established a puppet regime. China retaliated by invading Vietnam, provoking a short and inconclusive war. The United States, which had gone to war in Vietnam in 1965 to contain China, found itself in the ironic and morally dubious position in the mid-1980s of indirectly supporting China's efforts to contain Vietnam and sending humanitarian aid to an unlikely assortment of Cambodian bedfellows, including the notorious Pol Pot.

THE WAGES OF VICTORY

In Vietnam itself, the principal legacy of the war was continued human suffering. The ultimate losers, of course, were the South Vietnamese. The bloodbath predicted by some Americans did not occur, but many of those South Vietnamese who remained in Vietnam endured poverty, oppression, and forced labor. As many as 400,000 suffered the horror of "reeducation" camps, some for as long as ten years. More than 1.5 million so-called boat people fled the country after 1975. Some perished in flight; others languished in squalid refugee camps scattered throughout Southeast Asia. Around one million eventually resettled in the United States. Most of them had to give up all their personal possessions merely to escape, and many left family behind. The popular stereotype of the Vietnamese-Americans was one of assimilation and overachievement, the "model minority." In reality, many remained unassimilated and lived near or below the poverty line, depending on minimum-wage jobs or welfare. The new immigrants also endured alienation, encountered prejudice from Americans for whom they were a living reminder of defeat, and suffered from the popular image of the successful Asian, which implied that the unsuccessful had only themselves to blame.

In one of the most cruel ironies of a war that had more than its share of irony, the NLF, or at least some of its members, lost the war as well, despite the fact that many of them had played key roles in the victory. Hanoi moved quickly at the end of the war to reunify the country under the tight control of the Communist party. It disbanded the front organizations—including the NLF—that had been created to fight the Saigon regime and the Americans. The NLF army was merged with the North Vietnamese Army in a way that its separate identity was destroyed. Some of the southerners who had led the struggle and had suffered heavily in the process were considered a threat and dealt with accordingly. Non-Communists in the PRG were quickly purged. Some endured persecution; others, in time, fled. To affirm its legitimacy, the new regime soon openly boasted of what it had repeatedly denied during the war—its instrumental role in creating and running the southern insurgency.

Even for the ostensible winners, victory was a bittersweet prize. Despite the heavy-handed methods employed, unification was at best difficult to achieve. Historic differences between north and south were exacerbated during three decades of war, and it was impossible to force the freewheeling and resilient south into a made-in-Hanoi mold. Just as it resisted American direction in the 1960s, southern Vietnam continued to resist outside influence, complicating the task of consolidation. There were even signs that, in the classic tradition of the East, the ways of the conquered had rubbed off on the conqueror. The corruption and Western consumer culture that epitomized Saigon during the American war carried over to postwar Ho Chi Minh City, where the black market continued to flourish and bribery was necessary to accomplish anything.

The Hanoi regime achieved its goal of hegemony in Indochina, but only temporarily and at a cost it could not afford. In time, it became bogged down in its own quagmire in Cambodia, where for a decade it waged a costly and generally ineffectual counterinsurgency war against stubborn Cambodian guerrillas. The Vietnamese in 1991 happily accepted a United Nations–sponsored agreement that provided for their withdrawal from Cambodia and for the holding of elections to form a coalition government. Vietnam's occupation of Cambodia further strained already bad relations with China, the United States, and other nations of Southeast Asia, leaving it diplomatically isolated and entirely dependent on the Soviet Union.

For all Vietnamese, the most pressing and enduring legacy of the war has been economic deprivation. Thirty years of conflict, especially the destruction visited on north and south during the American war, left the entire nation a shambles. The situation was made much worse by continued high military expenditures and by the regime's ill-conceived and disastrous efforts to impose communism, force industrialization, and collectivize agriculture. In the immediate postwar years, the economic growth rate lagged around 2 percent, and per capita income averaged around $100. "Waging a war is simple," premier Pham Van Dong lamented, "but running a country is difficult."[27]

Responding to necessity and emulating Gorbachev's perestroika (reconstruction), a more pragmatic and reformist regime dominated by southerners launched in the mid-1980s a program of *doi moi,* or renovation. The new regime hoped to stimulate growth by freeing up the economy, by providing some capitalist incentives, and by seeking foreign investment. Hanoi even attempted to promote economic development through tourism. Vietnamese leaders still claimed to be pursuing socialism, but they talked more and more like capitalists, proclaiming the goal of a prosperous country in which people could be rich.

Doi moi brought modest gains. Agriculture flourished under the new system, and by the end of the century Vietnam was the world's second largest exporter of rice. The parallel, or unofficial, economy also prospered for a time, especially in the cities, where there were signs of an incipient boom. Foreign investment jumped, making up for the termination of external assistance after the collapse of the Soviet Union in 1991, and the growth rate increased to around 7 percent. There were significant increases in the production of consumer goods and foreign trade.

Huge problems persisted. Despite the "tiny economic miracle" of the mid-1990s, Vietnam remained one of the world's poorest countries. The infrastructure was in horrible shape, and the economy suffered from ineffective management and a lack of capital and technology. Per capita income rose only to $376 by the end of the century, and there was high unemployment. The growth rate lagged, and foreign investment declined. Although Vietnam was rich in natural resources and blessed with a high literacy rate and a people with a strong work ethic, its economic potential was nevertheless limited by rising overpopulation, a shortage of skilled labor, inadequate public services, an omnipresent and creaking govern-

[27]Quoted in Stanley Karnow, *Vietnam: A History* (New York, 1983), p. 9.

ment bureaucracy, and corruption reportedly as pervasive as that in South Vietnam at the end of the war.[28]

The problems at century's end raised serious doubts about the future of what was called "market Leninism." Whether real economic growth could be achieved in an oppressive political climate remained much in doubt. Intent on insulating itself from the changes that had destroyed communism in the Soviet Union and Eastern Europe, the regime staunchly refused to couple economic reform with political freedom and continued to infringe on basic rights. Traditional fears of interaction with foreigners reinforced instinctive suspicions of globalization. An aging party leadership continued to stake its legitimacy on its "revolutionary heroism" in defeating the French and Americans. But its appeals increasingly fell on the deaf ears of a population 85 percent of which was under forty years of age and many of whom saw the old enemy, the United States, as the model of modernity. In addition, many Vietnamese, including veterans, were increasingly disillusioned that the sacrifices made during the war had not brought rewards in terms of a better life.[29] For the nation as a whole, the great promises of victory in 1975 had not been realized.

THE AGONY OF DEFEAT

For America's allies, the war had consequences that exceeded the size of their contribution. In Australia, participation in Vietnam led to sharp internal divisions and conflict, and failure to recognize the contribution of those who served left a legacy of bitterness among veterans. In New Zealand, despite the small size of the commitment, the war aroused widespread opposition and eventually provoked a major foreign policy debate that raised searching questions about the nation's role in the world and especially its relations with the United States. For South Korea, participation in Vietnam produced enormous economic benefits, helping to stimulate its rise as

---

[28]Andrew Pierre, "Vietnam's Contradictions," *Foreign Affairs,* November/December 2000, 69–86.

[29]Robert K. Brigham, "Revolutionary Heroism and Politics in Postwar Vietnam," in Charles E. Neu (ed.), *After Vietnam: Legacies of a Lost War* (Baltimore, Md., 2000), pp. 85–104.

a major economic power. Since the end of the war, the government has remained silent about its role. Only with the emergence of democracy in recent years has Vietnam become a subject for open discussion. Long alienated veterans who have borne their anger in silence now speak openly of the "blood money" earned at the price of those lives who "fuelled the modernization of the country."[30]

Although the United States emerged physically unscathed, the Vietnam War was among the most debilitating in its history. The price tag has been estimated at $167 billion, a raw statistic that does not begin to measure the full economic cost. The war triggered an inflation that helped undermine, at least temporarily, America's position in the world economy. The war, along with Watergate, also had a high political cost, increasing popular suspicion of government, leaders, and institutions. It discredited and crippled the military, at least for a time, and temporarily estranged the United States from much of the rest of the world.[31]

Much like the effect of World War I on the Europeans, Vietnam's greatest impact was in the realm of the spirit. Like no other event in the nation's history, it challenged Americans' traditional beliefs about themselves, the notion that in their relations with other people they have generally acted with benevolence, the idea that nothing is beyond reach. It was a fundamental part of a much larger crisis of the spirit that began in the 1960s and that raised searching questions about America's history and values and marked a sort of end of American innocence.

The fall of Saigon had a profound impact. Some Americans expressed hope that the nation could finally put aside a painful episode from its past and get on with the business of the future. Among a people accustomed to celebrating peace with ticker tape parades, however, the end of the war left a deep residue of frustration, anger, and disillusionment. Americans generally agreed that the war had been a "dark moment" in their nation's history. Some comforted themselves with the notion that the United States should

---

[30]Jeffrey Grey and Jeff Doyle, *Vietnam: War, Myth, and Memory* (St. Leonards, Austral., 1992), especially pp. 137–150; Roberto Rabel, "The Vietnam Decision Twenty-Five Years On," *New Zealand International Review* 15 (May/June 1990): 3–11; *New York Times,* May 10, 1992.

[31]Two recent efforts to assess the legacy of the war are Arnold R. Isaacs, *Vietnam Shadows: The War, Its Ghosts, and Its Legacy* (Baltimore, Md., 1997), and Neu, *After Vietnam.*

never have become involved in Vietnam in the first place, but for others, particularly those who had lost loved ones, this was not enough. "Now it's all gone down the drain and it hurts. What did he die for?" asked a Pennsylvanian whose son had been killed in Vietnam. Many Americans expressed anger that the civilians did not permit the military to win the war. Others regarded the failure to win and to support an ally as a betrayal of American ideals and a sign of national weakness that boded poorly for the future. "It was the saddest day of my life when it sank in that we had lost the war," a Virginian lamented.[32] The fall of Vietnam came at the very time the nation was preparing to celebrate the bicentennial of its birth, and the irony was painfully obvious. "The high hopes and wishful idealism with which the American nation had been born had not been destroyed," *Newsweek* observed, "but they had been chastened by the failure of America to work its will in Indochina."[33]

In the immediate aftermath of the war, the nation experienced a self-conscious, collective amnesia. The angry debate over who lost Vietnam, so feared by Kennedy, Johnson, and Nixon, consisted of nothing more than a few sharp exchanges between the White House and Capitol Hill over responsibility for the April 1975 debacle. Perhaps because both parties were so deeply implicated in the war, Vietnam did not become a partisan political issue; because the memories were so painful, no one cared to dredge them up. On the contrary, many public figures called for restraint. Vietnam was all but ignored by the media. It was scarcely mentioned in the presidential campaign of 1976. "Today it is almost as though the war had never happened," the columnist Joseph C. Harsch noted in late 1975. "Americans have somehow blocked it out of their consciousness. They don't talk about it. They don't talk about its consequences."[34]

Those 2.7 million men and women who served in Vietnam were the primary victims of the nation's desire to forget. Younger on the average by seven years than their World War II counterparts, having endured a war far more complex and confusing, Vietnam veterans by the miracles of the jet age were whisked home virtually overnight to a nation hostile to the war and indifferent to

[32]Jules Low, "The Mood of a Nation," Associated Press Newsfeature, May 5, 1975.
[33]"An Irony of History," *Newsweek*, April 28, 1975, 17.
[34]Joseph C. Harsch, "Do You Recall Vietnam—And What about the Dominoes?" *Louisville Courier-Journal*, October 2, 1975.

their plight. Some were made to feel the guilt for the nation's moral transgressions; others, responsibility for its failure. Most simply met silence. Forced to turn inward, many veterans grew profoundly distrustful of the government that had sent them to war and deeply resentful of the nation's seeming ingratitude for their sacrifices. The great majority adjusted, although sometimes with difficulty, but many veterans experienced problems with drugs and alcohol, joblessness, and broken homes. Many also suffered from post-traumatic stress disorder, the modern term for what had earlier been called shell shock or battle fatigue. The popular stereotype of the Vietnam veteran in the immediate postwar years was that of a drug-crazed, gun-toting, and violence-prone individual unable to adjust to civilized society. When America in 1981 gave a lavish welcome home to a group of hostages returned from a long and much-publicized captivity in Iran, Vietnam veterans poured out their bottled-up rage. They themselves constructed a memorial in Washington to honor the memory of the more than 58,000 comrades who did not return.[35]

Within a short time after the end of the war, Vietnam's place in the national consciousness changed dramatically. The amnesia of the immediate postwar years proved no more than a passing phenomenon, and by the mid-1980s the war was being discussed to a degree and in ways that would have once seemed impossible. Vietnam produced a large and in some cases distinguished literature, much of it the work of veterans. Hollywood had all but ignored the war while it was going on, but in its aftermath filmmakers took up the subject with a vengeance, producing works ranging from the haunting *Deer Hunter*, to the surreal and spectacular *Apocalypse Now*, to Oliver Stone's antiwar epics, to a series of trashy films in the 1980s in which American superheroes returned to Vietnam to take care of unfinished business. No television leading man was worth his salt unless he had served in Vietnam. The Vietnam veteran, sometimes branded a "baby killer" in the 1960s, became a popular culture hero in the 1980s, the sturdy and self-sufficient warrior who had prevailed despite being let down by his government and nation. Millions of Americans each year went to the stark

---

[35]For two very different perspectives, see Christian G. Appy, *Working-Class War* (Chapel Hill, N.C., 1993) and B.G. Burkett and Glenna Whitley, *Stolen Valor* (Dallas, Tex., 1998).

but moving V-shaped memorial on Washington's Mall, making it the most visited site in the nation's capital. Denounced by critics as a "black wall of shame" when it was under construction, the memorial evoked a profound emotional experience for many visitors and became a means of healing, a place for recognition of the costs of war. In 1993, a memorial was added to honor the 265,000 women who served in the military during the Vietnam War. In courthouses and communities across the nation, memorials were constructed to honor those who had served.

THE SEARCH FOR LESSONS

Nowhere was the impact of Vietnam greater than on the nation's foreign policy. The war shattered the Cold War consensus that had existed since the late 1940s, leaving Americans confused and deeply divided on the goals to be pursued and the methods used. Even before it had ended, the traumatic experience of Vietnam, combined with the apparent improvement of relations with the Soviet Union and China and a growing preoccupation with domestic problems, produced a drastic reordering of national priorities. From the late 1940s to the 1960s, foreign policy had consistently headed the ranking of national concerns, but by the mid-1970s it placed well down on the list. The public was "almost oblivious to foreign problems and foreign issues," opinion analyst Burns Roper remarked in late 1975.[36]

The Vietnam experience also provoked strong opposition to military intervention abroad, even in defense of America's oldest and staunchest allies. Polls taken shortly before the fall of Saigon indicated that only 36 percent of the American people felt the United States should make and keep commitments to other nations, and only 34 percent expressed a willingness to send troops should the Russians attempt to take over West Berlin. A majority of Americans endorsed military intervention only in defense of Canada! "Vietnam has left a rancid aftertaste that clings to almost every mention of direct military intervention," the columnist David Broder observed.[37]

[36]Quoted in Charles W. Yost, "Why Americans Seem Disillusioned by Foreign Affairs," *Louisville Courier-Journal*, October 26, 1975.
[37]David Broder, "Isolationist Sentiment Not Blind to Reality," *Washington Post*, March 22, 1975.

The indifference and tendency toward withdrawal so manifest immediately after the war also declined sharply in the next decade. Bitter memories of Vietnam combined with the anger and frustration of the 1979 Iranian hostage crisis to produce a growing assertiveness, a highly nationalistic impulse to defend perceived interests, even a yearning to restore the United States to its old position in the world. The breakdown of détente, the steady growth of Soviet military power, and the use of that power in the Horn of Africa and Afghanistan in the late 1970s produced a profound nervousness about American security. The defense budget soared to mammoth proportions in the early 1980s, and support for military intervention in defense of traditional allies increased.[38] Under the leadership of President Ronald Reagan, the nation embarked on a new global offensive against the Soviet Union and its clients.

The new nationalism was still tempered by lingering memories of Vietnam. Many Americans remained deeply skeptical of 1960s-style globalism and dubious of such internationalist mechanisms as foreign aid or even the United Nations. Fifteen years after the end of the war, a whopping majority still believed that intervention in Vietnam had been a mistake, producing strong opposition to military intervention abroad. Thus in the aftermath of Vietnam, the public mood consisted of a strange amalgam of nostalgia and realism, assertiveness and caution.

In the very different climate of the 1980s, the debate over Vietnam that had not taken place at the war's end assumed a central place in the larger and at times quite vocal debate over U.S. foreign policy. The basic issue remained the morality and wisdom of intervention in Vietnam. Concerned that in a new and even more dangerous Cold War a resurgent militance might lead to further disastrous embroilment, liberals urgently warned of the perils of another Vietnam. Fearful, on the other hand, that the so-called Vietnam syndrome had sapped America's will to defend legitimate interests and stand firmly against the evil of communism, some conservatives, including most notably President Reagan, spoke out anew on what they had always believed was a fundamental reality: that, as Reagan repeatedly proclaimed, Vietnam was "in truth a noble war," a selfless attempt on the part of the United States to save a

[38]Adam Clymer, "What Americans Think Now," *New York Times Magazine,* March 31, 1985, 34.

free nation from outside aggression. Other conservatives conceded that the United States might have erred in getting involved in Vietnam in the first place, but they went on to insist that an important interest had been established that should have been upheld for the sake of U.S. credibility throughout the world.

The second great issue on which Americans also sharply disagreed concerned the reasons for U.S. failure in Vietnam. Unwilling to concede that success had been beyond reach, many of the leading participants in the war concluded that America's failure had been essentially instrumental, a result of the improper use of available tools. General Westmoreland, Admiral U.S. Grant Sharp, and others blamed the "ill-considered" policy of "graduated response" imposed on the military by civilian leaders. They argued that had the United States employed its military power quickly, decisively, and without limit, the war could have been won. Some conservatives indeed concluded that timid civilian leaders had prevented the military from winning the war, a view that worked its way into the popular culture. "Sir, do we get to win *this* time?" the larger than life movie hero Rambo asked upon accepting the assignment to return to Vietnam and fight the second round single-handedly.[39]

Other Americans viewed the fundamental mistake as the choice of tools rather than the way they were used, and they blamed an unimaginative military as much as civilians. Instead of trying to fight World War II and Korea over in Vietnam, they argued, the military should have adapted to the unconventional war in which it found itself and shaped an appropriate counterinsurgency strategy. Still other commentators, including some military theorists, agreed that military leaders were as responsible for the strategic failure as civilians were, and they argued that instead of mounting costly and counterproductive search-and-destroy operations against guerrillas in South Vietnam, the United States should have used its own forces against North Vietnamese regulars along the seventeenth parallel to isolate the battlefield in South Vietnam from the northern threat.[40]

[39]William C. Westmoreland, *A Soldier Reports* (Garden City, N.Y., 1976), p. 410; U. S. Grant Sharp, *Strategy for Defeat* (San Rafael, Calif., 1978).

[40]Comments by Robert Komer in W. Scott Thompson and Donaldson Frizzell, *The Lessons of Vietnam* (New York, 1977), p. 223; Harry G. Summers, Jr., *On Strategy: The Vietnam War in Context* (Carlisle Barracks, Pa., 1981).

The lessons drawn were as divergent as the arguments advanced. Those military leaders who believed that the United States failed because it did not act decisively formulated in the 1980s a set of rules for intervention (or, in most cases, nonintervention) that came to be known as the Powell Doctrine, named for General Colin Powell, a veteran of two Vietnam tours who served as national security adviser under Reagan and subsquently as chairman of the Joint Chiefs of Staff under Presidents George Bush and Bill Clinton. Under this doctrine, troops would be committed abroad only as a last resort and only if it was plainly in the national interest to do so. Objectives must be clearly defined and attainable. Public support must be assured, and overwhelming force must be employed to achieve certain, swift, and complete victory.[41] Those observers who believed, on the other hand, that the basic problem had been the formulation rather than the execution of strategy insisted that military and civilian leaders must examine more carefully the nature of the war they were fighting and formulate more precisely the ways in which American power could best be used to attain the nation's objectives.

Such "lessons" depended on the belief systems of those who pronounced them, of course, and those who had opposed the war in Vietnam drew quite different conclusions. To some former doves, the fundamental lesson was never again to intervene in Vietnam-like situations in the Third World. Some commentators warned policy makers to beware the sort of simplistic reasoning that had produced such dogmas as the domino theory and the Munich analogy. Others pointed to the chronic weakness of South Vietnam and admonished that even a superpower could not save allies who were unable or unwilling to save themselves. For still others, the key lessons were that American power, however great, had distinct limits and that to be effective, U.S. foreign policy had to be true to the ideals on which the nation was founded.

Throughout the 1980s, the ghost of Vietnam hovered over an increasingly divisive debate on the proper U.S. response to revolutions in Central America. Shortly after taking office in 1981, Reagan committed U.S. prestige to defending the government of El Salvador against a leftist-led insurgency, in part in the expectation that

[41]George C. Herring, "Preparing *Not* to Refight the Last War: The Impact of the Vietnam War on the U.S. Military," in Neu, *After Vietnam*, pp. 72–75.

success there might exorcise the Vietnam syndrome. When the quick victory did not materialize, the administration expanded U.S. military aid to El Salvador, created a huge military base in Honduras, and launched a not-so-covert war to overthrow the leftist Sandinista government of Nicaragua. The administration insisted that the United States must support non-Communist forces to avert in Central America the bloodshed and misery that followed the end of the war in Vietnam. At the same time, the military and the Defense Department made clear that they would not go to war under the conditions that had prevailed in Vietnam. On the other side, dovish critics ominously and repeatedly warned that U.S. intervention in Central America would lead straight into a quagmire like Vietnam.[42]

The issues were squarely joined in the Persian Gulf War of 1991, which seemed at times as much about Vietnam as about Saddam Hussein's conquest of Kuwait. Americans who opposed going to war to liberate Kuwait warned that "Iraq was Arabic for Vietnam" and predicted a Vietnam-like quagmire in the desert. President George Bush vowed from the outset, however, that this war would not be "another Vietnam," and he and his military advisers, many of whom had fought in Vietnam, conducted the Gulf War largely on the basis of the Powell Doctrine. The president made clear that American troops would not be forced to fight with "one hand tied behind their back," as had allegedly been the case in Vietnam, and the military employed maximum force to ensure a speedy victory. Media coverage was rigidly censored to prevent, as many claimed had happened in Vietnam, its stimulating antiwar sentiment. When the United States and its allies swiftly and decisively defeated Iraq, Bush exulted in a euphoric victory statement: "By God, we've kicked the Vietnam syndrome once and for all!"[43]

The president's eulogy turned out to be premature. To be sure, success in the Gulf War helped restore the nation's confidence in its military institutions and weakened inhibitions against military intervention abroad. It did not, however, expunge deeply encrusted

[42]George C. Herring, "Vietnam, El Salvador, and the Uses of History," in Kenneth M. Coleman and George C. Herring (eds.), *The Central American Crisis* (Wilmington, Del., 1985), pp. 97–110.
[43]George C. Herring, "Refighting the Last War: The Persian Gulf and the 'Vietnam Syndrome,' " *New Zealand International Review* 16 (September/October 1991): 15–19.

and still painful memories of an earlier and very different war. The president's own actions made this difference quite clear. In refusing to drive on to Baghdad and seek total victory over Iraq, Bush himself heeded fears of the Vietnam-like political entanglements and military quagmire that might result from involvement in an alien and hostile area.

In the aftermath of the Gulf War, the ghosts of Vietnam still lingered. Emotional debates in 1993 and 1994 over possible military intervention in the brutal ethnic conflict in the former Yugoslavia called forth old and still bitter memories. A journalist surveying opinion in the American heartland in May 1993 found "an abiding fear that the Balkans are another Vietnam, a deep-seated angst that tends to outweigh concern that another holocaust is in the making."[44] In part because of perceived lessons of Vietnam, President Bill Clinton kept a discreet distance from the Bosnian conflict.

Americans expressed little opposition when Bush sent U.S. troops on a mission of mercy to war-torn Somalia in late 1992, but when those troops in the fall of 1993 became caught in the cross fire of Somalian politics and eighteen Americans were killed, the specter of Vietnam again rose like a storm cloud over the nation. The fear that Somalia might become another Vietnam forced a rapid American pullout from that troubled nation, making it abundantly clear that the ghosts George Bush claimed to have buried still haunted the nation.

That conclusion was affirmed once again in Clinton's 1999 war in Kosovo, in the Balkans. Many historical analogies competed for attention in that conflict. Memories of the appeasement of Hitler at Munich and the horrors of the Holocaust provided compelling arguments to do something to stop Serbian ethnic cleansing in Kosovo. But if the World War II analogies pushed Clinton and his advisers toward war, it was the more recent and personally far more searing experience of Vietnam that dictated how they would fight. The president and many of his top aides had protested that war. They were haunted by its memories, especially by the fear of getting bogged down in intractable political situations in strange and distant lands. Thus to reassure a presumably nervous public

[44]B. Drummond Ayres, Jr., "In American Voices, a Sense of Concern over Bosnia Role," *New York Times,* May 2, 1993.

Lessons of a Lost War
This March 1999 cartoon by Pulitzer Prize winner Joel Pett of the *Lexington (Ky.) Herald-Leader* highlights the way in which lessons from the Vietnam War and other historical analogies were used in the making and waging of the war in Kosovo and suggests the elusive and often conflicting nature of such lessons.
© 1999 Joel Pett, Lexington Herald-Leader. Reprinted by permission.

and minimize the political risks to his already embattled administration, Clinton once at war relied exclusively on air power. He even affirmed publicly that ground forces would not be used.

Critics of the war from the political right and left responded with dire warnings, based on different readings of the Vietnam analogy. Some warned of a step-by-step descent into a quagmire, a frequently used codeword for Vietnam. Others claimed that Vietnam had made clear that bombing by itself could not erode the will of a determined foe. Still others, such as former Vietnam prisoner of war and Arizona Republican senator John McCain, invoked the Powell Doctrine, insisting that "You don't get into a conflict unless you are willing to exercise all means necessary to winning it."

The analogy-filled debate on the war in Kosovo produced some fascinating role reversals and some very strange bedfellows, suggesting that, as a new century approached, old positions were shifting. Such changes can be explained partly by partisanship, but something deeper was also at work. Some liberal doves who had opposed the Vietnam War on moral grounds now argued that American power should be used to combat evil and promote good in the world and supported military intervention in the Balkans. With the end of the Cold War, on the other hand, conservative hawks who had supported the global crusade against communism had little enthusiasm for intervention in places where the United States did not appear to have vital interests.[45]

The ongoing debate over U.S. involvement in Vietnam raises as many questions as it answers. Many of the so-called lessons are based on historical givens that can never be proved. Whether the more decisive use of military power could have ended the war satisfactorily without causing even more disastrous consequences remains at best unprovable. Whether the adoption of a more vigorous and imaginative counterinsurgency program at an earlier stage could have wrested control of the countryside from the NLF can never be known, and the ability of the United States to implement such a program in an alien political culture is at best highly questionable. That the United States exaggerated the importance of Vietnam, as liberals have suggested, seems clear. But their argument begs the question of how one determines the significance of a given area and the even more difficult question of how one assesses at an early stage the ultimate costs of intervention.

Each historical situation is unique, moreover, and to extract lessons from one and apply them indiscriminately to another and very different event is at best misleading. The Central American crisis of the 1980s resolved itself in a way that confounded the dire predictions, drawn from Vietnam, offered by each side in the U.S. political debate. America's military success in the Persian Gulf War and in Kosovo reflected more the unique conditions of those conflicts than the successful application of lessons drawn from Vietnam. The one valid lesson that might be drawn, therefore, is to view all historical lessons with a healthy dose of skepticism.

---

[45]George C. Herring, "Analogies at War," in Albrecht Schnabel and Ramesh Thakur, eds., *Kosovo and the Challenge of Humanitarian Intervention* (Tokyo, 2000), pp. 347–359.

In light of their perceived victory in the Cold War, Americans may increasingly be tempted to view the Vietnam War as an anomaly. The collapse of the once-feared Soviet Union and its empire and the demise of communism left the government of Vietnam an apparent anachronism, one of a handful of regimes clinging to a discredited doctrine. In this context, Americans may come to regard the Vietnam War as little more than a tactical setback in what turned out to be a strategic victory, a lost battle in a war eventually won.

In the new post–Cold War world order, Vietnam may even come to seem irrelevant. The crises of the new era bear little resemblance to those of the Cold War. The conflicts that provoke debates over possible intervention are primarily ethnic and tribal. For the United States, no vital interests appear to be at stake, and there is little or no profit to be gained from involvement. The main arguments advanced for intervention are to stop the human suffering, feed the hungry, or bring order out of chaos.

Much can be learned from the American experience in Vietnam: the difficulties of intervening in a foreign civil war; the pitfalls of incrementalism; the perils of underestimating an enemy; the importance of knowing what kind of war one is fighting; the dubious morality, however noble a nation's intentions, of making a commitment it may not be prepared to see through; the limits of public tolerance for questionable uses of military power abroad; a long list of dos and don'ts in the raising and handling of an army.

Although it does not permit precise lessons and may seem increasingly irrelevant in today's world, Vietnam nonetheless yields enduring cautionary principles that should be kept in mind as the United States proceeds into a new and uncertain era. First is the centrality of local forces in international crisis situations. Whether the United States won the Cold War is arguable, and the role of the containment policy in that outcome will long be debated. That containment was misapplied in Vietnam, however, seems beyond debate. The United States intervened to block the apparent march of a Soviet-directed communism across Asia, enlarged its commitment to halt a presumably expansionist Communist China, and eventually made Vietnam a test of its determination to uphold world order. By wrongly attributing the conflict to external sources, the United States drastically misjudged its internal dynamics. By intervening in what was essentially a local struggle, it placed itself at the mercy of local forces, a weak client, and a determined adversary.

What might have remained a local conflict with primarily local implications was elevated into a major international conflict with enormous human costs that are still being paid. Local conditions may be even more important today when the main challenge for U.S. foreign policy is not to influence relations between states but to affect events within them. These forces will vary drastically from one situation to the next, but the point is clear: we ignore them at our own peril.

Second is the limits of power. As Somalia suggests, even so-called humanitarian interventions can lead to intractable political challenges. Stopping wars requires settling the political questions over which they are fought. Ending chaos or anarchy involves guaranteeing borders or establishing government machinery where none exists. In Vietnam, such tasks ultimately proved beyond the ability of the United States. This will not necessarily be the case elsewhere, but Americans must recognize that such interventions, at the very least, will be complicated and costly. They will involve us in the "poisonous tangle of local politics."[46] They will not lend themselves to the quick fixes we seem to prefer. Vietnam offers no easy instruction to deal with such situations. It should stand, however, as an enduring testament to the pitfalls of interventionism and the limits of power.

America's failure in Vietnam and the tragedy that resulted also make clear what can happen when major decisions are made without debate or discussion. One unfortunate Cold War dictum was that foreign policy decisions were too important to be left to Congress and the public. For such reasons as well as his own personal agenda, Lyndon Johnson took the nation to war in Vietnam by stealth, deceiving the public as to his intentions and what he was actually doing. A compliant Congress quietly acquiesced, and even those legislators who understood and were profoundly skeptical of Johnson's policies unwisely stood with him out of fear or out of partisan and personal loyalty. For Richard Nixon and Henry Kissinger, dissent was tantamount to treason and secrecy was a modus operandi. They refused even to take much of their own government into their confidence. Democracy is admittedly messy, and debate can delay decisions or produce results based on compromise. On the other hand, as

---

[46]Michael Mandelbaum, "The Reluctance to Intervene," *Foreign Policy* 95 (Summer 1994): 3–18.

Robert Mann has concluded, America's war in Vietnam makes clear the "kind of tragedy that can result when presidents . . . enforce their foreign and military policies without the informed support of Congress and the American people."[47]

THE UNENDING WAR

Conflict with Vietnam did not end with the fall of Saigon in 1975. In marked contrast to the magnanimity it showed toward Germany and Japan after World War II, the United States was neither gracious nor generous in defeat. For nearly two decades, it continued to treat Vietnam as an enemy, and sporadic efforts to "normalize" relations got nowhere.

The United States took a hard line from the outset. Except for a handful of dove members of Congress committed to reconciliation and a few businesses interested in drilling for offshore oil, no constituency pressed for normalization, and no organized groups expressed interest in it. On the other hand, a deep-seated residual American bitterness toward Vietnam, the legacy of frustration and defeat, stood as a major obstacle to reconciliation. With government support, a powerful lobby had emerged to demand from the Vietnamese a full accounting of Americans missing in action. Amply financed, skilled at propaganda, and vocal in its opposition to normalization, it played on the emotions of a people unaccustomed to failure and demanded that the Vietnamese be held to strict accountability. The approach of a presidential election in a mood of barely suppressed anger made Vietnam an especially delicate issue in the first months after the war.

The original strategist of normalization, Secretary of State Henry Kissinger, set the tone for postwar U.S. policy toward Vietnam. Weary from six years of frustrating negotiations and embarrassed by the failure of his policies, Kissinger was in no mood to compromise. Privately condemning the Vietnamese as "the most bloody-minded bastards" he had ever dealt with, he insisted that the United States must not appear too eager for normalization and must not make unilateral concessions. Ever the geopolitician,

---

[47]Robert Mann, *A Grand Delusion: America's Descent into Vietnam* (New York, 2001), p. 731.

Kissinger confidently predicted that Vietnam's deteriorating relations with China and its fear of dependence on the Soviet Union would work to the advantage of the United States. If Washington "played it cool," the "logic of events" would force Hanoi to accept its terms.[48]

From the outset, the Ford administration thus took a tough position. The United States extended to all of Vietnam and Cambodia the wartime embargo against North Vietnam. Insisting that Hanoi had "massively violated" the Paris agreements, the Ford administration claimed to be under no obligation to furnish the reconstruction aid Nixon had promised "without condition" and even denied that promises had been made. In 1975 and 1976, the administration vetoed Hanoi's application for membership in the United Nations. It made normalization contingent on Vietnam's restraint toward its neighbors and demanded a full accounting of U.S. soldiers missing in action (MIAs). Under stern pressure from right-wing challenger Ronald Reagan for the Republican nomination, the normally conciliatory Ford played to the galleries, denouncing the Vietnamese as "pirates" and accusing them of being "cold and callous" on the MIA issue.[49]

Perhaps the best opportunity for normalization came in 1977. The new Democratic administration of Jimmy Carter was eager to liquidate numerous long-standing Cold War issues and especially to put the Vietnam War to rest. It also hoped through an accommodation with Vietnam to promote peace and stability in Southeast Asia. To show good faith, the United States relaxed its opposition to the admission of Vietnam to the United Nations, eased travel restrictions on Vietnamese, and permitted private organizations to furnish humanitarian aid to Vietnam. Backing away from the position of its predecessor, the administration asked only for the fullest possible accounting of MIAs. A dovish mission to Vietnam headed by labor leader Leonard Woodcock secured from the Vietnamese the establishment of an office to help deal with MIA issues, and both sides sensed the possibility of reconciliation.

---

[48]Memorandums of Kissinger conversations with Montgomery Committee, November 14, 1975, and March 12, 1976, Kissinger/Scowcroft File, Box A1. See also T. Christopher Jespersen, "The Bitter End and the Lost Chance in Vietnam: Congress, the Ford Administration, and the Battle Over Vietnam, 1975–1976," *Diplomatic History* 24 (Spring 2000): 265–293.

[49]*Washington Post,* September 12, 1976.

The same sort of misunderstanding and miscommunication that had complicated U.S.–Vietnamese relations since the 1940s destroyed the démarche of 1977. Deducing from the Woodcock mission that the United States was fully committed to reconstruction aid, the Vietnamese, to facilitate an agreement, did not make such aid a specific precondition for normalization. In fact, they continued to feel that the United States was morally obligated to provide the assistance Nixon had promised, and they had even calculated the sum into their economic plans. Thus when Carter, misunderstanding apparent Vietnamese flexibility, publicly stated that the United States did not owe them anything, they responded angrily. Totally misreading the mood in the United States and certain that antiwar forces would compel the administration to give in, they released Nixon's letter to the press and demanded U.S. compliance with his promises. The move aroused deep antagonism in the United States, and the House voted after a ten-minute debate to renounce Nixon's promises and bar any aid to Vietnam. The Carter administration immediately backed off.[50]

Facing imminent crises with China and Cambodia and eager almost to the point of desperation to come to terms with the United States, an embattled Vietnam in 1978 proposed normalization without preconditions. There was even serious talk of selecting a site for an American embassy in Hanoi.

This move toward reconciliation was the victim of major shifts in world politics in the late 1970s. The Carter administration, its hopes of ending the Cold War long since abandoned, moved steadily toward a new phase of confrontation with the Soviet Union. To have available the so-called China card in this new Cold War, the administration was set to open formal diplomatic relations with Beijing, and some U.S. officials feared that any effort to reconcile with China's enemy Vietnam might jeopardize this more important move. In any event, Carter's Russophobic national security adviser, Zbigniew Brzezinski, viewed Vietnam as a Soviet proxy and normalization as a peripheral issue. Vietnam's own actions contributed to the breakdown. A Soviet-Vietnamese treaty signed in November 1978 seemed to confirm the suspicions of Brzezinski and other hard-liners. A massive exodus of "boat people," many of them descending upon already

---

[50]Nayan Chanda, *Brother Enemy: The War after the War* (New York, 1986), pp. 136–160.

jammed refugee camps in the region, further poisoned American attitudes toward Vietnam and, along with the Vietnamese invasion of Cambodia, aroused anger, fear, and concern among other Southeast Asia nations, undermining one of the major rationales for accommodation with Hanoi. The administration decided to shelve normalization, leaving Vietnam no alternative to moving deeper into the Soviet camp. As the Cold War intensified after 1979, any prospect of reconciliation vanished.[51]

While normalization languished in the 1980s, the POW/MIA issue took on the power and mystique of a religion. In fact, the actual number of MIAs and the percentage of MIAs to casualties were far lower in the Vietnam War than in previous American wars. Most MIAs were air personnel who disappeared under circumstances that made their survival and the subsequent location of their remains difficult if not impossible, and each year in the rugged terrain of Indochina it became harder to find and identify remains. The linkage of MIAs to POWs muddled an already complicated issue, suggesting that any of the missing might be prisoners. Roughly one-half of the more than 2,000 service personnel listed as POW/MIA were known to have been killed in circumstances where the body could not be recovered. Between 1975 and 1993 various congressional and executive groups studied the issue intensively and produced not a shred of evidence that a single American was being held captive in Vietnam. For the United States to demand a full accounting of MIAs from an enemy—especially a victorious enemy with whom it was still technically at war—was quite without precedent in the history of warfare.

Still, the issue would not go away. The Nixon administration had originally raised it as a means of rallying public support behind an increasingly unpopular war. In doing so, it created a monster that would turn on the government with a vengeance. Spurred by recurrent reports of sightings of live Americans behind the bamboo curtain, the increasingly powerful POW/MIA lobby kept up a drumfire of criticism of Hanoi—and Washington. The potent National League of Families of American Prisoners and Missing in Southeast Asia created before the end of the war a stark black and white POW/MIA flag with the inscription "You Are Not Forgotten," which in time

[51]Ibid., pp. 263–296; Steven Hurst, "Regionalism or Globalism? The Carter Administration and Vietnam," *Journal of Contemporary History* 32, no. 1 (1997): 81–95.

flew above the White House, in the Capitol Rotunda, and over state office buildings, the only flag of a political lobby group to be so honored. Sensationalist films such as *Rambo: First Blood, Part 2* and *Missing in Action* boosted popular acceptance of the myth. American suspicions were also played on, a Senate committee concluded in 1993, by "charlatans and opportunists" who built a "cottage industry out of the despair of bereaved families." Hanoi did its part by periodically doling out remains when it was expedient to do so. As late as 1993, 57 percent of those Americans polled believed that service personnel were alive and being held captive in Indochina. The myth of abandoned prisoners of war held captive by Indochinese Communists and rescued by American superheroes served urgent postwar needs for redemption, vindication, and reempowerment. It was as though Americans believed that something of themselves had been lost in the war and needed to be rescued. The myth was also used to demonize the Vietnamese and delay ending the war. It became a reason for refusing to come to terms with defeat. Responding to the surge of public interest, the Reagan administration after 1982 operated on the assumption that Americans were being held captive, gave the issue the "highest national priority," and insisted once again that Vietnam provide a *full* accounting.[52]

In the mid-1980s, Vietnam went to remarkable lengths to accommodate the United States. With an estimated 300,000 MIAs of their own, the Vietnamese must have considered the American position quite outrageous. But they were anxious to break out of their isolation, increasingly concerned about their growing dependence on the Soviet Union, and eager for Western aid to promote *doi moi*, and they saw little choice but to comply with U.S. demands. They therefore permitted increasing access for Americans to search for MIAs and offered cooperation to try to resolve outstanding issues.

By this time the Reagan administration had launched a major offensive against Communist nations across the world, and it was not inclined to accommodate Vietnam. The United States eagerly accepted Vietnamese offers of cooperation but continued to insist on a full and complete accounting of the soldiers missing in action, and it linked normalization to Vietnamese withdrawal from Cambodia and a final peace settlement there. U.S. policy was no doubt

[52]Bruce Franklin, *M.I.A., or Mythmaking in America* (New Brunswick, N.J., 1993); Isaacs, *Vietnam Shadows*, pp. 128–136.

in part motivated by a desire to punish the nation that had embarrassed it. The Reagan administration may also have hoped, by squeezing Hanoi, to topple a Communist "domino," winning by economic means the military victory the United States had been denied and thereby easing the stigma of defeat. In addition, although public opinion polls indicated growing support for normalization and business groups increasingly promoted it, the administration saw little to be gained politically and feared antagonizing the still powerful MIA lobby.

U.S. policy actually hardened under Reagan's successor, George Bush. The Bush administration set out an elaborate "Road Map" that outlined various phases for normalization, each contingent on what Washington considered satisfactory progress in resolving outstanding MIA cases. The United States went so far in 1991 as to block French efforts to help Vietnam economically through the International Monetary Fund. Perhaps never before in the history of warfare had a loser been able to impose such harsh "peace" terms on the ostensible winner. "One day Vietnam may overcome the consequences of having won its war against America," the London *Economist* noted in 1991. "The Americans are putting off this day as long as possible."[53]

NORMALIZATION AND BEYOND

By 1994, that day seemed finally at hand. Vietnam had long since met most of the conditions on the Bush Road Map, withdrawing from Cambodia and taking extraordinary steps of cooperation in locating MIAs. American military teams dug up the Vietnamese countryside, interviewed villagers, and even researched Vietnamese archives in a new and grisly form of body counting. The embargo broke down, and other nations profited from the sale of American goods in Vietnam. Spokespersons for U.S. business, including the powerful National Association of Manufacturers, the U.S. Chamber of Commerce, and the *Wall Street Journal*, clamored for lifting the embargo lest the Japanese and other rivals beat America in the race for markets and investments. Public opinion polls indicated firm support, if not great enthusiasm, for normalization.

[53]"Weighing Up Vietnam," *The Economist*, October 19, 1991, 27.

President Bill Clinton still moved cautiously. His record as an opponent of the war and an avoider of the draft was a major campaign issue in 1992, and he, like his predecessors, hesitated to provoke the still formidable MIA lobby. In July 1993, the Clinton administration stopped blocking international loans to Vietnam and began stationing diplomats in Hanoi to help American families seeking information about missing service personnel. In September, the administration allowed U.S. firms to bid on projects financed by the World Bank, but it kept the embargo in place. Finally, in February 1994, Clinton lifted the embargo, and the United States and Vietnam set about establishing liaison offices in Hanoi and Washington.

The results in terms of trade were limited. American corporations such as Pepsico, Boeing, and United Airlines rushed into Vietnam. Thirty companies opened offices the day after the embargo was lifted, starting the battle for Vietnamese hearts and wallets. The American shoe company Nike became Vietnam's largest foreign employer. But the cumbersome Vietnamese bureaucracy posed a major obstacle to investment and development, and by 1999 the United States ranked only eighth among foreign investors. Largely because of Vietnamese foot-dragging, a trade agreement was not signed until 2000. High tariffs on Vietnamese goods sold in the United States and Vietnam's lack of most-favored-nation status limited the amount it could sell, thus ultimately limiting its ability to buy U.S. goods. In any event, Vietnam did not have much to sell, and with a low per capita income there were sharp limits to what it could buy. U.S. exports averaged only $300 million from 1996 to 1999, roughly only three days of American exports to Japan.[54]

Full normalization came in 1995. In late 1994, in a major symbolic act, the Vietnamese returned to the United States the now crumbling and rotted-out embassy in Ho Chi Minh City, once an imposing symbol of America's vast power in Vietnam, subsequently a symbol of its frenzied and humiliating departure. In a notably brief and deliberately subdued ceremony in January 1995—ironically, following toasts drunk with Russian champagne—the two nations agreed to open liaison offices in Washington and Hanoi, a move that permitted them to fly their flags in each other's capitals for the first time in years. Finally, in July, President Clinton announced his intention to establish full diplomatic relations. In an

[54]Pierre, "Vietnam's Contradictions," 80–82.

act richly symbolic of the spirit of reconciliation, the United States subsequently sent to Hanoi as its first ambassador Douglas "Pete" Peterson, a former POW who had previously visited that city as an involuntary guest at the notorious "Hanoi Hilton" prison. In a technical sense, at least, America's longest war had ended.

In both countries in the ensuing years, there were signs that people and governments were coming to terms with the war. The outflow of refugees from Vietnam slowed to a trickle, and some Vietnamese who had settled abroad began to return home to visit. Some even talked about going back to build a new Vietnam. What the Vietnamese called the American War continued to be celebrated as a source of nationalist pride, but there was little animosity toward Americans themselves. Indeed, in a country where a large majority of the population had been born after the war ended, most Vietnamese were too busy trying to cope with the present to dwell on the past, and the bonds formed with allies and enemies in war seemed to offer some prospect for a unique and mutually fruitful relationship.

Americans also seemed to be coming to terms with a long and painful war. The anger and bitterness subsided, and the war seemed to be passing into history. Most veterans seemed to have made their peace with the war. Some even returned to Vietnam to revisit old battlefields and duty stations. Actress Jane Fonda and former Secretary of Defense Robert McNamara, two of the most controversial figures of the war, offered apologies for their actions. Despite the so-called Vietnam Syndrome and the Powell Doctrine, the United States by the year 2000 had thousands of troops scattered across the globe. In the presidential campaign, the first in which all major candidates came from the Vietnam generation, the war was no more than a subtext. Some former hawks and doves softened their positions on the war, and a crude national consensus seemed to be emerging "that the war was a tragic mistake and that . . . those who fought and died in Vietnam were brave young men who deserve this country's respect and gratitude."[55]

Still, on both sides the wounds had not entirely healed. The United States sprayed 20 million gallons of herbicides and defoliants, including Agent Orange, on about 14 percent of southern

---

[55]David W. Levy, "Closure: How the National Discussion of Vietnam Will Eventually Be Resolved," *The Long-Term View* 5 (Summer 2000): 144–148.

Vietnam, and an estimated 1 million Vietnamese, including as many as 150,000 children, suffer from birth defects, miscarriages, and various illnesses possibly attributable to the chemicals. An estimated 3.5 million land mines still litter the countryside of South Vietnam and, along with other unexplored ordnance, take a huge toll in deaths and casualties each year. While Americans used high tech methods to search out their few remaining MIAs, some Vietnamese families employed psychics to locate the remains of their loved ones.

In the United States, as well, the war's influence did not entirely go away. America's continuing obsession with Vietnam was manifest in the sheer volume of popular culture, by one estimate 12,000 nonfiction titles, 1,400 personal narratives, 250 films. It seems certain that should any of the troops stationed in hot spots around the world come under fire or should there be calls to send troops into an active combat zone, the ghosts of Vietnam will rise again. Although the POW/MIA lobby seems to have lost much of its clout, the search for remains of the 1,966 soldiers still listed as missing goes on; in April 2001 seven Americans were killed in a plane crash while conducting a search, the last American casualties, one hopes, of the Indochina Wars. Although the search seems increasingly futile, no president wants to take responsibility for stopping it. Even as the nation moves toward some kind of consensus, deep divisions on the war's meaning and lessons remain, especially among those who participated in it. McNamara's apology provoked cries of outrage from veterans and antiwar protesters alike. In the mini-debate that occurred on the twenty-fifth anniversary of the end of the war, former journalist Neil Sheehan insisted that the United States was fortunate to have lost the war because the loss had made Americans a more skeptical and cautious people and therefore spared the country further misadventures abroad. On the other hand, former Secretary of State Henry Kissinger bemoaned the way the war had sapped America's will for global leadership.[56]

President Bill Clinton's visit to Vietnam in November 2000, the first trip there by an American president since Richard Nixon visited the troops in 1969, symbolized these crosscurrents. It was an important step in the process of reconciliation. Clinton was the first post-

---

[56]Neil Sheehan, "Silver Linings," *Boston Globe,* April 30, 2000; Henry A. Kissinger, "The Long Shadow of Vietnam," *Newsweek,* May 1, 2000, 47–49.

war president to visit Vietnam. He stayed four days, longer than is customary for such visits, and the Vietnamese government, in an act without precedent, permitted his speech to be broadcast over national television. He did not apologize, as some Vietnamese and Americans had urged, recognizing the obvious political explosion such a step could set off. But he showed a rare sensitivity to Vietnamese feelings. The theme of his visit was "Vietnam is a country, not a war," an obvious fact that Americans in their self-absorption have never quite grasped. "The history we leave behind is painful and hard," he said. "We must not forget it, but we must not be controlled by it." He visited a site at which Americans and Vietnamese together painstakingly sifted through dirt in search of fragments of bone that might help identify Americans. He also expressed concern for the Vietnamese still missing and provided thousands of pages of documents to help the search. In Hanoi and Ho Chi Minh City he drew huge crowds, and his visit represented a sort of closure.

The visit also made clear, however, that the process of reconciliation between Americans and Vietnamese and among Americans themselves is not over. "Why didn't he go before?" some veterans snarled, making clear the continuing divide in the Vietnam generation between those who went and those who did not. The Vietnamese insisted that the United States should assume greater responsibility for such war-related problems as land mines and victims of Agent Orange. When Clinton gently chided the Vietnam government about its human rights record and pressed it to permit greater personal freedom and open itself to globalization, Vietnam's communist leaders charged that the imperialist Americans were once again seeking to impose their will on a sovereign nation.

Twenty-five years after the last helicopter departed the rooftop of the embassy in Saigon, more than a half century after U.S. Army officers joined Ho Chi Minh in proclaiming the independence of Vietnam, America's longest war had formally ended and the two nations were seeking to reconcile. But the ideological and cultural divides that had helped bring on the war in the first place and had made it so difficult to end still remained.

PRONUNCIATION GUIDE OF VIETNAMESE WORDS

An Loc, *battle of* [ahn-lok]
Annam [ahn-nahm]
Ap Bac, *battle of* [up-bahk]
Ban Me Thuot, *battle of* [bhan-may-twoot]
Bao Dai [bow-dye]
Bay Vien [bay-vyen]
Ben Tre [ben-tray]
Bien Hoa, *attack on* [byen-hwah]
Binh Xuyen [bin-swyen]
Bui Diem [boo-ee-zyem]
Cam Ranh Bay [kahm-rahn]
Cao Bang [kow-bahng]
Cao Dai [kow-dye]
Chieu Hoi Program [chyoo-hoy]
Cho Lon [chah-luhn]
Con Thien, *battle of* [kohn-tyen]
Dak To, *battle of* [dahk-toh]
Da Lat [dah-laht]
Da Nang [dah-nahng]
Danh va dam, *strategy of* [dahn vah dahm]
Diem, Ngo Dinh *See* Ngo Dinh Diem
Dien Bien Phu, *battle of* [dyen-byen-foo]
Doi Moi [doy-mye]
Duong Van Minh [zwahng-vahn-meen]
Giap, Vo Nguyen *See* Vo Nguyen Giap
Haiphong [hye-fawng]
Hanoi [hah-noy]
Hmong Tribe [hmawng]
Ho Chi Minh [hoh-chee-meen]
Hoa Hao [hwah-how]
Hon Me [hahn-may]
Hue [hway]
Khanh, Nguyen *See* Nguyen Khanh
Khe Sanh, *battle of* [kay-shahn]
Ky, Nguyen Cao *See* Nguyen Cao Ky
Lao Dong [loud-awng]
Le Duan [lay-zwun]
Le Duc Tho [lay-dook-taw]
Le Loi [lay-loy]
Loc Ninh [lok-neen]
Minh Mang [meen-mahng]
Minh, Duong *See* Duong Van Minh

Minh, Ho Chi *See* Ho Chi Minh
Mu Gia Pass [moo-zah]
My Lai, *village of* [mee-lye]
Nghe An [ngay-ahn]
Ngo Dinh Diem [ngoh-deem-zyem]
Ngo Dinh Kha [ngoh-deen-kah]
Ngo Dinh Nhu [ngoh-deen-nyoo]
Nguyen Ai Quoc [ngwen-eye-kwuck]
Nguyen Cao Ky [ngwen-kow-kee]
Nguyen Chanh Thi [ngwen-chahn-tee]
Nguyen Khanh [ngwen-kahn]
Nguyen Van Thieu [ngwen-vahn-tyew]
Nha Trang [nyah-trahng]
Nhu, Madame [nyoo]
Nhu, Ngo Dinh *See* Ngo Dinh Nhu
Pham Van Dong [fahm-vahn-dohng]
Phan Boi Chau [fahn-boy-chow]
Phan Huy Quat [fahn-hwee-kwaht]
Phuoc Long [fook-lawng]
Pleiku [play-koo]
Quang Tri [kwang-tree]
Qui Nhon [kwee-nyahn]
Saigon [shye-gone]
Song Be [shawng-bay]
Tan Son Nhut Airport [tun-shun-nyut]
Tet Offensive [tayt]
Thich Quang Duc [teek-kwahng-dook]
Tran Hung Dao [trun-hung-dow]
Tran Van Huong [trun-vahn-hwahng]
Trieu Au [trew-oh]
Trung Sisters [trung]
Truong Dinh Dzu [trwahng-deen-zoo]
Vang Pao [vahng-pow]
Van Tien Dung [vahn-tyen-zoong]
Vietcong [vyet-kohng]
Vietminh [vyet-meen]
Vietnam [vyet-nahm]
Vinh [veen]
Vo Nguyen Giap [vaw-ngwen-zahp]
Vung Tau [voong-tow]
Xuan Loc, *battle of* [swun-lok]
Xuan Thuy [swun-twee]
Yen Bay Revolt [ee-yen-bay]

Suggestions for
Additional Reading

[A comprehensive bibliography can be found on pp. 322–340 of the third edition of this book and also on the *America's Longest War* website. This selective bibliography includes the standard works on the war and the most important items published since 1995.]

GENERAL

Excellent introductions to the historiography are Gary R. Hess, "The Unending Debate: Historians and the Vietnam War," *Diplomatic History,* 18 (Spring 1994), 239–264; and Robert J. McMahon, "U.S.-Vietnamese Relations: A Historiographical Survey," in Warren I. Cohen, *Pacific Passage: The Study of American-East Asian Relations on the Eve of the Twenty-First Century* (New York, 1996), 313–336.

Some of the most useful reference works are Stanley I. Kutler (ed.), *Encyclopedia of the Vietnam War* (New York, 1996); and Spencer C. Tucker, Jr., (ed.), *Encyclopedia of the Vietnam War: A Political, Social and Military History* (3 vols., Santa Barbara, Calif., 1998). The most comprehensive guide to the already massive literature on the war (up to 1990) is Lester Brune and Richard Dean Burns, *America and the Indochina Wars, 1945–1990: A Bibliographical Guide* (Claremont, Calif., 1992).

The State Department's *Foreign Relations of the United States* volumes on Vietnam are the most important documentary source. Now published through the year 1966, they are exhaustively researched and superbly edited.

The various editions of the *Pentagon Papers* are still useful, although the analyses done by the Pentagon historians in 1967 are now dated and the documents are limited in number and coverage. The best introduction remains Neil Sheehan et al., *The Pentagon Papers as Published by the New York Times* (New York, 1971). *The Pentagon Papers (The*

Senator Gravel Edition) (4 vols., Boston, 1971) is the most usable of the larger editions. *United States-Vietnam Relations, 1945–1967: A Study Prepared by the Department of Defense* (12 books; Washington, D. C., 1971) contains the most documents but is awkwardly arranged, poorly printed, and full of deletions. George C. Herring (ed.), *The Secret Diplomacy of the Vietnam War: The Negotiating Volumes of the Pentagon Papers* (Austin, Tex., 1983) is an annotated edition of those papers dealing with peace initiatives.

Two multivolume studies in progress deserve special mention. William Conrad Gibbons, *The U.S. Government and the Vietnam War: Executive and Legislative Roles and Relationships* (4 vols.; Washington, D.C., 1984–) is based on exhaustive research in U.S. documents and does far more than the title suggests. R. B. Smith, *An International History of the Vietnam War* (3 vols.; London, 1983–) seeks to place U.S. and Vietnamese decisions in an international context.

Many of the classic, one-volume studies of the war have been written by journalists who served in Vietnam as correspondents, and most of them subscribe to the "liberal-dove" point of view. David Halberstam, *The Best and the Brightest* (New York, 1972) brilliantly profiles key U.S. policymakers and provides shrewd insights into their mindset. Frances FitzGerald, *Fire in the Lake: The Vietnamese and the Americans in Vietnam* (Boston, 1972) romanticizes the Vietnamese communists but properly emphasizes the vast cultural divide between Americans and Vietnamese. Stanley Karnow, *Vietnam: A History* (New York, 1983) remains especially useful for insights drawn from the author's journalistic experience in Southeast Asia. Neil Sheehan, *A Bright Shining Lie: John Paul Vann and America in Vietnam* (New York, 1988), uses the legendary army officer as a vehicle to study the entire war. A third generation of works subscribing to a similar point of view includes A. J. Langguth, *Our Vietnam: The War 1954–1975* (New York, 2000), a splendidly written account; and Robert Mann, *A Grand Delusion: America's Descent into Vietnam* (New York, 2001), which highlights the role—or non-role—of Congress.

Among the best one-volume accounts by historians are Marilyn Young, *The Vietnam Wars, 1945–1990* (New York, 1991) and Robert Schulzinger, *A Time for War* (New York, 1997).

The "liberal-dove" interpretation has come under challenge from conservative "revisionists." Guenter Lewy, *America in Vietnam* (New York, 1978), defended the United States against charges of war crimes and argued that with a different strategy the war could have been won. Norman Podhoretz, *Why We Were in Vietnam* (New York, 1982), concluded that the war was unwinnable but the cause just and the effort worth making. More recently, Michael Lind, *Vietnam: The Necessary War* (New York, 1999) agrees that the war should have been fought and argues, curiously, that it could have been lost better.

From the political left, Gabriel Kolko, *Anatomy of a War: Vietnam, the United States and the Modern Historical Experience* (New York, 1985), offers a particularly searching analysis of Vietnamese society.

There are a number of valuable studies of Vietnam during the thirty-year war. Among the best are William J. Duiker's *The Communist Road to Power in Vietnam* (Boulder, Colo., 1981) and his shorter but more up-to-date *Sacred War: Nationalism and Revolution in a Divided Vietnam* (New York, 1995). William S. Turley, *The Second Indochina War: A Short History* (New York, 1985) is still useful.

THE FIRST INDOCHINA WAR, 1945–1954

Among the best accounts of the origins of the Vietnamese revolution are David Marr's superb trilogy, *Vietnamese Anticolonialism* (Berkeley, Calif., 1971), *Vietnamese Tradition on Trial* (Berkeley, Calif., 1982), and *Vietnam 1945: The Quest for Power* (Berkeley, Calif., 1995). William J. Duiker's magisterial *Ho Chi Minh: A Life* (New York, 2000) is indispensable.

The standard account of the politics and diplomacy of the First Indochina War remains Ellen Hammer, *The Struggle for Indochina, 1945–1954* (Stanford, Calif., 1966). Bernard Fall's classic *Street Without Joy* (New York, 1972) dramatically depicts the frustrations met by French military operations. Lloyd C. Gardner, *Approaching Vietnam: From World War II through Dienbienphu* (New York, 1988), puts events in Indochina in the larger context of relations among the western allies.

The origins of U.S. involvement in Vietnam are well covered in Ronald Spector, *Advice and Support: The Early Years* (Washington, D.C., 1983), the first volume of the U.S. Army's superb official history of the war; and in George McT. Kahin, *Intervention: How America Became Involved in Vietnam* (New York, 1986). Mark Bradley, *Imagining Vietnam & America: The Making of Postcolonial Vietnam, 1919–1950* (Chapel Hill, N.C., 2000), represents the best of the new Vietnam scholarship, using Vietnamese and American sources and thoroughly analyzing from the perspective of each nation the obstacles to meaningful relations. The critical American decision of 1950 is analyzed from different perspectives in Robert M. Blum, *Drawing the Line: the Origins of the American Containment Policy in East Asia* (New York, 1982) and in Andrew Rotter, *The Path to Vietnam: Origins of the American Commitment to Southeast Asia* (Ithaca, N.Y., 1987). The ambience of these years is best captured in two older books, Robert Shaplen, *The Lost Revolution: The U.S. in Vietnam, 1946–1966* (New York, 1966), and Graham Greene's classic novel, *The Quiet American* (London, 1955).

For Dien Bien Phu, Bernard B. Fall, *Hell in a Very Small Place* (Philadelphia, 1966), and Jules Roy, *The Battle of Dienbienphu* (New York, 1965), remain the standard accounts, while Vo Nguyen Giap, *Dien Bien Phu* (Hanoi, 1962) offers a Vietnamese perspective. Robert F. Randle, *Geneva 1954: The Settlement of the Indochinese War* (Princeton, N.J., 1969), should be supplemented with Francois Joyaux, *La Chine et le reglement du premier conflit d'Indochine, Geneve 1954* (Paris, 1979).

THE ERA OF NGO DINH DIEM, 1954–1963

The best overall study of South Vietnam during the Diem era remains Robert Scigliano, *South Vietnam: Nation under Stress* (Boston, 1964). The U.S. nation-building effort in the Eisenhower years is well covered in David Anderson, *Trapped by Success: The Eisenhower Administration and Vietnam, 1953–1961* (New York, 1991). John Ernst, *Forging a Fateful Alliance: Michigan State University and the Vietnam War* (East Lansing, Mi., 1998) and Joseph Morgan, *The Vietnam Lobby: American Friends of Vietnam, 1955–1975* (Chapel Hill, N.C., 1997) are two valuable monographs.

The origins and nature of the insurgency in South Vietnam in the late 1950s have been a source of heated controversy since that time. Douglas Pike, *Viet Cong: National Liberation Front of South Vietnam* (rev. ed.; Cambridge, Mass., 1972), emphasizes the importance of organization in the success of the NLF. Carlyle Thayer, *War by Other Means: National Liberation and Revolution in Viet-Nam* (Boston, 1989) is a more recent study. Jeffrey Race, *War Comes to Long An: Revolutionary Conflict in a Vietnamese Province* (Berkeley, Calif., 1972) and Eric Bergerud, *The Dynamics of Defeat: The Vietnam War in Hau Nghia Province* (Boulder, Colo., 1991), two studies of the insurgency at the provincial level, are essential to understanding the war.

John F. Kennedy's policies, actual and contemplated, have been the subect of especially vigorous controversy in recent years. John M. Newman, *JFK and Vietnam* (New York, 1992), contends that Kennedy had developed a secret plan for withdrawal from Vietnam, a point of view popularized and encased in conspiracy theory in Oliver Stone's film *JFK*. Lloyd C. Gardner and Ted Gitinger, *Vietnam: The Early Decisions* (Austin, Tex., 1997), contains essays challenging this argument. Fredrik Logevall, *Choosing War: The Lost Chance for Peace and the Escalation of War in Vietnam* (Berkeley, Calif., 1999), David Kaiser, *American Tragedy: Kennedy, Johnson, and the Origins of the Vietnam War* (Cambridge, Mass., 2000), and Lawrence Freedman, *Kennedy's Wars* (New York, 2000), reject the notion of a secret plan, but speculate that had Kennedy lived he might have avoided a major escalation of the war, Kaiser the most passionate—and least persuasive. William Prochnau, *Once Upon a Distant War* (New York, 1995) chronicles the conflict between government and press in these early years.

THE SECOND INDOCHINA WAR, 1964–1968

Lyndon Johnson's decisions to escalate the war, not surprisingly, have also provoked controversy. Robert Dallek, *Flawed Giant: Lyndon Johnson and His Times* (New York, 1998), stresses that the dictates of the containment policy left Johnson little choice, while the Logevall and Kaiser books cited above emphasize that he had options. H. R. McMaster, *Dereliction of Duty: Lyndon Johnson, Robert McNamara, the Joint Chiefs of Staff, and the Lies That Led to Vietnam* (New York, 1997), as the title suggests, is a harsh indictment of the system and the personalities. Yuen Foong Khong, *Analogies at War—Korea, Munich, Dien Bien Phu—The Vietnam Decisions of 1965* (Princeton, N.J., 1992) provides an insightful analysis of the way history is used—and especially misused—in making important policy decisions. Michael Beschloss (ed.), *Taking Charge: The Johnson White House Tapes, 1963–1964* (New York, 1997) provides many insights into Johnson's thinking during these critical months. Edwin Moïse, *Tonkin Gulf and the Escalation of the VietNam War* (Chapel Hill, N.C., 1996) is the authoritative account of that important episode.

For Johnson's management of the war, *see* Larry Berman, *Lyndon Johnson's War* (New York, 1989); George C. Herring, *LBJ and Vietnam: A Different Kind of War* (Austin, Tex., 1994); and Lloyd C. Gardner, *Pay Any Price: Lyndon Johnson and the Wars for Vietnam* (Chicago, 1995).

Recent important works by and about "the principals," Johnson's key advisers, include Robert McNamara's controversial memoir, *In Retrospect: The Tragedy and Lessons of Vietnam* (New York, 1995); Kai Bird, *The Color of Truth* (New York, 1998), a joint biography of William and McGeorge Bundy; and Thomas Zeiler, *Dean Rusk: Defending the American Mission Abroad* (Wilmington, Del., 2000).

A vigorous debate on the reasons for U.S. failure in Vietnam erupted during the war years and has continued unabated. For an introduction to the subject, *see* George C. Herring, "American Strategy in Vietnam: The Postwar Debate," *Military Affairs*, 46 (April 1982), 57–63. Two major participants, (General) William C. Westmoreland, *A Soldier Reports* (Garden City, N.Y., 1976), and (Admiral) U.S. Grant Sharp, *Strategy for Defeat* (San Rafael, Calif., 1978), insisted that restrictions imposed by civilians prevented the military from winning. Andrew Krepinevich, *The Army and Vietnam* (Baltimore, 1986), William Colby, *Lost Victory* (Chicago, 1989), and Larry Cable, *Conflict of Myths* (New York, 1986), and *Unholy Grail* (Andover, Eng., 1991), on the other hand, indict the military for its conventional thinking and suggest that a counterinsurgency strategy might have succeeded. Harry G. Summers, Jr., *On Strategy* (Carlisle Barracks, Pa.,. 1981), and Bruce Palmer, Jr., *The Twenty-Five Year War* (Lexington, Ky., 1984), criticize civilian and military leaders for failing to think strategically and argue that a true conventional war strategy isolating North from South Vietnam might have worked. Jeffrey Record, *The Wrong War: Why*

We Lost in Vietnam (Annapolis, Md., 1998), persuasively counters all these arguments, blaming America's failure more fundamentally on its misunderstanding of the significance and nature of the war, its underestimation of the enemy, and its overestimation of its own political stamina and military prowess. John Prados' valuable collection of essays, *The Hidden History of the Vietnam War* (Chicago, 1998), reaches similar conclusions.

The classic studies of the air war are Mark Clodfelter, *The Limits of Air Power: The American Bombing of North Vietnam* (New York, 1989), and Earl H. Tilford, Jr., *Setup: What the Air Force Did in Vietnam and Why* (Maxwell Air Force Base, Ala., 1991), both sharply critical of the strategic thinking of airpower advocates.

The best study of the various pacification programs remains Douglas S. Blaufarb, *The Counterinsurgency Era: U.S. Doctrines and Performance* (New York, 1977), although the more critical D. Michael Shafer, *Deadly Paradigms: The Failure of U.S. Counterinsurgency Policy* (Princeton, N.J., 1988) is also useful. For the especially controversial Phoenix Program, *see* Dale Andradé, *Ashes to Ashes: The Phoenix Program and the Vietnam War* (Lexington, Mass., 1990), Douglas Valentine, *The Phoenix Program* (New York, 1990), and Mark Moyar, *Phoenix and the Birds of Prey* (Annapolis, Md., 1977).

Important specialized studies include Harold G. Moore and Joseph L. Galloway, *We Were Soldiers Once . . . and Young* (New York, 1992), a stirring account of the 1965 battles of the Ia Drang; John M. Carland, *Stemming the Tide* (Washington, 2000), good on early military operations; Jeffrey J. Clarke, *Advice and Support: The Final Years* (Washington, D.C., 1988), an authoritative study of the Vietnamization program; Bergerud, *Dynamics of Defeat*, a major book with implications beyond the single province it studies; and Robert Buzzanco, *Masters of War* (New York, 1996), an excellent analysis of civil-military relations.

The war has produced a huge and distinguished personal literature. Christian G. Apply, *Working-Class War* (Chapel Hill, N.C., 1993) is a fine scholarly analysis of the G.I. experience. Among the classic memoirs are Philip Caputo, *A Rumor of War* (New York, 1977), Michael Herr, *Dispatches* (New York, 1977), and David Donovan, *Once a Warrior King* (New York, 1985). For the perspective of the support troops, the REMFs, *see* Joe P. Dunn, *Desk Warrior* (Needham Heights, Mass., 1999). The best of the fiction include James Webb, *Fields of Fire* (New York, 1978), and Tim O'Brien, *The Things They Carried* (New York, 1990). The oral histories are also legion. Wallace Terry, *Bloods* (New York, 1984), deals with African-American soldiers, Otto Lehrack, *No Shining Armor* (Lawrence, Kan., 1991) with Marines, and Kathryn Marshall, *In the Combat Zone* (New York, 1987), with women. Kim Willenson, *The Bad War* (New York, 1987), and Myra McPherson, *Long Time Passing* (New York, 1984) explore through oral history the experiences of the entire Vietnam generation.

Peter Edwards with Gregory Pemberton, *Crises and Commitments* (Sydney, 1992), and Edwards, *A Nation at War* (Sydney, 1997), are an excellent official history of America's most important ally, Australia.

One of the least studied and most important topics is the American interaction with and impact on the South Vietnamese. George C. Herring, " 'Peoples Quite Apart': Americans, South Vietnamese, and the War in Vietnam," *Diplomatic History*, 14 (Winter 1990), 1–24, is an introduction. Useful memoirs are Nguyen Cao Ky, *Twenty Years and Twenty Days* (New York, 1976), Tran Van Don, *Our Endless War* (San Rafael, Calif., 1978), and Bui Diem, *In the Jaws of History* (Boston, 1987). Le Ly Hayslip with Jay Wurts, *When Heaven and Earth Changed Places* (New York, 1989), is a moving account of a young Vietnamese woman victimized by all sides.

Reversing the old saying, in the Vietnam War the losers have written the history, and there is also a shortage of material on the North Vietnamese and National Liberation Front. Duiker's biography of Ho Chi Minh is essential, although Ho was not a key figure in policy making after 1963. Peter McDonald, *Giap: Victor in Vietnam* (New York, 1993), and Cecil Currey, *Victory at Any Cost: The Genius of Vietnam's Gen. Vo Nguyen Giap* (Washington, D.C., 1997), are useful biographies of this legendary figure. General Tran Van Tra, *Ending the Thirty Year War* (Washington, D.C., 1983) offers important insights into North Vietnamese and NLF strategy late in the war. David Chanoff and Doan Van Toai, *Portrait of the Enemy* (New York, 1986), is based on interviews with former NLF and NVA soldiers. Truong Nhu Tang with David Chanoff and Doan Van Toai, *A Vietcong Memoir* (Boston, 1985) is a valuable firsthand account by a non-communist NLF leader who fled Vietnam after 1975. Bui Tin, *Following Ho Chi Minh: Memoirs of a North Vietnamese Colonel* (London, 1994) is an important memoir by a soldier who participated in major events from Dien Bien Phu to the fall of Saigon. The important role of women is discussed in Sandra C. Taylor, *Vietnamese Women at War* (Lawrence, Kan., 1999). The horrors of the war from the perspective of a Vietnamese soldier are movingly chronicled in Bao Ninh's novel, *The Sorrow of War* (New York, 1996). Robert K. Brigham, *Guerrilla Diplomacy* (Ithaca, N.Y., 2000), is a first-rate monograph based on Vietnamese sources that makes clear the complexity of the relationship between the NLF and Hanoi and the conflicts that often divided them. The story of the Ho Chi Minh Trail is well told in Richard L. Stevens, *Mission on the Ho Chi Minh Trail: Nature, Myth, and the War in Vietnam* (Norman, Okla., 1995), and John Prados, *Blood Road: The Ho Chi Minh Trail and the Vietnam war* (New York, 1999).

Excellent studies of North Vietnam's relations with its major allies based on research in Soviet and Chinese archives include Ilya V. Gaiduk, *The Soviet Union and the Vietnam War* (Chicago, 1996), Qiang Zhai, *China and the Vietnam Wars, 1950–1975* (Chapel Hill, N.C., 2000), and Chen Jian,

"China's Involvement in the Vietnam War, 1964–1969," *China Quarterly*, 142 (June 1995), 357–387.

The numerous abortive peace initiatives have received much attention in recent years. A recent account based in part on interviews with North Vietnamese participants is Robert S. McNamara et al., *Argument Without End: In Search of Answers to the Vietnam Tragedy* (New York, 1999).

On American public opinion, John E. Mueller, *War, Presidents, and Public Opinion* (New York, 1973) ably compared the wars in Korea and Vietnam with interesting results.

The best general analyses of the antiwar movement and its impact are Charles DeBenedetti and Charles Chatfield (assisting author), *An American Ordeal: The Antiwar Movement of the Vietnam Era* (Syracuse, 1990), Tom Wells, *The War Within: America's Battle Over Vietnam* (Berkeley, Calif., 1994), and Melvin Small, *Johnson, Nixon and the Doves* (New Brunswick, N.J., 1988). For a contrary view, *see* Adam Garfinckle, *Telltale Hearts: The Origins and Impact of the Vietnam Antiwar Movement* (New York, 1997). Rhodri Jeffreys-Jones, *Peace Now!: American Society and the Ending of the Vietnam War* (New Haven, Conn., 1999) is an important new study that assesses the role of social groups in the ending of the war. Terry H. Anderson, *The Movement and the Sixties* (New York, 1995), and Maurice Isserman and Michael Kazin, *America Divided: The Civil War of the 1960s* (New York, 2000), discuss the antiwar movement in the broader context of an era of protest.

Valuable monographs include Mitchell K. Hall, *Because of Their Faith: CALCAV and Religious Opposition to the Vietnam War* (New York, 1990); Kenneth Heineman, *Campus Wars: The Peace Movement at American State Universities in the Vietnam Era* (New York, 1993), Andrew Hunt, *The Turning: A History of Vietnam Veterans Against the War* (New York, 1999), and James Dickenson, *North to Canada—Men and Women Against the Vietnam War* (Praeger, 1999). David Farber, *Chicago '68* (Chicago, 1968) is excellent. James W. Tollefson, *The Strength Not to Fight* (Boston, 1993) is an oral history of conscientious objectors.

The impact of the war on the Vietnam generation is ably analyzed in Lawrence A. Baskir and William A. Strauss, *Chance and Circumstance* (New York, 1978), but *see also* James Carroll, *An American Requiem: God, My Father and the War That Came Between Us* (Boston, 1996), a compelling personal account of the way the war divided families. James E. Westheider, *Fighting on Two Fronts: African Americans and the Vietnam War* (New York, 1997) reaches some surprising conclusions.

Important scholarly work on the erosion of congressional support for the war has been done in recent years. Mann's *Grand Delusion* is a good place to start. Randall Woods, *Fulbright: A Biography* (New York, 1995) is a first-rate biography of a key figure. Gregory Olson, *Mansfield and Vietnam* (East Lansing, Mich., 1995) is also useful.

Not surprisingly, the Tet Offensive of 1968 and the policy debate it set off have attracted a great deal of attention. Don Oberdorfer's classic account, *Tet!* (Garden City, N.Y., 1971) should be supplemented by Marc Jason Gilbert and William Head (eds.), *The Tet Offensive* (Westport, Conn., 1996). Much of the early analysis stopped with Johnson's March 31 speech, ignoring the very important aftermath. Ronald H. Spector, *After Tet: The Bloodiest Year in Vietnam* (New York, 1993), provides an excellent military history of this important phase of the war.

The role of media coverage, especially at Tet, has been one of the most controversial issues from a war filled with controversy. Robert Elegant, "How to Lose a War," *Encounter,* LVII (August 1981), 73–90, and Peter Braestrup, *Big Story!* (2 vols., Boulder, Colo., 1977), are two critical accounts by journalists who were there. Clarence R. Wyatt, *Paper Soldiers: The American Press and the Vietnam War* (New York, 1993), Daniel C. Hallin, *The "Uncensored War": The Media and Vietnam* (New York, 1986), and William M. Hammond, *Reporting Vietnam: Media & Military at War* (Lawrence, Kan., 1998), are excellent scholarly studies. Chester J. Pach, Jr., "Tet on TV: U.S. Nightly News Reporting and Presidential Policy Making," in Carole Fink et al., *1968: The World Transformed* (Washington and New York, 1998), 55–81, is valuable.

On the horrors of My Lai, *see* Michael Bilton, *Four Hours in My Lai* (New York, 1992), and David L. Anderson (ed.), *Facing My Lai: Moving Beyond the Massacre* (Lawrence, Kan., 1998).

NIXON, KISSINGER, AND THE END OF THE WAR

Nixon and Kissinger sought to ensure, with Winston Churchill, that history would be kind to them because they would write it. Each wrote huge memoirs. Nixon's *RN: The Memoirs of Richard Nixon* (New York, 1978) is defensive but useful for the material it includes from his papers and diaries. Kissinger's memoirs, *White House Years* (Boston, 1979), *Years of Upheaval* (Boston, 1983), and *Years of Renewal* (New York, 2000), in all a whopping 3955 pages, comprise perhaps the longest memoir even written by an American public official and are based on papers that Kissinger has prevented others from using. Among the accounts of top Nixon advisers, H. R. Haldeman, *The Haldeman Diaries* (New York, 1994), reveals much about the mood and modus operandi of the Nixon White House. Stanley Kutler, *Abuse of Power: The New Nixon Tapes* (New York, 1997) deals mainly with Watergate, but has important material on Vietnam.

Stephen E. Ambrose, *Nixon* (3 vols.; New York, 1987–1992) is a competent Nixon biography, and Anthony Summers, *Arrogance of Power: The Secret World of Richard Nixon* (New York, 2000) is senationalist but contains useful new material. Walter Isaacson, *Kissinger: A Biography* (New York, 1992) is excellent.

Scholars are now beginning to get around the restrictions on sources left by Nixon and Kissinger and produce important—and generally very critical—analyses of their Vietnam policies. Jeffrey Kimball, *Nixon's Vietnam War* (Lawrence, Kan., 1998), is excellent, and Larry Berman's *No Peace, No Honor: Nixon, Kissinger, and Betrayal in Vietnam* (New York, 2001) is superb on the peace negotiations. Joan Hoff, *Nixon Reconsidered* (New York, 1994), Melvin Small, *The Presidency of Richard Nixon* (Lawrence, Kan., 1999), and William Bundy, *A Tangled Web: The Making of Foreign Policy in the Nixon Presidency* (New York, 1998), deal with much more than Vietnam but are valuable for that subject also.

There are only a handful of specialized studies on the war during the Nixon years. Lewis Sorley, *A Better War: The Unexamined Victories and Final Tragedy of America's Last years in Vietnam* (New York, 1999), overstates its case but contains valuable information on the war as perceived from General Abrams's headquarters. David Rudenstine, *The Day the Presses Stopped: A History of the Pentagon Papers Case* (Berkeley, Calif., 1996), and Dale Andradé, *Trial by Fire: The 1972 Easter Offensive* (New York, 1995), are good on those important topics. Luu Van Loi and Nguyen Anh Vu, *Le Duc Tho-Kissinger Negotiations in Paris* (Hanoi, 1996), is essential for the secret negotiations.

AFTERMATH AND LEGACIES

The best analysis of the postwar war is Arnold R. Isaacs, *Without Honor: Defeat in Vietnam and Cambodia* (Baltimore, Md., 1999), a highly critical study by a journalist who was there at the time. Van Tien Dung, *Our Great Spring Victory* (New York, 1977), is a frankly exuberant memoir by the architect of the North Vietnamese triumph. Nguyen Tien Hung and Jerrold Schecter, *The Palace File* (New York, 1986), is an invaluable account of the last years of the Thieu regime. P. Edward Haley, *Congress and the Fall of South Vietnam and Cambodia* (Rutherford, N.J., 1982), persuasively rebuts Nixon and Kissinger's efforts to blame Congress for losing the war. Stephen T. Hosmer, et al., *The Fall of South Vietnam* (New York, 1980), is based on interviews with South Vietnamese leaders.

For Laos during the Second Indochina War, *see* Jane Hamilton-Merritt, *Tragic Mountains: The Hmong, the Americans and the Secret Wars in Laos, 1942–1992* (Bloomington, Ind., 1993), and Roger Warner, *Backfire: The CIA's Secret War in Laos and Its Link to the War in Vietnam* (New York, 1995), and *Shooting at the Moon: The Story of American's Clandestine War in Laos* (1997). The tragic aftermath in Cambodia is treated in Ben Kiernan, *The Pol Pot*

Regime: Race, Power, and Genocide in Cambodia Under the Khmer Rouge, 1975–1979 (New Haven, Conn., 1996.

Postwar Vietnam is covered in Gabriel Kolko, *Anatomy of Peace* (London, 1997), and in Robert Templar, *Shadows on the Wind* (1998). The best account of the continuing conflict in Indochina after the fall of Saigon remains Nayan Chanda, *Brother Enemy: The War after the War* (New York, 1986).

T. Christopher Jespersen, "The Bitter End and the Lost Chance in Vietnam: Congress, the Ford Administration, and the Battle Over Vietnam," *Diplomatic History,* 24 (Spring 2000), 265–296, and Steven Hurst, "Regionalism or Globalism? The Carter Administration and Vietnam," *Journal of Contemporary History,* 32 (1977), 81–95, analyze the diplomacy that delayed normalization for two decades. The crucial MIA issue is scathingly critiqued in H. Bruce Franklin, *M.I.A. or Mythmaking in America* (New Brunswick, N.J., 1992).

Recent attempts to assess the legacy of the war for the United States include Arnold R. Isaacs, *Vietnam Shadows: The War, Its Ghosts, and Its Legacy* (Baltimore, Md., 1997); Charles E. Neu (ed.), *After Vietnam: Legacies of a Lost War* (Baltimore, Md., 2000); and "Legacies of Vietnam," *The Long Term View,* 5 (Summer 2000).

Hien Duc Do, *The Vietnamese Americans* (Westport, Conn., 1999) is a recent effort to analyze the experience of the refugees.

The veterans are dealt with from very different perspectives in Robert J. Lifton, *Home From the War* (New York, 1973), and B. G. Burkett and Glenna Whitley, *Stolen Valor: How the Vietnam Generation Was Robbed of Its Heroes and Its History* (Dallas, Tex., 1998).

Efforts to probe the cultural legacy of Vietnam can be found in Fred Turner, *Echoes of Combat: The Vietnam War in American Memory* (New York, 1996); Jerry Lembcke, *The Spitting Image: Myth, Memory, and the Legacy of Vietnam* (New York, 1998); and most successfully in Tom Englehardt's excellent, *The End of Victory Culture: Cold War America and the Disillusioning of a Generation* (New York, 1995).

Index